W9-ADR-452

VENERABLE ANCESTOR

THE LIFE AND TIMES OF TZ'U HSI, 1835–1908, EMPRESS OF CHINA

BY

HARRY HUSSEY

Dolphin Books
Doubleday & Company, Inc.
Garden City, New York

Printed in the United States of America

To my Grandson
Harry Joseph Hussey

FOREWORD

My interest in China began with the visit of a missionary to our village in Canada when I was a small boy. The missionary had lived in China for a number of years but had returned to America to unite the Christian churches in what he called the Fourth Crusade, a crusade to conquer China for the Cross as the earlier crusades had attempted to conquer the Holy City. Unlike the earlier crusades his crusade was to be peaceful penetration. But as I now recall that enthusiastic old man and his frequent references and admiration for the armored knights and their victories in Palestine I am afraid it was to be peaceful only because of necessity. I am sure he would have preferred to have led an armed host against what he called the evil forces of Satan in China.

The missionary stayed more than a week in our village, holding daily meetings much like the revival meetings that were so popular at that time. I missed the first one but his story was ably relayed to our family by my father. I showed such an interest in the missionary that I was allowed to attend all the successive meetings. This rather unusual eagerness was mistaken as a hopeful sign of an interest in religion. Unfortunately this was a mistake which my family and the local church realized soon after the departure of the missionary and the return of my former reluctance toward attending church. As for converting the Chinese, I distinctly recall my fear at that time that the missionary might somehow be able to convert the Chinese and make them like ourselves before I had an opportunity to see them as they were. I later found that I had little need to worry over such a possibility.

While the missionary evidently did not succeed in organizing his Fourth Crusade he did succeed in disorganizing my entire life. He took me out of my peaceful village and made me a wanderer over the face of the earth. He crowded out of my child mind the story of King Arthur and his knights and such other stories I was supposed to read, and replaced them with the *Travels of Marco Polo*, a copy of which had somehow found its way to our village. He made China my first choice among foreign nations. While I have come to know and admire many other foreign countries, China remains today my first choice as the place for a home, with the exception of my mother country Canada. Nor am I alone in this. I have yet to meet the person who has come to know the Chinese who does not admire them, or the person who has lived in Peking for two years or more who does not want to continue living in that city, sometimes for life.

The missionary was a most convincing speaker. Though I have come to know Peking as I know no other city, and the Peking I know is many times more interesting than the city described by the missionary, yet whenever I think of Peking it is the missionary's picture of it that most often comes first to my mind. The picture he painted has stayed with me all these years, even though I later found that his description was more interesting than accurate. He had never actually seen Peking; he told us only what others had told him, but he told it very convincingly. So convincingly that he started me dreaming that someday, somehow, I must see that wondrous city of the Orient—about as improbable a dream for a small boy living in a village in Canada at that time as for a boy of today to dream of someday visiting the moon. But even my wildest dreams did not approach what one day was to be a fact: that Peking, the city of my dreams, would be my home for more than half my life. I knew at that time that it would take a miracle, a miracle as great as any I had ever been told, to make it possible for me even to visit Peking.

But such a miracle did happen.

The miracle was a bomb that dropped from the sky, in the form of a cablegram from Dr. John R. Mott, asking me if I would make a trip to China for his organization. I accepted immediately. I gave up my architectural work which I had so laboriously built up, gave up my home, and everything else I had in America, and never returned to any of them again except for short visits. Within three weeks I was on board the *Tenyo Maru* bound for Shanghai. It was only later that I realized that Dr. Mott had also asked me to visit Japan, Korea, the Philippine Islands, and Russia. It was China that was the magic word in that cablegram.

To make this visit to China even more enjoyable I found that I was to be accompanied by Mr. Fletcher M. Brockman, a Y.M.C.A. secretary and missionary, and one of the finest men I have ever known. I was to work out the plans for a number of buildings that the International Committee of the Y.M.C.A. intended building in the above-mentioned countries. On the boat Mr. Brockman suggested that I also visit as many as possible of the missionaries in China to assist them with the plans for their new buildings. This I gladly agreed to do as a small contribution to the mission work in China. It resulted in my visiting most of the large cities and provinces of China under the guidance of Mr. Brockman, who knew China and the Chinese people as few white men ever did. He seemed to have friends, Chinese friends, everywhere, who took us into their homes and gave me the opportunity to see Chinese family life.

These visits to the inland cities of China proved to be so interesting and enjoyable that for many years, whenever I could get away from Peking, I used such time to make other trips. My only object was to see more and learn more of China and the Chinese people. Most of the trips were made with only an interpreter, a cook, and a mule driver with his cart—the famous Peking cart. I tried to avoid all foreigners, preferring to spend the nights in Chinese inns, occasionally a Chinese home, but more often in Chinese temples, where I found I was always welcome. In all the many days that I have spent in the interior of China I have never met with anything but kindness and generosity, even though I belonged to a race that was not popular at that time.

The months I spent with Mr. Brockman and the many trips I made into the interior gradually removed most of the prejudices and foolish ideas I had about China and the Chinese people that I carried with me on my first visit to that country.

As my prejudices against the Chinese people decreased, my desire to live the rest of my life in Peking increased. Soon after my return to China, on my second visit, I found the house I wanted through the kindness of Mr. W. H. Donald, that well-known adviser to the Chinese Government for more than forty years. I bought it almost at sight just a little more than thirty-five years ago.

It was not until some time later that Mr. Donald and I realized that we had bought the residence of one of the officials of the late Ch'ing government. Like all Chinese homes it is a group of buildings, the principal buildings forming the sides of a number of courts. It is a fairly old building, in pure Chinese architecture of the style of about the time of Emperor Tao Kuang (1782–1850). It is located within the red wall of the Imperial City, a stone's throw from the Forbidden City, a section of Peking that was formerly restricted to officials and attendants of the court.

All my neighbors, except one who was a eunuch, were Manchus, and most of them, including the eunuch, later became my friends. The eunuch's wife was one of the most beautiful and, curiously, one of the most popular women in our neighborhood. My servants were all Manchus, some of them from the palaces of the Manchu families who had had to curtail their establishments after the death of Empress Tz'u Hsi.

I am an architect. My work in Peking at that time was the designing and the supervising of the construction of the buildings of the Union Medical College for the Rockefeller Foundation. This brought me in early contact with the three Manchu princes from whom the land for the buildings was purchased. I was able to do a few favors for these princes which they considered of much greater value than they were. They became my friends, especially Princess Yu, the head of one of the most important of the Manchu clans and owner of the Yu Wang Fu. We razed the buildings forming this palace and used the land for the principal buildings of the present

Medical College, destroying such beautiful buildings that it might almost be called vandalism. Princess Yu became my adviser and almost my guardian on all things Chinese until her death many years later.

These Manchus introduced me to other Manchu families. Through them I met Emperor P'u Yi and attended some of the functions connected with his wedding, when he married two beautiful Manchu girls at the same time. His brother and his wife, both artists, came often to my home, usually with presents of some of their best paintings.

When these Manchus noticed my interest in the life of Empress Tz'u Hsi and the Ch'ing emperors they arranged for me to visit at various times the palaces in the Forbidden City, the Imperial City, and the Summer Palace area. They showed me Empress Tz'u Hsi's jewels, including the famous necklace of one hundred and eight perfect pearls, so large that I hesitate to describe them. I saw her paintings, her clothes, and her rooms as they were when she lived in them; also her musical instruments, including a fine porcelain flute that she often played to entertain herself and her friends.

As I saw how this great empress lived and the simple things she enjoyed, and listened to the stories of her kindness and her generosity, to her little vanities and love of beautiful clothes, told by people who had known her intimately, she gradually became a warm, interesting human being, instead of the hard, cruel, and scheming ruler that had so often been described to me.

I was also greatly interested when they showed me the palaces of the imperial princes and their earlier emperors. While the palaces of these emperors and princes were usually of enormous size and elegance, the large buildings were used only for entertainment purposes; the princes and their families actually lived in smaller quarters, often not much larger than those of the middle-class merchants. Of particular interest was the Round Palace, where Kublai Khan gave such wild parties for his fierce Mongol warrior chiefs and entertained Marco Polo more than two hundred years before America was discovered. Much more beautiful was the little palace, the mosque and famous bathroom that the scholarly

Emperor Chien Lung built in a vain attempt to please and win the affections of famous Fragrant Princess. I was also shown the island palace of Emperor Kuang Hsu and the prison palace of his adored Pearl Concubine. I often sat for hours in the Pearl Concubine's favorite seat, under the flowering crabapple tree in her private courtyard, writing many of the notes for this story and dreaming of the great events that had taken place in that group of buildings.

As I completed my commissions for the Americans and British I found myself doing more things for the Chinese. My position on the Commission of Inquiry of the League of Nations as a member of the Chinese delegation made it necessary for me to attend many of the meetings of the League in Geneva. On these visits to Europe and America I undoubtedly bored my friends many times with my too-frequent stories of the Chinese, the Manchus, and the Empress Tz'u Hsi. Probably to stop this annoyance, a number of my friends suggested that I put my stories in a book so they could all read them.

When I mentioned this suggestion to my Manchu friends they also urged me to do this, fortunately for my vanity for an entirely different reason. They wanted someone who was not too prejudiced against them to tell the world of the life and achievements of their Empress. They were particularly proud of the many times she had outwitted the cleverest foreign diplomats that were sent to China by the Western powers. They offered to give me access to their private papers, their diaries, their libraries, and their personal assistance in collecting the necessary material to add to the notes I had been making since my arrival in China.

We started on our search into the life of Empress Tz'u Hsi. Unfortunately we were stopped by the Japanese invasion of North China. Later, the attack on Pearl Harbor and World War II made it necessary for me to leave China for a number of years.

On my return to China at the close of the war I found the Manchus were even more eager that I continue this work. We started immediately to gather together the organization we now knew would be necessary to secure all the information we required. In this we were given every possible assistance by the director, the chief librarian, and the staff of the National Library. They helped us select the members of our staff; they gave us access at all times to their priceless collection of Chinese, Manchu, and Mongol manuscripts and books. The libraries of the several universities and the language school were also open at all times to our research men.

Our staff was divided, or it divided itself, into two sections. One section, under the leadership of a noted Chinese scholar who had spent most of his life in the libraries of China, searched the libraries and books in private collections for every scrap of information that could be found relating to the life of the Empress Tz'u Hsi. He and his men also spent considerable time in interviewing Chinese professors of history and other Chinese who were formerly connected with the Chinese Government.

The other section, under the direction of an old Manchu scholar, searched the government records and interviewed members of the old Manchu families. The old Manchu could do this, as he was related in some way to most of them. He was a member of one of the oldest and most important Manchu families, but he hid his identity under a Chinese name. It was not until almost the last day I spent in Peking that he told me his real name and connections and then only when he realized that I had guessed his family and clan. I will keep his secret, not because he has anything in his life or family that he is ashamed of, but the feeling is still strong in some places against the old ruling families of the Manchus and, as he said, he has to earn a living for himself and family.

As one of our problems was to locate the records we required from the scattered files of the old Manchu Government, we were fortunate in having this Manchu gentleman helping us. He and his boyhood friend had spent most of their lives in the Department of Records of the old Imperial Government. As they were both students with little else to do, they had read most of the important records and had made copies of some of the more interesting ones.

The Forbidden City and the government departments had been looted three times during the past fifty years. The government of the new Republic of China had put little value on the old records. Many of these records had been used for fuel; the remaining records are rapidly disappearing. But even in such confusion, if given twenty-four hours' notice, these two old men could usually dig out almost anything we required. If they could not find it, it just did not exist. Even for an Oriental that old man had a remarkable memory. He apparently knew the exact location of every manuscript or book in any of the many public or private libraries in Peking.

Next to his memory his most distinguished characteristic was his insistence on the accuracy of every piece of information that we collected and used which related in any way to Empress Tz'u Hsi. He was our watchdog. All the other members of our staff, including myself, stood in awe of him. Some of the men claimed that he could smell a lie or inaccurate statement. Given one night—he never seemed to require sleep—he could prove the accuracy or inaccuracy of any statement submitted to him. He spoiled many a good story for us by proving it was not true, and at such times he never budged an inch. He was so stubborn that I often wanted to put him out of the office and never see him again. But more often I was worried by the fear that he might get sick, might leave us, or even die before our work was completed. I knew, we all knew, that it would have been almost impossible to complete our work without him.

Unfortunately in our investigations we unearthed a number of incidents in the private life of Empress Tz'u Hsi that we, and especially the Manchus, wished we did not have to tell the world. At times our great woman showed some of the disastrous weaknesses of her sex combined with the impersonality of a dictator. After days of discussion (the Manchus never settle anything in a hurry) they agreed that if we were to give a true picture of her life we would have to include all such incidents in our story. This was because they realized that for a superwoman who had crowded everything fine and feminine out of her life to do the great things she did would be but natural, but for a small woman, possessing all the charms and frailties of an attractive woman, which she was, to do such things would be extraordinary.

We must mention one more old man who was of great assistance to us. He was a hermit scholar, a Chinese, who had given his entire life to the study of the lives of the late Ch'ing emperors, including Empress Tz'u Hsi. He lived fifteen or more miles west of Peking and was far too old ever to leave his chair again, but he was always willing to receive our men and to help us with additional information or with his criticisms on any subject or story that we presented to him.

Naturally we ran into many difficulties in our work. We soon found that the first thing Empress Tz'u Hsi did when she secured power was to attempt to destroy every record of her early life of poverty and the fact that her father had died in prison for a serious crime against the government. While these facts were known to a number of Manchus she made it very unpopular or risky for anyone to discuss them in public or even privately. The result was to open the gates for a deluge of rumors and falsehoods that were far more damaging to her reputation than the actual facts would have been. But they made our task more difficult, as we had to collect and carefully study every story of this nature, and there were many such stories. We did not want to miss any grain of truth they might possess, or did we want to be later accused of omitting such stories because we did not know they existed.

Let us look at one or two typical stories of this nature that are often repeated in Peking and have found their way into a number of foreign books. A good friend of mine, a high official and a fine Chinese scholar, spent considerable time in securing and bringing to me what he considered was proof that Empress Tz'u Hsi had been the mistress of a wealthy Chinese before she entered the palace as an imperial concubine.

We showed my friend that we knew all about this "rich Chinese"; that his name was Wu Chin-t'ang and that he had been of considerable assistance to Empress Tz'u Hsi when she was preparing to enter the palace, but in doing this he was repaying a debt he owed her grandfather. We were able to throw considerable doubt on the truthfulness of this story when we showed my friend that Wu Chin-t'ang was more than eighty years old when he first met Empress Tz'u Hsi, that he was not a rich man but a very poor man, and that he had raised the money he gave Tz'u Hsi's mother from friends and relatives, who hoped to reap a profit from their loans when the young girl became an imperial concubine. We also showed my friend the many and the exceedingly intimate nature of the examinations and a list of the names of the people who made them before the young girl was accepted even as a candidate for entrance to the palace. My friend then expressed his conviction that someone had misled him.

Another friend brought to our office what he thought was proof that Empress Tz'u Hsi was neither a Manchu nor a Chinese but was of foreign blood, born in one of the Russo-Siberian tribes in Siberia, and so was Russian. This story so enraged our Manchu that it took the entire office force several hours to calm him sufficiently even to answer such an insult to the Empress and the Manchu race. But when he was able to talk he so buried my friend with the government records of her father's and mother's family and the place of birth of Empress Tz'u Hsi that my friend decided the information he had collected must have been about some other empress.

Probably there is no question about the Empress Tz'u Hsi that has been more often discussed and on which there is so much inaccurate information as the place of her birth. Even her own nephews confessed to me that they did not know where she was born. Chinese writers have attributed to her a variety of birthplaces. Most foreigners will tell you that she was born in a hutung they call Pewter Lane. While it is true that her mother did live for a time in Pewter Lane, it was nearly forty years after the birth of her famous daughter, and after her two sons had become dukes and wealthy enough to purchase a fine home for their mother. These same people will usually tell you that the Empress was born in extreme poverty, practically a slave girl of the slums, evidently overlooking the fact that in China, as in other countries, slum girls are born in the slums, and not on Park Avenue.

But we were not entirely unsympathetic with these writers in their effort to locate the birthplace of the Empress after the difficulty we ourselves experienced in deciding this important question. Even though we knew every home her father and mother had lived in from the time of their marriage until their deaths, our group came near to breaking up trying to decide the birthplace of Empress Tz'u Hsi. Unfortunately for us, the family moved from Chiao Kao Kow to the less desirable Tz Ssu Tiao just three months before the birth of the Empress. The Manchus, keeping true to tradition, claimed she was born in the home on Chiao Kao Kow where she was conceived. They proved this by many references to their old writings; they even had the opinion of the mother of the Empress to support their claim. The Chinese, with more noise but less authority, claimed the birthplace of a child was where it was "caught," or, as we would say, first saw the light of day. When the argument had lasted most of the day and showed every evidence of lasting most of the night, I suggested the compromise of including both places, giving the reason for doing so, and letting the reader decide for himself where she was born.

While Empress Tz'u Hsi was able to destroy many of the early records of her family and enforce a strict taboo on any discussions of her place of birth and early life as long as she was alive she could not stop her family and others from talking after her death. Nor could she entirely stop her old mother, during her lifetime, from bragging a little on certain occasions about the many hardships she and her daughter passed through before her daughter became a great woman. A not-over-brilliant brother could also be induced to talk at times when he thought he was with discreet friends. Many of the Manchus wrote in the secrecy of their diaries a number of things about the Empress they dared not mention in public. Most of these diaries are now in the possession of their children, and were read by our old Manchu or his assistants.

But the most reliable information about the early life of the Empress came from government records, which were so numerous and so often duplicated that even the power of an Empress could not destroy all of them. The Manchu Government of China was apparently greatly overstaffed during the reign of the later Ch'ing emperors, owing to the fact that every male Manchu was either in the army or in the government. Families of influence in China, as in many other countries today, often secured safe positions in the government for their sons instead of the more dangerous and disagreeable positions in the army, which were liable to take them to the wars on one of the distant frontiers of China.

In order to keep this large number of office holders employed, very complete records were kept of every transaction connected with the government, especially of the funds handled by the Treasury Department. As every Manchu drew a pension from the government a record was kept of his birth, name, place of residence, position held, salary received, and any change in his place of residence. As the father of the Empress was an officer in the army from the time of his marriage until his death in prison in Nanking we had little difficulty in following him and his family in their many changes in residence.

The Department of Justice and the Board of Punishments also kept a complete record of every person accused or convicted of a crime. Unfortunately we also found considerable material about the father of the Empress in the records of these government departments. The date and place of birth of every Manchu girl were also carefully recorded, as every Manchu girl was subject to call for service in the imperial court or as a candidate for imperial concubine. Although Empress Tz'u Hsi was able to destroy all evidence in this department of her own birth, we could trace the birth of the other members of her family.

We met with some unusual characters and had a number of interesting experiences when interviewing the members of the old Manchu families. An outstanding characteristic of all Manchus is their good nature. But even our old Manchu became annoyed when, after days of searching in the far northeastern corner of the city, he found the man he was looking for was the peanut seller just two blocks from our office. This old man, the sole owner and entire staff of a peanut shop that measured less than four feet square, was the direct descendant of emperors. He was born a prince and brought up in one of the imperial palaces and, but for a peculiar turn of the wheel of fortune, might have been an emperor—a worried, unhappy emperor, instead of the best-natured, most happy, and best-liked man on the entire street.

Neither space nor the patience of the reader will permit me to tell more of the interesting people who passed through our office. But I cannot resist telling of one more odd character who added considerably to our fund of information on the court of Empress Tz'u Hsi.

This man was the grandson of one of the best-known eunuchs of Empress Tz'u Hsi's court. While some might doubt that eunuchs ever had grandsons, a few of them did. There are records of eunuchs who took the precaution of having a son before becoming a eunuch in order to have someone to carry on the name and to look after the family graves. The more common and more popular custom was for a eunuch, if and when he became wealthy, to adopt a son, usually the son of one of his brothers.

The father of this particular Manchu was the adopted son of one of the most powerful and most hated officials of the later Ch'ing Dynasty. Many of the accusations against this eunuch are now believed to have been greatly exaggerated, but his name is still prominently connected with the worst scandals of Empress Tz'u Hsi's reign. Many now believe that his greatest fault was such an intense loyalty to his mistress that he believed any crime was justifiable if it were in her interest.

The grandson of this eunuch wanted, above all things, to defend the name and record of his famous grandfather, especially against the charges that he had unlawfully accumulated a huge fortune. In listening to his story we detected a slight suspicion that this latter accusation hurt the family most because it was not true. While the son and the grandson of the eunuch had led creditable lives and were fairly successful in their professions, the entire lack of worldly goods seemed amply to disprove at least this latter accusation. We could use little of this man's interesting story, as he had scant or no proof of his statements, but he did give us a number of clues that we investigated and later found of value.

In our search for information on the life of Empress Tz'u Hsi and the prominent people of her time we interviewed the descendants of more than seventy of the Manchu, Mongol, and Chinese families who had played important parts during the long life of the Empress. Of these more than twenty were the families of imperial princes, direct descendants of the Ch'ing emperors.

Each person we interviewed, every member of our group, and many friends outside our organization, assisted us in every possible way. Our staff gave their time and energy far beyond the value of any compensation they received. Most of these people were urged on by the hope that by their contribution a few more people in the outside world might get to know and better understand the Manchu people and their great Empress Tz'u Hsi.

HARRY HUSSEY

CONTENTS

VENERABLE ANCESTOR

THE TREK OF THE TUNIS PEOPLES

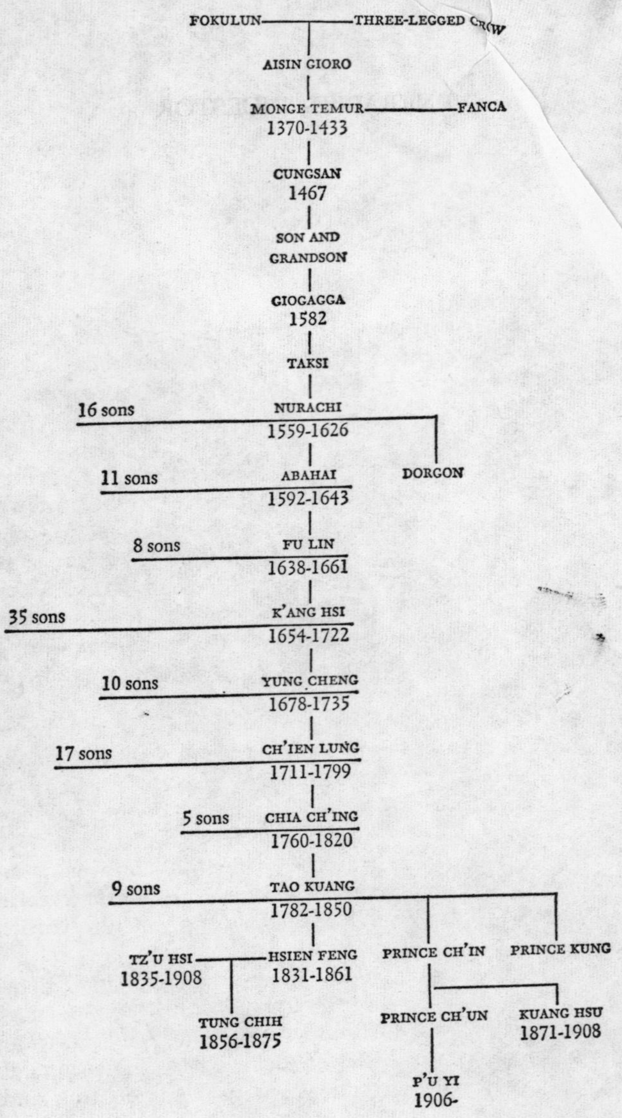
FOKULUN
THREE-LEGGED CROW
AISIN GIORO
MONGE TEMUR
1370-1433
FANCA
CUNGSAN
1467
SON AND
GRANDSON
GIOGAGGA
1582
TAKSI
16 sons
NURACHI
1559-1626
DORGON
11 sons
ABAHAI
1592-1643
8 sons
FU LIN
1638-1661
35 sons
K'ANG HSI
1654-1722
10 sons
YUNG CHENG
1678-1735
17 sons
CH'IEN LUNG
1711-1799
5 sons
CHIA CH'ING
1760-1820
9 sons
TAO KUANG
1782-1850
TZ'U HSI
1835-1908
HSIEN FENG
1831-1861
PRINCE CH'IN
PRINCE KUNG
TUNG CHIH
1856-1875
PRINCE CH'UN
KUANG HSU
1871-1908
P'U YI
1906-

1. THE MARK OF THE FOX

An old Manchu prophecy states that the rule and supremacy of the Aisin Gioro clan would someday be ended forever by a woman of the Yehonala clan bearing the mark of the fox.

The place was one of the old sections of the Tatar city of Peking, out near the Hsi Chih Men, the gate in the northwest corner of the city, where the poorer Mongols and Manchus lived. The time was the Double Tenth, the tenth day of the Tenth Moon of the fifteenth year of the reign of Tao Kuang, November 28, 1835, as the Western peoples reckon time. It was the Hour of the Tiger (four o'clock in the morning)—the hour in which so many people are born and so many people die in China.

A frail and discouraged young Manchu woman occupied one of the small rooms of the courtyard with the crooked crabapple tree, the smallest courtyard of a house on Ta Ssu T'iao Hutung, the property of Grandfather Wong, owner of the Jade Spring Well. Grandfather Wong was up early that morning. A child was being born to the Manchu woman and Grandfather Wong was much worried. He was afraid that both life and death would greet the rising sun that eventful day.

As with the birth of most Chinese children more than a hundred years ago, the Manchu woman was sitting up straight on the Chair of New Life, supported by an old woman and suffering as all women suffer at such a time. She was far too poor to employ a regular midwife, so she had only this kindly old woman, Grandmother Wei, to help her when her time came. Grandmother Wei possessed one of the few Chairs of New Life in the neighborhood. She had volunteered to loan to Hwei T'ai T'ai this chair with the big hole in the bottom and to "catch the baby" when it arrived.

The little Manchu woman was afraid, very much afraid. She was very young. It was her first baby, and she wanted some of her own people with her that night, but they lived far in the north and so could not be with her. She wanted most of all her husband. She wanted him to assure her he had been only teasing when he told her, three mornings before, that he had seen a black fox run across the courtyard. This was usually considered a bad omen. She was superstitious, and although she did not believe him at the time, she had been thinking often of the black fox during the long night. The story seemed true to her now, and this made her more afraid.

She also wanted her husband to tell her that he would not be too cross with her if their first baby was a girl child and not a man child, as she knew he wanted. She was sure her baby was going to be a girl. Grandmother Wei, with the instinct of an old woman who had helped bring many babies into the world, had told her so. This also worried her. She found it easy to worry and be afraid as she spent that long, cold November night in pain and loneliness. She thought often that night of her husband Hwei Cheng. She knew he had not always been a good husband to her; he was careless and selfish and left her alone very often. But even as Hwei T'ai T'ai suffered bringing Hwei Cheng's child into the world, she recalled his wonderful smile and the few times he had been tender and kind. She loved her husband and longed for him very much that night.

The neighbors knew her husband had not been home for two days. They could have told her he was at the Ch'ing Yu Club, the club for the celebration of Excessive Bliss, where, although it was against the law, the men smoked opium or "foreign dirt," as the Chinese called it. The neighbors could also have told her he would not be home for another two days, as they were experienced in what "foreign dirt" did to husbands. The Manchu woman had the sympathy of all her neighbors. They were as poor as she, some even poorer, so they could offer her little assistance. But they could meet at Grandfather Wong's well and curse Hwei Cheng for not being with his wife at such a time. And curse him they did, loyally, loudly, and at great length. The little Manchu woman had the gift, so noticeable in the women of her clan, of making friends.

Grandfather Wong usually pretended to pay little attention to the neighborhood indignation meetings held so often at his well, but he always had his bench close enough to miss little that was said. He would have had a hard time missing anything said that morning, for all the women talked at the top of their voices.

This custom of holding such meetings began almost with the beginning of the Chinese race. It served to protect women and has always played an important part in the life of Chinese women of the lower classes, especially in the villages. Custom ruled, as custom rules most things in China, that if any woman were abused by her husband, regardless of how much she might care for him or how much pride might prompt her to conceal her ill-treatment from the neighbors, she had publicly to proclaim before all who cared to listen that she had been beaten or otherwise abused by her husband. The scorn of the neighbors thus made many a henpecked husband hold his hand, regardless of how much the good wife might have deserved a few judicious blows.

But the meeting at Grandfather Wong's well that morning was unusual; not the wife, but all the other women of the neighborhood were making the accusations. This was so unusual that Grandfather Wong openly and unashamedly joined the crowd. The little Manchu woman had made a good friend of Grandfather Wong, the seller of sweet water from the Jade Spring Well.

Hwei T'ai T'ai had been married only a little more than two years, but they had been years of unhappiness. Soon after her marriage to the attractive young Manchu, Hwei Cheng, she found her husband was not always the smiling and kindly young man he appeared to all his friends. She found that his associates were young men of unsavory reputation who frequented gambling houses and brothels. It also soon came to her knowledge that her husband was intimate with a young woman called Orchid, whom he visited often outside Ch'ien Men and whom he had known before they were married.

Among her other duties, Hwei T'ai T'ai had to take care of her husband's father, an almost helpless old man who lived with them. This she did willingly, and as custom required of her, although the old man was often surly and bad-tempered. All this made her unhappy.

A little joy had come to her when she found that she was to become a mother. This always makes a Manchu or a Chinese woman happy. She thought it would make her husband more attentive, but he left her alone even more often than before and her joy soon turned to ashes in her mouth. Shortly after she found she was going to be a mother her father-in-law died. She was ashamed at the inner pleasure it gave her when she realized he could no longer berate and torment her; but she had to hide her relief and to weep and look unhappy because this was the custom of her people.

The death of the old man proved to be not a blessing but another misfortune. It was then that Hwei T'ai T'ai found that her spendthrift husband had secretly mortgaged their little home to pay some of his debts. Their home on Chiao Tao K'ow Hutung[1] was all that had remained to them of the once large Hwei estate. It had been the home of the number-one concubine when the Hwei family was wealthy and had concubines and many servants. To the Manchu woman it was a beautiful home, as it had two courtyards, two fine old trees, and a high wall which made it quiet and restful. Hwei T'ai T'ai had been happy in the thought that her baby was going to be born in what was to her a fine house close to the yamen of the commander of the Yellow Banner Corps and the many big homes of that select neighborhood. In later years she always gave Chiao Tao K'ow Hutung as the birthplace of her first child on the principle that a child's birthplace was really the home where it was conceived, not necessarily where it first saw the light of day. She little knew how much confusion

[1] Now Tung Ta Chieh.

she was causing for the future biographers of her daughter.

After the old man's death they had had to sell their house to pay more of her husband's debts and to provide money for the fine funeral Hwei Cheng insisted on giving his father. When she protested and told him they should not spend all their money on a showy funeral when they had no home and were soon to have their first baby, he reminded her that his father was a member of the Yehonala clan of the Manchu Bordered Blue Banner and must have a funeral in keeping with the greatness of his clan.

After all the funeral expenses had been paid no money was left, and, moreover, they had to find a new home. Peking was very prosperous and crowded at that time, because of troubles on the borders of the empire and no houses were to be found for the small rent Hwei Cheng could afford. His cousin, Tien Chen, had also recently lost his home on Ta Ssu T'iao Hutung. Although he had no right to do so, he let Hwei Cheng and his family move into one of the small courtyards of his former great house. It was unlawful for a Chinese to own property in the Tatar city after its capture by the Manchus but Wong Tso-min, or Grandfather Wong as we know him, had loaned much money to the Tien family; and Tien Chen, the last remaining son of that family, being unable to pay off the mortgage, had had to hand over to Grandfather Wong the title deeds of the property, thus making Wong the actual owner.

Hwei T'ai T'ai did not like her new home, as it was in the northwestern section of the Tatar city and far from all her friends. It was also a very small and unattractive house compared to the one on Chiao Tao K'ow Hutung. She thought Fate had been very unkind to her. She did not realize at that time that in acquiring her new home she also acquired Grandfather Wong, Soothsayer Fu, and other friends who were to be of more value to her than any fine house could possibly have been.

At first Grandfather Wong did not feel very friendly toward Hwei Cheng and his wife. In fact, he considered them very much of a nuisance when he found that in acquiring his new property he had also inadvertently acquired an impoverished

Manchu family. He knew that he could not legally force them out. It had been the law of China for many centuries that no man can ever be evicted from his home, even if he is unable to pay his rent, regardless of who owns the property.

As his "go-between" had been unable to persuade the Manchu family to leave, Grandfather Wong had decided to break all custom and talk to the Manchu woman himself. In that he made a great mistake. After two minutes' talk Grandfather Wong was astonished to hear himself promising Hwei T'ai T'ai that she could stay in her home as long as she wanted and that she need not worry about the rent. He could never understand how he came to make such a promise, and he knew very well he would never be able to make his wife, Wong T'ai T'ai, understand it either, as according to custom she was the manager of the home.

Now Grandfather Wong was worried, greatly worried, over the Manchu woman. In fact, he was worrying more over the birth of that little Manchu child than he had worried over all his own eleven children. He, too, knew that the child soon to be born in the courtyard with the crooked crabapple tree was going to be a girl. His friend, Soothsayer Fu Sheng-hsien, had told him so several days ago, and it never occurred to him to doubt the soothsayer's superior knowledge. He also knew what that would mean to the little Manchu woman: more scoldings and more neglect, regardless of how many indignation meetings the neighboring women held at the well. Hwei Cheng, the husband, was immune to such meetings, as he realized he could not be more disliked by his neighbors no matter what he did.

Grandfather Wong had kept his information to himself. He thought he was the only one who knew it, but in this he overlooked Grandmother Wei and her intuition in such matters. She had told the Manchu woman, who was resigned to the inevitable. In this time of her great distress Hwei T'ai T'ai did not care whether she lived or died. But it took only the first cry of that little mite of humanity, the cry caused by the lusty spanking administered by Grandmother Wei, to bring back to the mother not only the desire but the determination to live. That little cry was more than just the first cry of her firstborn. It seemed to her like a voice from the gods. It was a prophecy of the future. It was a miracle that kindled a flame of courage and ambition, a flame that filled the mother completely and was never to flicker for one moment so long as breath remained in her body. In fact, it was to keep death away as long as her first-born daughter needed her.

Old Grandmother Wei had brought with her her most precious possessions, practically her only possessions, two old snuff bottles. These were meant to bring good luck to the new mother. One bottle was of red porcelain; this she put in the right hand of the woman. The other was a clear bright green glass bottle, her favorite; this she put in the left hand of the woman so that in her suffering she could grasp them hard and lighten the pain. The green bottle had fallen from the woman's hand and little Erh, a young girl helping Grandmother Wei, picked it up and placed it on the window sill.

Hwei T'ai T'ai lay on the k'ang, only partially conscious. The first cry of the infant roused the mother just as the sun came over the roof of the building across the courtyard. The first rays passed through the bottle on the sill and cast a bright green path of light across the bed. Not recognizing the source of the light, the mother took it for a good omen, a sign from the gods. She cried out: "Ta Ts'ui, Ta Ts'ui [Green Jade, Green Jade]!" From that moment, regardless of all the grand names and titles the world was to give her daughter, to the mother she was always Ta Ts'ui. Unfortunately Ta Ts'ui is among the many Chinese words that few foreigners ever learn to pronounce correctly, so we will call her the English equivalent, Green Jade, until we can give China's last great empress the title by which she was to be known to the world twenty-six years later.

Grandfather Wong and his friends were destined to play an important part in the early life of Green Jade. He was the head of the family that owned and operated the Jade Spring Well. This was more than just a well where one bought sweet water; it was an institution. Even the Wong family could not tell its age, but they could show the history of twelve generations of Wongs that had continuously operated the well. Earlier records were lost when a fierce band of Mongols, on one of their raids into China, had burned the Wong home.

The well was close to the great Hsi Chih Men. In fact, the location of the gate is said to be owing to the desire of the builders to put it near the Jade Spring Well. Through the Hsi Chih Men entered the richly laden camel trains from Tatary, Turkestan, and beyond. It was the gateway to Nankow Pass, to Sinkiang, and Mongolia, and to all the countries bordering on the Gobi Desert. It was the gate often used by emperors, princes, officials, merchants, and common people when they visited any of the numerous palaces, temples, and hunting grounds on the western plains and in the western hills. Everyone, even the Emperor, stopped for a cool drink of water from the Jade Spring Well when they passed through the Hsi Chih Men. They all knew Grandfather Wong and all appeared to have time for a few words with him.

Supplying sweet water to camel trains, to the mules and horses of the Mongols, and to travelers was only part of Grandfather Wong's business. It might be called his foreign business. His everyday business in which he was most interested was to supply water to the people in that section of Peking. He had many customers, among them the breeders of goldfish, who often came long distances to obtain Jade Spring water because they believed their goldfish were brighter in color and multiplied faster in the water from Grandfather Wong's well. Teahouses and restaurants claimed Jade Spring water made the best tea. Most of the water was delivered to users by wheelbarrow or two-wheeled carts made especially for this purpose. Many people came to the well with jars of their own. All the water was drawn with wooden buckets. No pump was ever allowed in that well and the water was never permitted to come in contact with metal of any kind. When one looked down the well at noon, it took but little imagination to see that the color of the water was that of the clearest green jade.

Grandfather Wong had some peculiar ideas about the well. To say it was part of his very life would be putting it mildly. If necessary, he would have died for that well without the slightest hesitation. Yet he believed that the Wong family owned only the well itself; the water belonged to all the people, and he charged only for the service of bringing the water out of the well. Water was free to all who wanted to drink it and to those who brought their own jars to be filled. Grandfather Wong charged only the camel and mule trains, the sheep and the goatherds, who watered their animals at his well, and the professional sellers of water. To all others, man or beast, water was free.

The Jade Spring Well was not only a place to buy sweet water, it was also the social center of the neighborhood, as necessary a part of the city as was the magistrate's *yamen* (official residence), and a lot more popular. Instead of going to the magistrate, the poor often brought their disputes to Grandfather Wong. He was a good judge, as he knew all the family secrets of his customers. His decisions were seldom questioned.

Not far from the well, Wei, a man from Shansi province, had his teahouse. This was a gathering place in the evening for all the men of the neighborhood when their work was done. Here they met to drink a few cups of tea and to discuss the local and national problems of the day. Grandfather Wong was there every evening to pass on anything of interest he might have learned from the travelers who had halted at his well. Strangers stopping in that part of the city for the night were welcome at the teahouse where, in return for entertainment, they told of the world outside the great walls of Peking. Every village and town in China had one or more such teahouses which were the center of the community. Traveling merchants, actors, soldiers, and officials stopped there and spread news from one village to the next. This system of teahouses made the average Chinese of one hundred years ago, without newspapers, amazingly well informed on local and national affairs. At the time of Green Jade's birth the most important matter for discussion in the teahouses was the news from Canton, where the behavior of foreign sailors and traders was causing much uneasiness, soon to culminate in the so-called Opium War with Great Britain.

Grandfather Wong had many friends, but one stood far

above the others. This was his sworn brother, Soothsayer Fu Sheng-hsien, a man closer to him than any member of his own family. Other countries miss much in not having the custom of sworn brothers. It is a custom in which two or three young men of similar education and standing make a compact, swearing to stand by each other throughout life. As the sworn-brother oath is seldom—if ever—broken, this assures every man who has sworn brothers of a few friends he can count on absolutely, no matter what happens.

Soothsayer Fu and Grandfather Wong were about the same age. What that age was no one could guess. In a country such as China, where old age is respected and has many privileges, both men and women often exaggerate the evidence of old age. But these two men were really very old. They had known each other since childhood. Each was equally wrinkled, but whereas Grandfather Wong's wrinkles were marks of gentleness and good will to all, Fu's wrinkles were etched in by suffering and disappointments. He had had many sorrows in his life and had seen many things a man should never see. Fu had few friends, but Grandfather Wong knew him for the kindly old man he really was.

Soothsayer Fu's paying business was picking lucky days for weddings, funerals, days on which to start a journey, dig a well, or take a new concubine. He was often engaged to pick a lucky location for a new house, a grave, or to plant trees, for he knew where the Feng Shui were right or wrong. He was also the letter writer of the community.

While he earned his living and supported his family by these activities, his hobby, his joy, the real satisfaction of his life was to study the stars, planets, and other celestial bodies and to weigh their effects on the lives of men.

Grandfather Wong often joined his friend in the study of such things but he was a rank amateur compared to Soothsayer Fu, whose local name signified The Man Who Caught the Golden Turtle, meaning: "He who has accumulated wisdom."

Grandfather Wong and Soothsayer Fu had long practiced the art of carrying on a serious, interesting conversation with the use of the fewest possible words. They had reached a point quote many similar experiences from the long history of Buddhism. To him the vision foretold the return to earth of the spirit of one of the past great emperors or empresses; most probably that of Empress Hsiao Tz'u. He explained to his friends that this spirit had been waiting a long time for a suitable body to occupy in order to return to this earth. It had now entered the body of the little Manchu child born at the time of the vision. Nothing could be clearer.

Grandfather Wong and Soothsayer Fu did not wait the three days for the proper visiting day to call on the newborn babe and its mother. Together with the priest they visited Hwei T'ai T'ai that evening to tell her the great news. They were rather taken aback to find that she was not astonished; she already knew she had given birth to a wonder child, a daughter of the gods. They only confirmed her in her own opinion and gave her the details of Soothsayer Fu's vision.

2

Green Jade was fed the story of Soothsayer Fu's vision with her mother's milk. The mother told her the story almost every day of her childhood and also later, whenever Green Jade required a little extra courage to carry her through difficult times.

Without doubt the vision of Soothsayer Fu had a remarkable influence, perhaps the deciding influence, on the life of Green Jade. It made her a good student. It gave her the confidence, courage, and determination she required so many times in her long life. It changed the previously shy, timid Hwei T'ai T'ai into a woman of force worthy to be the mother of a great empress and the grandmother of two emperors. It made Grandfather Wong into a generous landlord; from that day the Manchu woman and her family lacked nothing that he could give from his scanty supplies.

Soothsayer Fu and the Buddhist monk later taught Green Jade the Chinese characters, the simple stories of China, the history of the Manchu race, and the religion of Buddha.

All this Soothsayer Fu is reputed to have related in a written history which is the basis of the tales told of Green Jade's childhood.[2]

Though born in poverty, Green Jade was a true daughter of the Yehonala clan, one of the oldest clans of the Manchus, an imperial clan that traces its lineage without break back to Hsiao Tz'u, the wife of Nurhaci and ancestress of all the Ch'ing emperors who sat on the Dragon Throne of China.

Nurhaci, who lived in the seventeenth century, was one of the greatest of the Manchu leaders before they invaded China. He boasted descent through Monge Temur (the earliest of their chiefs of whom written records exist) and from the legendary maiden Fokulun. She, with two of her sisters, lived in the forest on the bank of the Mutan River that flows along the foot of the Long White Mountain, an early home of the Manchu race. The three maidens were bathing in the river when a three-legged crow dropped a red cherry into the hands of Fokulun, the youngest. Fokulun ate the cherry and, although a virgin, became pregnant. When she became large and could not keep her secret any longer she informed her sisters and asked them what to do. The two sisters replied: "We have all three eaten of the drug of immortality. Your condition is Heaven's will. Wait until your body is light again, then you can fly back to heaven." The two sisters returned to their celestial home. Fokulun stayed in the woods and was cared for and fed by a great white wolf.

When her son was born, Fokulun realized that he was a child of the gods, that he was sent to this world to be a peacemaker, and that he must join the men of the world to carry out his destiny. She wove a basket of reeds from the riverbank, placed the babe in it, and left it among the bulrushes. When the water rose, the basket floated down the river. It came to rest at a point where three families were fighting to see who would be head of the clan. When they saw the child, so evidently a gift from the gods, they stopped fighting and appointed him their leader. He grew to manhood, established his capital at Otoli, and took the name of Aisin Gioro, the

[2]The learned Manchu and Chinese scholars I have consulted agree that such a book was written. Many have said they have seen one, but up to this date I never have.

name of the imperial family of the Manchus to the present day.

How surprising that the early Manchus, who could have had no contact with the literature of any country beyond their own borders, should thus have combined the stories of Moses in Egypt, Romulus and Remus, and of the virgin birth in Palestine in describing their origin. But this legend appears in the earliest Manchu writing and was even told around the campfires long before the Manchus had a written language.

How did these Manchus, with a mixed population of less than six hundred thousand, with little culture, no wealth—horsemen with few implements of war—how did such a people with such a humble origin develop the skill to conquer a country of more than three hundred million people? At that time China was the largest, most wealthy, and supposedly the strongest military country in the world. Not only did the Manchus conquer the country but in a comparatively short time they won the respect, the co-operation, and the loyalty of the people they had conquered. The Manchus gave China the best government it had had for centuries. They improved the living conditions, extended the borders of the country, and raised China to its highest point in area, population, wealth, prestige, the arts, and social culture.

To attempt to understand better these people and if possible to discover the spark of greatness that made the Manchus and their sons and daughters the unusual people they were, let us go back and make a short study of their origin. Let us follow them in their slow, painful, and hard upward progress from a small, unimportant group of primitive people living in what is now the most barren part of the Gobi Desert to the Dragon Throne of China.

Let us turn to the stories and songs that the storytellers of these people have been telling for centuries and which are still being told today. The storytellers tell us that the people we now call Manchus are of the Tungus peoples of the Mongol race. They tell us they were the first people created by the gods, the gods that still live in the black, mysterious mountains in the direction of the noonday sun, Tibet. Soon after the waters receded from the earth, the gods gave them the valleys of the Tungus and Yenisei rivers for their home. Here their people lived for more moons than there are hairs on a woman's head. At that time their homeland was the most desirable country in the whole world, as it was well watered, grew all the food they required, and was warm both summer and winter.

In these fortunate surroundings the early ancestors became rich and selfish. They forgot the teachings of their gods and their gods forgot them, forgot to send the rains and the warm winds as formerly from the east and south. Instead, the winds came from the northlands and were cold. The ground became hard and frozen. Only snow fell from the sky. Many of the young of their women and their mares died in the womb. Men and women sickened and died because they had no food to put in their bellies.

As the rich lands gradually changed into the Gobi Desert, the dinosaur, the saber-toothed tiger, the mastodon, and other semi-tropical animals, including men, that formerly were plentiful in Mongolia, had either to adapt themselves to their new environment, migrate, or die.

Man alone of all these animals seems to have survived. Some of the people stayed, adopted new ways of living, and became the great Mongolian race. Others, like the Tungus, left their homes and traveled eastward in search of the warm winds and rains that formerly came from that direction. They pushed ahead of them the weaker tribes that occupied the lands through which they had to pass. They pushed these tribes eastward to the shores of the Pacific, and ultimately across the seas to America. Here Asiatic folklore apparently substantiates the theories of anthropologists concerning the origin of the American Indians.

While the Tungus pushed those in front of them, the hungry tribes behind pushed the Tungus until they, too, finally came to the coast. As they were land people and could go only where a horse could take them, they went no farther.

Their leader, Aisin Gioro, united the tribes, welcomed the homeless people from the plains, formed them into one group, and established their boundaries on the Sungara and Amur rivers, with the Long White Mountain as the heart of their new lands.

From this time the Tungus were to be known by a number of different names, far too many for us even to list; but generally, and for the longest period, they were known as Nuchens. It was not until shortly before they invaded China that they adopted the name Manchu.

The Nuchens appear to have spent most of their time in fighting, either in defense of their own territories or in the less-admirable occupation of attempts to steal territory from their neighbors. They succeeded in gradually welding themselves into what might loosely be called a nation—at least a nation of sufficient importance to gain the notice of China, their powerful neighbor to the south.

Recent excavations show that during some part of this period the Nuchens ceased to be tent-dwelling nomads and built themselves cities with market places, fine palaces, and comfortable homes. A list of the presents or tribute they sent to the chinese emperors at this time consisted of fine furs, precious stones, leather goods, horses, stone arrowheads, and other articles that suggest a fairly cultured people.

While the Nuchens reached a point of comfort in their homes and some elegance in their attire, it cannot be claimed that they ever came near the level of the civilizations of the Chinese or the Egyptians. This was probably owing to the difference in climate and to the fact that the Nuchens were horsemen. They could go anywhere a horse could take them. But a seat on a horse is a very poor place to work out a formula in mathematics or the plans for great buildings or great cities. Until after their conquest of China they never advanced much beyond the horseback period. But in that they were superb. Their inventions were connected with horsemanship. Among those were the reintroduction of the stirrup and the short bow. These accounted for many of the victories and ultimately made the Tatars the terror of Europe.

To those whose definition of a "gentleman" is one who does no manual work, the Nuchen would seem worthy of high rank. He was probably the earliest and the most persistent gentleman in history. Whether rich or poor, he was a warrior and a huntsman and would do little else but fight and hunt. He never stooped to farming or trade. While the Nuchen women did do certain things that might be called manual labor, such as the preserving of meats and foods (a talent which they have to this day), and were obedient in most things to their husbands, they, too, were superb riders. They could use the bow and arrow as well as the men, and whenever necessary they fought with equal bravery alongside their sons and husbands. They showed at a very early date the courage and the independence which were to be so noticeable during the Ch'ing Dynasty.

The language of the Nuchens gradually grew from a mixture of many dialects into a distinct language of their own. In the development of their written language they were assisted by a number of Tibetan scholars. Chinese reports mention that in the year A.D. 713, during the reign of Emperor Hsuan Tsung of the T'ang Dynasty, a Nuchen envoy arrived at the Chinese court with many presents and that his credentials were written in the Nuchen language. It also adds that only one man, the poet Li Po, in all the Chinese court could read the Nuchen script.

The Tungus-Nuchens were from the very beginning of their history monotheists, some being Shamanists. They worshiped, or, more accurately, acknowledged one Supreme Deity. But this did not stop them from taking the precaution of having a number of lesser or personal gods—gods that they felt free to call on at any time of the day or night for assistance on matters that were too trivial or of such a nature that they might not wish to discuss them with the Supreme Deity. They also considered it the duty of the ruler to keep the relations with the Supreme Deity on a satisfactory basis. These personal gods were men or women who had been prominent for good works and generosity while living on this earth. Nor were they in any way narrow-minded in the selection of such gods. They selected them even from their enemies. The theory was that persons who had been kindly and willing to do good deeds in this world would, they hoped, be equally willing after death to help a poor supplicant. The Nuchens did not become Buddhists until after their conquest of China, and then only after a careful comparison of all the religions known to them at that time, including Christianity.

This gradual rise of the Nuchens from a semi-wild Mongol tribe to a fairly cultured nation above the level of all their neighbors, except the Chinese to the south, was shown in many ways. They employed Tibetan and Chinese teachers for their children. They stopped the barbarous custom of leaving the dead on platforms on the plains to be disposed of by the elements, the birds, and animals, as practiced by the Mongols, and substituted burial in the ground and later cremation. The Nuchens probably reached their greatest pre-Chinese height late in the twelfth century. Before Genghis Khan started his campaigns against western Asia and eastern Europe and made his home base safe by destroying his neighbors, including much of the nation of the Nuchens. He destroyed all the walled cities of the Nuchens, their culture, and almost the entire nation. Only two great walls, which, like the Great Wall of China, failed to hold back the Mongol horsemen, and the ruined walls of a few forgotten cities, remain in present-day Manchuria as proof of the engineering skill and early culture of the Nuchens.

The Nuchen tribes continued to pay tribute to the Mongols until Nurhaci became strong enough to stop tribute both to the Mongol chiefs and to the Ming emperors of China. Nurhaci (1559–1626) had three wives entitled to the name Ta Fujin, or Great Empress, a number of secondary wives who were called Fujin, without the Ta, which meant "great," and concubines almost without number. Not much is known about his first wife except that she was the mother of two of his famous sons, Cuyen and Daisan. His second wife was the mother of Dorgon. She committed suicide at the death of Nurhaci to accompany and serve him in the next world. His third wife, Empress Hsiao Tz'u, was the mother of Abahai and the grandmother of Fu Jen, the first Ch'ing emperor of China. This empress is of particular interest to us, as it was her spirit that the Buddhist monk claimed had entered the body of Green Jade at her birth.

Nurhaci did many things for the Nuchens. Probably his greatest accomplishment was the defeat of the Yehe tribe and the capture of the Liao-yang district from the Chinese. Both the Chinese and the Mongols recognized Nurhaci as emperor and the Nuchens as a separate, independent nation, the first time they had been so recognized in their long history.

To strengthen his new nation Nurhaci reorganized the army and introduced the Eight Banner system. This system not only assigned every male to one of the eight banners but also the families of the warriors. In this way the entire population was united in one war machine, creating an almost invincible fighting nation. The banner system continued until the fall of the Manchus nearly three hundred years later.

Nurhaci, with his several younger brothers, his sixteen sturdy fighting sons, and innumerable fighting grandsons, supplied his share of warriors for this army. He also built protecting walls around some of his principal cities. After several moves he finally established his capital in Mukden and did much to make it the fine city it was at the beginning of this century.

The great ambition of Nurhaci's life was the conquest of China, a dream that would have been considered an impossibility by anyone except the Nuchens.

Nurhaci finally considered he had completed the organization of his nation for a successful war against the Chinese. He had met and defeated the best Chinese armies the Ming emperors had sent against him. He had captured the Liaotung Peninsula from the Chinese and had driven most of the Chinese soldiers beyond the Great Wall at Shanhaikwan. His spies had told him that the people of China were dissatisfied; rebellion had broken out in many of the provinces. To Nurhaci it was evident that the "Mandate from Heaven" for the Ming Dynasty was running out; it was the time to strike. And strike he did, but he evidently struck too soon. He did not find the conquest of China so easy or so quickly accomplished as he had expected. He won a few victories but he met with a disastrous defeat when he encountered the main Chinese army using cannon and other European firearms furnished them by the Jesuits and Portuguese. Nurhaci retired to his capital in Mukden and died a few days later from an illness largely brought on by chagrin over his defeat and the loss of his army.

His death occurred in 1626—six years after the landing of the Pilgrims on Plymouth Rock.

Abahai (1592–1643), the eighth son of Nurhaci, became Emperor after a short period of joint control with his brothers, succeeding his father. He realized that China could not be conquered by a sudden raid or one battle as Nurhaci had evidently planned; that such a huge empire could only be conquered by a long and carefully planned campaign. He started this campaign by first making his base secure, by defeating his enemies on his borders. He conquered Korea. In fact, he conquered it twice. The second time he made it a vassal state, which it remained until taken from the Manchu Empire by the Japanese in the Chino-Japanese War of 1894–95. He then attacked the Mongols on his western front and forced them into an alliance which they loyally kept as long as the Ch'ing Dynasty existed. Evidently when Emperor Abahai conquered a country it stayed conquered. He imported Jesuit missionaries from Macao to teach him to make cannon and other modern war equipment. He added to and made other improvements in the organization of the Eight Banners started by his father.

Equally important were his efforts to unite his own people into a closer and stronger nation. The people he now ruled over included many tribes that were not the original Nuchens. In 1635 Abahai ordered that the name Manchu be used to describe the people of his nation. Abahai hoped that its use would also somehow conceal the lowly origin and raise the prestige of the dynasty which he now called the Ch'ing Dynasty.

While Emperor Abahai was always more of a soldier than a scholar he did continue to employ Tibetan scholars to improve the written language of the Manchus. He also welcomed the many Chinese scholars, political leaders, and even military officers who were banished from China in considerable numbers or considered it advisable to leave that country because their ideas were too advanced or were otherwise objectionable to the Ming emperors and their dying government. In this way the Manchus acquired some of the most advanced and greatest scholars of China. As the Manchus, like all oriental people, were eager for a modern education, many of these exiles became teachers to the leading families. The result was that Manchu princes, like Dorgon and several of his brothers, were well versed in Chinese history, culture, religion, geography, and the arts before they ever saw China. This contributed much to the success of the Manchus after they conquered China, as these men, especially Dorgon, realized that the Chinese culture and family system represented a civilization higher than their own. They were willing to accept it, and so made few changes in the social and political structure of China when they organized their new government for that country.

Instead of making any large-scale frontal attacks on China with huge armies, Abahai sent a number of raids into China under his brother Dorgon. As the Manchus were never able to capture the heavily fortified Great Wall at Shanhaikwan, he sent these raiding parties through Mongolia and into China through the Nankow Pass. On one raid they reached the walls of Peking but made no attempt to attack the city. On another raid they captured and sacked Tsinan Fu, the capital city of Shantung province, and Paoting Fu, capital of Chihli province. These attacks were not intended as means of conquest but as raids for loot and to weaken the power of the Ming Emperor. In this they were successful. Abahai died before he accomplished the conquest of China, but he lived long enough to see that the fall of the Chinese Empire to his Manchus was inevitable. He died on September 21, 1643.

In the meantime the Mings had been driven from Peking by the bandit Li Tzu-ch'eng, who proclaimed himself Emperor and succeeded in getting considerable support from the eunuchs and some officials of the old Ming court. But Li knew that to hold Peking he must either destroy or ally himself with General Wu San-kuei, at that time defending Shanhaikwan against the Manchus under Dorgon. Wu had under his command one of the best-equipped armies in China.

Li Tzu-ch'eng began negotiations with General Wu San-kuei by seizing his father, his family and, more important, his favorite concubine, Ch'en Yuan-yuan, known to history as Lady Ch'en. This made it difficult for General Wu to decide on the proper course to follow. But after a considerable number of notes had passed between the two parties, in which each tried to deceive the other, one trying to gain time, the other to gain back his sweetheart, Li Tzu-ch'eng finally decided he had become strong enough to defeat General Wu San-kuei. He broke off further negotiations by sending the general a friendly little note telling him he had given the general's concubine, Lady Ch'en, to the heir apparent to "dally with as he pleased." Li added that Wu need not worry over this, as it really would not make any great difference to him anyway since he, Li, was marching against him with an army and expected to capture and hang him in a few days.

General Wu San-kuei was now between the armies of Li Tzu-ch'eng on the south and the Manchu armies under Dorgon on the north. This time he had no difficulty in making up his mind. He arranged a meeting with Dorgon and offered him a large part of China if Dorgon would join and assist him in driving the bandit Li Tzu-ch'eng out of Peking. Dorgon was perfectly willing to drive anyone off the Dragon Throne of China. This had been his aim for years. But he asked in return for his assistance not part but all of China. General Wu accepted. Together they captured Peking and drove the bandit Li into the western provinces, where he was killed by one of his own followers. Poor General Wu was never reunited with his lovely Lady Ch'en. Many pictures have been painted, many poems written, and many stories told of the love of General Wu for Ch'en Yuan-yuan and his efforts to find her during the rest of his life.

At the death of Abahai, Dorgon was the unanimous choice of the Eight Banner princes and the war chiefs to succeed his brother. They wanted a mature man and a tried general as head of the nation. But Dorgon refused because of his loyalty to his brother, who, he thought, would naturally want his son to succeed him. Dorgon's first act after entering Peking when he had the Dragon Throne of China at his disposal was to send for Fu Lin, son of his brother Abahai, and have him proclaimed Emperor of China under the name of Shun Chih.

After the conquest of Peking, it took many years and much hard fighting to conquer the entire country. The story is that when the Chinese had finally to make peace with their Manchu conquerors, they sent one of their oldest and wisest generals to negotiate on their behalf. The old general astonished the Manchus and infuriated the Chinese by proposing that as the Manchus were the victors they must have the fruits of victory. They must be the superior race, must under no condition be required to do any of the manual work of the country or enter into business of any kind. The Chinese must be the laborers and serve the Manchus for all time.

This, naturally, pleased the Manchus; but when the Chinese heard these conditions they wanted to kill the old general who, they claimed, had given them into slavery. The old general answered: "No, not slavery, but mastery. In three hundred years the Manchus will have to beg for their bread."

The general was a poor prophet! He missed the count by thirty-two years. If any people ever lost a war and won the peace, this old Chinese general accomplished it for his people. Today the Chinese are again masters, and the Manchus are begging their bread.

3

Let us return to little Green Jade.

We left her on the day of her birth just as Grandfather Wong and Soothsayer Fu so unceremoniously rushed in on her mother to tell of the vision.

They later found that Soothsayer Fu had held back a piece of information he had learned that morning. He had not even told his friend Wong. He was afraid to do so before he had consulted the old charts again. When the Manchu baby was shown him he noticed, as the mother also had noticed, that the child had a peculiar mark on her left breast. It was a birthmark—rather a faint discoloration of the skin that Green Jade was to carry to her grave. But Fu saw in the birthmark something the others did not see. He distinctly saw the outline of a fox.

He knew very well that "the mark of the fox" was the mark either of a good or evil omen, and he decided to find out which it was before telling his friend. Two more days of fasting and study made it clear to him. He found an old Manchu prophecy made at the time the imperial Aisin Gioro clan almost wiped out the Yehonala clan, reducing it to eight families. This prophecy stated that the rule and supremacy of the Aisin Gioro clan would someday be ended forever by a great woman of the Yehonala clan bearing the mark of the fox. Fu understood this to be but one more evidence that Green Jade was favored by the gods. To the mother this mark of the fox was an ever-present reminder of the high destiny ahead of her daughter.

The first five years of Green Jade's life were much like those of millions of other girl babies born in China a hundred years ago. She passed through the usual childhood illnesses with the help of, or rather in spite of, the customary Chinese remedies. She suffered the many equally dangerous formalities young children born in China have to endure. On the third day after birth she was given her first bath. Not a nice warm bath in a warm room. Green Jade was bathed in cold water and exposed to the cold air according to rules laid down by her Manchu ancestors more than a thousand years before she was born, and which tended to weed out the weaklings. She had no privacy at her first bath. The whole neighborhood was invited to the ceremony, which, by custom, was presided over by the old woman who had assisted in bringing the baby into the world. As the importance derived from occupying the center of the stage at this rite was probably the only reward Grandmother Wei received for her services, she saw to it that no part of the ritual connected with the first bath was omitted.

The mother and Grandmother Wei proudly showed all guests that Green Jade was a true "blue-bottomed" Manchu. Her little bottom was as blue as if she had been sitting in indigo, the mark of a lineal descendant of the godchild, son of the maiden Fokulun. As this and the sign of the fox on her left breast had to be shown to every guest, it must have taken the protection of the gods to have saved little Green Jade from death by exposure that November day.

She was weighed at this ceremony and every month of the first year to see that she was not "running away." If the baby lost weight, it was believed that spirits were grabbing it. Then false scales might be brought into use in an effort to fool the spirits. This precaution was not necessary with little Green Jade; she gained weight from the first.

Like all children in China, even the poorest, on the twelfth day Green Jade had to pass through another ordeal, the Day of Gifts. A bigger celebration was held one month after birth. This was planned apparently more for the parents and neighbors than for the child. A theatrical troupe was hired to entertain the company. Games were played in the courtyard with the crooked crabapple tree. Colored cakes were eaten. All was gay and amusing. Green Jade received many presents. These consisted of bright-colored clothes, bracelets, bells, and children's games. Grandfather Wong and the neighbors planned and paid for this celebration as Hwei Cheng, as usual, was too occupied with his friends and gambling companions to evince interest in his wife and daughter.

A big celebration occurred on Green Jade's first birthday. This was also a neighborhood affair. As so many children in China die during their first year, this celebration is particularly gay and noisy, as it is felt that if the child has survived the first twelve months it has a good chance of reaching middle or old age.

As soon as she was old enough, Green Jade, like all other children in China, had to do her share of household duties. She had to run to the shops to purchase the day's requirements of garlic, cabbage, sweet potatoes, and occasionally a small piece of meat. The meat seller was a Mohammedan named Hei Yu, who sold only lamb and mutton. Hei Yu used to tease Green Jade by pinching her nose, which was larger and more prominent than that of the average Chinese child. Hei Yu is the only one of Green Jade's friends of Ta Ssu T'iao Hutung whom we will meet again after she became Empress.

As a little child, Green Jade wore the same bright red trousers and blue jacket, silk for special occasions and cotton for every day, as the girls of Ta Ssu T'iao Hutung wear today. Green Jade was always rather small for her age. She was beautiful even as a child, with bright eyes, a quick temper, and full of curiosity. The old women whose mothers or grandmothers claimed to have known Green Jade as a child tell many stories about her early life, passed down by word of mouth and undoubtedly added to with the telling. From some of these stories we know that Green Jade played games with other children of her age, more often with the boys, in the large vacant lot directly in front of Grandfather Wong's dwelling. The old people tell that Green Jade soon became the leader of her playground. This we can well understand. In the first days of spring, like the children of other lands, they played marbles. Later they played a curious game which consisted of kicking a small shuttlecock with the inside of the foot, keeping it continuously in the air. They also chased dragonflies. Most of all, they enjoyed flying their large bird-like kites.

But Green Jade did not have so much time for games as the other children. As long as Soothsayer Fu lived, she had to study. Fu and the Buddhist monk insisted on this and became her teachers. This she did willingly, for she enjoyed learning to write the ornamental Chinese characters and to paint simple flowers with the brush Fu made for her. When she was four years old the Buddhist monk started her on the study of the *Four Books* that every educated child in China has to learn and must be able to recite from beginning to end.

The best time of Green Jade's whole day was when she accompanied Grandfather Wong to watch the great gates of the city close at sunset. To Wong this was almost a religious rite. Green Jade was seldom up in time to see the gates opened at sunrise, but Grandfather Wong had not missed seeing the gates opened at sunrise and closed at sunset for more than sixty years. They were huge gates, eight or ten inches thick and armored both sides with steel plates held in place by large gold-lacquered bolts. It took several men to move them. To Wong these gates and the high wall that surrounded Peking meant order, protection, and security. Dynasties might come and go, but the city's wall and gates stayed and were part of his very life. He and little Green Jade always stood in silence as the great gates swung shut, not to be reopened until sunrise.

Green Jade had many things within view of her home to stir that quick imagination of hers. She had but to turn to the southeast on a clear day to see the enormous White Dagoba, the monument built by the first Ch'ing Emperor to honor the visit of the Dalai Lama to his court. In sunshine or moonlight, the Dagoba glows like the bud of a great white lotus.

A little farther to the southwest Green Jade could see the five pavilions on Prospect Hill, the massive gates, red walls, and yellow roofs of the numerous palaces of the Forbidden City. She could not see the palaces, libraries, and museums on the shores of the three lakes within the grounds of the Imperial City, but Grandfather Wong, Soothsayer Fu, and the Buddhist monk told her about these magnificent buildings when they described to her the glories of her native city and her native land. Remembering the prophecy concerning her destiny, she pictured herself living there someday.

Her father, Hwei Cheng, paid so little attention to his family that we have so far paid little attention to him. At the time of Green Jade's birth he was a young man, not more than twenty-two or -three years old. He was very good-looking, always well dressed, regardless of his financial position, had an attractive personality, and a smile that made friends for him even faster than he lost them by his dissolute ways. That smile, his love for fine clothes, and his ability as a musician were about the only things he passed on to his daughter. She was to keep them her entire life.

By birth Hwei Cheng belonged to one of the oldest and most important of the imperial clans, but his particular family had dwindled in size, importance, and wealth for several generations. He was an only son, and seems to have had no relatives except his father, a sister, and the cousin T'ien Chen, who had somewhat casually provided the quarters in Grandfather Wong's house.

Hwei Cheng's father, like his father before him, was division chief of the fifth rank in the Board of Punishments. This was a position that paid only a small salary but carried considerable influence. The fact that Hwei Cheng's father held such an influential position and yet remained a poor man seems to prove that he was either very honest or very incompetent. Majority opinion favors the latter supposition. But he did at least one great thing for his descendants: he was able to save the life of a neighbor named Wu Chin-t'ang who was being tried in his court for some serious crime. Wu Chin-t'ang never forgot this and was of great assistance to Green Jade and her family many years later after the death of both her father and her grandfather. Without Wu Chin-t'ang's assistance it is probable that Green Jade would never have passed the examinations for entrance into the court of Emperor Hsien Feng.

Hwei Cheng was an average high-born Manchu young man of his day, fond of hunting, archery, falconry, boxing, and most games of chance, but he had no fondness whatever for work of any kind. He had a small position in the army, which paid him a salary, most of which went to the upkeep of his extravagant manner of living. His income was not large enough for him to live as he wished, so he added to this by gambling and occasionally selling his influence in his father's court. His friends were mostly the idle, fun-loving sons of the old Manchu families, to whom he was a good companion.

We know little about the family of Green Jade's mother, except a long list of the names of grandfathers, great-grandfathers, and great-great-grandfathers. She also was of a high Manchu family which had produced noted military leaders. It is to her mother's family that most historians give credit for Green Jade's unusual ability and exceptionally strong constitution. About the only thing of interest connected with this family, beyond war records of men in battles the world has never heard of, is the report that one of them was buried with a golden head. The explanation of this extraordinary occurrence is that at the opening of the eighteenth century a Chinese secret society suddenly appeared in many parts of the country. It apparently had agents and members everywhere, even in the Emperor's private living apartments, where they succeeded in regularly leaving messages. The society was organized to strike terror into the Manchus by unusual murders. They killed in the most unlikely places and at the most unusual times, but only in one way—they always decapitated their victim. This was bad enough for a Manchu or Chinese who wants his body in one piece when he dies, but the society added to the horror by keeping possession of the head. The head of the victim could never be found. As every Chinese expects to meet his ancestors after death, how could he do this with dignity without a head? To rectify this serious condition, the Emperor furnished all such victims with a golden head to be buried with the body. This was probably carved of wood or stone and covered with gold leaf. Whether the good intentions of the Emperor satisfied the ancestors is not mentioned in any of the books written on this subject.

At the time of Green Jade's birth her father neglected both his wife and baby daughter. When Grandfather Wong tried to tell him of Soothsayer Fu's vision, he scoffed, saying he did not believe in such old women's tales. But as Green Jade began to develop into a beautiful child with a quick, intelligent mind and gained many friends in the neighborhood, Hwei Cheng began to take an interest in her. He sometimes accompanied her and Grandfather Wong to see the gates closed for the night. But he often teased her about the great woman she was going to be someday, which annoyed both Green Jade and her mother. To them the soothsayer's vision was sacred. Hwei Cheng never gained his daughter's confidence. Neither did Hwei Cheng become popular with the neighbors—honest people who expected every man to support his family. They had little use for a man such as Hwei Cheng, who spent the allowances he received from the treasury in gambling and buying fine clothes for himself. With the sure instinct of the uneducated, they detected that Hwei Cheng was not an honest man or a courageous one.

4

After years of intrigue and using the influence of his cousin Tien Chen and that of his other friends, Hwei Cheng finally succeeded in securing an official position to his taste. He was appointed Commissioner for River Conservancy in the city of Ch'en Chow Fu in Honan province, approximately a month's journey from Peking.

Hwei Cheng was very pleased with this appointment, as he believed that in the provincial towns, where competition was not so keen, he could, with the aid of his many Peking friends, rapidly work up to an important position and in a few years return to the capital as a high official.

Green Jade did not want to leave Peking and all her friends. She thought Peking the most wonderful city in the world. It would have been difficult to have made her understand that the many changes in residence, the many army camps she would live in, the many different people she was to see and know, and even the many disappointments and hardships she was to suffer during the next ten years were all necessary experiences to prepare her for the exalted position she was destined to occupy.

Green Jade's mother, Hwei T'ai T'ai, with greater experience and more faith in the peculiar ways of fate, and with the resignation of all Chinese women, accepted the change without comment, although she feared that most of the hardships of the next few years would fall on her. Ta Feng, or Phoenix, her second daughter, had been born on Green Jade's fourth birthday. Her third child and first son was just one year old when Hwei Cheng secured his appointment. Fortunately for Hwei T'ai T'ai's composure, it was not difficult to travel in China with a family of five a hundred years ago.

As anxious as Hwei Cheng was to secure an appointment, he showed no great desire or haste to leave Peking. But after all the excuses for delay he and his friends could invent were exhausted, the day of departure was finally fixed. He and his family were to leave with a large military train from Peking on the third day of the Ninth Moon of the twenty-second year of the reign of Tao Kuang. According to Western reckoning, this was October 7, 1843.

All their belongings, including presents from friends, were loaded on two military carts. Most of the civilians traveled in Peking carts, but the family of Hwei Cheng, being an official, rode in mule-borne sedan chairs. The Peking cart of that day had rich trappings and was usually drawn by a large mule. It was probably one of the most ornate, picturesque, and uncomfortable vehicles that has ever been invented. To Green Jade and the family, the sedan chairs represented a first experience in luxury and rank. They enjoyed traveling as the family of a commissioner.

Having friends leave on a long journey is no ordinary event in China. It calls for a real celebration. When all of Hwei

Cheng's friends, the neighbors, and Green Jade's playmates gathered at the Hsi Chih Men to see them off, it created a considerable traffic jam. Enough firecrackers were set off to win a battle if the powder used in them had been fired from guns.

But celebrations even in China have to end sometime. Green Jade bade a tearful good-by to Grandfather Wong and Soothsayer Fu. As the family finally started on their long journey to the south and she passed through the great gates, she wondered if this would be for the last time in her life. But being young, hardly were the towers of the Hsi Chih Men out of sight than her spirits rose again. She began to enjoy the journey. She gave up the sedan chair and was soon sitting in the least dignified but only comfortable seat in a Peking cart, at the point where the shafts meet the body.

From here she could see the entire countryside—a new experience for her, as she had seldom been outside the walls of Peking. She could also see many other travelers passing up and down the Great Road that connected the capital with all the great cities of central and southern China. Over this road came governors to report to the Emperor, generals to tell of the progress of the war with the British, and embassies bringing tribute from many foreign countries to the court of the Ch'ing emperors.

At that time, only a few years after Stephenson had built the first successful steam railroad and when most of the traveling done in England and America was by coach or on horseback over rutted, unpaved roads, China had probably the best internal transportation system to be found in any country on the globe. For centuries the Chinese had been busy connecting rivers and cities by the Grand Canal and by thousands of miles of lesser canals. With a fine system of highways and resthouses at convenient distances, it was possible for travelers to reach any city in China in comparative comfort. The great trunk roads of China at that time rivaled or probably excelled anything the Romans ever built. They were described by a member of the Macartney Mission in 1793 as being paved with granite blocks ten feet and more in length, eighteen inches in width, and ten to twelve inches in thickness, laid on a solid cement base. There were bridges of white marble with graceful arches, carved as though they were part of the entrance to a palace instead of a span over a river. Many of these bridges, like the Marco Polo Bridge west of Peking, are still in existence, though in some instances the rivers they once spanned have altered their courses or dried up. The lovely springing arches of snow-white marble now overlook market gardens in the old river courses where blue-clad Chinese farmers toil among their rice, peanuts, and sweet potatoes.

The Hwei family found several other families of officials also traveling in the military train. Hwei Cheng, with his ability to make friends everywhere, was soon on cordial terms with another Manchu family of about his own station, called Chang En-li. They had a daughter named Hsiao Tieh, or Small Butterfly, who was about the age of Green Jade, and two or three younger children. It was not long before the older children were crowded into one Peking cart, leaving the sedan chair to the other members of the family. Green Jade and Small Butterfly quickly became sworn friends. They were to spend many happy hours in Ch'en Chow Fu.

Within a few days it was evident that the sedan chairs and civilian carts could not keep pace with the military train that traveled night and day, so orders were given allowing the civilians to travel more slowly. They continued under strong guard, however, as the White Lilies, a strange name for a band of bandits, were threatening the Great Road at several points.

The mule driver of the children's cart was one of those kindly and friendly old souls one meets so often driving carts in China. He explained many things about the country that were strange to the city girls. It was a particularly interesting time of the year: the farmers had harvested most of their crops and were in the midst of the autumn celebrations. Country fairs were being held in many of the towns and villages. These fairs were most interesting to the two city-bred families. Green Jade and Small Butterfly particularly enjoyed the village theaters.

All the plays were the classic plays of China. Most of them had been popular for centuries. The actors spoke in a strange stage form of Chinese, much of which was probably not understood by anyone in the audience. But the villagers had no need to understand the words; all of them knew the story of the plays by heart, having learned them as children. And woe to the troupe that attempted to introduce anything new! The people wanted only plays showing their familiar war heroes or love stories showing the loyalty and courage of their great women of the past. Only occasionally were plays shown that pictured treachery or other weaknesses of human nature. All the actors were men. The Chinese had learned long ago that the stage apparently was not a good place for men and women to work together in portraying other people's weaknesses.

The village fair still plays an important role in the life of millions of Chinese who live in small towns and villages. The Chinese have no weekly rest day as other people have on Sundays, but take their holidays at the new year and during the autumn fairs after their farm work is ended for the year. These fall fairs are in addition to the weekly fairs held mainly for the sale of their produce. The fall fairs are larger, often lasting for days and usually include many forms of entertainment, such as trapeze performers, contortionists, strong men, trained bears, fortunetellers, and invariably the flea-and-beetle circus. The supply of fleas is plentiful in China.

The farmers attend the fair in family groups and seem to spend much of the time looking for their lost children.

In the fair crowd, Green Jade watched, the older people and the boys were dressed in new blue cotton clothes; the girls usually in bright red trousers and blue jackets. As all the blue cloth was dyed with indigo raised by the farmers and the cloth was woven, dyed, and made into garments by the women, the pleasing result was that no two families appeared to have clothes of the same style or shade of blue. There was also a sprinkling of Mongol monks in bright yellow robes, and Tibetan or Buddhist monks in maroon. The color of the clothing of the crowds was more than matched by the color of the farm produce on exhibition – orange-colored persimmons, green melons, pink and maroon apples, yellow yams, and great quantities of many other kinds of fruit and farm produce. Green Jade and the other children had little money to spend, but enough to buy candied fruit on a stick, roasted chestnuts, and colored drinks, all equally potent in giving children the usual stomach-ache.

After three weeks' journeying the travelers came to the crossing of the Yellow River. Too treacherous for navigation, except on the upper reaches, and always ready to change its course, overflow, and drown thousands of villagers, the Yellow River is called, not inaptly, the Sorrow of China. It has never been tamed. The summer floods have always been able to wash out any bridge the early engineers built at the point where the Great Road crossed the river. The bridge had been washed away a few weeks before the military train from Peking arrived, so the carts were taken across the river by ferry.

At this point they changed to the Great East-West Road that connects Shantung province and the coast with Sian Fu, Lanchow, and the other cities of western China and Tibet. By this road they finally reached Ch'en Chow Fu without further adventure.

Hwei Cheng and Chang En-li found Ch'en Chow Fu a much more interesting and attractive city than they had expected or had believed a city in the interior of China could be. They were learning a lot about their country since their departure from Peking. Ch'en Chow Fu was, and still is, a walled city. While the walls of the city and the four gates are not so large or so magnificent as those of Peking, they are ample for its protection. It lay in the center of a large grain-growing area of Central China.

Hwei Cheng held the position of commissioner and was inspector of the grain the government purchased for the army, having under him a small police force and a number of clerks. He seemed to be a different man since leaving Peking; he paid more attention to his family. He even began to teach Green Jade her lessons, but as a teacher he was not very successful. What was more important, he took his work seriously. Chang En-li had a good influence on him, pointing out that the quickest way to be promoted was to make a success of his present position and get favorable reports from the magistrate, his superior.

The families of Hwei Cheng and Chang En-li were able to secure good homes fairly close to each other in the Manchu section of the city. Green Jade and Small Butterfly spent hours together, busily investigating everything. Green Jade did not have much time for amusement, as her mother insisted that she continue her studies. In this her father agreed, and he secured good teachers for her. Small Butterfly joined her in some of her studies, but although about the same age, she was far behind her in all subjects, as Green Jade was an exceptional student.

Hwei Cheng profited by Chang En-li's advice and received his first promotion in less than a year. He was appointed a sub-magistrate of a higher grade in the city of Tehchow in Shantung province.

The journey to Tehchow presented few difficulties. The family traveled by cart over the Great Road to a small town on the Grand Canal, where they transferred to a comfortable canal boat for Tehchow, a journey sixty miles to the north.

Their first view of the Grand Canal was a great event. The Chinese consider the construction of their Grand Canal a more important engineering work than their Great Wall. It certainly served a more useful purpose. The canal was started before 540 B.C. and had been added to, straightened, enlarged, and improved until at the time the Hwei Cheng family first saw it, it was a thousand miles in length and the main means of transportation between North and South China. It was at the very height of its usefulness to China. Its decline started with the development of coastwise transportation.

Tehchow was much smaller than Ch'en Chow Fu, but it was an important customs stop on the canal for all goods passing in or out of Shantung province. It was also an important government purchasing depot and transfer point for army supplies. Hwei Cheng was in charge of the customs—a position of considerable significance. Her father's position enabled Green Jade to learn a lot about the Grand Canal and all the strange ships and strange people that passed up and down that great waterway. The very first day she had made friends with her father's assistant, who took her with him when he examined ships and cargoes. That little mind of hers was storing up a lot of information about China and the Chinese people.

A few months after his arrival in Tehchow, Hwei Cheng

had the good fortune to be put in charge of the presents the government and officials of Shantung province were sending to the Dowager Empress Kung Tz'u on her forty-fifth birthday anniversary. He remained in Peking three weeks. He saw Emperor Tao Kuang, renewed old friendships, and made such a good impression at court that he secured the appointment of subprefect in the city of Hangchow Fu, the southern terminal of the Grand Canal. This was a very high position for a man of his age and experience.

When Hwei Cheng returned to Tehchow and told the family of their good fortune they were all immensely pleased. Hangchow Fu, next to Peking, was the most interesting city in all China.

The journey to Hangchow Fu on one of the official government boats was very comfortable and interesting. The family now traveled in all the luxury and prestige befitting a high government official. This Hwei Cheng enjoyed to the fullest. He had always been a well-dressed man and he liked nothing better than to show off his new Peking clothes and position before the officials who came aboard to pay their respects to the new prefect at every town and city through which they passed. Little Green Jade was also beginning to show a love for fine clothes and did a little strutting herself in the new gowns her father had brought from Peking. Hwei Cheng was proud of his handsome, talented daughter.

The family did not have to go ashore to enjoy sightseeing. The upper deck of their government boat, with its gay-colored awning, made an ideal place from which to view the countryside. They were passing through Shantung province, the very heart of China and one of the most highly cultivated parts of the country. It was the land of Confucius. They passed within sight of the sacred mountain of Tai Shan near the foot of which lies the famous temple of Confucius and the cemetery where even today any descendants of the Great Teacher can be buried. Little Green Jade could tell her family, even her father, many things about China's great philosopher that she had learned from teachers. Before reaching the sacred mountain they stopped one day at Tsinan, capital of the province. Little did Green Jade dream that one of the events which was to have considerable effect on her life would take place in that city when her servant and friend the eunuch An Teh-hai was beheaded by the governor of Shantung a few years after she became Empress.

Two weeks after leaving Tehchow, Hwei Cheng and his family reached the Yangtze River, China's greatest waterway, which divides the country into North and South China. Almost 10 per cent of the world's population live in the watershed of the Yangtze. Hwei Cheng was making a very leisurely journey, enjoying every minute of the luxury and pleasures of official life. No town was too small for the boat to stop at, no town too small to tender him some kind of reception, which he was always careful to return. He was making a good impression by his pleasant manners and extensive entertaining. Favorable reports were being sent back to Peking about the new subprefect. While Green Jade and the rest of the family were seldom included in these entertainments, it gave them time to see more of the towns and countryside than they would have been able to see on any ordinary trip, especially as the captain had appointed himself their guide. Several days were spent waiting for an opportune time to cross the river which at that point was—and still is—dangerous for frail houseboats. There were so many interesting things to see on the great river that Green Jade and Phoenix could hardly be persuaded to sleep the two nights they were in sight of the Yangtze.

One more day and they reached the city of Soochow, admired so much by Marco Polo. Here they stopped two days. Soochow, the City of Earth, and its neighbor Hangchow Fu, the City of Heaven, are considered by the Chinese their two most beautiful cities. They claim that from Soochow comes everything that is beautiful: the most beautiful girls, the most beautiful silks, and the most beautiful of everything that can be made by skilled craftsmen. From it, today, come the famous sing-song girls of Shanghai.

As Soochow has been twice destroyed since the days Green Jade spent there, the city she knew resembled more that which Marco Polo visited than it did the modern city of to-day, so we will let him describe it.

Marco Polo wrote: "Suju [as he called it] is a very great and noble city. The people are idolators and subject to the Great Khan and have paper money. They possess silk in great quantities from which they make gold brocade and other stuffs. The city is passing great and has a circuit of sixty li [twenty miles]. It has merchants of great wealth and an incalculable number of people. There are also in this city many philosophers and leechers, diligent students of nature. And you must know there are six thousand bridges, all of stone and so lofty that a galley, or even two galleys at once, could pass underneath one of them. Everything remarkable comes from this city: fine pictures, fine carved work, fine silks, and fine ladies. When the Emperor visited the city, the citizens laid the streets with carpets and silk stuffs, but the Emperor dismounted and made his train do the like, not to ruin the beautiful fabrics."

One can well imagine how the famous silk shops of Soochow interested the entire Hwei Cheng family as they still do the visitor of today. Green Jade was showing a decided liking for fine clothes and now that they had money and a free-spending father she could indulge in such luxuries for the first time in her life.

Four more days and they were in Hangchow Fu. Their journey was ended. They were met be a large group of officials and given the usual welcoming banquet. They were installed in their official home in the Manchu section of the city and supplied with a staff of servants in keeping with Hwei Cheng's position. The family had come a long way from the days when they occupied the two little rooms in Grandfather Wong's humble home.

Hangchow Fu was another of the canal cities of China. It was much larger than Soochow and its charm was in its fine lakes, palaces, temples, and places of amusement. Its people were traders, not craftsmen; they depended on Soochow for the beautiful silks and ornaments its people were so fond of wearing. As Hangchow Fu was completely destroyed by the Tai Ping rebels a few years after the arrival of the Hwei family and again later by the Republican armies and mobs in their war against the Manchus, we will have to rely again on Marco Polo's description of Hangchow Fu. As it was also a canal city it appealed to the Venetian visitor. While undoubtedly the city had decreased much in both size and wealth from the time of Marco Polo to the time Hwei Cheng arrived there its main characteristics were probably much the same.

Marco Polo wrote of it as follows: "The city is without dispute the finest and noblest in the world. It is so great that it has a hundred li [thirty-three miles] in compass, with a large lake within its boundaries. There are in it twelve thousand bridges of stone, for the most part so lofty that a great fleet can pass beneath them. Let no man marvel at so many bridges, as the city stands as it were in the water and surrounded with water with many canals within the city and requires so many bridges to give free passage about. The wealth of the merchants is so enormous that no man could form an estimate thereof. They live as nicely and delicately as though they were kings and queens. The people are idolators. Both men and women are comely and for the most part dress in silk. The city has three thousand baths with hot water which is supplied from springs. The people take great delight in bathing, for they are a cleanly people. They have a custom that as soon as a child is born they write down the day, the hour, and the planet under which it was born so that everyone among them knows the day of its birth. It has a total of one million six hundred thousand houses. There is one Christian church belonging to the Nestorian Christians. The ocean comes within eight miles of the city and a great river connects the city with the ocean."

Such was the city in which Hwei Cheng and his family were to spend the next five years. A city of pleasing surroundings, a city of beautiful homes and wonderful gardens, lakes, and hills given over to the enjoyment of the people. It was a pleasant city to live in, with no great extremes of climate. The people were more gay, more friendly, and less formal than in Peking. Many different kinds of fruit and every form of farm produce grew in abundance within a few miles of the city. As it was an ocean port, the products of the sea and of the neighboring provinces and countries were also available to its people. The family of Hwei Cheng was now living in probably the most pleasant city of all China, they had a fine official position, wealth, and many friends. The gods had truly been kind.

It took Green Jade just two days to find a girl friend of her own age; another two days and they were sworn friends for life. The friend was a Manchu girl, called Pao Chu, Treasured Pearl, the daughter of one of the officials in Hwei Cheng's department. She was also from Peking but had lived two years in Hangchow Fu. Treasured Pearl took great delight in showing Green Jade the city.

When the two girls tired of seeing the shops and workmen, they visited the inner and outer West Lakes to look at the wonderful palaces built along the shores and on the hills behind. They visited the old pagodas and the ancient ruins of the Sung palaces.

But again Green Jade had to study, as did her sister and two small brothers. Her father engaged several teachers to instruct them in Chinese characters, painting, music, and the classics. He was careful in the education of his children, especially seeing to it that they learned to speak only the pure Mandarin dialect. In this search for proper teachers a man named Li Weng-yang was recommended to him. He had been dismissed from government service for some fault. However, Hwei Cheng liked the man and employed him. This proved a fortunate choice. Li Weng-yang taught Green Jade the entire time she was in Hangchow Fu. Although Li Weng-yang was a Chinese, he was a student of Manchu history, and he taught Green Jade the history and legends of her people as well as much Chinese history. He also discovered in her a talent for painting and encouraged her in the art. It was owing much to the scholarship and abilities of this tutor, her extended travels, and the opportunities her father's position gave her to meet many important men, that Green Jade became the great woman she was. She never forgot Li Weng-yang. After she entered the imperial palace she recommended him to the court officials so highly that he was sent for and became an imperial tutor. He was Green Jade's faithful friend and adviser until he died several years after she became Empress.

Hwei Cheng liked his work and life in Hangchow Fu. He enjoyed everything that gave him power and prestige. His first taste of influence was so great that he devoted his entire time and effort to securing further advancement. He worked hard, attended strictly to the affairs of his department and, to the astonishment of his wife, became a very good official. He continued to make friends easily, did much entertaining, dressed well, and was popular. Unlike most of the local officials who entertained in the large restaurants overlooking the lake, he more often followed the Peking custom and invited his friends to his own home, especially after he moved to a larger place in the hills overlooking the West Lake. He had become rather proud of his good-looking wife and handsome daughter. Although they were not always permitted to attend these entertainments, Hwei Cheng usually managed to let his guests meet them in some way. This was to be of great value to Green Jade and her mother a few years later. His elder daughter had also become of great assistance to him in his official duties, as she already began to show an unusual ability in interpreting and framing official documents.

The position of Hwei Cheng, subprefect of Hangchow Fu, had now become so important that he had to do something to raise the prestige of his family. Since his father had died he had no other relatives to invite to Hangchow Fu. After many talks and discussions with his wife, they decided he should take a number-two wife, or a concubine. Such a thing was rather expected of a man of the standing of Hwei Cheng. He would soon be looked on as a tight-fisted man if he did not follow the custom, as all men were supposed to have as many wives as they could reasonably afford.

The wives of a Chinese family take pride in the number of wives their husbands possess. Almost the first question asked by two old Chinese women when introduced to each other is: "How many Tender Ones are there in your home?" The answer to that question places the family socially and financially. A concubine would also be of considerable assistance to Hwei T'ai T'ai in the management of what was fast becoming a rather large household.

The concubine finally selected was a quick, rather good-looking girl of about twenty, named Autumn Cloud. She proved to be a welcome addition to the family, and was soon well liked by Green Jade, Phoenix, and their two brothers. It was agreed that Hwei Cheng had again made a wise decision, as he always did whenever he consulted and followed the advice of his wife.

Time passed quickly in Hangchow Fu for the entire family; Hwei Cheng continued in popularity with all his associates, and Green Jade made rapid progress with her studies. Hwei T'ai T'ai worried a little as her elder daughter began to show some of the weaknesses of her father in her love of fine clothes and the tendency to take too much pride in her position. She seemed to be forgetting too soon her early life and days of poverty in Peking. Hwei T'ai T'ai was developing, as most Manchu women do in later life, into a rather solid, clear-thinking woman. She was not too pleased with the rapid advancement of her husband. She knew he was in reality a weak man. Hwei T'ai T'ai's only aim in life was the promotion of the career of Green Jade. For that she would have sacrificed anything—her husband's career, even the husband himself. She still had absolute faith in the signs she had seen that early November morning in Peking.

While Green Jade was beginning to show a domineering attitude and often quarreled with her friends, with her father's concubine, and with her sister and brothers, she was always respectful and kind to her mother, whom she recognized as the real head of the family. Soon Autumn Cloud gave birth to Hwei Cheng's third son and fifth child, who was given the name of Foniyinbu.

5

Emperor Tao Kuang, from whom Hwei Cheng had received his first government appointment, ruled China for thirty years, from 1821 to 1851. He was the father of Emperor Hsien Feng, who later became the husband of Green Jade and the father of her son.

The troubles that occurred in this reign really started when the first foreign trader with his armed soldiers and sailors set foot on the shores of South China. This should not have caused such serious difficulties, as the Chinese people were not at that time anti-foreign nor had they been against the foreign trader. Marco Polo and the Venetians who had accompanied and followed him were traders and had been well received. So were the Arab traders from the Red Sea, the traders from Muscovy and the countries of the eastern Mediterranean.

Many foreigners were also at that time living peacefully in China. The Jesuit fathers had been welcomed to China by an early emperor, as were also Buddhist teachers from India, Mohammedans from Asia, Nestorians from the Near East, and Greek Catholics from Russia. All these were peacefully preaching their different religions. The leaders of all these groups, including the early traders, had had audiences with the emperors. Some were friends of the emperors.

But the trader and his companions who came later by sea were evidently men of a very different character. No official of China, not even the city magistrates, would receive them or any foreign government official who attempted to speak for them. At least they would not receive them as equals. The reason for this is evident. These new traders, if traders they could be called, believing that the easily gathered wealth, or loot, of the countries of South America, the Philippine Islands, India, and Java was exhausted or was closely controlled by European governments, were turning their attention to China, one of the few independent oriental countries left and the richest of them all. The Chinese emperors had been informed of this by their Jesuit advisers, who were always opposed to the British and to many other European nations. They knew they were dealing with men who they feared were more anxious for territory than for trade. They knew how the East India Company had broken up and conquered India. Now this same company was attempting to secure a foothold in South China. The French were rapidly gaining complete control of Indo-China and the British were doing the same in Burma, both countries then under the protectorate of China.

The Chinese officials were finally persuaded to allow a limited amount of trade with the merchants of Canton. To facilitate this trade, the foreign merchants were allowed to establish a number of *hongs* or trading warehouses on certain specified locations of the bank of the river at Canton. The Chinese officials soon found that they had made a grave mistake. Instead of the foreigners confining themselves to their hongs, as agreed, they made their way into every part of the city and neighboring countryside. The life of the city soon became one series of brawls and street fights between the foreign sailors and soldiers and the citizens. It soon was unsafe for a Chinese woman or man of the better class to walk the streets of his own city.

This was the era when the crews of foreign ships, especially for the long voyages to the Orient, were made up of kidnaped sailors, men from the dregs of the slums and prisons of Europe, often bought from agents as the ship captains bought their other supplies. These sailors landed in Canton after months at sea, with bad food and without even the sight of a woman. They were usually drunk, dirty, with long, unkempt beards and hair, dressed only in trousers, and went about armed and traveled in noisy gangs. As they were in a heathen foreign country they thought they did not have to behave. It does not take much imagination to see the impression such men made on the Cantonese, the small, peaceful, inoffensive Chinese we see so often on our streets in America. Nor to realize the effect of the stories of these sailors when they were exaggerated as they passed from mouth to mouth until they reached every town and village in China. It was the "red-haired foreign devils" who made the worst impression, and the term *Hung Hu-tzu* used to describe them at that time is still used to describe a bandit or one of the lowest type.

In addition to this, the Chinese authorities had another serious complaint—the opium trade. For some years the British East India Company had been illegally importing opium into China. This traffic had grown until it amounted annually to more than two million pounds sterling—a large sum at that time. The Chinese Government made many protests against this trade to the British Government, but all protests were ignored. The Chinese also claimed that the foreign ships were kidnaping Chinese citizens for the rubber and sugar plantations of other parts of the Orient.

Such was the background for the so-called Opium War which occurred during Green Jade's childhood. While opium is most often mentioned as the cause of this conflict, there is little doubt that there would have been a war even if there had been no opium question. The Chinese wanted to drive everything foreign out of their country. They wanted to end the conditions then existing in Canton. They wanted to be able to protect their own citizens in their own country. They wanted to stop the importation of opium that was already having a disastrous effect on their people. They believed that with their forts and the size of their armies they could defeat the British battleships and any army the British could transport the long distance from England.

The British also had many grievances. They could not forget the blow to their pride and dignity caused by the refusal of Emperor Chia Ch'ing to receive Lord Amherst, the representative of the British King. They wanted more ports opened to foreign trade and all existing trade restrictions removed. They wanted the Chinese officials to receive their government and trade officials on an equal footing and in a manner becoming their position.

The British believed that with their more modern equipment and their battleships they could easily defeat the military forces of China. The British proved to be the better prophets—they did defeat the Chinese.

The Treaty of Nanking, which ended this war, forced China to open more ports to foreign commerce and to remove many restrictions on foreign trade. It forced China to cede the island of Hong Kong to Great Britain and to pay an indemnity. The opium question, supposedly the cause of the war, was not even mentioned in the treaty.

The Treaty of Nanking, made in 1842, brought the Opium War to a close, but it did not put an end to the animosity toward foreigners. This went on smoldering, continuing to flare into various small riots in the port cities, where foreign sailors and traders came in contact with the Chinese.

Shortly before Emperor Tao Kuang's death, trouble broke out in Kwangtung and Kwangsi provinces—trouble which was to play a decisive part in Green Jade's destiny.

Tao Kuang was succeeded by his son, Hsien Feng, then twenty years old. Only a few weeks after the youthful Emperor ascended the Peacock Throne, Hwei Cheng was sent on another official mission to Peking. He was presented to the new Emperor, to whom he expressed thanks for his promotion. As usual, he made a good impression on all the officials in Peking, and especially on the Emperor, who was ingenuously impressed by Hwei Cheng's fine clothes, his easy manners, and his apparent knowledge of conditions in the south.

At that time all Peking was worrying about the Tai Ping rebellion, which was gaining headway. Hwei Cheng, who had just enough knowledge to be able to talk and an inveterate desire to please, gave the officials at the capital the information they wanted to hear. He assured them they had no cause to worry: the ever-glorious Manchu armies would soon be able to clear the country of the infamous Tai Ping leader and his followers. By making himself appear a man of wide experience and wisdom, Hwei Cheng succeeded in securing another promotion, that of military Tao T'ai of the five Fu districts on Anhwei province. This gave him authority over more than fifty magistrates. It was a very high position, next in importance to that of governor of a province. It would seem that it pays to be the harbinger of good news, even though the news may not be true.

Hwei Cheng's new headquarters were at Wuhu, an important city on the south bank of the Yangtze River, about seventy miles southwest of Nanking.

After two weeks of farewell receptions and banquets given by his friends in Hangchow Fu, "eating his way out of town," as it is called, Tao T'ai Hwei Cheng loaded his family, his servants, and all their belongings on a government boat and started on another triumphal journey on the Grand Canal. They stopped off again for a day at Soochow, where officials gave a large banquet to the new Tao T'ai. The wives of the officials similarly honored Hwei T'ai T'ai and her daughters.

Hwei Cheng did not bother to stop at the small towns on this trip. He visited only the larger cities, where he could meet officials more nearly of his own rank. The snob in Hwei Cheng was beginning to show, as was his love of money. As long as he strove for promotion he was willing to spend all the money he had on banquets, presents, and other ways of gaining friends, looking on money so spent as a good investment. Now that he had secured the highest position he probably would ever hold he began saving his money, letting others give banquets and presents to him. His wife, Hwei T'ai T'ai, noticed this with increasing uneasiness. She knew Hwei Cheng better than he knew himself.

The two days they were in Nanking were spent in entertaining. Here Tao T'ai Hwei Cheng was the host, for most of the officials entertained, such as the Viceroy and his friends, were of higher rank and were men he felt he had to cultivate if he was to expect good reports from them, Wuhu being fairly close to Nanking. Nanking was also destroyed by the Tai Ping rebels and is now much smaller than the city Green Jade and her family explored so thoroughly the two days they spent there. Here they saw the great tomb of the first Ming Emperor, the Purple Mountain, and many other historical spots of the city that has been the capital of China on several occasions.

All journeys must end sometime, even in China. They arrived in Wuhu four weeks from the day they left Hangchow Fu. After the usual receptions they finally settled in their new home, the best they had ever occupied. Tao T'ai Hwei Cheng was the highest government official in Wuhu, outranked only by the governor of the province in Anking. Wuhu was a small city but a pleasant one to live in, as it was a port city on the Yangtze River. The climate was good and the surrounding country produced almost every variety of fruit and other farm produce.

From the first day Tao T'ai Hwei Cheng arrived in Wuhu, as a matter of fact even before he arrived, he appeared a different man. He was no longer the pleasant, friendly subprefect. He became the rather overbearing military Tao T'ai and made few friends in Wuhu, a city where he was to need friends desperately. Rumors soon circulated that the new Tao T'ai was a seeker after money; that he was accepting bribes from magistrates and wealthy businessmen.

While Hwei T'ai T'ai had always been anxious for him to save part of the money he was spending so freely in Hangchow Fu, she did not like the means he was using to secure money in Wuhu. But he did not listen to her advice or did he talk things over with her as he had formerly done. He knew she would not approve of his actions, so why ask her?

Hwei T'ai T'ai began to prepare for the trouble she knew would come someday. She urged her husband to buy expensive jewelry and silks for her and for her daughters. This he was willing to do, as it kept her from asking too many questions. These things she stored away unknown to him and to the other members of her family.

A few days after their arrival in Wuhu, Green Jade was overjoyed to learn that her father had arranged for the family of her friend Treasured Pearl to be transferred to that city. As they grew older both girls spent more time at their studies. Green Jade was now deep in the history of the Manchu race and the Ch'ing Dynasty, taught her by another fine old Manchu scholar.

Green Jade and Treasured Pearl also looked forward to a real wedding, the first in which they were to take part. After several months of negotiations the family had finally chosen a wife for Treasured Pearl's eldest brother. The bride was a girl from Peking and was expected to arrive in a few weeks. The boy's family had not seen the bride since she was a small child, but they knew her family well.

After all the formalities for the proposed wedding of Treasured Pearl's brother had been performed, the report of the Mei Jen (Go-Between) received and approved, the names of the bride and groom written on red papers and placed before the ancestral tablets for the information of the ancestors, and the usual presents exchanged between the two families, the bride and a number of her relatives arrived in Wuhu. A lucky day was selected for the wedding, which was to take place in the home of a relative of the bride.

As both were prominent families, the wedding was the occasion for several days of feasting, theatricals, and other forms of amusement. The actual wedding ceremony was held in the evening and was rather brief, without any religious ritual of any kind. Mildly following the custom of the wild Manchus of early days, when they usually stole their brides from neighboring tribes, the groom and his young friends rode on gaily-decorated horses at a mad gallop to the home of the bride. To increase this illusion the groom and his friends were at first not well received by the bride's family. They went through a number of ceremonies suggesting a battle before the groom was allowed to enter the house. The actual ceremony was simple. It consisted of the groom, after saluting the bride, publicly declaring before those present and his ancestors that he took this woman as his wife. The bride in like manner accepted him as her husband. They made no promises of any kind to each other. The master of ceremonies in this case was Tao T'ai Hwei Cheng, but it could have been any friend. All during the ceremony the bride's head and face were hidden by a covering of red silk.

When the ceremony was completed the groom again saluted the bride and walked out of the room, followed by his new wife. He once more saluted as he and his friends mounted their horses and returned to his home. The bride was put in a bridal chair and, accompanied only by her maid, was carried to the groom's home. On arrival she was met by the groom, saluted again, and taken into the house where her maid removed the red covering from her face and the husband had his first view of his wife. Together they walked slowly into the room of the little household shrine and kneeling before it they thanked heaven and earth for all the favors they had received and implored continued blessings throughout their lives.

Tao T'ai Hwei Cheng soon had his office in Wuhu organized and running smoothly. He felt himself most secure in his official position and saw visions of soon becoming a man of wealth and importance.

At this time, when the gods seemed to be smiling on the Hwei family as they had never smiled before, Fate suddenly struck again. The little cloud that had been forming in the sky to the south and which Hwei Cheng had so optimistically described to the Emperor suddenly developed into a furious storm that was not only to destroy Tao T'ai Hwei Cheng utterly, but almost all China. The Tai Ping rebellion, smoldering for months in Kwangtung province, suddenly broke into fierce flame throughout South China. In its early days the movement seemed to be just another rebellion against the Ch'ing Dynasty and a financial crusade against the religion and ancient customs of China, of which there have been so many.

Hung Hsiu-ch'uan and his Tai Ping armies now began to sweep northward, destroying every city that opposed them and massacring many of the inhabitants. They destroyed temples and other holy places and did everything possible to spread terror among the people. They had well-organized fifth columns that sprang up in cities miles ahead of the advancing armies. These groups would start riots and announce that the Tai Ping armies were only a few miles from the city. Because of the lack of rapid means of sending messages these rumors caused much panic in cities often hundreds of miles from the nearest Tai Ping army.

One of the most successful panics of this nature was begun one night in Wuhu. Many people were killed and large fires were started in several parts of the city. The inhabitants knew of the terrible massacres in cities captured by the Tai Ping rebels, and as they thought the hostile armies were only a few miles away, the whole city was in panic. In this emergency Tao T'ai Hwei Cheng showed himself the inefficient man and coward that he was. As military Tao T'ai he should have assumed command of the city; instead, he left his post and rushed to his home in fright. He wanted to take his family and flee the city immediately. It would have been well if he had, but Hwei T'ai T'ai and Green Jade, who was now sixteen, were not cowards. They persuaded Hwei Cheng to return to his office and to think of his position as leader of the people.

Hwei Cheng found his department deserted. Some of his men were fighting in the streets; others, living in the more dangerous sections of the city, were rescuing their families. As Hwei Cheng sat alone in his office his fears returned. He was certain the city would be captured by the Tai Ping rebels. Then the idea occurred to him that if the city was going to be captured, looted, and destroyed, the rebels would also take the government gold and silver that were in his strongbox. Why should he not take them first? With the city destroyed, no one would know who had taken it; all would believe that the gold and silver had been seized by the rebels.

The opportunity looked to Hwei Cheng like a gift from the gods. He was never slow in following up an idea, especially one that promised gain. His private cart was at the door. The driver soon summoned another cart and in a short time both carts were loaded. Curiously enough, Hwei Cheng also took the government seals; why, it is hard to understand. By so doing he may have thought he was protecting the government, as it would have been very inconvenient if the seals of the Tao T'ai office should fall into the hands of the rebels.

When he reached home he told his wife and Green Jade of his plans. He had to have their assistance, as they had to go with him. Though Hwei Cheng put the scheme in the most plausible light possible both women saw that not only was it dishonest, but it also endangered the entire family. They pointed out that he was risking not only his own life but their lives as well.

They told Autumn Cloud and the children. All fell at his feet and with tears implored him to return the money immediately before it was missed. But Hwei Cheng had been building too many air castles filled with the things he was going to do with the money to change his plans. He was a very stubborn man at times and was sure the Tai Ping armies would capture Wuhu. He ordered his family to get into the carts he had waiting. They obeyed as any Manchu family would have done.

By morning they were several miles southwest of the city,

following the river road to a small town where Hwei Cheng knew they could cross the Yangtze by ferry. They reached the ferry about one o'clock. Three hours later Hwei Cheng had all the carts and the family across the river. As none of them had had any sleep for two days they stopped in a little village inn for the night—rather poor accommodations after their luxurious home in Wuhu. The following morning they headed north, evidently intending to take the Great Road to Peking. Hwei Cheng was so certain that Wuhu had been captured and destroyed and that his flight would not be noticed in the confusion that he apparently made no effort to conceal his identity or to take a less-frequented route.

Meanwhile the uprising in Wuhu had been suppressed and many of the rioters caught and hanged. It was learned that the Tai Ping armies were more than a hundred miles from the city. Hwei Cheng's absence from his office was not considered unusual the first day; it was thought that he was looking after government affairs in some other district. But when rumors reached the office that he and his entire family had fled the city an investigation was ordered. It was soon found that the seals and a considerable amount of gold and silver were missing. This was reported to the governor at Anking and to the Viceroy at Nanking.

It did not take long to trace the missing Tao T'ai Hwei Cheng. When he arrived at the town of Lintanyi he was met by a number of police officers who asked him to come to the magistrate's office for questioning.

This was a very unexpected and terrible blow to Hwei Cheng, who had thought himself safe from arrest. He was so paralyzed by fear that he made a very poor showing before the magistrate. He and his whole family were put into prison and a petition was sent to the high court at Anking. The governor ordered Hwei Cheng's release, as he was a high military official and so could not be legally arrested by the civil authorities, but he was immediately rearrested by the Viceroy of Anhwei, Kiangsu, and Kiangsi provinces, and ordered imprisoned at Nanking. His family was released, however, and moved to a Buddhist temple close to the prison in that city. The prisons in China at that time were much like those in

Europe a hundred years ago. The families of prisoners were free to go in and out of the prison at any time to visit their relatives.

Apparently Hwei Cheng was never brought to trial and many of the curious facts of his case were never proven. It was fortunate for Green Jade and her mother that he was never found guilty of the theft of government property. If he had been so convicted, Green Jade would never have been accepted as a candidate for entry into the palace six months later.

Hwei Cheng was given very lenient treatment by the Viceroy and it was understood that he would be released as soon as his family replaced all the money taken from the treasury. At first this did not appear much of a difficulty, as Hwei Cheng had had little time or occasion to spend much of the gold and silver he had taken from Wuhu. But when an accounting was made it was found that the amount of money missing was several thousand taels more than was found in Hwei Cheng's possession when arrested. This was a tremendous sum for that time. The only explanation for the disappearance of this money was that it had been stolen by the cartmen, or, more likely, someone in addition to Hwei Cheng had robbed the treasury in Wuhu that night of the panic.

Hwei Cheng became so sick from fear and disappointment at the sudden collapse of all his plans that he could give no assistance of any kind to his family in this new crisis.

As Hwei T'ai T'ai also became ill because of worry and the hardships she had passed through since they left Wuhu, the entire responsibility fell on Green Jade. She was just sixteen years old when this terrible blow struck her family—rather young to have such a load suddenly placed on her shoulders. But apparently she never wasted a minute in self-pity over the collapse of all her fine dreams. She remained absolutely loyal to her father and supplied him with every comfort she could secure. She rallied every resource they had. She sent Autumn Cloud to Wuhu to find and bring to Nanking the jewelry and other valuables Hwei T'ai T'ai had put away as security. These were sold, as was everything else the family possessed. The money gained by these means was only a small part of the sum required to pay Hwei Cheng's debt, but, such as it was, it was all handed over to the Viceroy. Green Jade was still confronted by the problem of paying for food and other necessities for her family of seven persons.

6

Truly it looked as if the fortunes of Green Jade and her family could not fall lower than they were that November morning, the Double Tenth, her birthday. However, Fate dealt her yet another severe blow: her father died suddenly that same day. As long as he was alive and available for trial and punishment, the treasury officials did not press too hard for the repayment of the money. But Hwei Cheng's sudden death changed all this. Now the Viceroy demanded the complete sum of the debt before he would let the family have possession of Hwei Cheng's body.

Only a Chinese or a Manchu can understand how serious a situation this created for Green Jade and her family. No other people are so anxious that the family be united in death. A very large sum of money had yet to be raised, a sum so large it appeared an impossible amount for them to obtain. But Green Jade and her mother, who now had recovered from her first shock, decided that they would raise the money, get possession of Hwei Cheng's body, and take it to Peking for honorable interment in the burial place of their ancestors, even if this were the last thing they did in their lives. Nothing else in the whole world was now so important to these two determined women.

Green Jade wrote Li Weng-yang, her old teacher in Hangchow Fu, told him her difficulties, and asked him to call on their friends to loan her as much money as they could. This was not considered an unusual request in China, where friends are well accustomed to helping one another in all financial difficulties. Everyone understood and sympathized with the daughter's determination to redeem her father's body for burial in the family tombs. Li Weng-yang wrote a similar letter to the father of Treasured Pearl in Wuhu. He hardly needed to be told of the difficulties Green Jade and her family were in, and he worked equally hard to raise a large sum which he sent to Green Jade. She called on the Viceroy, who contributed generously. Other officials were also very liberal in their gifts; apparently few could resist Green Jade. But the final amount was still many hundreds of taels short. The family was fairly starving as every *cash* they received went to the treasury. In desperation Green Jade left the family in charge of Autumn Cloud and sent her mother to Wuhu, while she herself made the hard trip overland to Hangchow Fu, where the family had many friends. There she raised the balance of the sum required, but when the debt was paid nothing was left for food or transportation to Peking with the body.

Green Jade found an old boatman named Li who was almost as anxious to go to the north as she was. He wanted to get his boat and his family out of reach of the Tai Ping rebels, who were now actually threatening Nanking and who were already seizing all river craft they could lay their hands on. To Li, his boat was his most valuable possession, in fact his only possession. It fed all the mouths of the Li family. He was so anxious to leave the Yangtze River that he offered, after some persuasion by Green Jade, to transport the entire Hwei Cheng family with all their possessions as far as Tungchow just for the food necessary for himself, his wife, a daughter about Green Jade's age, and two younger boys.

Before leaving Nanking, Autumn Cloud suggested it would be better both for the family and herself if she returned to her own people and did not burden the Hwei family further to provide for her. This was a generous offer. The whole family had become very attached to her and disliked very much to see her leave them, but it seemed such a good plan for all concerned that they agreed to it. They had little they could give her as a parting gift, but Autumn Cloud wanted little. Much as they hated to part with Foniyinbu they let her take her baby boy with her, the last son of Hwei Cheng, who, as such, really belonged to the Hwei family. This was the kindest thing they could have done for Autumn Cloud. It made her very happy, as she now had a son to take care of her in her old age. She was a very contented woman when she left for Hangchow Fu.

The officials in the office of the Viceroy who knew the story of Tao T'ai Hwei Cheng gave Green Jade and the family the present of a fine coffin for her father, a coffin worthy of a military Tao T'ai. It was a thoughtful and generous gesture which solved one of Green Jade's most difficult problems.

As it was now near the end of the First Moon, the month of the Chinese New Year, and as the Grand Canal was free of ice, Green Jade insisted on loading the boat and starting on the journey though she had only enough money to purchase food for four or five days. The old boatman knew this was not wise, but he was under Green Jade's spell and let her eagerness override his caution.

To earn money for food for all on board Li's boat, Green Jade and Phoenix used their fine voices to sing at the boat landings for the few coins the crowd would toss to them. But in spite of all their efforts they did not have one cash either for food or to pay the canal dues when they arrived at Chink'ow, where the Grand Canal joins the Yangtze.

At dusk of the second evening after their arrival at Chink'ow a man on horseback approached the canal and in a loud voice asked for the boat of Tao T'ai Hwei. Li answered that he had the family of Tao T'ai Hwei on his boat. He was asked to call the head of the family. When Hwei T'ai T'ai informed him that she was the head of the Tao T'ai's family, the horseman gave her six hundred taels, saying it came from the magistrate. Hwei T'ai T'ai told him there must be some mistake, but the horseman assured her there could not be a mistake; there could not be two men with the name of Tao T'ai Hwei in all China. She asked for the name of the magistrate and was told it was Wu T'ang. Thinking that the magistrate must be a friend of her late husband and was sending the widow the customary burial present, she accepted the money and sent him a note of thanks.

But the curious thing was that there actually were two Tao T'ai Hweis. The man the money was really intended for was Tao T'ai Hwei from Chekiang province. He had been on an official visit to Peking and was returning to his post. Being short of money, he had sent a note to his friend Magistrate Wu T'ang asking for a loan of six hundred taels. For some unknown reason the message was delayed. He waited over a day, then as he could wait no longer he left for Chekiang on the very day the boat with Green Jade and her family tied up at the same dock.

When Magistrate Wu T'ang received the note of thanks he realized the mistake his servant had made. He was furious and declared he would get his money back. But one of his friends who had made some inquiries told him that Hwei T'ai T'ai had a very beautiful daughter on the boat who had been registered at the Board of Rites for entry into the palace. She might become influential at court one day, the friend suggested. Why make an enemy of her by demanding the return of the money? It would be wiser to let the family keep it and have her for a friend. The magistrate saw the wisdom of this advance and followed it to his profit. Green Jade never forgot Wu T'ang's kindness. Later she rewarded him by making him Viceroy of Szechuan province, and whenever he visited the court she showed him many favors.

With the six hundred taels they now had enough money to reach Peking. They had no more financial difficulties, but Green Jade and her mother must often have compared the humble way they were now traveling with the luxurious journey they had made down the same canal only a few years before. As their boat moved slowly northward Green Jade and her mother discussed the many changes in their fortunes during the last eight years. They had risen from dire poverty to great luxury and were now back where they started. It would have been difficult to convince Green Jade that Fate was only giving her another lesson, a severe and hard lesson, to prepare her for the even harder problems she would have to solve in the future.

Although the future looked dark and uncertain, neither Green Jade nor her mother ever lost faith in Soothsayer Fu's vision and the prophecy that Green Jade would someday be a great lady, perhaps even an empress.

This was not the foolish dream it would have been for a girl in her circumstances in a Western country. China's system of plural marriages at that time made the dreams of someday becoming even an empress possible for every Manchu girl. But Green Jade had something else on which to build her hopes. She had a vision and prophecy in which she had absolute faith.

Fortunately for Green Jade and her pride, the fact that they were in mourning required them to wear the cheapest cotton clothes; these were the only clothes they possessed, as everything else had been sold in Nanking.

While their boat was tied to the dock at Tientsin, Green Jade and her family saw their first "foreign barbarians" from over the seas. Two young white men were at the landing watching the traffic on the canal. They evidently had not been long in China. They wore foreign clothes and could speak only a little Chinese. They were accompanied by a young Chinese of about their own age who interpreted for them. Green Jade and Phoenix were much interested in the foreigners. They wanted to talk to the two young men but Hwei T'ai T'ai would not allow this. She had heard too many shocking stories about white men. The girls had the boatman inquire why they were in Tientsin, at that time closed to foreigners. He found they were from Shanghai and had received a permit from the governor to accompany a Chinese friend making a short visit to his old home in Tientsin. They had assisted him in bringing his family and valuables from Shanghai to escape the Tai Ping rebels.

Although forbidden to talk to the barbarians the two girls stood as close to them as they could, listening to the questions the young men were asking the boatmen and which the young Chinese interpreted for them.

The two white men made a good impression on the sisters. While the girls did not like their ugly clothes and their harsh voices, they did like their frank faces, their clean look, and their tall, slim bodies. The girls had been told and expected to find every barbarian dirty, with unkempt red beard, hairy, coarse in appearance and behavior, and intoxicated. Here were two young men quiet in their behavior, certainly not intoxicated, and who showed not the least tendency to steal Chinese girls. Green Jade and Phoenix learned they were from the Flowery Flag country (America), a country that had never fought against the Chinese, and that they were learning the

Chinese language so they could tell the Chinese about their religion.

This increased the girls' interest. What they had been told somehow did not seem to apply to these young men. Green Jade evidently did not yet have the prejudice against all barbarians and all missionaries that she was to have later. But little did the two missionaries dream they were standing close to the woman who was to be accused of being a bitter enemy of their religion fifty years later.

At Tungchow, the northern terminus of the Grand Canal, thirteen miles east of Peking, they had to leave the old boatman. They had become very fond of Li and his family. After dividing such presents as they had, they loaded their meager belongings and the coffin into carts and started over the Great Road to Peking.

They sent a messenger ahead to find Tien Chen, the cousin of their father and their only relative in Peking. Tien Chen met them at the Ch'i Hua Men with the bad news that it was against the law to bring a coffin into Peking. They were told to leave the coffin in a temple outside the city until the time for burial. As Green Jade's family did not have sufficient money to pay for the service of the temple or for a proper burial at this time, they determined in some way to get the coffin into the city and keep it in their home until they could secure funds for the funeral.

They decided to try a less-guarded entrance, the Tung Pien Men, a smaller gate leading to the Chinese section of Peking. However, here they found the same difficulty, so they stopped for the night at the Ho T'ien Inn. Tien Chen tried all the next day to get the necessary permission to bring the coffin into the city but failed. Green Jade was furious. During the past months she had solved so many more difficult problems than dealing with a few gatekeepers that she took charge of the negotiations, saying: "I have my own way to treat these slaves." The arrogance that was to become so noticeable in her in later life was beginning to show.

Green Jade remembered that the gates of the city were always closed at the exact moment the big bell in the bell tower announced sundown. A few minutes before sundown she sent the cart with their personal belongings through the city gate. Once through, she spread out all her belongings in the yard of the customs officials for their inspection. She argued so much and made the officials so annoyed that they decided to search every piece of her baggage. While the customs men were busy with the search, the cart carrying the coffin passed unnoticed through the gate with the crowd that was hastening to get into the city before the gates clanged shut.

Once inside the city, the driver turned the cart around to face outward. It looked as though he were taking a body outside the city for burial. The customs officials began to curse Green Jade for making them search all her luggage for nothing. She was ready for them and cursed them back for delaying her with their foolish examination of her baggage while all she was trying to do was to get out of the city to bury her father. She started crying in a loud voice. The crowd, not knowing the circumstances but always ready to help anyone against officials, took Green Jade's side and threatened the customs men for holding up a poor little girl who was only trying to bury her father. Just then the great bell tolled and the gates closed. The customs officials, alarmed at the proportions the incident had assumed, were only too glad to tell Green Jade to take her baggage and coffin any place she wanted so long as it was a great distance from them.

As it was now too late for the family to reach their old home on Ta Ssu T'iao Hutung, the only place in Peking where they could expect to find friends, they stopped at a small inn. Their cousin Tien Chen, now reduced to living in one room near Ta Ssu T'iao Hutung, could not help them. Early the next morning Green Jade and her mother left the three children at the inn and made the three-mile trip across the city to Ta Ssu T'iao Hutung. Here they met great disappointment. During the eight years they had been absent from Peking a number of local riots and disturbances had occurred in that section of the city. Grandfather Wong was dead and his family scattered. The only one of their old friends they could find was the Mohammedan meat seller, Hei Yu.

Hei Yu was very pleased to see them again. He did everything he could to help them. This was not much, as he had lost most of his possessions during the riots and was now almost as poor as the Hwei family. But he and Cousin Tien Chen did find four small rooms for them in a tiny courtyard. It was even a much poorer place than the one Green Jade was born in but it was the best they could afford. By evening they were settled in their home.

Three days later, with the help of their two friends, the coffin was removed to the family burial ground, where it was left unburied; the actual funeral had to wait until years later, when they could afford a proper ceremony. Their last money was now spent, but it took more than that to discourage Green Jade and her mother. They had been through this experience before. To earn a living they now offered to mend or make clothes. Hei Yu brought all the garments he and his family had that required mending and he persuaded his neighbors to do the same.

Some writers claim that even with the two women working in this way, many hours a day, they could not earn enough money to buy food for their family of five, and that Green Jade and her sister hired themselves out as professional criers at funerals. This was considered about as low an employment as could be found.

But again, when things looked blackest, Fate stepped in to help them. It has been told that Hwei Cheng's father, Ching Juei, was once able to help a neighbor, Wu Chin-t'ang, who was on trial for his life before the court where Ching Juei was employed. Wu's son, Wu Wen-chen, heard that the family of Hwei Cheng had returned to Peking and were in need of assistance. He decided that this gave him the opportunity to return the favor their grandfather had done his father. Wu Wen-chen was a Chinese and held the position of supervisor on the estate of Prince Cheng—a position of importance and influence but with small financial returns.

Wu called on the Hwei family, moved them to a small but much better place on Ta Erh T'iao Hutung belonging to Prince Cheng which he could let them have for a very small rental. With Prince Cheng's influence, Green Jade's elder brother was admitted to a cavalry school which paid a salary of one and a half taels a month. The younger son was placed in a school for Manchu boys. This greatly improved the condition of the family, but the women still had to take in sewing to purchase enough food for the family.

Wu Chin-t'ang was still alive, but a very old man. When his son told him of the return of the Hwei family the old man paid them a visit. He was very pleased with Green Jade. When he learned she had registered for entrance to the palace he told them the entrance examinations had been set for the first week in July, only a few weeks distant, and that if Green Jade were to be successful she had to have a new dress, new shoes, hair trimmings, cosmetics, perfumes, and many other things. The cosmetics and perfumes were expensive but necessary, as Green Jade could not appear at the palace without them. All Manchu girls of the better class more than eighteen years of age covered the entire face and the exposed part of the neck with a thick layer of white powder and much pink coloring whenever they appeared in public. This hid the face as completely as if the girls wore a veil and was done even though Manchu girls usually had very beautiful complexions. Without powder and paint they felt undressed.

The suggestion of old Wu added one more problem to the heavy load the two women were already carrying. But they knew that somehow Green Jade would take that examination, and they were right. Three days later old Wu called again. He had persuaded several distant relatives that it might not be a bad investment for them to help provide the money for clothes and other necessities for Green Jade's palace examinations. From them Wu had collected enough money so that Green Jade was able to dress as well as her competitors. Although some writers have claimed that Wu Chin-t'ang adopted Green Jade, the facts were just the opposite. Green Jade adopted the old man Wu. She called him "Grandfather Wu" from the very first visit he made on the family. After she became Empress she saved Grandfather Wu's son from severe punishment when Prince Cheng and his entire household were convicted for their connection with the Su Shun conspiracy.

It was not until after Green Jade had received the official

notification to report for the examinations that she learned how close she had come to being barred from ever entering the palace. When Emperor Ch'ien Lung revised the rules for the "selection of beauties for the court" he included a provision that no daughter of an official convicted of a crime against the government could be registered. Once every three years the Board of Revenue notified the governors of the provinces, the commanders of the Eight Banner Corps, and other officials in Peking to prepare a list of young Manchu girls who could qualify for the palace examinations. This list had to give the name of the Banners of the girls' parents, the official positions of their fathers, grandfathers, and great-grandfathers, and the special qualifications of the girls themselves.

This order from the Board of Revenue was received by the governor in Anking on the tenth day of the tenth month of the thirtieth year of the reign of Tao Kuang, that is before Tao T'ai Hwei Cheng fled from Wuhu. The governor, being a good friend of Hwei Cheng, immediately sent the name of Green Jade to the board with his highest recommendation. Even then her name would probably have been taken from the list if the new Emperor Hsien Feng had not on his own initiative altered the rule that would have postponed the selection of the candidates until after the end of the twenty-seven months of mourning for the death of his father. This would have brought the date of submission of the names of the candidates long after Green Jade's father was imprisoned in Nanking. The governor would hardly have dared recommend the daughter of an official then in jail, even if he had not yet been convicted.

Another curious coincidence is that in less than a year from the time the Hwei family left Wuhu that city was captured by the Tai Ping rebels, almost entirely destroyed, and practically every Manchu living in the city was massacred. As Treasured Pearl and her family and all the other neighbors of the Hwei family were killed it is probable that Green Jade and her family would have met the same fate if the gods had not intervened. They would not have escaped if Tao T'ai Hwei had not been a coward and fled the city that night of the first riots.

It is difficult for anyone who has followed the life of Green Jade thus far not to believe that the gods were watching over her. Her whole life from the time of her birth seems to have been a series of experiences, some of them very hard, to prepare her for the great life she was now entering. The vision the morning of her birth, whatever it may have been, gave Green Jade and her mother the courage necessary to carry them over obstacles that would have defeated any woman without absolute faith in her destiny. Friends and funds were forthcoming when they were necessary. The family escaped death at Wuhu almost by a miracle. Her name was submitted and accepted by the Board of Revenue only because a rule was altered that had never before been altered. She was provided with the clothes necessary for her appearance before the Board of Examiners when there seemed no possible way of securing them. She was given a mind far above the average girl of her time and an education which was to make her stand out above all the other concubines in the Imperial Palace. Apparently the gods had the intent to make her Empress of China.

7

The weeks that followed the receipt of the money from Grandfather Wu were busy weeks for Green Jade and her family.

Cloth for the new dresses had to be chosen and purchased and the dresses made. This was done almost entirely by her mother and herself. Both were now good seamstresses. A teacher from the court had to be employed to teach Green Jade how to comport herself before the Board of Examiners, how to answer the questions she would probably be asked, to show her how to dress and put on the make-up for her face, and even how to walk. Green Jade had spent so little time in Peking that she was not familiar with Peking styles and court life, but, as usual, she was a good pupil.

She learned from her teacher about the two classes of candidates entering the palace, the Hsuan Hsui Nui and the Hsuan Kung Nei. Only candidates of the Hsuan Hsui Nui had the opportunity to become concubines to the Emperor. Candidates of the second class chosen annually served the Empress and the concubines of the former Emperor. Some of these were old ladies of great influence and importance, but also of uncertain temper. Green Jade also learned that only a small number of the girls examined ever succeeded in becoming a Hsuan Hsui Nui, as the number of candidates was more than the number of girls required. Getting into the palace was not the simple or easy thing Green Jade had imagined it to be.

Unfortunately no amount of adversity, no taste of poverty seemed able to lessen Green Jade's vanity and her desire to show off her good looks and fine clothes, a trait she inherited from her father. Even before the examination she was already parading before the neighbors in an overbearing way.

The great day for the examination finally arrived. Early that morning, in the first week of June, the entire neighborhood was excited by the arrival in their poor hutung of a mule cart sent from the palace, escorted by a number of eunuchs. Green Jade was treated with great respect, placed in the cart, and taken on her long ride to the Yuan Ming Yuan, a considerable distance from the city.

What were her thoughts as she rode to an audience with the Emperor that would decide her future life? Certainly they were not fearful. It would take more than such an event to put fear in the heart of the girl who had shouldered such weighty responsibilities in Wuhu and assumed the leadership of her family. She had too much faith in her destiny to fear anything.

When Green Jade entered the Yuan Ming Yuan she was taken directly to the Hall of High Mountains and Long Rivers. Here she and the other candidates were presented, one at a time, to the Emperor. Each presentation lasted only a few minutes. Each candidate had previously been questioned at length by the Board of Examiners. Green Jade had no difficulty with any of the questions asked her, as she probably was the best-educated girl examined at that time. But she had not been prepared for the thorough physical examination she also had to pass. Although this was carried on in a small private chamber by a group of women, Green Jade was more embarrassed than ever before in her life.

After the board made its recommendations and Green Jade had returned to her home, she knew that her life would be spent in the palace. But as yet she did not know in what capacity. The successful candidates had to wait two months for formal approval and final classification by the Empress Dowager. The intervening time was spent largely in making clothes and attending the small parties friends and relatives insisted on giving to the candidates. In this way Green Jade met and made friends with some of the other concubines before they entered the palace.

Some writers claim that in those two months she also met Jung Lu, the handsome young guardsman of about her own age with whom she was to be closely associated after she entered the palace and until his death more than fifty years later.

While Green Jade awaits the imperial decision let us review her character as we have come to know it.

She was a mature woman, although only seventeen years old, when she entered the palace. That she was unusually beautiful and had a very attractive smile is without question; too many have testified to that for us to have any doubt. She was of average height for a Manchu girl, about five feet one inch, and weighed one hundred and five pounds. Most foreigners who saw her in later life described her as being tall, but they apparently did not look at her feet. At all receptions and official meetings she wore a Manchu shoe with a high heel which was not where one would expect it to be but in the center of the shoe. This added almost four inches to her actual height. She was not the round-faced beauty that so many Chinese admire. Like most Manchus, she had a slightly longer face and a fairly good-sized nose, the same nose that the Mohammedan Hei Yu had pinched so often when she was a child. But the large, piercing, almost black eyes and the warm smile were her most-noticeable and most-admired features. She possessed a good voice, sang well, and played a number of musical instruments, including the flute. She was a good student and had an education probably equal to or better than most of the imperial princes. She certainly excelled them in experience and in handling difficult problems and in her knowledge of China and the Chinese people. Of foreign countries and customs she knew practically nothing and she was rapidly acquiring a very deep prejudice against everything foreign. She was fond of reading, especially books on the history of the Manchus and the Ch'ing Dynasty. She was a fair painter of flowers and many of her paintings are still shown in Peking. She was exceptionally proficient in making large Chinese characters. She was fond of the theater and is credited with writing several of the plays that were later produced in the palace theaters. But she is never mentioned as a serious writer and she was the only Ch'ing ruler who failed to publish a collection of poems or some other literary work of merit. However, her decrees and mandates are still considered masterpieces of legal prose.

Even at an early age she began to show many contradictions in her character. As we have seen, she had unusual courage and the ability to make quick decisions. She showed imagination in forming plans and a strong determination in carrying through any policy she favored. She made friends easily, especially of older men, and was usually very loyal. Her friends in turn remained loyal to her regardless of how she treated them. She was not always truthful, she had a quick temper, and could be cruel. She was vain and loved display and formality, especially in everything connected with the court. She was always kind to inferiors and apparently never failed to reward anyone who had helped her or her family in the days when they needed help so badly.

Finally, through Prince Cheng, Grandfather Wu heard that Green Jade had been successful in the examinations and had been selected an imperial concubine designate of the first group. As soon as this became known she and her mother had many friends. Distant relatives they had never heard of, and who had not paid the slightest attention to them when they needed assistance, now called and were very friendly. Interestingly enough, they were well received by Green Jade and her family. The two brothers were promoted to positions in the army that paid them a sufficient salary so the family could move to a much better home at Fang Chia Yuan, inside the

Ch'i Huan Men. Later, when the younger son was made a duke, this house became known as Duke Hwei's palace. The family lived in it until it was destroyed by the Boxers in 1900, when they moved to Hsi La Hutung or, as foreigners called it, Pewter Lane. As the Hwei family was living in Pewter Lane when foreign writers first came to know them, the latter assumed that Green Jade had been born in that street. This, we now know, was not correct.

Those were very happy days for Green Jade, the first happy days she had enjoyed for a long time. She believed without the slightest doubt that she would someday be a great empress and would rule the court she was to enter in a few weeks. All her dreams and the vision of Soothsayer Fu were coming true. Would she have refused her future honors if Soothsayer Fu could have shown her at this time the price Fate was to make her pay for success? If she could have known the many disappointments and sorrows that were to come to her as Empress and mother would she have hesitated? If she could have foreseen the day when she had to approve the execution of some of her best friends, and if she could have heard the terrible accusations that were to make her hated by the entire world, would she have flinched from the tasks ahead? Any other woman would have without a doubt, but not Tz'u Hsi. The future Empress of all China was a courageous woman.

The number of successful candidates for the Hsuan Hsui Nui was finally fixed at six. An imperial decree ordered the first three girls to report at the Yuan Ming Yuan on the third day of the Ninth Moon. They became pins, or concubines of the second class. The next two girls were ordered to report on the twenty-first day of the Ninth Moon. At this time Green Jade, sixth in rank, was appointed a concubine of the third, or lowest, class. She thus found herself last on the list instead of first, as she had planned. It was her first and one of her few failures.

From the day the imperial decree was issued the home of the Hwei family was guarded by soldiers from the Inner Three Banner Corps. They pitched a gaily-colored tent at the front gate to the joy of all the small boys in the neighborhood. Two elderly maidservants were sent from the palace to show Green

Jade how to arrange her hair and to dress properly and also to instruct her in the ceremonial customs to be followed when she met the Emperor.

When the yellow cart finally arrived for Green Jade, she and her mother realized that they were parting for a long time. Although it was the one thing both of them had been working and praying for since Green Jade was born, the love between mother and daughter proved for that hour, at least, stronger than their love for power and wealth. Mother and daughter clung to each other and could not be separated. They cried for a long time, paying no attention to the urging of the eunuchs, who knelt on the floor, begging the mother to let her daughter go.

Finally Green Jade said: "Mother, do not worry. Remember how much we suffered together with our poverty. It is better that we leave each other for a short time than that we suffer poverty again together. I will someday be a great woman, as you and I know. Then I will pile up a hill of gold and ask you to sit on the top of it." A prophecy and a promise she was to keep. She left her mother and all the neighbors still weeping.

The cart carrying Green Jade was accompanied by a considerable number of mounted soldiers, eunuchs, and officials from the Ministry of the Imperial Household. They were taking no chances on losing or having anything happen to one of the new concubines of the Emperor. When the young officer in command of the guard, who, according to some accounts, was the handsome Jung Lu, saw the condition of the Hwei family and the sorrow at the parting between mother and daughter, he took pity on the family and ordered that horses be provided for the two brothers that they might accompany their sister as far as the entrance to the palace.

Naturally this delighted the boys. Instead of returning home after seeing Green Jade pass through the Yuan Ming Yuan gates, they went to the home of their cousin Tien Chen. To comfort their mother they bought some cakes and in giving them to her told her they were a present from the Emperor with whom, they added (entirely out of their imaginations), Green Jade had won immediate favor. The story of this outrageous lie was brought back to the palace by one of the servants and immediately spread through the women's quarters. Green Jade became fearful of the consequences to herself. When Empress Hsiao Chen saw her weeping she told her not to mind because her brothers had told a lie to their merit. It was not for profit to themselves but only to comfort their mother. This seems to indicate that a friendly and rather informal relationship had already developed between the lowly concubine and the Empress. This is not so extraordinary as it might appear, as Hsiao Chen was younger than Green Jade.

Green Jade's first friend in the palace was Li Pin, also known as Tatala, the daughter of General Wen Hsiang. She was the first girl selected and for a time was the favorite of the Emperor. When Green Jade told Li Pin how worried she was about her mother, because she had so little food, Li Pin sent word to General Wen Hsiang, who immediately called on the Hwei family and sent them both rice and money. It was found that Hwei Cheng was of the same banner as General Wen and that they had been friends in their younger days. Li Pin and Green Jade soon became sworn sisters. Green Jade began thus early to build up her organization within the palace.

When Green Jade entered the palace she created many problems for herself and one for us. Our problem is what to call the young girl who had just entered the court of the Ch'ing emperors. All concubines and most of the officials in the palace were called by their official positions, and Green Jade changed her name twice during the first year and three times the next two years. As it would be difficult to recognize or follow her under so many names we will continue to call her Green Jade, the name her mother always used. We shall use this name until she becomes an empress. Then we shall be more respectful and call her Empress Tz'u Hsi.

2. THE CH'ING EMPERORS AND THEIR COURT

If we are to understand the life of Green Jade at the court of the Ch'ings, to understand why she sometimes succeeded and sometimes failed, we must know more about that court, the emperors and empresses, princes, princesses, concubines, statesmen, scholars, warriors, and eunuchs who composed it. We will not attempt to go too deeply into the lives of these interesting Manchus; that would take far too much time. But we should know a number of important things about them if we are to understand how a young girl, eighteen years old, without influential kinsmen or friends, could, in six years, become the dictator of the Chinese Empire. In Green Jade's small but sturdy body Nature or Fate or some other powerful force had somehow renewed the spark that had made the early Ch'ing emperors such great men, great conquerors, and great statesmen.

As Green Jade wandered through the gardens and gazed at the scores of blue lakes, the bright-colored pagodas, pavilions, and palaces that made up the fabulous Yuan Ming Yuan, which covered an area even larger than the entire city of Peking, her thoughts must often have turned to the tales she had been told of the Manchus and the founders of the Ch'ing Dynasty. From what we know of her forceful character it is not unlikely to suppose that of all the Manchu heroes Green Jade accorded first place to Dorgon, the warrior conqueror of Peking. His exploits, daring, subtlety, and competent statesmanship would assuredly have won her admiration.

As we know, Dorgon played an important part in placing the Ch'ing emperors on the Dragon Throne. Though never an emperor, no Manchu ruler did more for the establishment and perpetuation of the Ch'ing Dynasty or to make possible the rule of an empress such as Tz'u Hsi. To know Dorgon is to understand how the descendants of Nurhaci were able to rule China for nearly three centuries. To know Dorgon we must go back a few years, to the time of the death of Nurhaci and the crowning of his son Abahai.

At the time of his father's death, Dorgon was only fourteen years old. His mother, the favorite wife of Nurhaci, committed suicide the day her husband died so she could accompany him into the next world. Dorgon thus lost both father and mother on the same day—a great tragedy in a young boy's life. Because of this, Emperor Abahai took especial interest in his young half brother. He treated him like a favorite son. He saw that he received his education from the best teachers available. These were Chinese scholars who taught the young Manchu Chinese history and Chinese culture. The Emperor took him on most of his campaigns, taught him statecraft and war. He called him the "Wise Warrior," and when Dorgon was old enough Abahai placed him in charge of an army. It was Dorgon who led most of the raids into China. It was Dorgon who was given the difficult task to attempt to force a way through the defenses of the Great Wall at Shanhaikwan. He led the first Manchu armies that entered Peking and he seized the Dragon Throne for the Manchus.

Dorgon was appointed Regent until his nephew Emperor Shun Chih became of age. Under the title of "Imperial Uncle Regent" he was the absolute ruler of China at the very time China and the Ch'ing Dynasty needed a strong, wise leader. He was always considerate and loyal to the boy Emperor. He once ordered executed a group of army officials who had conspired to overthrow the young ruler and place him on the throne. He continued many of the institutions and practices of the Ming emperors and invited a number of Chinese officials of the Ming court to join his government. By these wise measures he perpetuated valuable Chinese customs and consolidated the nation. He restricted the power of the eunuchs, made personal property safe, and reduced taxation. In his Household Rules and Regulations which were to govern the personal and official acts of future emperors and princes for more than two centuries he gave China her first constitution.

Dorgon's good judgment and unselfishness are shown in his reasons for refusing the throne in favor of his young nephew. He pointed out that he was primarily a military man and that with the use of cannon and guns, first employed in the Manchu armies in his conquest of China, the tactics of war had changed. He said the science of war and the science of governing an immense empire such as China had become too complicated for any one man to be a master of both. He repeated the old Han proverb: "A man may conquer an empire on horseback, but a man cannot rule an empire on horseback." He stated that in future military men must be trained in war and emperors must be educated in history, literature, religion, and the art of government. When his associates complained that the new Emperor was too young to occupy the throne in such turbulent times, he replied that they were fortunate in having an emperor young enough to be trained in the new art of government and not a man of experience too old to learn. And he saw to it that his nephew, the Emperor, did so learn.

But apparently Dorgon overlooked or forgot to apply the same pacifying process to the Manchu princesses. Those fierce, warlike daughters of fighting princes and war chiefs whom the Manchus brought to China as wives or mothers remained the same courageous, independent, and militant women they had always been. There was not one emperor in the long history of the Ch'ing Dynasty who did not have at least one of these courageous, outspoken women as an empress, empress dowager, or both, to dominate his reign.

The Ch'ing conquerors also gave China a system of government that was the law of the land as long as they ruled it. Instead of forcing their own system on China they showed themselves broad-minded statesmen by adopting much of the system of government already in operation at the time of the conquest—the system the Mings and earlier dynasties had slowly worked out. China has always been fortunate in that no new dynasty ever wiped out the religion, the customs, or the governmental system of its predecessors. They have usually built shrewdly on the structure of the former dynasty in the same way that they added to the ancient palaces and cities.

At the head of the nation stood the Emperor, who received his authority from Heaven. At that time the country was divided into fifteen provinces, each ruled by a governor who received his appointment from the Emperor. Each province was divided roughly into ten *hsien* or districts, and each hsien was under a magistrate appointed by the governor. The magistrate ruled through the headman of the family or village. By this system the emperor, governor, magistrate, and headman of the family were each answerable to the authority immediately above him. The headman of a family held about the same authority over those below him, and had about the same responsibility for their welfare, as the Emperor had for the governors who were his immediate inferiors.

The Emperor was responsible to Heaven for the proper government of the country. He, in turn, held the governors responsible for the government of the provinces and gave them the necessary authority to keep the peace, administer justice, and collect taxes. The governor passed this responsibility and authority on to the magistrates. The magistrate held the headman of each family responsible for all the obligations of the family to the government and for the conduct of each member of the family. A whole family could be punished for the criminal act of any one of its members. The military organization of the country was entirely separate from the civil government, being under viceroys appointed by the Emperor. Any officials or men of prominence, or in theory any citizen of China, had the right to send a petition or memorial to the government or even to the Emperor on any subject that warranted such a document.

Great honor, often more honor than salary, was attached to each of the government offices. In times of peace the positions were attractive and much sought after, as they gave social standing, prestige, and often possessed lucrative opportunities. But in times of rebellion, banditry, or even floods and other such disasters, a position of authority often caused its holder uin. This simple form of government proved very China; some students have described it as prob- nost economical and most efficacious system of gov- levised for a large country by any people in history. e to the statement that the Manchus governed a with two men, which, if true, compares favorably housands of officeholders that now seem necessary only a small part of a province.

ı princes were taught from childhood that the Em- received his mandate to govern from Heaven and that he was accountable to Heaven for all his acts as emperor. They were also taught that the Emperor held the country in trust from his ancestors, to whom he would have to answer when he met them in the celestial regions. They strongly believed this, and the fear of doing anything that would bring disgrace to their dynasty usually made every Ch'ing emperor, regardless of the kind of private life he led, a very conscientious ruler.

In addition to these heavenly restraints the Emperor also had a few earthly rules to follow. He had to govern in strict accordance with the Household Rules of the Ch'ing Dynasty. For this he was answerable to the imperial family or clan. He had two governing bodies: the Nei Ko, or Cabinet, and the Chun Chi Ch'u, or Grand Council. The Grand Councilor was the highest official in China, next to the Emperor. The decisions of these two were usually approved by the Emperor with the little imperial red dot which he always placed on all official papers. In addition to the above, there were the Censors, an independent and courageous board that stood between the Emperor and his people. The Censors were the watchdogs of all the other officials, and though members of this body were often punished for their courage, they seldom hesitated to speak out to condemn any corrupt or inefficient officials—even a Grand Councilor or, on occasion, the Emperor himself. Courage was the tradition of their office and the Censors seldom lacked it. We shall see that they frequently censored even Empress Tz'u Hsi when she was at the height of her power.

The rank of any official in China could be told at a glance by the button on his hat. The highest official wore a ruby or a plain red coral button. From the red button the colors ranged downward through plain coral, transparent blue, op transparent crystal, white porcelain, smooth gold, ca to plain gilt with the Shou character of the ninth and rank.

The Ch'ing rulers also continued and improved the tr tional civil-service examinations for the selection of gover ment officials. China had been selecting her officials in this way for many centuries before any other people attempted such a democratic system. These examinations were open to any boy or man in China who could qualify. The farmer's son and the viceroy's son had equal opportunity. Each was required to sit in identical small cubicles and write answers to the same set of questions. If successful, each received the same award. The preliminary examinations were held in the local hsien. The successful candidates were then sent on to the examinations held in the provincial capitals. The successful candidates of these provincial examinations went on to the national examinations, which were held in Peking.

In Peking there were accommodations for about eight thousand candidates. Each candidate had to provide himself with candles, food, and such other things as he would require for three days. He occupied a small cubicle about seven feet by four and no one was allowed in or out during the examinations. It often proved to be a physical as well as a mental test, and it was not unusual for candidates to die during the examinations. But the reward for successful candidates was so great that many competed for the honors. As there was no age limit, middle-aged men also entered the examinations, which were held every three years, and often continued to do so until they became old men. Cases have been known where a son, his father, and grandfather took the examinations at the same time.

The results of the Ch'ing leaders' decision to educate future emperors of China as scholars and administrators instead of military commanders and the emphasis they now put on the development of a strong civil government soon became evident in the court life at Peking. Ch'ing emperors were commanders in chief of the armies in name only. While they sometimes accompanied the armies on nearby campaigns, no Ch'ing emperor after Abahai ever again actually led any of the great Manchu armies that were to conquer so many distant parts of Asia.

Most emperors became scholars and left notable works of literature. Shun Chih, the first Ch'ing emperor, spoke the Chinese language as well as he spoke his native Manchu. He adopted Chinese customs and religion so completely that, it was reported, he finally gave up his throne to become a Buddhist priest.

As emperors and court took greater interest and pride in cultural subjects, so did the Manchu youth of the land. As one result, interest in military affairs dwindled. The greatest pride of the early Manchus had been in their ability as soldiers. This was originally the only profession open to highborn Manchus. But during the reigns of the later Ch'ing emperors it began to be looked on as no honor to belong to the army, with the result that the army no longer attracted the able young men as it had done in the past. Thus the empire failed to keep pace in military affairs with the rest of the world. Foreign observers and writers have always claimed that the Ch'ing Dynasty degenerated because the Ch'ing emperors became scholars instead of great warriors. The Ch'ing Dynasty did not become weak because it could not produce great men. It was weakened by a number of internal uprisings and insurrections and the attacks of stronger military nations from over the seas and because China had placed culture above war.

Shun Chih, the first Ch'ing emperor, seems a curious offspring from such a warlike father as Emperor Abahai and an equally fierce mother, Empress Hsiao Chuang, until we recall the system of education Dorgon introduced for his training and for that of the later Ch'ing emperors. Shun Chih was the first product of that system of education.

He apparently was a rather delicate boy; some say he suffered from tuberculosis. But this did not stop him from being fond of riding, archery, and other games so popular with the Manchu princes of that time.

He was a studious and extremely conscientious ruler. From childhood he was interested in religion. In 1651 he came in contact with the famous Jesuit missionary, Father Adam Schall, who cured the Emperor's mother of a severe illness. He had many long discussions with Father Schall and showed himself an eager searcher for the truth in religion. He often summoned the priest to the palace in the middle of the night to discuss religion. He listened patiently to the good father's attempts to convert him to Christianity and he sometimes attended mass in Father Schall's church.

The Emperor had similar talks with Hsing Tsung, a well-educated young Buddhist monk. He was a stranger to the religions of both teachers, but he agreed with them in their belief that there was but one God. He also joined them in advocating the Golden Rule as the rule of life for all men. The Emperor could understand the Christian theory that the Son of God was the "Sin Bearer" of all peoples as he, the Emperor, the Son of Heaven, believed he was the "Sin Bearer" of his people.

The Emperor carefully weighed Father Schall's declaration that Christianity was eternal and unchangeable against Hsing Tsung's statement that Buddhism was changing daily and that a religion which was suitable to the primitive man would not serve the requirements of the modern man who had, by many successive reincarnations, advanced both spiritually and mentally. Father Schall condemned all other religions and preached that Christianity and faith in Jesus Christ provided the only road to salvation. Hsing Tsung claimed that just as there were many different colors of cows but the milk from all was the same color, so there were many roads to Nirvana or salvation. A man, the Buddhist taught, should choose the road most suitable to him, be it the worship of idols, Christianity, Mohammedanism, or any other. All streams, the Buddhist taught, led to the same ocean. Father Schall condemned the worship of idols in the strongest terms. Hsing Tsung defended their use, stating that idols served the common man as a flag served an army; it focused man's devotion on his God as a flag focused man's devotion on his country. He affirmed that an idol was not a substitute for God but only a means of assisting the mind to dwell on God, and that any image with which man invests the Formless One of the Supreme Being is an idol. The uneducated man scrawls a head on a piece of wood or stone and calls it *his* god; the educated man shuts his eyes and builds an image in his mind and calls it his god. Both are idols. Neither one can be condemned without condemning the other.

Father Schall condemned and forbade the ancestor worship of the Chinese. Hsing Tsung praised ancestor worship for its power in keeping the family together, for developing respect toward parents, and for its resultant good to the nation. The Emperor compared the harsh "Thou Shalt Not" of the Christian commandments to the mild suggestions of Buddhism that all men should cultivate the five cardinal virtues—purity, self-control, detachment from worldly things, truth, and nonviolence. The Emperor was not attracted by the Christian idea of heaven as a reward for a good life and hell as a punishment for a bad life. Hsing Tsung told him that Nirvana was for all, that while some might take a longer time to reach this perfection all would finally attain it. After lengthy consideration of these arguments, the Emperor decided that only Buddhism supplied a satisfactory explanation why man was in this world. Therefore he chose to become a Buddhist. He even began to think that he might have been a Buddhist monk in one of his previous incarnations.

The death of his favorite wife, Empress Hsiao Hsien, turned his attention more completely to religion. The relation between the Emperor and Hsiao Hsien is only one of the many beautiful love stories of the Ch'ing emperors, some of which rival the great romances found in Western literature. The body of the Empress was cremated with elaborate Buddhist ceremonies. The Emperor grieved so over her death that he announced his intention to shave his head and become a monk. He was temporarily dissuaded from this by Hsing Tsung, who urged him to remain on the throne.

The last four days of Shun Chih's life are shrouded in mystery which even today has not been entirely removed. The official records show that the Emperor died of smallpox in 1662, his body cremated, and his ashes buried in the Tung

Ling, the Eastern Tombs. There is a tomb there for Emperor Shun Chih, but many people claim that it is empty.

The story most popularly believed is that after the death of his beloved Empress the Emperor forsook the throne and retired to a temple in T'ien T'ai Shan. This is undoubtedly true. The court, believing it was but a passing fancy and that he would return within a reasonable time, kept his absence a secret. When he finally died in the temple his death was announced in the usual way, and as though he had never left the palace in the Forbidden City. He was given a state funeral and a burial ceremony was held in the Eastern Tombs.

The story goes on to say that in reality the monks, following the Emperor's wishes, embalmed and then lacquered his body and placed it on a throne in the Temple of the Heavenly Terrace, where it remains to this day. This seems probable and explains the extraordinarily lifelike lacquered figure, which truly seems not a statue but an actual human body. It is relacquered and clothed in new royal robes every year. The mummy bears a very close resemblance to the portraits of Emperor Shun Chih that are occasionally hung in the Imperial Museum. The temple is a favorite sight-seeing spot for all visitors to Peking.

2

Shun Chih was succeeded by his son, known as Emperor K'ang Hsi, who is generally recognized as the greatest of the Ch'ing emperors. He was born when his father was only seventeen and his mother fourteen years of age. It is said he was chosen Emperor largely because he had miraculously recovered from small pox and so was not liable again to contract this disease, which seems to have been one of the most dreaded sicknesses of the upper-class Manchus at that time.

K'ang Hsi extended the borders of China far to the south, added Formosa to the empire, conquered parts of Mongolia, and stopped Russian encroachments in the north. The war with Russia resulted in the first treaty China ever made with a European nation.

K'ang Hsi is known even more for his peaceful accomplishments than for his conquests in war. He encouraged the arts in every form, and with the help of the Jesuit Fathers corrected the Chinese calendar and made the first complete survey of China. For these valuable services and for introducing quinine to China, the Emperor gave the French priests a large piece of land within Peking on which they built their first cathedral. Unfortunately the prestige the Christian Church had gained under Emperor Shun Chih and continued to enjoy under Emperor K'ang Hsi was lost by the stubborn stand the Church took on the question of ancestor worship and other traditional Chinese customs. In condemning and forbidding converts to practice these rites the very foundations of the Chinese home were undermined. By this attitude the papal legate, Charles Tournon, in carrying out the orders of the Vatican, lost for the Church an opportunity to convert the Chinese emperors and the court to Christianity.

K'ang Hsi's mother died when he was very young. He was brought up by his grandmother, the Empress who had helped Dorgon put Fu Lin on the throne in Mukden before the Manchus conquered China. Empress Hsiao Chuang was very kind to little K'ang Hsi. She proved a real mother to him and for this won his lifelong gratitude. When K'ang Hsi became Emperor he made her his Superior Empress Dowager. Even when she was an old woman he took her on many of his tours of inspection and always listened to her wise advice. She interfered little in politics, but she did relieve him of his household and domestic duties. She died at the age of seventy-five and was buried with full imperial honors.

K'ang Hsi had a very high opinion of himself. According to Father Ripa, the Emperor considered himself a very good painter, calligrapher, poet, musician, and mathematician. The good father had some doubts on all the above claims but these he was careful to conceal until long after K'ang Hsi's death.

The Emperor also considered himself a superman and felt it his duty to produce as many descendants as possible. In numbers he did very well, as he had thirty-five sons. Twenty-five of these reached manhood and nineteen were living at the time of his death. But there seems to have been few supermen among them. Yung Cheng, his fourth son and successor, was considered below the average ability of Ch'ing emperors. Of the others, five died in prison, and two more would have had the same fate if they had not escaped. But K'ang Hsi's accomplishments were real and far-reaching and outnumbered his faults, which were small and largely owing to his vanity. He died in 1722 after sixty-one years on the throne, the longest reign in Chinese history.

K'ang Hsi's successor, Emperor Yung Cheng, suffers in comparison with both his father and his son. His mother was a maidservant who was elevated soon after his enthronement and became Empress Hsiao Kung. Yung Cheng was well educated, he chose wise councilors, and was one of the most conscientious workers of all Ch'ing emperors. He read all the memorials presented to him, often making witty and interesting comments on the margin of the papers. He kept strict watch over the national revenue and over officials. As an administrator he was admirable. It was in military affairs that he failed, losing much of the territory won by his father. Most Chinese writers look on Yung Cheng as a jealous, cruel, and unjust Emperor who nevertheless introduced a number of beneficial reforms. His reign was but a bridge between the two great Emperors K'ang Hsi and Ch'ien Lung.

Ch'ien Lung, 1711–99, the fourth Emperor of the Manchus, is known as one of the ablest and wisest emperors in the long history of China. He came to the throne at twenty-four and ruled sixty years, at which time he abdicated so as not to reign longer than his grandfather K'ang Hsi. He was the favorite grandson of K'ang Hsi, who took a great interest in his education. Ch'ien Lung was successful in all his military campaigns, regaining the territory lost by his father and adding Tatary, Tibet, Burma, and Sungari to China. He even defeated those savage fighters, the Gurkhas, in his campaign against Nepal. How he got his army across the great mountains into Nepal is still one of the mysteries that puzzle modern military experts.

His domestic life was almost free from scandal. He was very fond of his first wife. His second wife became a Catholic nun. His most famous affair with women and one of the few defeats he ever suffered was his unsuccessful attempt to break the will and win the "Round-Faced Beauty" known as the Fragrant Princess.

China and Ch'ien Lung had heard much of this famous woman who fought so valorously beside her husband against the Chinese armies in their invasion of Sungari. The princess was captured when her husband was killed, and at Ch'ien Lung's orders was brought unharmed to Peking. He was greatly pleased with her, but the admiration seems to have been entirely one-sided. The beautiful captive drew a dagger and tried to kill the Emperor at their first meeting. She repeated the attempt at every future opportunity.

Ch'ien Lung, like most men, thought he knew the ways of women and believed her attitude would change in time. As no woman had ever resisted his advances for long, why should this Mohammedan princess? To shorten the time as much as possible, he loaded her with gifts. These she proudly refused. He then built for her in the Sea Palace area one of the most beautiful palaces in Peking. He even added a Moslem mosque, an exact copy of her favorite mosque in Sungari, built where she could see it from her window when repeating her prayers. However, all these attentions failed. The Fragrant Princess refused to be won. The Emperor visited her often, always taking necessary precautions against attack, but she refused even to talk to him and would answer none of his questions.

After the Fragrant Princess had been in Peking a little more than two years and Ch'ien Lung had apparently not made the slightest progress in his wooing, his mother, Empress Dowager Hsiao Sheng, determined to take a hand in the affair, which she thought unbecoming to the Emperor's dignity. She commanded the Fragrant Princess to attend her at the Palace of Motherly Tranquility. After the usual courtesies, the Empress Dowager bluntly asked the Fragrant Princess what her intentions were toward the Emperor. The Fragrant Princess as bluntly replied that her intentions were to avenge the death of her husband by killing the Emperor, but that so far she had had no opportunity to do so, as she was closely watched.

This was perfectly understandable to the old Empress Dowager. She would probably have done the same herself in the same position. Accordingly, instead of having the obdurate princess strangled, as she had planned, she graciously allowed her to commit suicide. The princess thanked her, kowtowed three times, and without a moment's hesitation ended her life in the way approved by Japanese noblemen. They bred strong women in Mongolia and Manchuria in those days.

Emperor Ch'ien Lung mourned her death for two years. He raised her to the rank of a number-three concubine, an honor which it is unlikely the Fragrant Princess would have appreciated. Copies of a fine portrait of her in full armor by the Italian painter Castiglione can be bought even today in the shops of Peking.

Castiglione was a Jesuit brother, one of a number of very brilliant men, including astronomers, and mathematicians, whom the Church sent to China. In addition to his two portraits of the Fragrant Princess, Castiglione painted many other subjects, including two justly renowned pictures of Ch'ien Lung's famous One Hundred and Eight Horses.

Ch'ien Lung did many notable things, only a few of which we can record. He received the Macartney Mission sent to China by George III in 1793. Lord Macartney was evidently an ideal man to head such a mission. He was dignified, diplomatic, and had great respect for the old Emperor. To avoid the difficult problem of the kowtow, Ch'ien Lung received Lord Macartney and his staff informally in his huge hunting tent. They had two meetings in Jehol and another in Peking, where many rich presents were ceremoniously exchanged. At the Peking meeting Lord Macartney presented his petition asking for many things, among them the right to establish a permanent legation in Peking and for more Chinese ports to be opened to British trade.

All of Macartney's requests were denied in probably one of the most polite and yet firm refusals of any diplomatic document ever passed between two nations. In his reply the Emperor pointed out that Lord Macartney represented only one of the many minor kings beyond the Western ocean, that China was the center of the universe and produced everything she required within her own borders and so had no use for any of the things the Western countries wanted to sell. But as the Western nations seemed to be desirous of securing the blessings of a higher civilization and required tea in order to exist, he stated that he would allow that trade to continue at Canton.

The visit of Lord Macartney's mission was a failure, unfortunately only the first of many failures in the diplomatic relations between China and the Western nations.

The Ch'ien Lung period is probably best known to foreigners by the porcelain, cloisonné, enamel, metal work, silks, paintings, and other forms of art that were made in such high quality and quantity during the reign of this remarkable ruler. Many of the best pieces in existence today bear the little poem which the Emperor composed and inscribed on beautiful things he approved. Ch'ien Lung built a number of fine palaces and parks in the neighborhood of the capital city. But he did more than encourage art and build palaces, he reformed the government, curbed the eunuchs, and strengthened the civil-service examinations.

Ch'ien Lung died at eighty-nine, having outlived most of his sons. In the National Library at Peking can be found the 35,000 volumes of his diary. In these beautiful books every other page is a drawing to illustrate the page of manuscript it faces.

With Ch'ien Lung's death one hundred and fifty years ago the decline of China began. Soon she was to be torn by revolutions, attacked by the Western powers, and her ports—even her capital—occupied by the hated barbarians.

Many scholars place much of the blame for this on Ch'ien Lung's successor, Emperor Chia Ch'ing, who, though a conscientious ruler, was somewhat overfond of writing long memorials which often led him into difficulties.

Probably his greatest failure with the most far-reaching effect on China was his handling of the Amherst Mission, which arrived in 1816. This was another mission from the British King, asking for the same privileges that Ch'ien Lung had denied Lord Macartney. Unfortunately Lord Amherst was far from being a pleasing diplomat as was Lord Macartney. Nor was Emperor Chia Ch'ing so experienced, polite, and dignified as his predecessor on the Dragon Throne.

Meanwhile the foreigners in Canton—sailors, soldiers, and traders—had proven themselves to be very poor guests of China with their many brawls, fights, and clashes with the Chinese population. The conditions then prevailing in Canton were a poor argument to persuade China to open more of her port cities to foreigners.

Lord Amherst was convinced that the way to treat an Oriental was to show force, determination, and, occasionally, bad manners. Unfortunately for his country and China he was opposed by an equally determined Emperor.

Lord Amherst took every opportunity to show that he, a representative of His Majesty King George III, could not be dictated to by any oriental potentate. He rudely threw the Emperor's schedule of entertainment out of order at the last moment. After the Emperor had ascended the throne to receive him, Lord Amherst sent a message that he was too ill to attend the audience. The Emperor then ordered him to send two subordinate envoys in his place. The reply came that they were too ill to attend. Strange as such a coincidence was, it was nevertheless true. All three Englishmen were suffering from exposure and the hardships of the journey. The Emperor unfortunately did not know this until later. But he had had experience of the use of illness as an excuse to avoid a meeting. It is one often used in China. He was furious at the Englishmen and canceled the entire program of entertainment. He refused to see Lord Amherst at a later date, and ordered the mission to leave Peking immediately. Two stubborn men had met with the usual results.

Either because the Emperor relented a little, or because he could not resist the opportunity to write another message, he sent a second communication to Lord Amherst in which he pointed out that he bore in mind that a lowly official of a country beyond the seas could hardly be expected to be familiar with correct court etiquette. He stated that he was pleased to pardon their remissness. He pointed out that the two missions sent by the English King must have caused considerable inconvenience and expense and he suggested that as his country put no value on nor had any need of the presents or the products of foreign countries the English King should send no more missions to China. It may be left to the imagination what effect this message had on the British envoy.

It soon became clear that the dignity of Great Britain had been hurt beyond repair. Sixteen years later Lord Napier appeared before Canton with a large British fleet to restore the prestige of Great Britain in the Orient and to take by force the concessions refused Lord Amherst.

This war, called the Opium War, occurred in the reign of the next Emperor, as has been told in an earlier chapter. The bombardment of Canton and the attacks on Chapu, Shanghai, and Chinkiang in which the Manchus fought a brave but losing defense were exciting events of Green Jade's childhood.

After the Opium War and during the latter part of his life the Emperor was sad and lonely. He felt his reign had been such a failure he asked that the customary inscription telling of his accomplishments be omitted from his grave. He knew he had accomplished little and had lost much. He died in 1850 and was succeeded by his fourth son, Hsien Feng, in whom we are greatly interested.

3. FROM CONCUBINE TO EMPRESS

When Green Jade prostrated herself before the Emperor on the day of her introduction to the Summer Palace to undergo her examination it is not unlikely that her eyes were not so modestly downcast that she did not get a good look at the young man whose concubine she aspired to become.

Fortunately for us an interesting contemporary description of Hsien Feng is to be found in M. N. Callery and Yuan's *History of the Insurrection in China*, published in 1853, when Hsien Feng had ruled two years and in the very year that Green Jade entered the palace.

"The Emperor is only twenty-two years of age. He is of middle height, and his form indicates great aptitude for bodily exercises. He is slender and muscular. His face, which indicates a certain degree of resolution, is chiefly characterized by a very high forehead and by an almost defective obliquity of the eyes. His cheekbones are very prominent and strongly marked. The space between the eyes is large and flat, like the forehead of a buffalo.

"Hsien Feng is of a stubborn and credulous disposition. In the midst of the most effeminate luxury he affects severity of morals. . . . His chief defect is a want of that exquisite tact which enables a prince to give everyone the exact measure of praise or blame which is his due. He is not endowed with a correct judgment, for amongst that multitude of attendants, eunuchs, concubines, and slaves who surround him he does not know how to distinguish those faithful counselors whose fate is bound up with the existence of his dynasty from mere adventurers who hover about every palace and who, having their fortunes to make, never give advice which is wholly disinterested. At once violent and weak, the young Emperor abandons himself to his favorites of the moment, and places blind confidence in the officials for the time being. . . ."

This was the man on whom Green Jade's present and future depended.

Hsien Feng, the seventh Emperor of the Ch'ing Dynasty, could well claim to be its most unlucky monarch. He inherited conditions for which he was in no way responsible and these produced problems he could not solve. His reign started with the Tai Ping rebellion which caused the loss of more than sixty million Chinese and drained the resources of the country almost dry. His reign ended with the Arrow War in which the magnificent Yuan Ming Yuan was looted and destroyed, the Emperor forced to flee from the capital, and China suffered the humiliation of having armies of the Western barbarians in control of Peking.

No other Emperor of China has probably been so violently and often so wrongly attacked by foreign writers. This was usually in an effort to justify some of the acts the foreign powers committed during his reign and during that of his son.

Hsien Feng's mother died when he was very young and he was cared for by Empress Hsiao Ching, the mother of his half brother, Prince Kung. She gave him the same care and affection as she gave her own son, for which Hsien Feng was grateful his entire life. The two brothers lived together, studied under the same tutors, hunted and played together, and became great friends.

It was generally understood that the younger brother, Prince Kung, was to be his father's successor. But when the two boys were summoned to receive the blessing and last instructions of their dying father, the Emperor in his delirium named the wrong son as his heir. As the final choice of a dying father was binding, Hsien Feng became Emperor. Had events been otherwise, the history of China might have been very different during the past century. Prince Kung was generally considered by foreigners to be the most brilliant and efficient statesman of his period.

At the time Hsien Feng became Emperor, nine years after the Treaty of Nanking, China was on the verge of disintegration. The treasury was empty. Famines and rebellion had broken out in several parts of the country. Officials were notoriously corrupt. These were difficult problems for a young and inexperienced boy of twenty to solve, but he met them courageously. He replaced most of the old officials, unfortunately not always with men of higher ability. He forced many of the dishonest officials to surrender their ill-gotten wealth which he used for military purposes.

He appointed and deposed generals until he finally found the right man in General Tseng Kuo-fan, governor of Hunan, who was recommended to him by Green Jade. Hsien Feng was the first Ch'ing Emperor to accept Chinese volunteers in the army in place of the Manchu Bannermen who had apparently lost their old military spirit. It is probable that Emperor Hsien Feng would have been able to crush the Tai Ping rebellion in a short time if China had not at the most critical period of the rebellion been attacked by the combined British and French military forces.

In studying the lives of Emperor Hsien Feng and Green Jade we must bear in mind that the Manchu court at that time was a very young court. The Emperor was but twenty years old when he ascended the throne. Prince Kung and the other imperial princes were his juniors. Su Shun, his boon companion, was a few years older. Several of his uncles were not much older than the Emperor. Even the Empress Dowager Hsiao Ching, mother of Prince Kung, who might be expected to be the restraining influence in the court, was only thirty-eight years old and often was the gayest of them all. It could hardly be expected that such a group of young people would at all times act prudently or conservatively. The group close to the Emperor enjoyed many parties and picnics, the theater, and other kinds of entertainment. Undoubtedly they were gayer than they should have been when China was in such a deplorable state.

But it was not for his life within the palace that Emperor Hsien Feng was most criticized. He was often accused of forsaking the gaieties of his court in company with Su Shun and others and spending afternoons and evenings in the pleasure houses outside Ch'ien Men. This is the gate between the Tatar and the Chinese cities.

The assumption which has been made by foreign writers is that the Emperor and his intimates spent their nights in houses of prostitution. This was not true.

When the Emperor slipped out of the side door in the red wall of the palace for an afternoon and evening of fun, as he often did, he found a Peking cart drawn by a fast white mule waiting for him. He was always in disguise but was careful to wear a yellow belt to show he was an imperial prince. Whether he fooled anyone by his disguise is doubtful; there were few secrets within the palace. But the disguise did remove the necessity for formality of any kind. It is also probable that sometimes the young men drank too much, but there was a trustworthy old eunuch always at hand to see that no harm came to the Emperor and that he got home safely.

The interesting story is told by an old eunuch that after Green Jade became the mother of Hsien Feng's heir, she and some of the other ladies of the court were puzzled as to why their husbands should enjoy spending their evenings outside Ch'ien Men regardless of how pleasant and elaborate the parties within the palace were. The ladies decided to take the risk of finding out what life outside the gates was like. With the help of the chief eunuch, and in spite of his protests, they persuaded the theater make-up eunuch to disguise them as princes. They then induced a couple of young princes to smuggle them out of the palace and take them to the places visited by the Emperor and his circle. To reduce the risk to themselves, the eunuchs probably had everything arranged so no accident could happen, and it is questionable how much of the life outside Ch'ien Men the ladies saw. But they did see enough to convince them that their rather formal, traditional parties under the watchful eye of the Empress Dowager could never entirely compete with the entertainment offered by the "Flowers outside Ch'ien Men."

The houses the Emperor and his friends visited on their afternoons and evenings away from the palace were places of very different character than the ladies had feared. In China the family selects the first wife for its sons, but generally the husband chooses, with the consent of his first wife, any additional wives he may desire. To fill this need for the better families in Peking certain women, often widows of officials who did not care to remarry, would take two or more young girls, usually relatives, educate and train them, and at the proper age introduce them to the young men of Peking. To make this introduction under the best possible conditions, a number of these women would often join forces and furnish a large building as a home and place for entertaining. These houses varied in taste, size, and elegance to fit the class of men their owners hoped to attract. Some of them were furnished with luxury and elegance. The girls were often better educated than the wives of the princes or other officials who visited them. They usually played a number of musical instruments, sang, danced, and were expert at various games. The jokes may at times have been a little more risqué than a princess would hear in the palace. Rumors were that some of the less conservative places had a Chinese version of a strip tease, but this was considered rather unusual. Dinners and banquets with good wine and song were the usual entertainment.

Prostitution had no place in such institutions. Probably no girls in China or any other country were more carefully watched over than these girls. They knew, and the women who managed them knew, that the girls' chance of being taken into one of the high families as concubines depended on their remaining virgins.

With the mistake some foreign writers have made in stating that Emperor Hsien Feng and his friends spent most of their nights in houses of prostitution, they also made the mistake of declaring that he had contracted there a social disease. They have given as evidence of this that he had only one child, evidently forgetting that many healthy men have no children at all. In fact, Hsien Feng had not one child but three—two sons and a daughter. The daughter married a well-known official. The younger son—by one of the concubines—died at an early age.

If we do not care to take the statements of his associates and of the doctors who examined him, all of whom denied the accusations, one can draw a conclusion from the fact that both his empresses and a number of his secondary wives, including the mothers of his children, lived to a healthy old age. This would seem to indicate that they did not suffer from any social disease.

Other foreign authors, taking their information from the southern or Cantonese writers who criticized all the Ch'ing emperors, describe Hsien Feng as a degenerate, a weakling, and a young man who gave his entire time to pleasure and neglected his duties. A careful study of the records of his reign, long talks with people who knew him well, and information from the diaries of some of his associates, prove he was no degenerate or weakling, but a conscientious young man trying to handle a situation that was beyond his ability to cope with.

Let us now return to the life and affairs of Green Jade, who seems to have succeeded in getting into difficulties almost from the first week she entered the palace. She was soon to find that everything connected with life at court was regulated by custom and the Household Rules of the Ch'ing Dynasty. And Green Jade was not accustomed to rules.

Each of the six new concubines was given a separate palace with all the servants and supplies necessary for a complete and independent home. Green Jade, being the lowest in rank, was naturally given the last choice of palaces and had the smallest number of servants. This she resented.

A few days after Green Jade's arrival, Empress Hsiao Chen decided to move out of the Palace of Long Life, the Yung Shou Kung, giving as her reason that she did not like its name. Green Jade immediately asked the Emperor for this palace.

She was not entitled to it. It was the best palace and should have been given to the highest-ranking concubine. But Green Jade apparently knew when and how to make her request and the Emperor gave the Yung Shou Kung to her. She moved in at once and probably could not resist showing the elation she felt. She had gained her point, but this did not make her popular with the other concubines or with the princesses. This was a very unwise thing for her to have done if she wished to make rapid progress in the court.

The next incident was more serious and might have ended her life in the palace. In many ways it is almost unexplainable. Empress Hsiao Chen was responsible for the health of the Emperor and his household and for running all domestic affairs within the palace. She often gave lectures to the concubines who were directly under her. In accordance with ancient tradition and the Household Rules, the palaces occupied by the concubines were so located that to reach any one of them the Emperor had to pass through the palace of the Empress. In theory she was supposed to direct him to the concubine he was to visit. No secrecy surrounded the Emperor's comings and goings. Everyone in that section of the palace knew which concubine was the favorite of the evening.

In one of her talks to the new concubines, the Empress mentioned that certain concubines of former emperors had gained great respect and honor by remaining virgins all their lives. She suggested that the young concubines should not use their charms too often on the young Emperor, let them sometimes entertain him in other ways when he visited them. Green Jade, who was already on very good terms with the Empress and was well aware that her standing in the palace largely depended on the Empress's approval, took this advice far too literally. When the Emperor called on her a few nights later, she told him of the Empress's advice and suggested they spend the evening in singing and playing musical instruments. This they did. As they were both good musicians, and Green Jade had an exceptionally good voice, Hsien Feng was not ill-pleased. Indeed, he went away with the impression that his number six was very pleasing.

But when she attempted to do the same thing the following night, the Emperor became angry. He had had enough music for the time being, as he promptly gave his number six to understand. Here Green Jade made an unfortunate mistake. Her quick temper betrayed her. She forgot she was talking to the Son of Heaven and not to an army officer of the provinces. She fell at Hsien Feng's feet and, with her ever-ready tears, the power of which she overestimated this time, urged the

Emperor to remember the Household Rules of his family governing the conduct of emperors with their wives.

But the Emperor was not interested in Household Rules at this time. He was furious. Green Jade then evidently lost what little sense she had as she advised the Emperor to return to his palace and sleep alone for a few nights. He left her, threatening never to return. He almost kept his promise, which would have been the end of all those fine dreams of Green Jade.

When she regained her senses and realized what she had done she was in despair. She was certain her whole future at court was ruined and even contemplated suicide. Little Li Pin, then the favorite concubine, knew something was wrong and called on her. When Li Pin heard the full story, she immediately informed the Empress. Together they calmed Green Jade and promised to intercede with the Emperor on her behalf. But despite the combined efforts of the Empress and Li Pin to reinstate Green Jade in favor, the Emperor did not call at the Yung Shou Kung again until six months had passed.

During those months Green Jade learned one lesson well. She learned that the manners and tactics of the army camp and provincial city would not be accepted in court life. She thereupon became a student of court ways. She had a very good teacher in the old eunuch Wang Ch'ang-yu.

Eunuch Wang had formerly belonged to Prince Cheng. Wu Ching-tang had persuaded the prince to give Eunuch Wang to Green Jade as her personal eunuch when she entered the palace. Prince Cheng was willing to do this, as he was fond of the kindly old man who had spent most of his life within the Yuan Ming Yuan. This was another of those fortunate events that were continually happening to Green Jade. Eunuch Wang soon proved to be much more than a servant. He became her friend and was her adviser as long as he lived. She would have made much slower progress, perhaps no progress at all in the complicated, selfish, and jealous life of the court, if it had not been for the wise counsel and constant protection of the old eunuch who had seen many favorites rise and fall.

While the Empress, Li Pin, and two of the concubines were

friendly to Green Jade, the two remaining concubines, both daughters of high officials, openly showed their dislike of her. They often reminded her haughtily that she was the daughter of an official who had died in prison. They also teased her about the name Green Jade that her mother called her—a name they thought suitable only for a child and not for an imperial concubine. This was probably correct, but it made Green Jade more bitter than anyone realized at the time. She never forgot the sneers she had been subjected to, and when she became an empress the first thing she did was to try to destroy every record of her life before she entered the palace. She forbade her mother to use the name Green Jade and sought to destroy every document pertaining to her father. Fortunately, she was not entirely successful in this, otherwise it would have been impossible to tell this story of her early life.

Empress Hsiao Chen, who helped Green Jade in many ways, was a remarkable young woman. It is hard to understand why Hsiao Chen showed so little jealousy toward the concubine whom she must have early recognized as a real rival for the affections of the Emperor and for influence in the palace. She was of higher birth, from a more influential family, and far outranked Green Jade. Foreign writers have attempted to show these two women as rivals and enemies, but we know that the Empress used her power to get Green Jade back into favor with the Emperor. The records show them working together as coregents for many years. They were close friends at least for the first fifteen or twenty years of their life within the palace. In later years, when both became older and more set in their ways, they did occasionally quarrel. But seldom were these differences so serious that the two empresses were not on good terms again within a few days. That such a long friendship could exist between these two women, so different in temperament, living under the conditions in which they spent their lives, speaks well for both of them and for the social order that was maintained in the palaces of the Ch'ing emperors.

The concubines in Hsien Feng's court were not allowed to lead a life of idleness. They were assistants to the Empress in running the huge household and each was responsible for certain duties. The Yuan Ming Yuan was more than just a group of palaces for the Emperor, the imperial princes, and members of the imperial clans. It was all that, but it was also the home of many hundreds of eunuchs, serving girls, and other employees. It included a group of manufacturing plants or villages which produced many of the things necessary in the operation of such an enormous establishment. One village was devoted to the raising of silkworms. In another the silk was dyed and manufactured into garments, shoes, and hats for the men and women of the court. The dwellers in another village made the clothes for the eunuchs and servants. The perfumes and cosmetics for the ladies were made within the palace. There were also schools for the children. In fact, the Yuan Ming Yuan was a city of several thousand people all apparently necessary for the upkeep and the operation of the imperial court.

While most of these activities were under the supervision of competent eunuchs, the Empress and the concubines were responsible for the management of the Emperor's household. The concubines also had to arrange banquets and other forms of entertainment for the Emperor and his friends and in addition had to continue their studies under private teachers. It was soon found that Green Jade was the best-educated girl in the palace. This made her ambitious to become even more learned in the history of her people, the rules and regulations of court life, and in the composing and writing of state papers.

At one time she was able to do a kindness to one of her old friends. When there was a vacancy for a tutor to the concubines, Green Jade recommended Li Weng-yang, who had taught her in Hangchow Fu and who later helped so materially at the time of her father's death. He later became a famous painter of birds and landscapes. Green Jade thus added one more faithful and useful friend to her palace group.

2

Six months passed since the Emperor visited Green Jade. At the end of that time he allowed the Empress and little Li

Pin to persuade him to attend a banquet they were giving in Green Jade's palace. Perhaps he was more anxious than he hoped they would notice to see again the young girl who had had the courage to defy him and about whom he had thought often in the last few weeks.

He found an entirely different Green Jade. She was now as polished in her manners as the most gifted lady in his court. He also noticed for the first time that she had an intelligent beauty that many of the other young girls lacked. Yes, he was glad he had let the Empress and Li Pin persuade him to be forgiving toward his number six.

It was not long before Hsien Feng was visiting Green Jade almost every night, having dinner with her and enjoying the musicals she gave. Sometimes the two were alone, but often the Emperor brought some of his friends, and several of the other concubines would be invited to join the gathering. On some occasions Green Jade had professional musicians, of whom there were many among the eunuchs.

Each palace was built about a courtyard. In summer the court was roofed over with bamboo mats to keep out the sun. In these shaded courtyards many of the social affairs took place, including theatrical performances, of which Green Jade was very fond. The actors were usually eunuchs trained for that purpose, but whenever any famous actor or troupe was in Peking, a command performance for the Emperor was arranged. She also arranged picnics on some of the islands in the lakes. At one of these picnics she met Prince Kung, half brother of the Emperor. He was two years older than Green Jade and soon became very much attached to her. Su Shun, an imperial clansman, was also often invited to the picnics. He was a little older than the others and was the playboy of the crowd. He was blamed for some of the wild parties he gave for the Emperor outside Ch'ien Men.

At the time Green Jade and her family lived in Hangchow and Wuhu, her father's young concubine, Autumn Cloud, who had formerly been an attendant in an opium house, was expert in cooking the small opium pellets just before they were put on the pipe. These pellets bubbled into queer shapes when held over a small flame and Autumn Cloud could make them take the shapes of various animals. Green Jade one day came accidentally upon the concubine cooking opium pellets for her father, and the procedure greatly interested her. She learned from Autumn Cloud how to cook opium and soon became expert at heating "The Paste of Increased Long Life and Realization of Desire" and forming it into odd shapes.

When the Emperor was spending one of his nights with Green Jade, he suggested they try a few pipes of opium. She agreed, and showed her skill in forming interesting figures with the pellets. The Emperor was much intrigued, never having seen the like before.

The use of opium is closely connected with sexual pleasure; it works on the mind in a way that kills the realization of time. Pleasures that actually take but a few minutes under the influence of opium appear prolonged for hours.

How much opium the Emperor and Green Jade smoked is not known, probably only as much as two normal young people would when trying a new craze. But it was enough to lay Green Jade open to the charge later made by her enemies that she gained her control over the Emperor by making him an addict. Most writers believe that it was only when the Emperor was suffering intense pain in the weeks before his death that he really became an opium addict. He was said to have been encouraged in this by the conspirator Su Shun.

The Emperor found Green Jade a sympathetic listener to the recital of his mounting troubles. The campaign against the Tai Ping rebels was going badly. His armies were being defeated on every front. The rebels were even threatening Peking. Green Jade knew army camps and gave him many intelligent suggestions. It is not known whether she knew General Tseng Kuo-fan personally or whether he had been mentioned to her by the Eunuch An Te-hai, who was making many suggestions to her those days, but it is certain that she did recommend General Tseng to the Emperor. His appointment was most fortunate. It proved the turning point of the war, for which the Emperor gave Green Jade much credit.

He found her equally valuable in state affairs. She read his official papers for him, helped him in writing his edicts, and in this way relieved him of much work and many worries, besides making herself well acquainted with the affairs of the empire. It was not long before she was directing his entire staff. She also urged him to drink less wine and to take better care of his health. Her influence on the Emperor was good. Our Green Jade was climbing fast.

On the advice of Eunuchs Wang Ch'ang-yu and An Te-hai, Green Jade began to pay more attention to her popularity with the other concubines and even with the eunuchs and servants. She gave them presents and did little favors for them. Eunuch Wang explained to her the value of good reports from the servants which often reached the Emperor. She even tried to make friends with Yun Pin, her one real enemy among the concubines.

In many respects the life of these young concubines was not unlike that of a group of American college girls. They were all on a strict allowance of money, supplies for their kitchens, silks and cotton goods for costumes, cosmetics, and perfumes. All were carefully doled out by the Treasury Department. Records of these disbursements are still available.

Like college girls, the Emperor's concubines usually spent in excess of their allowances, and we find many references to their borrowing clothes, money, and servants. Accusations of theft of these commodities are not lacking. The usual disputes that arose from these dealings were adjusted by the Empress.

Green Jade had now been in the palace three years. She had become the favorite of the Emperor and had made many new friends and was happy again. But she knew that the influence of a court favorite was brief. She was determined to rule not through the throne but from the throne. The one sure road to this position of power was for her to give birth to the Emperor's heir.

The Empress was childless, nor had any of the other concubines then conceived a child by Hsien Feng. This had given rise to repeated rumors that the Emperor could not have a child.

Again the gods came to the aid of Green Jade. In October of her third year in the palace she proudly announced that she was going to give the Emperor his long-desired heir. Naturally this dramatic news gave Green Jade's enemies, who had watched jealously her rise to prestige and influence, the opportunity to whisper that she was not above gaining her ambition by illegitimate means. Years later, after Green Jade became Empress Tz'u Hsi, her enemies revived these rumors, and the South China writers who always opposed the Ch'ing Dynasty went so far as to name the handsome young guardsman, Jung Lu, as the father of the Empress's son. This report was taken up and circulated by foreign writers. However, there is no evidence to be found that Hsien Feng ever questioned the paternity of his heir.

In April of the following year Green Jade's child was born. It was a son. Again the gods were kind. The Emperor was more pleased than he had ever been in his life. He raised Green Jade to be a Yi Fei, or concubine of the second class. All her friends rejoiced with her. Her position was now secure, as she was the mother of the prince who would probably be the next Emperor of China.

Even this apparently did not make the Empress jealous. She seemed to be almost as happy as the Emperor over the birth of an heir. Green Jade was sorry for her friend Li Pin, who wanted a baby very much. She suggested to the Emperor that it might have been the Yung Shou Kung that had brought her luck, and she asked his permission to give the palace to Li Pin to see whether it would be lucky for her. The Emperor was very pleased at this suggestion, though he may have had some doubts of the real reason for the offer. He knew generosity of this kind was not the strongest characteristic of any of his concubines. The Yung Shou Kung was by far the best palace available to concubines and Green Jade liked it very much—two facts which made her willingness to abandon it difficult to explain. He gladly gave his consent and Li Pin moved into the Yung Shou Kung. But it did not prove lucky for her; she never had a child. Green Jade's supremacy remained unchallenged.

Soon after Green Jade's son was born, her mother was invited to the palace to see her grandson. There were a few formalities that a grandmother had to perform at such a time, even though she be in humble circumstances and her grandson the son of an emperor.

She was well received by Green Jade, who remained very fond of her mother. The many hardships they had passed through together had drawn the two women close. The Empress was also kind to her, as were the concubines, except Yun Fei. Even the Emperor received Hwei T'ai T'ai and paid her proper respect as the grandmother of his son.

But this was only a formal meeting. It was not until nine months after the birth of her son that Green Jade was allowed by special permission of the Emperor to visit her mother.

On this occasion she rode in a yellow chair accompanied by several young princes, many eunuchs, and guardsmen. One can well imagine the excitement the procession caused in Hwei T'ai T'ai's humble home. Neighbors filled the street for blocks to see the mother of the future Emperor of China. Her mother and all the members of the family—they had many relatives now in these prosperous times—ranged themselves along the sides of the courtyard to greet their distinguished relative. Green Jade was given the seat of honor in the house and all the family, except her mother, kowtowed to her. A banquet was served by the eunuchs and, after many refusals and much urging, Green Jade took her place at the head of the table. Both mother and daughter were glad when the banquet was over and they could be alone for a long talk, the first real talk they had had in four years. Hwei T'ai T'ai must have recalled Soothsayer Fu's vision and prophecy. Green Jade was not only fulfilling the prophecy, she was keeping her promise never to forget her mother. Throughout her life she remained faithful to her family.

3

In spite of the birth of his heir, the year 1856 was not to be a lucky one for Emperor Hsien Feng or for China. It was the beginning of one of the blackest periods in the country's history. In this year the Tai Ping rebellion reached its greatest menace and the combined armies and fleets of Great Britain and France started their first attack on China.

The Tai Ping rebellion, which has been mentioned several times, exerted such a disastrous influence on the entire reign of Hsien Feng and the early part of Green Jade's regency that it needs to be more fully described at this time.

The Tai Ping rebellion had a very lowly beginning. It started with a little farmer boy, Hung Hsiu-ch'uan, born in a small village about thirty miles from Canton. He was an intelligent boy and showed such signs of brilliancy that a number of his relatives, though they were very poor, joined together and made such sacrifices as were necessary to give him an education. He tried several times to pass the Hsiu Ts'ai examinations but always failed. If he had been successful he would have qualified for an official position.

Like many others, he blamed his failure on lack of influence. He became bitter, dissatisfied, and anti-government.

Unfortunately for China and the whole world, while Hung Hsiu-ch'uan was in this frame of mind a number of small pamphlets, published in Chinese by missionaries urging all to become Christians, fell into his hands. One of the pamphlets attempted to describe the Christian God, the Holy Trinity, and the birth of Jesus Christ. This interested Hung Hsiu-ch'uan very much. He took to his bed and studied it for weeks. While in bed he claimed he had a vision and received a command direct from the Celestial Father and Heavenly Elder Brother of the Christians, making him the true lord of all nations and commanding him to destroy demons, restore the true religion, and save China from the Manchus.

Hung Hsiu-ch'uan got in touch with the Reverend Issachar Roberts, an American missionary in Canton, who gave him additional instruction in the Christian religion. Mr. Roberts failed to get Hung Hsiu-ch'uan to join his church and also unfortunately failed to give him a very clear idea of Christianity. In fact, Hung Hsiu-ch'uan soon began to enlarge and "improve" the Christian doctrine. He even began to instruct Mr. Roberts. While Hung could readily understand the doctrine of the virgin birth, as he had read a number of similar tales in Chinese literature, his mind balked at the theory of a celestial birth without a celestial mother. To the consternation of some of his missionary friends, he proceeded to give God a celestial wife. He soon went further and gave God another son, with the name of Heavenly King. This position he modestly assumed for himself. But he was not going to be a meek and lowly younger brother; he left that role to Elder Brother Jesus Christ.

He began calling himself Emperor of the Great Peace Celestial Empire, and started to raise an army. The dissatisfied, the criminal, bandits, robbers, and vagrants flocked to his standard. He soon had a considerable force drawn from every part of the provinces of Kwangtung and Kwangsi. A peculiar religious mania spread through this strange collection of the human dregs of South China. His soldiers shaved their heads, abstained from opium, alcohol, and even tobacco. They destroyed idols and temples, and attended daily religious services.

At the beginning the Tai Ping armies had a distinctly semi-Christian character which gained the sympathy and support of many of the Western missionaries and native Christians, who thought all China would soon be conquered for Christ. Many of these foreigners kept this view long after the Heavenly King and his armies showed themselves to be cruel, ruthless looters and murderers. Even today some foreigners regret that the Tai Pings were not successful.

Hung Hsiu-ch'uan and his armies soon gained great victories. As they swept northward and became stronger, Hung seemed to get more and more of his inspiration from the Old Testament rather than from the teachings of his Elder Brother of the New Testament. His soldiers, receiving no pay except loot, sacked and destroyed every city they captured, very much as the early Hebrews did in storming Jericho and other cities in Palestine. The country was terrorized. It is small wonder that Green Jade's father should have been seized with fear when the rumor came that the Tai Pings were advancing on Wuhu.

Hung's personal life also began to change with his success. He learned to like luxury and the ease wealth brings. He appointed five minor kings, or disciples, to carry on the active work of his campaigns while he retired to his harem and, wisely, seldom thereafter showed himself to his army or friends. He must have had some strange ability as a leader because with all his faults, weaknesses, and cruelties he was able to attract to his army and hold a considerable number of extremely able generals and officials who were men of character, ability, and standing, as evidenced by some of the letters written by Chinese Gordon.

It is not necessary to follow the campaigns of the Tai Pings in detail. They met with some defeats, but within two years they had captured all the great cities on the Yangtze River and controlled practically all of South China. They entered Wuhu just four months after Green Jade had left for Peking with her father's body.

On March 19, 1853, the Tai Pings captured Nanking and made it their Celestial Capital. Here Hung Hsiu-ch'uan received another mandate from his Celestial Adviser. This time he was appointed Emperor and thereafter saluted with the words "Lord of Ten Thousand Years." The little country boy who had failed in his examinations had gone far in three years.

From Nanking the Tai Pings sent two expeditions into North China and even threatened Peking. They held Nanking for nearly eleven years, longer than the entire reign of Hsien Feng, and inaugurated a number of important reforms. These were usually a combination of what Hung considered Christian teaching, largely from the Old Testament, and old Chinese customs with which he was much more familiar. He appears to have attempted to create a caste system in China so he could make different laws for different classes. He made marriage compulsory for all women, but gave them positions in both the government and the army. In this connection it is interesting to find that Mahomet had done the same thing. He had one rather large army composed entirely of women under the command of his sister as "Celestial Commander." Foot-binding, prostitution, opium, and tobacco smoking, use of alcohol, and gambling were prohibited. It was unfortunate that these partly inaugurated reforms so blinded a number of Americans and British living in China and many other misguided people in Europe and America that they continued to support the Tai Ping rebels and welcomed them as fellow Christians in spite of their record of massacres, rape, and robbery.

The Tai Ping uprising brought the names of three foreigners into prominence. The first was an American named Frederick Townsend Ward who organized a brigade of Chinese troops, foreign trained but officered by Chinese, to defend Shanghai. This later became known as the "Ever Victorious Army." Ward was well thought of by Li Hung-chang and other Chinese officials and he and his Ever Victorious Army won many victories over the Tai Pings. Ward was killed at Tzeki in 1862, fighting the Tai Pings, and has the distinction of having two graves. Fellow townsmen in his native United States show his grave in a little New England cemetery. Another grave is on the side of the sacred mountain of T'ai Shan, where the Chinese annually honor the memory of this American by decorating his grave with the traditional white paper.

Henry Burgevine, who succeeded Ward, was evidently a man of different character. He was later dismissed from command, and reportedly joined the Tai Pings. The most interesting man of the three was the famous Charles George Gordon. Chinese Gordon, as he was called, fought first against and later with the national armies of China. We shall hear more of him later in connection with the British and French attack on Peking.

4

It is now evident that from the very day Green Jade entered the palace she started to build a circle of friends and supporters on whom she could rely. She had the rare ability which all successful dictators must have of choosing the right people and attaching them to her cause. Certain men stuck to her through their entire lives, regardless of how she treated them.

She won the friendship and support of the Empress, who had every reason to be jealous of her, but who apparently never was. Li Pin, the Emperor's first favorite, was her best friend among the concubines. The old eunuch Wang Ch'ang-yu would have died for her at any time. Prince Kung, who well might have looked on her with distrust, was later to be her strongest supporter among the imperial princes. She avoided the Emperor's special friend, Su Shun, though he was the most attractive and brilliant official in the palace at that time. Her instinct warned her against his charm and whispered that he was not to be trusted.

This same infallible instinct led her to select the young lieutenant of the Palace Guard, Jung Lu, as someone she could use to great advantage. She detected in him, who was only one of a number of young officers—many of them superior to him in birth, wealth, and position—the qualities of loyalty and statesmanship that were to serve her throughout her rule.

To this group she later added General Tseng Kuo-fan, Li Hung-chang, and Yuan Shih-k'ai.

It must not be overlooked that in addition to these personages she had, during her life in the palace, the assistance of three important eunuchs—the loyal old Wang Ch'ang-yu, the brilliant An Te-hai, and Li Lien-ying.

Many people ask: Who were these eunuchs and why should China have had what seems such a disgusting and degrading system? Men like faithful, wise old Eunuch Wang are one answer to these questions. Most eunuchs were loyal and efficient servants. With no families of their own to become attached to, many of them developed an unusually strong affection and loyalty for those they served. This was in most cases returned by their masters. All eunuchs were Chinese; no Manchu ever became a eunuch. To see evidence of this master-servant affection one has but to visit some of the old imperial Manchu families in Peking today, or what is left of them, and see how they divide what little they have with the old eunuchs who served them in happier days. When Emperor P'u Yi was driven from Peking he fought little for his possessions but he fought hard yet unsuccessfully to secure protection and future welfare for the old eunuchs who had so faithfully served his family.

The system of eunuchs was not confined to China. For many centuries in most oriental countries eunuchs were employed in the harems and as servants in the palaces. They were also a part of the life of the Greeks and Romans. Eunuchs provided the adult soprano voices in the Sistine Chapel and in the papal choirs even until the time of Pope Leo XIII.

At the time Green Jade entered the palace about four thousand eunuchs were employed in the palaces, temples, and at court, and in a few of the larger palaces outside the Forbidden City. They filled every position—they were chambermaids, servants, cooks, mechanics, messengers, chair coolies, musicians, actors, and secretaries. While there were without doubt many disreputable and dishonest eunuchs, as there were also many other dishonest officials in the Ch'ing government who were not eunuchs, the great majority were ignorant, humble men, doing their duty to the best of their ability, afraid to do otherwise, as they knew no other employment was open to them if they were discharged from the palaces.

The general impression that eunuchs were deficient in courage or intellect is amply refuted by history. One of China's greatest admirals was a eunuch, as were many other famous officials under the earlier emperors. The difficulty in China was not that the eunuchs were not sufficiently intelligent; the greatest opposition to them was that many were too intelligent. Being intelligent and willing to work harder and longer than other officials and having no wives and children to distract them, they often gained high positions of influence and power entirely by their own efforts. That many eunuchs abused such positions of influence cannot be denied. The fall of the Ming Dynasty was attributed more to the influence of corrupt eunuchs than to any other single cause. But such eunuchs could gain positions of power only when the princes and other officials were negligent. Even the weakest of Chinese emperors would not have upheld such eunuchs if they had not been useful to him. It is also possible that many eunuchs were painted a little blacker by the historians than they actually were in order to hide the weaknesses of others. Eunuchs have seldom had anyone to defend them.

Two famous eunuchs, An Te-hai and Li Lien-ying, were closely associated with Green Jade during her life at court. The first, An Te-hai, is usually described as the most corrupt, most disliked, and most detestable official of the Ch'ing Dynasty, and no one has yet attempted to deny this.

He was not much older than Green Jade. He was a small man, extremely vain, usually dressed in loud clothes, and loved to give big, noisy parties. In later years he became insolent and cruel and delighted in mistreating such officials as were in his power. He demanded and received bribes and used every possible method to acquire money. He became one of the most powerful and most feared men in China during the early part of Green Jade's regency. The only thing that can be said in her defense in having such a man in her court was that he was young and still honest when she first knew him, and that he undoubtedly rendered her one of the greatest services any man ever did. He saved her life. Whether she knew much about his evil reputation is doubtful, as he controlled most avenues of information to her after he became powerful. She did receive many memorials denouncing him, but she evidently did not believe them, as she was always receiving memorials against some of her friends or advisers. But with every allowance made for her having such a man as An Te-hai as a friend and adviser, it remains one of the blackest blots on her character.

Green Jade first met An Te-hai through Eunuch Wang. The two eunuchs were probably relatives, as both were natives of Hocien Fu, the home of many palace eunuchs. When Green Jade was in difficulties over her acquisition of the coveted Palace of Long Life, Wang called in An Te-hai to help her, as the latter had great influence over the servants in all parts of the palace. It was an eventful meeting. Each seemed immediately to recognize in the other a possible strong ally. From that day An Te-hai became Green Jade's faithful friend and a valuable and powerful ally in her climb to power.

An Te-hai must have had a very quick mind and a strong instinct for judging the ability of people. When he first met Green Jade she was the least important of the new concubines, without friends or influence, not popular in the court, and had quarreled with the Emperor. Yet at his first short meeting with her he picked her out from all the girls in the palace as the one most likely to succeed. Without doubt he was ambitious and was already planning to become the head eunuch of the palace, the highest position he could ever hope to attain. Yet he risked all he wanted to be by joining Green Jade against the princes and officials in the Ch'ing court.

He evidently made his decision to link his fortune with that of Green Jade within a few minutes of meeting her. It was not by accident, but by sheer ability that he became one of the most influential officials of his time.

Naturally Green Jade and An Te-hai made no open alliance, or did they ever discuss or hint to each other that they should work together. But An Te-hai found many little ways of assisting the new concubine, and Green Jade soon found that in arranging theatricals, picnics, or other entertainments to hold the Emperor's interest the young eunuch was of valuable service. Meanwhile An Te-hai was slowly organizing all the eunuchs in the palace into groups he could control. He soon had his eunuchs as servants in every palace, in attendance at every meeting, as doormen at every official's gate. They became An Te-hai's spies. He was the best-informed man in the court.

Green Jade had need of this support—all the support she could get. In addition to the feuds and intrigues within the palace—some of which were incited by Su Shun and the imperial Prince Tung, whom she was never able to win to her side—there was the constant threat of the Tai Pings. The rebels held most of China between the Yangtze River and Canton. One disastrous result of this was that the government in Peking was cut off from news of what was then happening in South China.

The Treaty of Nanking, which opened the port and city of Canton to Western nations, had raised a bitter anti-foreign feeling in that city and throughout the province. This had grown year by year until now, in 1856, it had become a serious menace to peace. The British and the Chinese had many grievances against one another. These conditions were made worse by the leaders of both sides.

Yeh Ming-chen was the Viceroy of Canton. He was an enormous man, stubborn, overbearing, cruel, and violently anti-foreign. In spite of his unattractive appearance and extremely bad manners he was highly educated.

The Viceroy had many difficult problems to handle: the Tai Ping rebels were hammering at his northern gate and wanted nothing better than the opportunity to hang him. The foreign nations were at his front door with very much the same intention.

The British, who had the largest trade with Canton, probably more than all the other foreign nations combined, took the lead in all negotiations with Viceroy Yeh Ming-chen. The British trade commissioner then wanted all restrictions to foreign trade removed and all insults to foreigners ended. To this he received neither a reply nor any apparent results. A British sailor was killed in a village many miles from where he had any legal right to be. The British Fleet retaliated by looting and burning the entire village and threatened to do the same to the Viceroy's yamen.

Viceroy Yeh Ming-chen had about an equal number of grievances against the foreigners. He again wanted the illegal trade and smuggling of opium into China stopped. He demanded that the British cease smuggling guns and ammunition from Hong Kong to the Tai Ping rebels, who were using these weapons to attack him. The Viceroy also accused the foreigners of kidnaping Chinese coolies for work in their plantations in other parts of Asia. To all these demands, which were repetitious of China's demands at the time of the Opium War, the Viceroy received the same kind of answer as he gave the foreigners. Just when these bickerings between the Viceroy and the British commissioners were at their height the *Arrow* incident occurred.

The *Arrow* was a fast sailing ship called a *lorcha.* It was owned by Chinese, captained by a Chinese who was a British subject, and registered in Hong Kong, which gave it the right and protection of the British flag. The ship was operated for one business only, piracy. On that point there seems to have been no dispute. The *Arrow* enjoyed many years of very profitable business, regardless of the protests of the Chinese officials against the protection given by the British flag.

The British registration finally expired and was not renewed, but the *Arrow* continued illegally to fly the British flag. At the first opportunity after the expiration of its registration Chinese officials seized the ship and crew. The British commissioner protested against this insult to the British flag, even though this was illegally used, and demanded that the flag and the Chinese crew be turned over to the British consul. Unfortunately, the flag had been destroyed, so nothing could be done about that except to demand an apology. This demand on the Viceroy was accompanied by a threat to shell his yamen if it were not complied with within twenty-four hours.

This did not put the Viceroy in the best of humor, but there was nothing he could do about it. He sent the entire crew in heavy chains to the British consul, but unfortunately he omitted to send the apology. This infuriated the consul—people apparently get infuriated easily when they have the upper hand—and he returned all the prisoners to the Viceroy. The Viceroy thought they were playing a game with him—a game he did not like. He ended it by promptly beheading the entire Chinese crew, including the British-Chinese captain.

To old Sir John Bowring and Admiral Sir Michael Seymour this act by the Viceroy could only be answered by war. The admiral sailed up the river, and the poor old Bogue forts were captured again, as they had been so often in the past. The fleet shelled Canton, directing their aim particularly at Viceroy Yeh Ming-chen's yamen. The Viceroy countered by offering a reward of thirty dollars each for all British heads delivered to him, regardless of age, sex, or color.

Curiously, neither the Chinese Government nor the British Government had taken part in this war up to this time; it was a private war between the Viceroy and the commissioner. The British Government did not back up Admiral Seymour and the fleet was consequently forced to withdraw. The Chinese, not knowing the reason for the withdrawal, celebrated it as a great victory and the Viceroy was decorated.

But the British Government did not forget the affair of the *Arrow*. At the moment they had more important things to attend to in other parts of the world. When the most pressing of these had been solved the government sent Lord Elgin to China with full powers to settle all matters in dispute with Viceroy Yeh Ming-chen. The French Government sent Baron Jean Baptiste Louis Gros with similar instructions and authority.

After sending identical notes with identical demands to the Viceroy and getting identical notes of rejection from him, the combined French and British fleets began the bombardment of Canton for the second time. The Allies occupied the city. Viceroy Yeh, having no place to go and finding it impossible to conceal his huge bulk anywhere in Canton, was captured. He was sent to India and lodged in a villa called Tolly Gunge, a few miles from Calcutta, where he died the following year. While this treatment of the Viceroy may not be in strict accordance with international law, it was probably much better than he would have received from the Tai Pings and better than he had any reason to expect after his bloody career in the province of Kwangtung.

War was formally declared by the British in 1857. With the Tai Pings holding practically all of China south of the Yangtze and while most of the military resources of the national government were engaged against the rebels it looked like a fairly safe time to attack China. The British invited the Americans, Russians, and French to join them in this war. All refused except the French. The French joined for two reasons: they were at that time attempting to challenge the position of the British in the Orient and could not let the British reap the advantages of a cheap victory over China. They also wanted to improve their hold on Indo-China.

After capturing Canton the combined fleets sailed for Tientsin. The capture of Tientsin brought the war to the very gates of Peking, only eighty miles away. News of the disaster caused a panic in the capital. Exaggerated tales were told of the strength and ferocity of the foreign troops. In the unprotected Yuan Ming Yuan fear mounted. The Emperor, his family, and the families of all the other princes hurriedly packed and moved into the Forbidden City within its stout high walls.

The move ended the happy, easy life of the court at the Yuan Ming Yuan and the girlhood of Green Jade. They were to move back to the Yuan Ming Yuan for short periods the following year but never to the pleasant, carefree times they had enjoyed before the war cast its blight over North China.

In the meantime there was much work to do. The Emperor

and his advisers were spending sleepless nights. During this period Green Jade was constantly with the Emperor and was of the greatest assistance to him. She was the only one who had any influence over him. She read the long reports for him, and her alert mind was quick in picking out and giving him only the important parts. She helped him with his mandates and edicts, as she had become very expert in composing such state papers. She also watched over his health and kept his idle friends from bothering him.

We do not know how much of the advice Green Jade offered was good and how much was bad. We do know that on one most important decision the Emperor was called on to make her counsel was disastrous. When the first agreement was offered to China by the Allies, the Emperor spent several sleepless nights trying to make up his mind to sign or not to sign. In his overwrought state he rushed to the palace of Green Jade. Here, more like a boy than a Ch'ing emperor, he fell on his knees, buried his face in Green Jade's lap, and sobbed out the story of his predicament. She reminded him that a Ch'ing emperor might die, but no Ch'ing emperor could sign away an inch of the land that had been entrusted to him by his ancestors. This advice proved to be a very grave mistake. But it was the mistake of a strong woman. Emperor Hsien Feng did die but he never signed a treaty giving an inch of territory to the hated barbarians.

In order to get the "foreign devils" out of Tientsin the Emperor appointed three commissioners to negotiate with Lord Elgin and Baron Gros. A preliminary agreement was reached which was to be confirmed and signed at Shanghai the following year. When it came time to sign the treaty the Manchu Government, as usual, caused many delays in an attempt to have certain conditions altered. Lord Elgin lost all patience with both the Manchu officials and his French allies and ordered the fleets to sail back to Tientsin.

This time when Lord Elgin attempted to recapture the Taku forts he was defeated, losing three vessels and three hundred men. The British and French fleets were forced to retire but returned the following year, greatly reinforced.

This time they landed at Ta Ch'ing Ho, a small port north

of Taku, and attacked and captured the forts from the rear. The Allies occupied Tientsin and in early September marched on Peking. The Manchu Army was defeated in two fairly heavy engagements between Tientsin and Peking. As practically all the Manchu forces were being used against the Tai Ping rebels in Central China, they could not hope to keep the foreign troops from reaching Peking.

Before the second engagement a number of British and French officers were with the Manchu Army negotiating under the protection of a flag of truce. As the engagement started before the foreign officers had an opportunity to return to their own lines, the Manchus held them prisoners, claiming the truce had been broken by the foreigners in starting the engagement.

5

When the British and French armies started their march on Peking and the Manchus found that they did not have the necessary military strength in the north to stop the advance of their enemies, it was decided to move the government to Jehol. This was a heavily fortified city in the mountains beyond the Great Wall, about one hundred and twenty-five miles northeast of Peking. Jehol was often used as a summer capital and hunting grounds by the emperors and so had ample accommodations for the Emperor and all his court.

Green Jade pleaded with Hsien Feng not to leave Peking. In this she was joined by the Empress, Prince Kung, his brothers, and a number of the ministers. They pointed out to the Emperor that Peking with its strong walls had never been captured by assault and that it could withstand the barbarians until sufficient forces could be brought from the south to drive them into the sea. Green Jade, having more faith and courage than the others, tried to shame the Emperor into staying by telling him that the barbarians would not dare to attack Peking if the Son of Heaven remained in the city, but he could not expect the barbarians to spare the city if the Emperor took the Sacred Palanquin and fled, leaving the ancestral shrines and the sacred altars unprotected.

Green Jade and the princes had another equally strong reason for wanting the Emperor to stay in Peking. Eunuch An Te-hai had been keeping them informed of a conspiracy which was being planned to banish from the court and kill, if necessary, the Empress, Green Jade, Prince Kung, and his brothers at the Emperor's death. As Hsien Feng had never been a strong man, and the complicated troubles of the recent years had overtaxed him, it was considered possible that he would not live much longer.

It seems that Su Shun, who was a very wealthy and talented man and had held almost every important position in the government, was watching with considerable uneasiness the growing influence of Green Jade. In her younger days he had entirely overlooked her as a possible rival, but now he recognized that she had great ability and was to be feared. She had never hesitated to show her dislike for him and his influence on the Emperor. He realized that if the Emperor should die her son would be appointed Emperor and she would become Empress Dowager and probably regent during her son's minority. This would give her great power and would also give the Yehonala clan control of the government.

Su Shun had little difficulty in pointing this out to Prince Tsai Yuan and Prince Tuan Hua, both efficient officials in high positions but members of the rival imperial clan. Green Jade and her friends knew that as long as the Emperor remained in Peking she and the Empress and Prince Kung would be in constant contact with the Emperor, while Su Shun and the older princes could see him only occasionally and then at formal meetings. But in Jehol this advantage would be reversed. There Su Shun had a large palace and was influential. At Jehol the court would be run more like an army camp.

Su Shun and his associates finally succeeded in persuading the Emperor to leave Peking by reminding him of the treatment the same British and French commanders had given to Viceroy Yeh Ming-chen. They also pointed out that his presence in Peking would give a greater incentive to the barbarians to capture the city and so in staying there he would only increase the burden of his military commanders. The Emperor by this time was a very sick man. Probably he knew that he had not long to live and that in staying in the Forbidden City he was endangering his son and his family. But even then he would not leave until the Chinese had lost their second battle and all knew that the Chinese armies were in no position further to resist the allied advance on Peking.

While Su Shun and his associates, now joined by the four Grand Councilors, were increasing their influence over the sick Emperor, Green Jade and her friends were not idle. Most of her followers and the lesser officials of the court had been ordered to remain in Peking, but Su Shun had no control over the Emperor's household, which was under the management of the Empress.

The Empress and Green Jade arranged to have themselves, the Emperor's son, and all his companions guarded by the Imperial Bannermen of the Guard. These troops were the best in China and were under the command of Jung Lu. They were all Manchus, mainly of the same clan as Green Jade and very loyal and devoted to her.

As the final order to leave for Jehol came rather late, there was no time to arrange an orderly departure. Everything was done hurriedly and in great confusion. The clothes, the jewels, and valuable possessions were crammed into the carts. In the excitement Green Jade lost her son, the future Emperor of China. She was sure he had been kidnaped and set up an alarm and a search. What must have been her consternation to discover that she had not only lost the future Son of Heaven but her only hope of advancement! It was some hours later that the little boy was found asleep in the cart of the Empress in the procession some miles ahead.

The refugees traveled rapidly, as they expected to be attacked by the cavalry of the allied armies. Rumor always had the Allies only a few miles in the rear.

They finally arrived in Jehol and were housed in the old palace buildings according to a plan arranged by Su Shun, which put the Emperor at such a distance from the Empress and from Green Jade that it was very difficult for them to see him or even communicate with one another. They now realized that their very lives were in danger. But it was at such times that the quick mind of Green Jade worked most effectively. She had Eunuch An Te-hai report to her every move and every conference of the conspirators. Through Jung Lu she sent daily messages to Prince Kung, who had remained in Peking to negotiate the treaty with the foreigners. But one can hardly say that Prince Kung assisted in negotiating the treaty, since the treaty was not negotiated. It was a demand on China, the terms of which Lord Elgin would not even discuss and which the Chinese had to accept under a threat to destroy Peking.

This treaty, among other things, called for a huge indemnity, fastened more completely on China the principle of extraterritoriality, and provided that foreigners could travel anywhere in China and not be subject to the laws of the country. It allowed foreign governments to establish legations in Peking. For the first time China was forced to legalize the importation of opium. Several additional ports, including Tientsin, were opened to foreign trade and residence.

The French added to the treaty the right of Christian missionaries to carry on their work in any part of China. An additional clause was later inserted to give missionaries the right to purchase and own property and to preach their religion anywhere in the empire under the protection of the government. This clause was later interpreted to extend protection to Chinese Christians. Many Christian leaders have expressed the opinion that these special rights did missionary work in China more harm than good. It gave strength to the claims of many Chinese that Christianity was being forced on them by the armies and navies of the Western countries.

These terms left the Manchu Government almost naked. Worse still, they had to reveal their nakedness to their own people and to the whole world, as the Allies would not leave Peking until the government issued a manifesto proclaiming to the world the conditions of the humiliating treaty. The overbearing attitude of Lord Elgin when he signed the treaty and when he had China at his feet did much to increase the resentment against him and all foreigners.

The story is told that at the first meeting of Lord Elgin and Prince Kung, the British commander appeared in undress uniform. He apologized for this attire, saying that his dress uniform had been lost when the Chinese sank one of the British ships. Prince Kung replied that he equally regretted that he was not properly robed, for the reason that Lord Elgin had destroyed all his clothes when he burned his private palace in the destruction of the Yuan Ming Yuan.

Meanwhile events were moving rapidly at Jehol. They might have moved disastrously for Green Jade but for the presence at that time in the Emperor's household of the young Eunuch Li Lien-ying. He was in almost constant attendance on the Emperor and kept Green Jade informed of all that was happening. In turn she sent word to Prince Kung that it was advisable that he hasten to Jehol with additional troops as soon as possible.

Hsien Feng was fast growing weaker. It was evident to everybody that he had only a few weeks, perhaps only days, to live. To relieve him of pain he was kept almost continuously under opium or other drugs. While in this condition Su Shun gradually poisoned his mind against Green Jade and the Empress. He accused Green Jade of improper relations with Guardsman Jung Lu while en route to Jehol.

How far the conspirators succeeded in convincing the Emperor of this is not known, but it is known that Su Shun, Prince Tsai Yuan, and Prince Tuan Hua did succeed in getting the Emperor to sign a decree appointing them regents upon the death of the Emperor. In a second decree Green Jade was forbidden any control over her son, the heir apparent.

In order to strengthen their position still further they induced the Emperor to write a decree authorizing Su Shun to force Tz'u Hsi to commit suicide on his death so that her spirit could accompany and minister to him in the celestial regions. A neat little arrangement!

At this point the gods again intervened. The imperial seals could not be found. Without them even the Emperor's decrees were valueless. Though guarded as the most precious and valuable things in the empire, the seals had been stolen from under the conspirators' very noses. This was not easy to accomplish, as there were at least ten, all of jade, very large and of considerable weight. All together they were more than one man could readily carry. It did not need many guesses for

Su Shun to make up his mind who probably had the seals, or at least who knew where they were hidden.

Su Shun knew also that he must not have this last decree in his possession when the Emperor died, as that would suggest either a forgery or undue influence. It had to be found on the person of the Emperor. Su Shun put it under the sick man's pillow.

Eunuch Li Lien-ying, who was massaging the Emperor at the time, saw all this. He was almost in panic over the danger to Green Jade, to whose interests he was already devoted. He feared the Emperor would probably die that very night. He stole out of the room, found Eunuch Wang, and told him the whole plot. Although it was then past midnight, Wang woke Green Jade and told her of her danger. She and the Empress discussed the situation the rest of the night. While they were still trying to find a solution the announcement came that the Emperor was dead. They went immediately to the death chamber. As the Empress bent over the body of her husband, unseen by anyone, she reached under the pillow. Her hand found and grasped the dangerous decree. She signaled to Green Jade, and together they burned the decree over one of the many candles that had been lighted for the dead.

The regents announced the Emperor's death. This was immediately followed by another decree in the name of the new Emperor, announcing his succession to the throne and appointing Prince Tsai Yuan as chief regent. The regents then published additional decrees, making their positions secure. However, none of these papers bore the imperial seal. Consequently they were not recognized by the Censors and other high officials in Peking. The Censors issued many memorials demanding that the regency be conferred on the Empress and the boy Emperor's mother as laid down by the rules of the Ch'ing Dynasty.

During all this time, while she and the Empress were being ignored and subjected to every slight by the conspirators, Green Jade showed her statesmanship and ability. Although fully informed by An Te-hai of every move the conspirators made, she kept her quick temper under control. She affected grief and a remote indifference and treated Su Shun and both princes with every deference to avoid unnecessarily arousing their suspicions. She held no conferences with the Empress, Jung Lu, or Prince Kung, but she was secretly in touch with them through Eunuchs Wang Ch'ang-yu and An Te-hai. She made no objection to any of the decrees issued by Hsien Feng or later by the regents. She let them arrange all the details for returning to Peking and the funeral of the Emperor. Soon even the wily Su Shun began to think he had overestimated the ability and fighting spirit of Green Jade.

But at the meeting of the imperial family and the regents she acted. With four new regents, who had been added to the board, there were also present the two brothers of the deceased Emperor, his widow the Empress, Green Jade, and all the other members of the court and imperial family who were required to confirm the funeral arrangements. Green Jade informed the assembly that according to the Household Rules of the Ch'ing emperors it would be necessary for the seven regents personally to accompany the body of the late Emperor to Peking. This the conspirators found, to their consternation, to be true. Green Jade also informed the assembly that, according to the same Rules, it would be necessary for her as Empress Dowager and for the Empress to proceed with the boy Emperor to Peking ahead of the funeral cortege. This was necessary in order that the boy Emperor and the two Empresses could meet the deceased Emperor and offer prayers and libations and perform other acts of reverence before the coffin at the gates of the capital city, as the Rules required.

All this the Regents found to be correct. The conspirators knew the danger of having the two Empresses and Prince Kung in Peking before they themselves arrived there, as they well knew by this time that the two Empresses had the missing seals. But again there was nothing they could do about it. There are stories that they attempted to ambush the Empresses' party on the way from Jehol to Peking but were unsuccessful in this, as Jung Lu and his bannermen were on their guard.

The Empress, Green Jade, and Prince Kung arrived in Peking several days in advance of the funeral cortege. Once they were safely within the Forbidden City the imperial seals suddenly reappeared. No explanation was ever made as to how they got there or where they had been.

The Empresses and Prince Kung now found themselves in a very strong position. They had the Emperor and the imperial seals and so could issue a few decrees themselves. Their decrees would be legally stamped and therefore would be accepted without question by the Censors as well as by the other boards of the government and the Chinese people.

Their first decree was the appointment of Emperor Hsien Feng's son as the new Emperor of China with the name T'ung Chih, "Universal Tranquillity." This was followed immediately by another decree issued by the Emperor appointing the Empress and his mother joint regents. The Empress was given the title Empress Tz'u An, meaning "Motherly and Restful." Green Jade was made Empress Tz'u Hsi, or "Motherly and Auspicious." They were also respectively called the Empress of the Eastern Palace and the Empress of the Western Palace.

With this solid legal foundation, Green Jade, now Empress Tz'u Hsi, prepared for the reception of the four conspirators on their arrival in Peking. A secret decree was issued in the name of the Emperor for the arrest of Su Shun and his associates.

In the meantime the funeral cortege slowly approached the capital city. Empress Tz'u Hsi sent a polite note to Prince Tsai Yuan asking about his health and as to the safety of the imperial coffin. She received an equally polite reply that they had arrived within ten miles of the city in safety. Tz'u Hsi sent a present to the coffin bearers for their arduous services, accompanying it with another note thanking Prince Tsai Yuan and his associates for their faithful devotion to duty.

The two princes knew exactly what such unnecessary politeness implied. It meant that Green Jade was in power again and was, in fact, challenging them. They also knew that it was death to the party that lost in the coming conflict. But they remained confident; they believed that their many friends in the government and in the army, with the great wealth of Su Shun, gave them more strength than anything Green Jade and her few friends could possibly muster. They did not know that most of their government friends were already helping the two empresses and that not one of the messages they had sent during the last ten days to their friends in the army had been delivered. All had fallen into the hands of Eunuch An Te-hai and his spies.

On arrival at the city gates, Prince Tsai Yuan dutifully announced his arrival to the boy Emperor. The Emperor, accompanied by the two Empresses, the two brothers of the late Emperor, and the other imperial princes met the coffin just outside the gates. The entire party knelt and performed the prescribed acts of reverence. Prince Tsai Yuan and his associates were received by the Emperor, the two Empresses, Prince Kung, and his brother with the greatest politeness and respect, which, however, deceived no one.

The Empress Tz'u Hsi now took charge of the proceedings. After again thanking the Grand Councilor and the regents for the services they had performed, she announced that their duties were now completed and that they were relieved of their positions. Prince Tsai Yuan attempted to point out that as he had received his appointment from the Emperor Hsien Feng before the latter's death, neither she nor anyone else had the authority to dismiss him from his position as chief regent. The Empress Tz'u Hsi replied to that argument by summoning Jung Lu and the guard and placing the regents under arrest.

As they could not see a single friend in the crowd or one soldier of the regular army, Su Shun and the other regents knew they were doomed. As they were marched away, Su Shun was heard to remark to Prince Tsai: "If you had let me kill that 'turtle' in Jehol when I wanted to we would not be in this fix today." (The word "turtle" is the most insulting word in the Chinese language and is untranslatable in its real connotation.) Prince Tsai Yuan and Prince Tuan Hua, as members of the imperial family, were generously allowed to commit suicide. Su Shun, who was only a clansman and who was disliked by many people, was executed. His enormous wealth was confiscated by the state and his family punished by banishment to the border provinces.

The two Empresses seemed a perfect combination as

coregents. Empress Tz'u An, the Empress of the Eastern Palace, who, however, chose to live in the Western Palace, was a quiet, rather retiring woman who was apparently satisfied to take charge of the household duties of the court and to let Empress Tz'u Hsi, who was neither quiet nor retiring and who made her residence in the Eastern Palace, handle the political side of their joint office. Empress Tz'u An did not seem to be jealous of her more active and more ambitious partner, whereas Tz'u Hsi was at times both jealous and dominating in her dealings with Tz'u An. But on the few occasions when Tz'u An did take a firm stand against Tz'u Hsi she usually gained her way. Tz'u Hsi evidently respected her and valued her friendship.

6

Of all the humiliations that China suffered during the Arrow War, not the least was the looting and destruction of the Yuan Ming Yuan by the Allies. This occurred shortly after the Emperor and his court had been forced to flee to Jehol.

It has been mentioned that the Yuan Ming Yuan during the summer months was the favorite home of the Emperor, the Empresses, and the imperial household and princes, as the Manchus were outdoor people who escaped from the city at every opportunity. The Yuan Ming Yuan consisted of more than thirty groups of buildings or villages and covered an area of more than twenty-five thousand acres.

There were no high walls to remind one of the restrictions of city life at the Yuan Ming Yuan as surrounded every other palace, temple, and important building in China. The villages and palaces were built for pleasure and good living. The villages were separated by artificial hills and connected by innumerable lakes, canals, and streams. The hills were covered with trees and shrubs of every description, placed, as Sir John Barrow wrote, ". . . not only according to size, but also the tint of their foliage." Sir John lived at the Yuan Ming Yuan in 1793, when he accompanied Lord Macartney's mission to Emperor Ch'ien Lung. Although Sir John saw many things on that visit to China that he did not admire, he did admire the magnificence of the Yuan Ming Yuan, the size and design of the buildings, the highly colored decorations, and, as he called them, the painted roofs. Sir John did not know that the brilliant yellow, blue, and green roofs of the palace were not painted; they were the famous glazed terra-cotta tiles of Peking.

Captain Charles Gordon, the well-known Chinese Gordon, visited one of the audience halls before it was looted. He wrote to his mother: "The whole interior of the building was lined with ebony carved in a marvelous way. The furniture consisted of a highly ornamented throne, large ornaments of solid gold, many high mirrors, clocks, musical instruments, books, and magnificent china of every description, heaps of silks and satin of every color, embroidery, and as much splendor and civilization as you will see at Windsor Castle. . . ." Praise, indeed, coming from an Englishman.

The first Yuan Ming Yuan was built by one of the early Ming emperors. It was added to by most of the later Mings and Ch'ings. Ch'ien Lung even built one village of Italian architecture, designed by Brother Castiglione, to show his friends how overseas people lived.

One village consisted of all the buildings necessary to hold court when the Emperor decided to meet his officials and foreign visitors in a less formal manner. In this group was one built in the form of a swastika on an island in the center of a small lake. One of the French officers who helped loot the palace called the Yuan Ming Yuan "the most magnificent group of buildings ever built by man for pleasure only. The Roman emperors never saw or even dreamed of anything that could compare with it. . . ."

The looting of the Yuan Ming Yuan is probably best described by Captain Charles Gordon. He wrote in another letter to his mother as follows:

". . . The people were civil to us, but I think the grandees hate us, as they must after what we did to the palace. You can scarcely imagine the beauty and magnificence of the palaces we looted and burnt. It made one's heart sore to burn them; in fact, the palaces were so large, we were so pressed for time, that we could scarcely plunder them carefully. Quantities of gold ornaments were burnt, considered as brass. It was wretchedly demoralizing work for an army. . . ." He wrote later: "Everybody was wild with plunder. My share of the looting was forty-seven pounds in addition to anything I could personally loot. Many did better than I did."

The actual looting of the buildings of the Yuan Ming Yuan does not seem to have been criticized or resented much by the Chinese; it was considered the usual and expected thing in a war at that time. But the burning and total destruction of the magnificent and valuable historical buildings have been generally condemned by most writers—both Chinese and foreign—as they were burned in retaliation, not to gain a military advantage. Baron Gros allowed his French troops to assist and share in the loot of the buildings but would not allow them to take any part in their destruction.

Several reasons have been given for destroying the buildings. The man who should know best why they were destroyed is Lord Elgin, who gave the order for their destruction. In his journal he wrote: "As almost all the valuables had already been taken from the palaces, the army will go there not to pillage but to mark by a solemn act of retribution the horror and indignation with which we were inspired by the perpetration of a great crime." The crime he refers to was the inhuman treatment and neglect of a number of British and French prisoners held by the Manchus. There is little doubt about their inhuman treatment as was later described by both the British and French survivors.

According to H. E. Wortham in his book *Chinese Gordon*, the object in destroying the buildings was to give the Chinese a lesson in civilization. If that was the aim it accomplished, its object—the Chinese conception of Western civilization—fell to as low a level as it could fall.

The Yuan Ming Yuan was always the favorite residence of Emperor Hsien Feng. It was at the Yuan Ming Yuan that Green Jade had her famous dog kennels, her prized goldfish, and the silkworms she took such pride in that she had the silk they made spun, dyed, and woven into some of the beautiful gowns she wore on state occasions, all done under her personal supervision.

If one of the objects in destroying the palaces was to impress the Emperor, as some writers claim, it failed, for the Emperor never saw the ruins. He had so many other worries and sad experiences at that time it is doubtful whether even the destruction of his favorite palaces would have added anything to his sorrows or lost pride.

With Green Jade it was different. The very first day she was able to leave Peking she visited the ruins of the Yuan Ming Yuan. She inspected the ruins of her favorite palace, the Yung Shou Kung, where she and the Emperor spent so many happy days together and where her son was born. She visited the ruins of every palace of the Emperor, every palace of her friends, the great halls, and the boats on the lake. The humble homes of the workmen, her kennels and all her dogs, even the trees and many other buildings and places she had loved so much, were gone.

When she saw all this destruction she was impressed, but not in the way the foreigners expected. She burst into tears not once but many times as she heard the story of vandalism from three old eunuchs who had loyally stayed with the palaces under their care while they were being looted and burned. She heard from them how a number of her old eunuchs had been killed by the foreign soldiers when they tried to defend her belongings, how the young servant girls and even the families of the younger princes who remained at the Yuan Ming Yuan had been treated during the terrible days and nights of looting and burning, how Prince Kung had lost all his own personal belongings and almost his life by staying to help the eunuchs and other servants, and how he escaped only by climbing the north wall after his own palace had been burned.

Empress Tz'u Hsi kept repeating: "How could they do it? How could they do such a thing? They must be the worst barbarians that have ever come to China in all her long history."

Is it unreasonable to believe that the idea that China should rid herself of all foreigners and all things foreign came to the young and saddened Empress at this time? And that the germ of her strong anti-foreign prejudice which was to influence her for the fifty years of her reign was planted in her mind by what she saw and heard that day in the ruined Yuan Ming Yuan?

4. TZ'U HSI'S LIFE IN THE FORBIDDEN CITY

It is doubtful whether Empress Tz'u Hsi ever had an hour of real discouragement in her entire life, but if she did it must have been the hour she spent in her sedan chair returning from her inspection of the ruined palace of the Yuan Ming Yuan. That day China's cup of bitterness must have appeared to her filled to the very brim.

The hated foreigner had forced his way into the Forbidden City and Western armies had occupied Peking for the first time in history. The Emperor had been obliged to flee from his capital and to die in exile. Every important coastal city had been forcibly opened to foreign trade and residence and subjected to the humiliations that Canton had suffered for years. The Chinese Government was helpless to protect its own people in their own country. Foreign governments were establishing legations within the shadow of the Forbidden City. Foreign religions could now be preached everywhere in the land. China could do nothing to stop this undermining of the very foundations of her civilization. Foreign citizens could now travel to all parts of China and not be subject to Chinese law or restraint. The Tai Ping rebels were in possession of many of the richest cities and provinces.

Certainly the prestige of China and the Ch'ing Dynasty could sink no lower. It looked as if the Manchus' "Mandate from Heaven" had run out.

But if Empress Tz'u Hsi was not discouraged as she slowly returned to Peking that cold December day most of the people of China were. To them the year 1861, the Year of the Rat, had been the blackest year in their lives—the blackest year of the Ch'ing Dynasty. In that year the Chinese people lost faith in their rulers, almost lost faith in themselves. In that year they were first to learn that China was not the Middle Kingdom around which all the other nations in the world revolved. The heavy tramp of the soldiers of the barbarians through the streets of the capital had shattered forever their belief in the superiority of China.

To the great mass of the people the Year of the Rat had brought even greater disasters than those that caused the government officials untold worry. It was a year of drought in some parts of the country, of floods in others, of rebellion, high taxes, and famine—a year in which millions died because they had no food. It looked as if the very gods had forsaken China.

But the black Year of the Rat eventually drew to a close and a new year dawned—the Year of the Pig, usually a lucky year. With this new year courage began to revive. No one knew why. Certainly there was nothing very evident at the time to give courage to anyone. But as one writer put it, "the worm turned for China, the first new year of T'ung Chih. (T'ung Chih was the six-year-old boy Emperor. The writer might have stated it more aptly: "The first year of Tz'u Hsi.") He was not referring to the humble worm that is supposed, ultimately, to turn and bite its tormentor. He was referring to the little earthworm that on New Year's Day the Chinese believe stops its downward progress into the earth to get away from the cold, turns, and slowly works its way upward to greet the spring sun and the warmth of a new summer.

With that new year the Chinese people also turned and faced their many problems with characteristic courage. Like the little worm, they gradually worked their way back again into the sunshine.

While the people of China, always optimistic, were looking forward to a better year in 1862, the problems and difficulties of the two Empresses seemed to be increasing. They had now been in power long enough to know that their hold on the government was very weak. This was particularly true of Empress Tz'u Hsi, against whom most of the criticism and opposition was being directed. The imperial princes knew they would have little difficulty in controlling Empress Tz'u An, regardless of any position she might occupy. They were equally aware that they could not hope to control Empress Tz'u Hsi. As long as she lived, she would be the government of China.

In discussing this period years later the Empress Tz'u Hsi said that the greatest difficulty she and Empress Tz'u An faced was that they did not know whom they could trust. They did not even know how far they could trust each other. They did know that Prince Kung had supported them during the Su Shun conspiracy only because he thought that with two young, inexperienced girls as coregents he, as Prince Adviser, would be the actual head of the government. How would he act now that he found he was mistaken? The Empresses also knew that many of the older and most powerful imperial princes and other Manchu officials of the rival clan, who had remained inactive during the Su Shun conspiracy, were now actively opposing them. The princes knew that if Tz'u Hsi remained head of the government the Yehonala clan would replace their own clan as the rulers of China. Many of the older, scholarly type of officials, curiously many of them Chinese, were opposed to breaking or making any changes in the rules of the imperial household established by Dorgon at the beginning of the Ch'ing Dynasty. These rules plainly forbade having a woman as regent. If the present government continued, they would have not one but two women regents. Worse still, they would have two very young women. These old men saw only disaster in such a situation, and they sent numerous memorials to the government protesting against both Empresses.

Tz'u An and Tz'u Hsi had many friends but these were mostly young men with little influence or military strength. They had, however, one great advantage over their opponents: they had the Emperor and the Great Seal in their possession and so could issue the only legal mandates and edicts. They also had a group of loyal eunuchs under An Te-hai and Li Lien-ying who kept them informed of every move and every meeting of the palace faction that opposed them. But above all they had in Tz'u Hsi a most brilliant mind and a competent person to be the head of the government at that time.

Her education, experience, and training far excelled that of any of the imperial princes. She was already showing her remarkable ability to make swift decisions and to act quickly in any emergency—a most valuable asset among the older officials of China, who always required time to study carefully any move before they would act.

The Tz'u Hsi who faced that fateful year of 1861 was a far different person from the young girl who had fled the Yuan Ming Yuan with Emperor Hsien Feng. The Su Shun conspiracy and the threat this was to her life and hopes had made a strong impression on her. She was no longer the impulsive, quick-tempered girl who had let her strong likes and dislikes influence her attitude toward men of importance. She realized that the Su Shun conspiracy was largely directed against her growing power and probably would never have arisen if she had not revealed her intense and jealous dislike of Su Shun and his supporters. She realized that now she had no one to assist her, not even Prince Kung, of the ability of Su Shun and the two imperial princes whom she had sent to their deaths. She never made that mistake again.

Probably at no other time in her entire life did T'zu Hsi show her cleverness and statesmanship more than during the early years of the first regency. She met the ministers and other officials only when coregent Tz'u An was present and then only from "behind the screen," so as not to remind them too frequently of her youthful appearance. All decrees and edicts were issued in the Emperor's name. She gave no receptions or audiences that would require the older Manchu princes to kowtow to her. She restrained the Board of Punishments and Prince Kung when they wanted to take drastic action against the friends and followers of the princes and the other conspirators. She pointed out that a few victims were better than many, that lives spared often made friends—strange words from the quick-tempered and vengeful girl of a few years ago. But this tolerant policy of hers did not extend to the women of Su Shun's household. She sought out and punished without mercy Su Shun's wife and concubines who had snubbed her when she first came to the palace.

But while keeping in the background, she was never idle.

She continued to cultivate the good will and friendship of her coregent. As Tz'u Hsi had very little if any liking for domestic affairs, she turned over the care and education of her son to Tz'u An. Later she was to regret this, but at the time it seemed a convenient arrangement.

With the aid of the three eunuchs, An Te-hai, Li Lien-ying, and old Wang Ch'ang-yu, she built up what was probably one of the best spy systems the imperial court ever had. It was from information gathered by An Te-hai and Li and passed on to her that Tz'u Hsi first learned of the Su Shun conspiracy against her life. This had made it possible for her to defeat the conspirators. After she became Empress, An Te-hai completed his organization and kept her fully informed on every important conference in the palace and the activities of every person in whom she was interested.

Through his eunuchs, An Te-hai had complete knowledge of every person who entered the Forbidden City, whom they saw, and the object of their visit. And as his spies were everywhere it soon became evident to the officials that the eunuch was a man to be feared. Li Lien-ying's eunuchs were the cooks, waiters, and boys in every household in the Forbidden City and the Imperial City. Eunuch Wang had boys or friends in every restaurant, club, public bath, and other places where men congregate outside the Forbidden City. Through these three chief eunuchs, any one of whom would have died for Tz'u Hsi without hesitation, there was very little that happened in the court or in Peking that the Empress did not promptly know all about. The advantage of having eunuchs in such positions was that they had access to the women's quarters in the palace at all times. She could see them and discuss matters informally with them without arousing suspicion.

Mention has been made several times of Eunuch Li Lien-ying, who was destined to have a great influence on the life of Empress Tz'u Hsi and the future of China. Tz'u Hsi had first noticed him as a very efficient and attentive young eunuch at the time the court was preparing for the flight to Jehol. He was then a rather good-looking youth, not more than seventeen or eighteen years of age, and had been in the Forbidden

City only a short time. He was quiet and retiring and in every way the opposite of Chief Eunuch An Te-hai. Tz'u Hsi inquired about him from Eunuch Wang and as the report was good she ordered that he be placed in attendance on her. This could not be arranged at the time, as Li Lien-ying was in attendance on the Emperor and was the one eunuch able to massage the Emperor in a way that brought some comfort to his ailing body. But Eunuch Wang had a long talk with him, and it was arranged that Li Lien-ying would serve Empress Tz'u Hsi when he could be released by the Emperor.

Many of Li Lien-ying's relatives still live in Peking, so it is easy to piece together his early life. Like many other eunuchs he adopted a boy, the son of his brother, to carry on his name and eventually to attend his grave.

Li was the fifth son of a very poor family of tanners and cobblers and in his early life was called Cobbler Li. The shop where he worked was in the neighborhood of the gate to the Forbidden City and because of its location many servants brought shoes there to be repaired. The young cobbler asked one day who were these men who were so well dressed and well fed, though evidently servants. He was told they were eunuchs. He gave the matter some thought and decided that here was a pleasanter life than cobbling. It is said that he himself performed the operation whereby he became a eunuch, using the sharp knife of his trade. If this is true, it marks him as a very brave man.

He was deeply religious and kept a Buddha in his room before which he invariably prayed before he went out and again when he returned. When asked the reason for such devotion he replied that when leaving the room he prayed to Buddha to bring him back safely, and when he returned he thanked Buddha for his safe return. Evidently Li was fully aware of the dangers surrounding a man in his position in the court of Tz'u Hsi.

Unlike the ambitious An Te-hai, Eunuch Li always knew his place. He was polite and deferential to everyone, even to the sons of officials, and always addressed them as master. One princess who served in the court relates that he was kind to the youngest servant girls, in spite of their lowly position.

He also appreciated the slightest favor from the ladies in waiting, even at the time when he was one of the most influential persons in China.

Li Lien-ying seems to have shown little desire for money or possessions. This is confirmed with much bitterness by his family, now living in poverty in Peking. He would not accept bribes or gifts of any kind from anyone for his personal use except the usual small seasonal presents. One of his weaknesses seems to have been an indulgence in opium, like most of the eunuchs who could afford such a luxury. They could hardly be blamed for such a habit, which evidently gave them pleasant sensations of a nature they could never hope to enjoy in any other way.

Eunuch Li had a sister usually known as Lady Li, who also served Empress Tz'u Hsi and stood high in her good graces. General Yuan Shih-k'ai and Li Hung-chang once tried to win Li's support for their new army plans by suggesting that they give his brother-in-law, the husband of Lady Li, a good position. Li refused their offer, saying: "Tell Yuan Shih-k'ai that my brother-in-law is a good man, humble, and without any education or ability to recommend him for high position. Please also tell Yuan Shih-k'ai not to tempt the simple, humble folk with positions that are beyond their ability and so would do them little good."

Like all eunuchs who were influential in court, Li Lien-ying had many enemies, especially among the Manchus, who resented a Chinese having so much influence. They seldom attacked his honesty but claimed his influence was not for the good of the country. It may have been so at times, but no one can deny that it was at all times in the interests of Empress Tz'u Hsi.

In contrast to the humility that marked Eunuch Li and which was the foundation of his mounting prestige, the arrogance of his fellow eunuch An Te-hai was rapidly bringing about his downfall. His power had grown until he practically controlled many of the departments of the government. He or his men had to be bribed even by high officials if they wanted to see the Empress or any other official in the palace within a reasonable time. He was soon suggesting candidates for positions in the government. He was overbearing, particularly to officials of the provinces. He was so powerful with the Empress and bragged so much about his influence with her that rumors spread that he was no eunuch but the lover of the Empress.

His arrogance became so great that Peking was no longer large enough for him. He wanted to show his importance to all China. He planned to do a thing no other eunuch had ever done before—to make a triumphal tour to many of the leading cities of the empire. The fact that it was against the law for a eunuch of the palace to leave Peking and the penalty for breaking the law was death made the trip more interesting to him. He would show all China that he was above the law.

He either secured a permit from the Empress or forged a permit allowing him to visit Soochow, the City of Beauty, especially of beautiful girls. Why a eunuch such as An Te-hai was always so fond of beautiful girls might be considered a mystery, but he was. He either borrowed or commandeered two government canal boats, loaded them with musicians, pretty girls, and many of his friends, and started a triumphal voyage down the Grand Canal. He demanded and received official entertainment at every important city through which he passed. In his conceit he even had many high officials kowtow to him, as they would to the Emperor.

When he reached the capital of Shantung province he met a governor of an entirely different character. When An Te-hai demanded an official reception he was given a reception, but not of the kind he anticipated. Governor Ting Pao-chen sent a company of soldiers and arrested An Te-hai and all his friends. The governor was highly incensed at the eunuch's assumption of imperial authority. He also knew that An Te-hai was unpopular with the officials in Peking. He himself had been a victim of the eunuch's arrogance on one of his visits to the court. The governor intended to execute the eunuch that very day, as he had the legal right to do, but some of his more conservative friends persuaded him first to report the incident to Peking. This he did by communicating with Prince Kung.

Prince Kung had also been looking for an opportunity to

get rid of An Te-hai. Therefore, instead of taking the governor's report to Empress Tz'u Hsi, who would never have allowed the execution of her favorite, he reported directly to the coregent, Tz'u An. After considerable effort he persuaded her to sign the decree ordering An Te-hai's execution. This was immediately sent by fast messenger to Governor Ting Pao-chen, who lost no time in carrying it out.

When Empress Tz'u Hsi learned of the order to execute her favorite servant she was furious. She countermanded it. This second order Prince Kung took care to send by slow messenger. Tz'u Hsi also demanded the instant dismissal and punishment of Governor Ting Pao-chen.

Tz'u Hsi was well aware that her enemies had been circulating the rumor that An Te-hai was not a eunuch at all, but her lover. This rumor had caused her considerable uneasiness. Now, Prince Kung informed her, the governor had effectually put an end to such gossip by exhibiting for five days the naked body of An Te-hai in the market place, where all the crowds could see that he was a real eunuch.

Empress Tz'u Hsi thought this over and her anger against the governor cooled. She began to see that he had served her cause very well. And An Te-hai with his arrogance and insatiable greed was becoming rather a nuisance.

Ting Pao-chen was not punished. Several years later Empress Tz'u Hsi graciously promoted him.

2

Tz'u Hsi fully realized the necessity of gaining the loyalty of Prince Kung, Prince Ch'un, and their three brothers, and endeavored to cultivate their friendship.

She found this difficult, as Prince Kung, now that he realized he had miscalculated in supporting her in Jehol, was unfriendly and at times behaved insolently toward her. On one occasion he hinted it was only through his support that she had attained her present position. The truth of this statement made it difficult for Tz'u Hsi to overlook. She said nothing but stored his remarks away in her mind for future action.

Prince Kung would sometimes presume on his high birth

and close relationship to the boy Emperor to enter the Throne Room before he was summoned or announced, though he knew this was against court rules. On one occasion he even asked Tz'u Hsi, before the whole Council, to repeat her instructions, pretending he had not heard them the first time—a serious breach of etiquette. He sometimes raised his voice, did not maintain a tone of respect, and did many other things Empress Tz'u Hsi was not liable to overlook or forget. But she kept her temper, as she knew that she was in no position at the time to enforce her authority.

In an effort to win his friendship and co-operation she bestowed one position after another on him until he was Grand Councilor (the highest post in the government), Prince Adviser to the coregents, head of the newly formed Foreign Office, and Prince of the Blood.

When these generous overtures failed to have the result Tz'u Hsi had hoped for, and Prince Kung grew more and more insolent, she decided some other means of reducing him to submission must be taken. She carefully awaited her opportunity. This came when on one occasion Prince Kung ventured to rise from his knees prematurely during a meeting of the Grand Council. This was a serious offense, as the kneeling position was required in order to protect the Emperor from assassination. Empress Tz'u Hsi immediately ordered the guards to arrest Prince Kung and escort him from her presence. She followed this with a decree accusing him of plotting against the safety of the coregents and the government, and relieved him of all his duties at court.

Later on, when she decided that she had punished him sufficiently and had shown him who was the real head of the government, she issued another decree in the name of both regents. In this she stated that the coregents had punished Prince Kung for his many breaches of etiquette and disrespect to the Throne only for his own good in order to save him and his family from the perils of a possibly greater crime and a greater punishment. But, the decree went on, as many friends of Prince Kung had petitioned that he be forgiven for his errors, the coregents in their generosity would permit him to be restored to some of his former positions. This was followed by another decree stating that as Prince Kung had been received in audience by the coregents, had prostrated himself and in tears asked forgiveness for all his mistakes, and as he seemed genuinely grieved at his misconduct, the coregents restored him to all his former positions except that of Prince Adviser.

Tz'u Hsi had no more difficulty with Prince Kung. She had judged his character accurately. After he was reinstated in his former positions he remained until his death in 1898 her loyal and valuable supporter. She called him "brother" (he was, in fact, her brother-in-law) and granted him many privileges. She adopted one of his daughters, who later became a great favorite in the court.

Only in the meetings of the Council and Cabinet did the Empress require strict adherence to all the formalities of her high position; in this she was adamant. At other times Prince Kung was treated as a member of the family. As with the members of most families, their friendly relations were not without a few breaks. This is shown by the fact that in his forty years of official life Prince Kung reached the position of Grand Councilor five times, and five times was dismissed from that position—something of a record. In fairness it must be stated that he was dismissed only three times by Tz'u Hsi. On the other two occasions she rescued and reinstated him.

Empress Tz'u Hsi handled Prince Ch'un in a different manner. She made him her loyal supporter by marrying him to her sister, Phoenix. He was never very brilliant or ambitious but he served Empress Tz'u Hsi faithfully in any position she forced on him.

Empress Tz'u Hsi also tried to add the three other brothers of Prince Kung to her intimate circle. Like all Manchu princes they were known by many names, but foreigners knew them as Prince Tun, the fifth brother, whose son got into disgrace and almost wrecked the Ch'ing Dynasty by openly joining the Boxers against the allied armies, Prince Chung, the eighth brother, and Prince Pu, the ninth brother. All were sons of Emperor Tao Kuang. Prince Tun was always a secret enemy of Tz'u Hsi.

No one knew better than Tz'u Hsi that in spite of anything she had done or could do to add to her strength her hold on the control of the government during the first few years of the first regency was extremely precarious. Her eunuchs were keeping her fully informed on the many plots and schemes that were being discussed against her. She knew how unpopular her appointment as regent was with the imperial princes and older officials within the court and how the many stories that had been circulated against her character in the teahouses of Peking had made her equally unpopular outside the court. There was a distinct feeling throughout China that the two regents had appointed themselves to positions that should not be held by women.

Tz'u Hsi also knew that if any attack were made against her it would come from within the palace. It would probably be sudden and with sufficient military force to overcome the Imperial Guard and would be completed far too soon for her friends commanding the armies in the south to be of any assistance to her. Even the possession of the boy Emperor and the Great Seals would be of doubtful value under such conditions.

At that time, before Tz'u Hsi had disciplined him effectively, Prince Kung was so plainly showing his dissatisfaction with her exclusive control of the government that she was not sure she could count on his support. It might be Prince Kung himself who would lead a revolt—a revolt in which the whole Aisin Gioro clan would rise against her.

She decided to build up a military organization which would be loyal to her. She knew she could count on the Imperial Bannermen of the Guard. They were mainly Manchus of her own Yehonala clan. But they were far too weak to be of much aid to her against the military forces the imperial princes controlled. However, the Bannermen would be a good, loyal nucleus for her new organization.

For a man to command such a force she must have someone she could absolutely depend upon. She decided that that man was the Guardsman Jung Lu. Their relations had gradually grown so close that many believed they were lovers. There is much to confirm this opinion, as will be seen later.

Jung Lu was born one year later than Tz'u Hsi. He was

neither a clansman nor a prince, but was of a very illustrious Manchu family. His grandfather was killed in battle fighting in Turkestan. His father and father's brother were joint commanders of the army fighting against the rebels in Kwangsi and both were killed the same day. Because of this Jung Lu inherited the honors and rank of his father. He is described as a remarkably fine-looking young man, especially in his guardsman's uniform. His duties took him often to the Yuan Ming Yuan when Tz'u Hsi lived there as a concubine. Whether they knew each other at the time is disputed. However, it is reasonable to presume that such a handsome young man would not have gone unnoticed by the young girls, including Green Jade.

In the several positions Jung Lu occupied before the flight to Jehol he had been a follower of Prince Kung. Tz'u Hsi knew this, but as she was at that time making every effort to win the permanent support of Prince Kung, she did not want to make her interest in Jung Lu too conspicuous. After she became Empress and when she was showing Prince Kung every attention she appointed him temporary commander and organizer of the new Peking Field Force and put Jung Lu on his staff. This force was the first military organization in China to be equipped with modern rifles and artillery and to be drilled in Western army tactics.

Tz'u Hsi decided that the force must be under her control. It was ideal for her purpose, as it would be permanently stationed in the neighborhood of the capital. She gradually improved Jung Lu's station until in 1864, when Prince Kung was promoted to a more important post, Jung Lu was made commander of the Peking Field Force. He led these troops on a short campaign against the rebels in Manchuria. Four years later, at thirty-two years of age, he was made lieutenant general of the gendarmerie of Peking, in addition to his command of the Peking Field Force. In this position Jung Lu could control and stop any military or other threat against the power of the coregents. Tz'u Hsi was now safe against any possible threats by Prince Kung and the imperial princes.

Within a year after Jung Lu was in complete charge of the Peking Field Force and even before he was in charge of the gendarmerie, Tz'u Hsi felt strong enough to challenge Prince Kung.

But even in her improved position it was a courageous thing for Tz'u Hsi to have so openly attacked a man of the standing of Prince Kung. While it was true that her friend Jung Lu was in command of the Imperial Guard and the Peking Field Force and was influential in the gendarmerie, these were new, untried forces. Tz'u Hsi knew that Jung Lu had served under Prince Kung and that according to Chinese custom his first loyalty should have been to his former chief. Yet she took all those risks and attacked Prince Kung when she knew that to lose was not only to lose her position as coregent but also, in all probability, her life.

At the time Tz'u Hsi stripped Prince Kung of all his positions and honors he was, without doubt, the most outstanding and most powerful man in China. But again the gods were with her; Prince Kung accepted defeat. He withdrew gracefully when he must have known that he had the power to crush her.

Some writers claim he accepted her authority because he lacked the courage to oppose her and that he was not the courageous and brilliant man that history claims him to have been. The more accepted explanation is that Prince Kung, like many others who surrounded Tz'u Hsi at that time, had come to recognize her unusual ability and to realize that if the Ch'ing Dynasty and China were to be saved the one person who could do it was Tz'u Hsi. No other explanation can be given why Tz'u Hsi, so difficult, unreasonable, and even disloyal to her friends, as she was on occasion, could hold the loyalty and co-operation of so many strong men and women who had every reason to dislike and oppose her. Her judgment of men was almost uncanny at times. She seldom, if ever, chose the wrong man for an important position.

The two Empresses were somewhat handicapped in their social life by the fact that they were in mourning for the Emperor during the first twenty-seven months following their return from Jehol. They had to live a life of austerity during that period.

According to custom, they shared the same palace—the

Palace of Eternal Spring. Tz'u An occupied the east side of the court and Tz'u Hsi occupied similar quarters on the west side. They shared a dining room with the boy Emperor, who was also in mourning and whose living quarters were even inferior to those occupied by the two Empresses. Their furniture was meager and poor. They had no table or chairs, and ate off a reed mat spread on the floor. When in their quarters they wore peasant dress, and to support the illusion that they were living the life of peasants the building they dined in was known as Chan Ts'u (Thatched House). Rather poor living conditions for the Son of Heaven and the two Empresses of the largest empire on earth.

In a further attempt to strengthen her government Tz'u Hsi swallowed her pride and recalled the four regents she had dismissed and almost executed. She gave them back their old positions as councilors and added Prince Ch'un and the three tutors of the Emperor to complete a council of eight. She was never very successful in winning the approval of the older imperial princes, the uncles of Prince Kung and his brothers. They were too old to accept the many changes she was making. Neither was she ever able to get the full support of the Censors. That board remained as it had always been—an independent and courageous critic of anybody or anything they considered not for the good of the country. Tz'u Hsi fought the Censors most of her life. She removed, banished, and even executed some of its members. But the Censors always survived to watch over and censor more severely any of her acts that did not meet with their approval.

This first government of Emperor T'ung Chih as organized by Tz'u Hsi did not make a very good impression on the representatives of the foreign nations who had recently established themselves in Peking. They found fault with the youthfulness of those in authority. They reported to their governments that the Emperor of China was a boy of six. The actual ruler was Empress Tz'u Hsi, an inexperienced woman of twenty-six. The Empress coregent was no older. The highest official in China, Prince Kung, was a man of little foreign experience and only twenty-eight years of age. He was assisted by his brother, Prince Ch'en, then just twenty-one. The foreign representatives also reported that not one of the Manchu government officials, or any of the advisers of the government, had ever been outside of China or its dependencies. They did not have the slightest knowledge of the outside world. All had strong prejudices against foreigners and everything foreign.

All these reports were true, but they were not the whole truth. The foreign observers had passed over the fact that the Board of Councilors included several older men of experience and three of the best scholars in the country. The Board of Censors also was composed of older men of ability and experience.

One other thing the foreign representatives did not see but which Tz'u Hsi knew well was that however weak the government of China appeared to be China still had great unity in her political system, in her provincial hsien and village governments. The family life of China remained strong and held the country together in this time of crisis. The heads and the permanent staff of the departments of the Imperial Government were doing their work as conscientiously as they had always done. These Tz'u Hsi was careful not to disturb. She, better than any other member of the imperial family, knew and understood their importance. The people of China were loyal to their emperors and their country. Though the emperors were of a foreign race their persons never required protection against the Chinese people. When they traveled they were accompanied by a guard of honor armed only with ancient traditional spears.

The immediate foreign menace was removed by the departure of the British and French fleets for Hong Kong and Europe. But Empress Tz'u Hsi and her associates knew that they might be recalled at any time, as the foreigners were openly discussing the possibility of dividing China among themselves, first into spheres of influence, and later into some more permanent form of control, as France was later to secure possession of Indo-China.

To solve China's foreign problems Empress Tz'u Hsi had first to unite the country and regain its prestige both at home and abroad by defeating the Tai Ping rebels. The country had to have peace in order to rebuild its destroyed cities and to regain the population and wealth lost by the Arrow War and the many years of internal disturbances.

The Tai Ping rebels had been greatly strengthened by the attack of the British and French armies on North China. They had also received a large supply of bombs and explosive shells from the foreigners—new war matériel the government troops did not possess at that time.

Tz'u Hsi greatly encouraged her generals by sending them additional troops and money, the latter being part of the confiscated wealth of Su Shun. She now had three successful generals: her nominee, General Tseng Kuo-fan, his even more noted younger brother General Tseng Kuo-ch'uan, and the well-known Li Hung-chang. Li Hung-chang was in command of an army which included the famous Ever Victorious Army then under the command of Henry Burgevine but later to be commanded by Chinese Gordon. The army under General Tseng Kuo-fan attacked Nanking and, after many battles, finally captured the city in July 1864. The rebellion was to drag on for another year or more but never again was it a menace to Peking. Empress T'zu Hsi's most pressing problem was solved.

As busy as Tz'u Hsi was in these days she took time to do a kindly act to an old friend who had assisted her in the past. Unfortunately this kindness resulted in tragedy, but through no fault of hers.

On the morning Emperor Hsien Feng's remains were escorted from Jehol to Peking a great crowd gathered to view the procession as it entered the gates. In that crowd was Hei Yu—Black Yu—the Mohammedan meat seller. While watching the ceremony, what was Black Yu's amazement to see that the Empress in the center of the group of princes and officials was the little Manchu girl he had known as Green Jade. He thought she recognized him. He walked the streets for hours dreaming of the great things that might come to him now that he had a friend who was an empress.

Unfortunately he could not keep his dreams to himself. He told all the neighbors, including the assistant in a small noodle shop a few doors away. This assistant was jealous of the good fortune of Black Yu and tried to take away some of his happiness by reminding him of the number of times he had pinched the nose of the great Empress in the game called "Pulling the Camel." He said that she probably remembered this, and Black Yu would be severely punished instead of getting any reward.

Poor Black Yu had forgotten about the nose-pinching and now it worried him. The more he thought of it the more he worried, especially when the noodle maker reminded him how much a man suffered while being sliced into thin pieces. Black Yu lost his appetite, became ill, and decided to run as far away from Peking as he could.

As a matter of fact Tz'u Hsi had recognized Black Yu in the crowd that morning and had decided to help her old friend in some way. At the first opportunity she sent two army officers from the local garrison to inquire about Black Yu and his family and to report to her. One can imagine how this inquiry alarmed the already frightened Black Yu. But two days later, when a very pompous officer appeared and ordered him to be at his home the following morning at ten o'clock to receive a communication from the imperial court, poor Yu thought his last day had come. The butcher was no scholar and so could not read the order. But he did see the big imposing seals and he knew by them that the order was from the palace and that the officers were from the army. He thought this could mean only one thing: he was going to be arrested and executed. He thought again of the death by slicing and, as he told his wife, "My soul almost ran out of my body." He took a few things and at midnight quietly disappeared from the neighborhood. When the gate was opened at sunrise he tried to leave the city, but the Manchu Yellow Banner troops were holding a review that morning and no one was allowed through the gates.

After Black Yu's wife missed her husband she locked the doors of the shop and, with the children huddled together, waited to be arrested. But instead of the expected officers, a group of eunuchs appeared with great quantities of food of every description, bundles of silks, cotton cloth, and money. They also brought Black Yu the offer of a small position in the palace as a reward for helping little Green Jade and her family when they needed help so badly. Too late the wife of Black Yu realized that someone had fooled her husband. A city-wide search was made for him but he could not be found. Late in the afternoon a coolie from a far corner of the city reported a body hanging from a tree. It was the body of poor Black Yu.

When word of this came to Empress Tz'u Hsi she grieved that her well-intentioned efforts had ended in such tragedy. She sent a large sum of money to the family and arranged for Black Yu's two sons to be taken into the army. She ordered a fine Mohammedan funeral and sent bearers from the court to the funeral of her humble friend.

Empress Tz'u Hsi also went to considerable trouble to save two other friends who had assisted her and her mother. These were the old man Wu Chin-t'ang and his son Wu Wen-chen, without whose help it is improbable Tz'u Hsi would have passed the examinations to become a concubine in the court of Hsien Feng. Wu Chin-t'ang and his son belonged to the family of Prince Cheng, a relative and supporter of Su Shun. When the prince and all his household were ordered punished for their connection with the leader of the conspiracy, Tz'u Hsi heard of this and immediately sent officers to rescue Wu Chin-t'ang, his son, and other families. Wu Wen-chen was given a position in the guard while the old man was retired on a pension.

In spite of all the kindly things Tz'u Hsi so often did for her friends, the stories most often circulated in the teashops of Peking and throughout China were usually of things detrimental to her reputation. In China, as in other countries, people apparently prefer to hear scandal rather than tales of virtue. Many of the stories can be traced to the evil Su Shun and his desire for revenge. Su Shun had taken advantage of an ancient custom to secure revenge on his enemy by further damaging her reputation. He did this in a way that could be neither stopped nor answered.

It will be recalled that the two princes associated with Su Shun in his conspiracy were allowed to commit suicide. This they did in the traditional manner. They called together their friends for a big banquet. At the close of the feast they mounted the table, fastened a silken cord around their necks and over the beam in the ceiling, then kicked the table from under them. There was a slight mishap with Prince Tuan Hua, who was an enormous man, so heavy that the silken cord broke. But he managed it in the second attempt.

But Su Shun was not an imperial prince. Moreover, he was probably the most hated man in China. He was ordered to be beheaded like a common criminal. But even common criminals in China are given one privilege before they die. While being driven through the streets of the city in an open cart on their way to the execution grounds they can call for anything they want and it is given to them. If it is food, they get it, though usually they choose to talk to the hundreds of curious folk who line the streets and no one can stop them. While most criminals sit in the cart with ashen faces, looking straight before them as if drugged (which sometimes they are), others take advantage of their privilege and discourse on subjects they would never dare openly discuss under ordinary circumstances. They relish to the full their one hour of complete freedom. This is always enjoyed by the public. It is part of the show.

Su Shun was one of the latter group, and the subject of his discourse as he rode to his death was the alleged sins of Tz'u Hsi. He repeated the old rumor that An Te-hai was no eunuch but the Empress's lover; that he, Su Shun, was being executed because he knew too much about her; that she had tried many times to induce him to have illegal sexual relations with her but he had refused and therefore she hated him.

Perhaps the crowds, knowing men, might have believed all these accusations if Su Shun had not added his refusal of Tz'u Hsi's proffered favors. But whether the public believed Su Shun or not, these accusations were to make interesting conversation in the teashops for many years.

3

After the end of the long period of mourning for Emperor Hsien Feng, the two Empresses and the boy Emperor moved out of the Thatched House into more comfortable palaces.

In fact both Empresses moved several times, as they were hard to please and neither liked the life in the Forbidden City. They sighed for the more comfortable and less formal life they had enjoyed at the Yuan Ming Yuan. Empress Tz'u Hsi finally chose the Liu Sui Tien, the Hall of the Fulfillment of Peace. Empress Tz'u An took up quarters in the P'ing An Shih, Chamber of Peace and Comfort. The young Emperor, with the indifference of a boy, was not very particular where he lived so long as it was close to the dining room and kitchens. All three still shared the same dining room. The two Empresses also did their secretarial work in the same building.

A list of the daily activities of both Empresses shows that they led very busy lives. The first meeting with their ministers was at four o'clock in the morning. Why they chose that unearthly hour no one seems to know, except that it followed tradition. Early-morning government meetings were continued even during the first few years of the republic.

In addition to the two Empresses and the boy Emperor a number of other important persons lived within the Forbidden City. First came an old concubine, the last living concubine of Emperor Tao Kuang. She died soon after the return from Jehol, but as long as she lived she received all the honors due her position and was treated with great respect by both the Empresses and the boy Emperor. Two of the young concubines who had entered the palace with Tz'u Hsi and who had treated her so badly—constantly reminding her that she was the daughter of an official who died in prison—had died. One hopes of natural causes. Tz'u Hsi's friend, little Li Pin, and one other concubine of Hsien Feng were still in the palace. They occupied an honorable position and were kindly treated by Tz'u Hsi and Tz'u An. There were also a number of other concubines of various ages who lived in one section of the palace grounds, though each had her own establishment. The ladies in waiting were the daughters of leading Manchu families and lived outside the Forbidden City. All these formed the social side of the court.

The imperial family employed more than three thousand eunuchs and five hundred serving maids. Most of these lived and worked within the Forbidden City and the Imperial City.

Peking has often been called the city of romance and mystery, a name it has well earned during its long history of more than three thousand years. But probably never in its history did it deserve that name more than during the fifty years Empress Tz'u Hsi controlled the destiny of the city and the country.

There has been an important city on or about the present site of Peking almost since the beginning of recorded history. Except for a few short periods, and under various names, the present Tatar city has been a capital for more than a thousand years, the home of emperors and the seat of government of a great empire. The present Tatar city was designed and built in those early years to house more than one million people within massive walls sixteen miles in length. Unlike most European cities that usually grew around a great castle or cathedral and so took a more or less circular form, the Tatar city of Peking was built according to a well-designed plan. It is a square city except for a slight variation in the northwest corner of the confining wall. Rumors are that it was deliberately built that way to avoid some old superstition about a square city. Its main streets are wide and straight, running north and south, with the hutungs and connecting streets east and west. Every street was laid out for proper drainage and with large sewers, many of which are still in operation today. Few other cities in the world were interested in sewers a thousand years ago. Peking can well claim to be one of the best-designed cities in the world.

When the Ch'ing armies entered Peking they found what is now the Tatar city almost deserted. The Chinese inhabitants had either fled or been driven out by the bandit Emperor Li Tzu-ch'eng. The Manchus did not allow the Chinese to return. They made the city into a home for the eight Manchu armies or Bannermen and their families. With the exception of those Chinese who were part of the Manchu armies, a small number of Chinese officials connected with the government, and a few selected tradesmen, no Chinese were allowed in the Tatar city until fairly recent times.

The Chinese were forced to live in the Outer City, south of

the Tatar city. Here is located the Temple and Altar of Heaven, the holiest place in all China, often described by the Chinese as the center of the universe.

Although the place immediately north of Ch'ien Men was usually open to the public, the plan of the Forbidden City actually starts with this great gate and extends north for two miles to Coal Hill, or Prospect Hill as it is more properly called. The Forbidden City is the center and very heart of the Tatar city. It is the reason for its existence.

The Forbidden City is divided into two parts. The central section contains great marble courtyards, large monumental buildings, including the Great Throne Room, two lesser throne rooms, and other buildings used only for the most formal and important ceremonies. As the Emperor had other buildings more appropriate in size and more conveniently located, the great buildings in the central section of the Forbidden City often remained idle during an entire reign.

The whole world should be thankful that the Chinese emperors of the early dynasties had the urge, the courage, and the genius to build the beautiful Forbidden City, the many courts, the high pink walls and massive gates, the pavilions and the great buildings with their carved white marble steps and balustrades, their red lacquered columns, cornices decorated with every color of the peacock and, above all, those glorious roofs with their gently curved lines, covered with bright Chinese glazed yellow tiles and decorated with ornaments of the same material and color. This group of well-designed and beautifully proportioned buildings has no equal in size and magnificence anywhere else in the world.

The remaining section of the Forbidden City is usually called the area of the Winter Palaces. During the rather short periods that Empress Tz'u Hsi had lived there as a concubine she had lived in the Ch'u Hsiu Kung, the Palace of the Storing of the Beautiful—rather an appropriate name for the separate living quarters of the imperial concubines.

Just south of the Wu Men and within the plan of the Forbidden City, but actually a part of the Imperial City, were two interesting parks open only to the imperial household. The western park had many goldfish pools, the famous peonies, and hundreds of other varieties of flowers. Here also was the She Chi T'an, the Altar of Harvest, second only to the Altar of Heaven as a holy place. It was the private altar of the Emperor and was used often, as many of the Ch'ing emperors seemed to have been deeply religious men. The floor of the altar is of earth of five colors, representing the five elements; the side of the terrace forming the altar is of white marble.

In addition to all the palaces described the imperial family also had less formal homes in the southern half of the Imperial City that bordered on the Nan Hai and Chung Hai, the South and Middle Lakes. Although this area was not in the Forbidden City it was part of the Imperial City, the most exclusive part. It was separated from the rest of the Imperial City by a high red wall. The palaces within this area were known as the Sea Palaces. Here, as at the former Yuan Ming Yuan, everything was less formal than in the Winter Palace. Friends of the two Empresses, the Emperor, and other members of the imperial household could be invited here to the theatricals, picnics, banquets, and other social affairs that formed a large part of the social life of the imperial household. The rocky hillside of the White Dagoba soon became as popular a place for picnics with Tz'u Hsi and her friends as the famous islands in the former Yuan Ming Yuan had been.

Every nook and building in this section of the Imperial City is closely connected with the life of Empress Tz'u Hsi. The two lakes together are about two miles in length and average about five hundred yards in width. In the summer they are almost completely covered with large white and pink lotus. Tz'u Hsi was very fond of early-morning boating parties. While the huge blossoms were in bloom, she went almost daily to see the lotus open at sunrise. There were so many flowers opening with the rising of the sun that one could actually hear them open, or so the Empress declared. As no fish were ever allowed to be taken from the lakes, goldfish of every size and color were plentiful and tame. They would take food from the hand. Who could blame Tz'u Hsi if she sometimes left Tz'u An alone "behind the curtain" at the early meetings with her ministers or kept them waiting a few hours while she was out on the lakes? It would be hard to imagine anything more pleasant than to be on the beautiful Southern Sea on one of the luxurious state barges, amid lotus flowers, watching the rising sun turn the yellow roofs of the many buildings and towers of the Forbidden City into the color of pure gold. Tz'u Hsi wrote two poems trying to describe her emotions on these early-morning parties. She also made a number of water colors of the lake and the lotus. Like all Ch'ing rulers, she loved the outdoors. She kept the state barges busy almost every day until late in the season. She is even said to have ordered the bombardment by her troops of the Legation Quarter in 1900 stopped to enable her to enjoy one of her boat rides undisturbed by the noise of cannon.

In addition to the lotus, the South Lake was also famous for the huge masses of giant pink and red peonies on its banks. The Chinese consider the peony the king of flowers. These peonies formed part of the rock garden on the east side of the lake, close to the "Bridge of Ten Thousand Years." Here Empress Tz'u Hsi had one of her several small "over-the-water" theaters that she had built and arranged in such a manner that the voices of the actors floated over the water and came softly to the small audience sitting comfortably and dining at tables almost hidden by wisteria vines. She built these theaters apparently for every season. One large over-the-water theater in the Pei Hai was so planned that not only did the voices of the actors come over the water but the audience sitting at the long dining table could enjoy a fine view of the reflection of the moon in the water. This theater was used only for the few days each month that the moon was full.

Close to the end of the bridge is the island and palace of Ying T'ai, which was to be the melancholy home of the young Emperor Kuang Hsu for the many years he was held prisoner by Empress Tz'u Hsi. To the south of this island is another gilded prison, the beautiful palace that Emperor Ch'ien Lung built to house and to hold that wild Sungarian beauty, the Fragrant Princess. All the palaces, bridges, and galleries in this area are famous for their beautiful carvings. The swastika, emblem of good luck and longevity to the Chinese, is the symbol most often found in the decorations.

Tz'u Hsi's favorite walk was along the western shore of the two lakes. In fine weather she walked under the old cedar trees planted centuries before by the Ming and even by the Mongol emperors. All her life long this was one of the Empress's favorite spots. She loved the shade of the great trees and the privacy they and the high wall of the Forbidden City afforded.

In her later years, and to her intense annoyance, this privacy was invaded. A public letter writer, who owned a little one-story house built against the outer side of the Forbidden City's wall, wanted more space and light for his occupation and built a small second story on his house. This came up above the top of the red wall. Its windows looked down into the Forbidden City and the path under the cedars where the Empress liked to walk. Annoyed as Tz'u Hsi was at this invasion of her privacy, she could do nothing to prevent it. In China even an empress cannot put a poor man out of his house. If she had presumed to send the military to destroy it, there would have been a riot in the neighborhood at such an outrageous infraction of custom in attacking a man's right to his home. Tz'u Hsi was well aware of what the Board of Censors would have had to say of such an act, and—regretfully—she submitted to the letter writer's survey of her cedars.

In wet weather Tz'u Hsi used the brightly decorated galleries she had built for her walks. In either case she had the beautiful Southern Lake at her feet, the Fairy Island or the Ocean Terrace near the center of the lake, the rock gardens on the eastern shore, and the wonderful buildings of the Forbidden City as a background. This was a walk indeed worthy of an empress.

It was this location which Tz'u Hsi chose for the private palace she built later to escape from the Winter Palaces. In front of it stands the Spirit Screen of gray carved brickwork that rivals in size and beauty the famous Nine Dragon Screen of the Pei Hai. Both sides of the screen are carved, showing an elaborate Chinese landscape with hundreds of figures, palaces, and lakes, not unlike the view one gets when looking northward from the site of the screen. The usual stone lions—ferocious, yet friendly—guard the entrance to the palace.

Like all imperial palaces, it contains a large main courtyard, reception and entertainment rooms, courts in the rear with living apartments. All the important rooms face south. It was the first building constructed by Empress Tz'u Hsi and is rather modest in size and elegance compared with some of those she built later. The palace is noted for its famous sandalwood carvings which even today give off a delicious perfume. These carvings are used as partitions but do not entirely shut off the view between the principal reception rooms. They are from four to six inches in thickness and are carved in the most elaborate designs. Though the carvings are cut entirely through the partitions, the artist has somehow contrived to create a different design on each side.

The most interesting building in the section of the Sea Palaces is the Tzu Kuang Ko, the Throne Room of Purple Effulgence. It has a fine gilded throne larger than most thrones. The most impressive objects in the large room are two black marble tablets with a fine inscription in both Chinese and Manchu characters. This palace was built by one of the early Ming emperors and was the throne room in which the representatives of the Mongols, tribute-bearing and other inferior nations, were received by the Emperor. Its magnificence was intended to impress these embassies. When the representatives of the European nations insisted on being received by the emperors of China they were given audience in the Tzu Kuang Ko. It was some time before they realized that in spite of their gold braid and resplendent uniforms the Emperor had been receiving them in a palace used only for representatives of tribute-bearing or inferior countries.

Directly north of the Sea Palaces is the Pei Hai, also called the Golden Sea, separated from the Chung Hai by the Jade Rainbow Bridge. The most striking monument in the Pei Hai, and one of the most striking in all Peking, is the White Dagoba, which crowns a hill on the Jewel Island in the center of the lake. It is an enormous bell-shaped monument, suggestive of a huge white lotus bud and visible from many parts of Peking. In bright moonlight it gives off a soft glow which has been the source of many legends. The hill on which it stands is supposed to have been miraculously moved from Mongolia, where it possessed certain magic powers. Genghis Khan built a Taoist temple on this hill for a teacher he had invited to Peking to instruct him. The present dagoba was built by the first Ch'ing emperor (who was also a student of religions and who later gave up his throne to become a Buddhist monk) to honor the first Dalai Lama to visit Peking. This accounts for its peculiar shape, which is not uncommon in Tibet.

At the eastern end of the Jade Rainbow Bridge is the Cheng Kuan Tien, the Circular Throne Hall. This was the palace of Kublai Khan, where he lived and died. It is described by Marco Polo as "the most beautiful palace in the whole world." It is now far from being the most beautiful palace in Peking, but one of the finest views may be seen from the upper terrace of the Cheng Kuan Tien. It was on this terrace that Kublai Khan gave many wild, elaborate drinking parties to his princes and other military leaders from the Gobi Desert and beyond. In Kublai Khan's time the present Pei Hai was but the park adjoining his Circular Palace. The park was heavily wooded at that time and according to Marco Polo these wild fighting men were very fond of animals and birds which they tamed and allowed to roam at will in the Pei Hai forest. Marco Polo particularly mentions the large numbers of swans, geese, ducks, and other wild fowl that made their permanent home on the lakes, which even then were famous for their lotus flowers. Through eight centuries these pleasure grounds have been cherished and carefully tended.

While Tz'u Hsi spent more of her time in the area of the Sea Palaces in the Southern and Middle Lakes and was to make this region almost as famous with her entertaining as Kublai Khan did the Pei Hai, she was also much interested in the magnificent buildings that bordered the latter lake. The hill of the White Dagoba was one of her favorite picnic grounds, easily reached by boat. She was particularly fond of visiting the Wan Fo Lou, which housed the largest Buddha in China, the Monastery of Ch'an Fu Ssu, the Altar of the Silkworms, built to honor the Chinese woman who, according to tradition, four thousand years ago taught her people how to raise the silkworm and weave its product into silk cloth. The Nine Dragon Porcelain Screen and many interesting buildings are also in the Pei Hai area.

The remaining part of the Imperial City, with the exception of a few temples, was occupied as homes and offices of army officers, special government officials, and others closely connected with the administration of the Forbidden City. There is one landmark that does not appear to belong to either the Forbidden City or the Imperial City but which dominates both. This is the high artificial mound known to foreigners as Prospect Hill. While it does not play any particular part in our story, except as the resting place of the emperors before burial, it was visited often by the imperial family, as a magnificent panoramic view of Peking and the surrounding country is obtained from the highest of its five pavilions. The last of the Ming emperors and his faithful eunuch committed suicide by hanging themselves from a tree on Prospect Hill. Chains were hung on the tree for many years to punish it for its part in the tragedy.

4

When the body of the Emperor Hsien Feng was brought from Jehol to Peking it was placed in the Ch'ien Ch'ing Palace within the Forbidden City to lie in state for ten days. During this period a number of elaborate sacrificial ceremonies were held before the coffin. As these services were held twice and sometimes three times a day, we will describe only a typical ceremony—the "Initial Major Sacrifice" that was held on the fifth day.

The official account states: "The sacrificial ceremony was attended by the Emperor, the two Empresses, and all the imperial princes and high officials and their families. The sacrificial offerings included eighty-one tables of meats, nine cases of pastries, twenty-seven sheep, and forty jugs of wine. The sacrifices that were burned for the deceased Emperor included two hundred and fifty thousand paper ingots, one hundred and forty-five thousand pieces of paper cash, fifty thousand pieces of paper gold and silver money, and ten thousand paper bolts of silk and satin." (The combined value of these paper sacrifices was only a few hundred dollars.) The description suggests that a very large crowd attended what were described as family sacrificial ceremonies.

On the completion of these ceremonies within the Forbidden City, the coffin was moved to the Hall of the Observation of Virtue, behind Prospect Hill, for the more public sacrifices. During this mourning period, which lasted one hundred days, no marriage ceremonies were allowed. Men were forbidden to sleep with their wives and any children conceived during the hundred days were considered illegitimate—probably the only illegitimate children in China. All banquets, theatricals, and other amusements were banned. The men could not shave their heads or wear silk clothes. The temple bells were tolled almost continuously. As long as the coffin of the Emperor remained in the Hall of Observation of Virtue sacrifices were made on all important holidays, birthday anniversaries, and other special days. The burial of an emperor was a serious event in old China.

As soon as the two Empresses had been appointed coregents they instructed Prince Kung to build a suitable mausoleum for the late Emperor. The Ch'ing emperors had two burying grounds, the Hsi Ling, Western Tombs, and the Tung Ling, Eastern Tombs; the latter were about ninety miles east of Peking. It was originally intended that the two grounds were to be used alternately, but this was not followed. The Tung Ling was chosen as the site for Hsien Feng's tomb, as he had always shown a preference for the Eastern Tombs. These tombs of the Ch'ing emperors are not to be confused with the better-known tombs of the Ming emperors, twenty miles north of Peking.

It took four years and an expenditure of ten million *taels* to build the tomb for Emperor Hsien Feng. While it is not the greatest of the Ch'ing tombs, it compares favorably both in design and size with most of them.

The entrance to the imperial tomb area starts with a large marble *p'ai lou* (arch) opening on the Triumphal Way, a wide-paved avenue nearly a mile in length. The avenue is protected by eighteen pairs of huge stone animals and giant men facing one another across the avenue. These figures consist of two pairs each of lions, camels, elephants, unicorns, horses, military men, scholars, officials, and eunuchs. Unfortunately this imposing array of sentinels was not effective in protecting the two fine rows of trees that originally lined the avenue. Since the days of the republic these trees have been stolen and sold, as has about everything else that could be moved from the tombs.

At the end of the Triumphal Way one passes through the Dragon and Phoenix Gate, a great red gate that opens into the Spirit Road, with more p'ai lous, marble bridges, and sacrificial furnaces. This avenue leads directly to the Great Courtyard, on each side of which are porticoes and small retiring and rest rooms. The north side of the courtyard is formed by the Spirit Hall, the principal building of the group. These spirit halls or sacrificial halls of the tombs are of enormous size. That of the Ming Emperor Yung Lo exceeds in size and magnificence even the Great Throne Room in the Forbidden City, making it the largest room in China and probably one of the largest in the world.

The sacrificial hall of the tomb of Hsien Feng stands on a raised marble terrace on which are bronze cranes, turtles, and deer. The most striking feature of the interior of the hall are the columns of Chinese laurel—the largest tree in China—that support the roof. They are fully three feet in diameter and are lacquered in gold and vermilion. The ceiling is of equally striking color, and with the gold-embroidered curtains give the room a mass of color instead of the more somber appearance one would expect. The principal furniture is the triple throne of yellow lacquer standing immediately behind the sacrificial table which holds the usual large candles, incense holders, and central urn.

Another door behind the throne leads to the courtyard of the tomb itself. This courtyard was planted with trees of many varieties. In it is the Soul Tower containing the tablet on which is inscribed all the various titles of Hsien Feng. This courtyard also contains another large sacrificial table, the furnaces for the burnt offerings and other sacrificial vessels.

The tomb itself, or the part that is visible above ground,

is a simple conical-shaped mound of earth called the City of Precious Relics. This mound is similar in every way except in size to the grave of the humblest Chinese. But while the mound of the tomb of the average Chinese is only a few yards in circumference, the mound of the emperors often exceeds more than a third of a mile in circumference. Beneath this huge mound of earth is the great dome-shaped vault containing the coffin; in the case of Hsien Feng, two coffins. Great care was taken in the construction of this vault to make it waterproof and strong against grave robbers. It is built of large blocks of granite. In design the front façade, at least, is much like the temples above ground, except that everything is in carved marble instead of wood, as with the temples. The coffin rests on a jeweled bed and is surrounded with treasures of jewels, precious stones, and the best work of the craftsmen of China. The door of the burial vault is one large slab of marble twelve inches thick, hinged with pin and pivot, as all Chinese doors are hung. This door opens inward. The floor of the vault slopes slightly upward and in it is cut a groove. A granite ball about three feet in diameter is fitted into this groove so that as the marble door is closed the granite ball follows the closing door. When the door is fully closed the ball drops for about a half of its diameter into a round slot, making it impossible ever again to open the door from the outside.

In 1917 I was requested to open several tombs for the imperial princes who wished to put several coffins together for better protection. Unable to force the door, we broke in through the ceiling of the vault and then opened the door.

In the fall of 1865 Prince Kung announced to the coregents that the tomb for Emperor Hsien Feng was completed. The Board of Astrologers was consulted and a propitious day for the funeral was selected. After another series of sacrificial ceremonies, including the Ghosts Festival, the boy Emperor, the two Empresses, and all imperial concubines met at the Kuan Teh Tien behind Prospect Hill to perform the final sacrificial ceremony before the coffin—the Farewell to the Soul.

On the following morning, the ninth day of the Ninth Moon, at the Hour of the Tiger (4 A.M.), the funeral procession started for the Tung Ling. The imperial coffin of catalpa wood, richly lacquered, was placed on a huge catafalque, draped in yellow embroidery, and borne on the shoulders of one hundred and twenty-eight men. In the procession were the princes, dukes, and ministers—all carried in richly draped chairs. There were in addition nearly eight thousand men carrying lanterns and various ceremonial articles, hundreds of Chinese, Tibetan, and Mongol priests, thousands of Imperial Household Guards, and the usual bands "to render sweet music."

When the procession arrived at the Ta Ch'iao or Great Bridge outside the Tung Chih Men, the cortege was joined by another funeral procession escorting the coffin containing the remains of Sakota, the first wife of Hsien Feng, who had died one month before he came to the throne. Her coffin had rested in a temple in the Ching An village for fourteen years until she could be buried with her emperor husband. It is not unusual for the Chinese to keep the bodies of members of the family for many years waiting for a proper time for burial. Although Tz'u Hsi's father had died more than ten years before his body was still unburied. The coffins containing the bodies are usually kept in a temple, but they are sometimes kept in the homes of the family, or placed in an enclosure of masonry in the fields.

The two funeral processions merged and continued in the direction of the Tung Ling, ninety miles to the east. The Emperor, the two Empresses, and the other members of the imperial family left the procession and returned to Peking soon after it joined the procession of Sakota. In four days the procession reached the Temple of Bounteous Blessings near the Eastern Tombs. Here the two coffins were brought into the temple and placed side by side, and for the next ten days, sometimes three times a day, a continuous series of sacrificial ceremonies were performed before them.

Emperor T'ung Chih, the two regents, the concubines, and the other members of the imperial family arrived at the Lung Fu Ssu (temple) on the tenth day and took up residence in the adjoining palace. Sacrifices were then made at the Temple of Heaven, the Temple of the Earth, the Temple of the Imperial Ancestors, in the Spirit Hall, and before the Gods of the Soil and the Grains.

By the twenty-first day of the Ninth Moon all the sacrifices were completed. The coffins were then placed on two dragon funeral carts and were slowly hauled on rails down the incline by the Emperor, the imperial princes, and a few of the grand ministers to their final resting place in the great domed chamber beneath the huge artificial mound of earth. The two coffins were laid on the marble jeweled bed and surrounded by a wealth of jewels, precious stones, silks, the usual pearl necklaces, and many wooden and paper figures of men, women and animals. The books and seals of the Emperor and Empress were placed to the right and left of the jeweled bed. After a short ceremony by the intimate members of the family they retired. Then the great marble doors of the tomb were slowly closed and sealed on the earthly remains of the seventh Emperor of the Ch'ing Dynasty and his consort.

An incident occurred—or was engineered at the burial services of Hsien Feng—that brought considerable loss of face to Empress Tz'u Hsi. Although Prince Kung had regained all his former positions and honors and had accepted Empress Tz'u Hsi as the leader of the dynasty and the government, his pride still smarted. His half brother, Prince Tseung, also thought he had a grievance or two against Tz'u Hsi. Together they persuaded the gentle and usually retiring Empress Tz'u An to demand her proper place at the final funeral ceremonies as the first wife of the Emperor. Just as the members of the imperial family were about to take their places for this important public ceremony, Empress Tz'u An, following Prince Kung's instructions, quietly informed Empress Tz'u Hsi that at the sacrificial ceremony she, as wife and Empress, would take her proper place in the center. The place at her right would be reserved for the spirit of Sakota, the first Empress, and as Tz'u Hsi was only a concubine at the time of Hsien Feng's death, she would take the place of a number-one concubine on the left, but slightly to the rear. All this was in strict accordance with the Household Rules.

The conspirators thought that by announcing this at the last moment Empress Tz'u Hsi would be so astonished she would have no time to object and would perforce take the humbler position allotted to her. But they underestimated the quick wit of Tz'u Hsi. She was neither embarrassed nor taken aback. After delivering a short lecture on etiquette and the Household Rules—which she knew better than anyone else in the imperial family, and could quote either for or against any proposition to suit her convenience—she calmly assumed the number-one position and put the Empress Tz'u An on her left. Then she indicated that the ceremony might proceed.

But while Tz'u Hsi was outwardly calm, the fact that her position had been so publicly challenged, and possibly the knowledge that she had been in the wrong, made her furious. She took the first opportunity to inform Empress Tz'u An and the imperial princes of her feelings. She emphasized this by refusing to return with them to Peking. She announced that she would take up her residence in the temple and there remain until the princes and Tz'u An should return and apologize to her for this affront. The cortege returned to Peking, leaving her at the tomb.

The question naturally arises: Why did not Prince Kung leave Tz'u Hsi at Tung Ling? Here, it would seem, was the opportunity he had been waiting for. The fact that a fortnight after the funeral he and the other princes with Tz'u An made the four-day journey to Tung Ling to offer the obdurate Tz'u Hsi their apologies seems additional evidence that Prince Kung recognized that only she could save China and the Ch'ing Dynasty.

As for Tz'u Hsi, how sure she was of her power and of her destiny to so tempt Fate!

5

While Empress Tz'u Hsi was giving most of her time to the building up of her government, choosing her officials from every part of China, she did not entirely neglect the social side of her court. Though she gladly left all the domestic duties, even the education of her son, to Empress Tz'u An, she believed her ladies in waiting were too important politically to be selected or trained by anyone but herself.

Her ladies in waiting were divided into two classes: the Nei Kung Feng, Inner Ladies in Waiting, and the Wai Kung Feng, Outside Ladies in Waiting. The Inner Ladies in Waiting were princesses and other young girls adopted by the Empress, and the imperial concubines. Each Inner Lady in Waiting had her own independent establishment within the Forbidden City. The older concubines had large palaces and were treated with great respect by Empress Tz'u Hsi. The younger concubines, and later even the Empress of the young Emperor, were treated more or less as servants and were in constant attendance on Tz'u Hsi.

Outer Ladies in Waiting were a large group who lived in their own homes outside the Forbidden City but who could stay within the palace for any length of time they desired. This group was important, as they were the wives and daughters of imperial princes and other leading Manchu families. They included the sister of Tz'u Hsi, who married Prince Ch'un, and the wives of prominent government officials. In addition to these ladies there were also attached to the household the two court artists, Madame Wang Cho and Madame Miao Chiahuei, who were given palaces. The sister of Eunuch Li was accepted as a member of this group; as "Big Girl Li" was neither the daughter of a prince nor of an official, her status was described as "woman guest." She must have been quite an unusual woman, as she was a favorite of Tz'u Hsi. Her presence, together with that of the two artists who were also of lowly birth, showed a democratic spirit one would hardly expect to find in an imperial palace. All these ladies, among the most beautiful and gifted in the country, made a gay and not always too dignified court.

The days of the first regency were far too full of national and international problems to give Tz'u Hsi sufficient time for many social or personal affairs. The gay court came later, during the second and third regencies, and after the death of Tz'u An, who had spent her time and influence to prevent all extravagant entertainment or anything else that called for spending much money. Tz'u An was also the watchdog of the morals of all the ladies of the court, including her coregent. Tz'u Hsi had apparently no interest in the morals of her court or any hesitancy in spending money, as is shown by her extravagances during the latter part of her life. The only record there is of her apparently taking any great interest in morals was the occasion when she went to considerable trouble to catch her favorite, Jung Lu, in the bed of one of the young women of the court, an almost unpardonable crime. Most Chinese writers claim that it was jealousy and not a high regard for morals that prompted Tz'u Hsi to take such drastic action on that occasion.

As careful as Tz'u Hsi was in choosing her officials and the ladies of her court, she was equally careful in the selection of her servants. She early learned the value of loyal eunuchs, as they had saved her life on more than one occasion. In addition to An Te-hai and Li Lien-ying, both of whom played important parts in the Su Shun conspiracy, she had six other eunuchs of equal loyalty and almost equal usefulness. First came old Wang Ch'ang-yu, to whom she was much attached. She always remembered how carefully he had watched over her in the early days to keep her out of trouble. Next to old Wang came Yang Chih-hei, who was the jester of the group. Whenever Eunuch Yang found his mistress crying, he would tell her funny stories and sing comic songs until he had her laughing again. The next most capable, if not the most popular of the eunuchs, was Ts'ui Yu-kuei, the chief spy among them. He was to be of particular value to Tz'u Hsi in later years, during the attempted revolt of Emperor Kuang Hsu. It was Ts'ui Yu-kuei who threw the beautiful Pearl Concubine down the well, as will be told later. The other eunuchs, Su Teh-lu, Chang Teh-lu, and Chang Teh-hai, though devoted to Tz'u Hsi, do not play any special part that is of interest to this story.

During the busy time of the first regency, Tz'u Hsi spent most of her recreation hours, especially during the winter months, attending theatricals or playing cards, chess, or dominoes with her ladies in waiting. Sometimes she would have as many as four or five tables of players at one time, as she always liked many people around her. The Chinese have a number of domino and card games in addition to mah-jongg and chess. All look simple, like so many things in China. It is only after one has played them five or six years that one learns how difficult they are. Chinese chess is sufficiently like the game played in the West to suggest a common origin, but to make the game more difficult the Chinese put a river down the center of the board which certain heavy pieces may not cross.

With the Empress of China playing, one might think that these games would be quiet and dignified, but they were not. The noise and the players' laughter at times could be heard across two or more courtyards. The games were played on a low, short-legged table and most of the players sat, oriental style, on the floor. Tz'u Hsi usually sat on a low three-legged stool, only a few inches in height, which she jokingly called her portable throne. She always claimed the north seat as the one which brought her luck. Her favorite game was "Opening the Treasury Box." "Pushing the Nine Card" she also liked.

Tz'u Hsi was clever at most things, but, like many other brilliant people, she was not sharp at cards. However, she never had a fair chance playing against the beautiful ladies of her court, as they made it a practice to rook her, stacking the cards against her. The eunuchs, who closely studied her moods, soon noticed that it did not matter how much money Tz'u Hsi lost in the course of an afternoon of play so long as she won the last few games. This left her in fine spirits and she would brag about it all the rest of the day. So the eunuchs, who shuffled the cards or dominoes, and the ladies worked it out so that Tz'u Hsi would lose the first fifteen hands but win the last five. They always played twenty hands. This satisfied everybody. The young girls who could not afford to lose the high stakes they played for won the most money, and the Empress won the last five games, which was what she wanted.

The Empress was always very good-natured at these games and stood on no ceremony with her ladies. They argued, quarreled a little, and joked much while playing. The eunuchs usually announced that the tables were ready for playing with the warning: "Venerable Ancestor, please beware, the Young Flowers say they are going to win today." To which Tz'u Hsi would usually answer: "The gods haven't decided yet who will win." Apparently she never discovered that while the gods had not decided who was to win the eunuchs had.

Even as a young Empress, Tz'u Hsi liked to be addressed as "Venerable Ancestor," as it implied that she was to be the foundress of a new line of emperors.

From childhood she was interested in the display of fireworks. Her mother's family had been manufacturers of fireworks during the reign of Tao Kuang, and they had always sent the Hwei Cheng family a huge box of fireworks and firecrackers for the New Year celebration. As a girl she saw the famous fireworks of Soochow and Canton. One of the first things she did when she became Empress was to order the governors of the southern provinces to send experts in the manufacture of fireworks to Peking, where she had the imperial household organize a special department and a factory which supplied the court with the finest fireworks available.

It is quite possible that even the indomitable Tz'u Hsi would not have had the courage to face her many enemies and difficulties during the first regency if she had known all the odds against her at that time.

During that period of uncertainty Empress Tz'u An, to whom Tz'u Hsi gave every reason to be jealous, held in her possession a decree in the handwriting of the late Emperor and sealed with the Great Seal. If Tz'u An had but shown it at any of the meetings of the Council it would have ended the career and life of Tz'u Hsi that very hour. That she did not use this decree against her coregent showed another admirable trait of this remarkable woman.

Like Prince Kung, she was often accused of lack of courage when she did not oppose Tz'u Hsi, but there is every reason to believe that she was the first to recognize and admire the unusual ability of her coregent. Like Prince Kung, she realized that Tz'u Hsi's ability was necessary to China at that time. That she possessed courage was proven on several occasions when she did oppose Tz'u Hsi, in several cases successfully. Of the two women Tz'u An was much the finer character. She was gentle, kindly, and generous, especially to the other women in the court. In all the criticisms of the imperial court of that time one finds none of Tz'u An. This is unusual in a country such as China, where everybody and everything are at times widely criticized.

As first wife of the late Emperor, Tz'u An outranked Tz'u Hsi officially as regent and as the legal mother of Tz'u Hsi's son, yet she gracefully remained in the background and let Tz'u Hsi direct the government and nearly everything else connected with the court. Tz'u An's personal sympathies were probably with the Aisin Gioro clan and the imperial princes in their opposition to Tz'u Hsi's efforts to make the Yehonala the ruling clan of China. It is unlikely that a young woman such as Tz'u An should not, at times, have been jealous of Tz'u Hsi, and sometimes resented the latter's arrogance. Yet, as far as is known, Tz'u An never attempted to use the decree which she had in her possession.

This decree was given Tz'u An by the Emperor over her protest. It seems that at the very time Tz'u Hsi stood highest with Emperor Hsien Feng and when she was of the greatest assistance to him, the Emperor recognized not only her unusual ability but also detected in her an almost uncontrollable ambition. He began to worry about the possible effect the ambition of such a talented woman would have on the court during a possibly long illness of his or after his death, when she would have the influential position of Empress Dowager. While the Emperor always admired Tz'u Hsi and spent more time with her than with Tz'u An, he believed that his first wife was much more reliable.

During the first weeks in Jehol the Emperor discussed his doubts openly with Tz'u An. The first wife tried to defend the concubine, but the Emperor, knowing that he did not have long to live, insisted on giving Tz'u An a decree which he bade her keep a secret from everybody. She was to use it only if she decided in her own mind that Tz'u Hsi's ambition or wild schemes endangered the empire or the dynasty. The Emperor wrote out the decree in his own hand and personally sealed it with the Great Seal, making it not only legal but an absolute command on the officials of China. It ordered the impeachment and death of Tz'u Hsi at any time Tz'u An thought these measures might be for the good of the state and should present the decree to the Council. As the command of an Emperor who was dead, this order could not be set aside or ignored by any Chinese official, regardless of his personal opinion or desires.

What a sword hung over the unsuspecting head of Tz'u Hsi! How fortunate for her that this powerful weapon was in the hands of a gentle, modest woman! Probably the very possession of such a weapon did much to make the latter more tolerant and lenient toward her coregent. Oddly, when the decree was finally brought to light, as will be told later, it destroyed the unoffending Tz'u An and not Tz'u Hsi.

The gods of China move in a mysterious way.

though three measures [illegible] the [illegible] of the [illegible]
[illegible] the [illegible] of the com-
mand of [illegible] Emperor who [illegible]
[illegible] ordained by any [illegible]
personal opinion [illegible]

[illegible] a word [illegible] half
[illegible] for that [illegible]
[illegible] the very [illegible]
[illegible] the [illegible]
[illegible] Council [illegible]
was finally brought [illegible] will be told later [illegible]
the [illegible] Table II.
[illegible] more [illegible]

5. MOTHER AND SON

The two coregents spent considerable time together after their return from the funeral of Hsien Feng, discussing events since the death of their mutual husband. True, there had been unpleasantness between them during the funeral ceremony, but they remained on friendly terms. Each knew she needed the other.

The year 1865 was drawing to a close. They had now been coregents through four eventful years. These had been particularly strenuous for Tz'u Hsi, as most of the difficulties and worries of the government had fallen on her shoulders. But there had also been triumphs enough to make both Empresses join with the Chinese people in believing that the new year—the Year of the Sheep—would be lucky for them and for all China. The country had every reason to look forward to the new year. It was at peace for the first time in fifteen years. The Tai Ping rebellion had been finally put down by Tseng Kuo-fan and his brother Tseng Kuo-ch'uan. Soothsayers prophesied good crops and general prosperity.

Tz'u Hsi was particularly pleased. She had reorganized the government and had gradually replaced all who opposed her. Some of the most famous scholars in China were now connected in some capacity with the government. There were also a number of the old conservatives to balance the younger men such as Prince Kung, Prince Ch'un, and their friends. Jung Lu was head of the troops in Peking and her friend Tseng Kuo-fan was within call with his armies if she should ever require his help.

But one little cloud was forming on Tz'u Hsi's horizon. She

had noticed that in her altercation with Tz'u An at the funeral of Hsien Feng her son, the boy Emperor, had taken the side of Tz'u An instead of that of his mother. It was hardly noticeable at the time, but later Tz'u Hsi realized its significance. She began to see that in giving all her attention to affairs of government she had neglected her duties as a mother. She was soon to learn that while she could control the imperial princes, old and young officials, and nearly every other man she ever met, she could not control her own son.

At twelve years of age T'ung Chih was showing the first signs of insubordination. The misunderstandings between mother and son were to cause the greatest unhappiness of Tz'u Hsi's life. They were the cause of the most damaging stories and rumors that were to be told against her.

It is evident that even at a young age Emperor T'ung Chih was beginning to rebel both against his mother and against the life he was forced to live shut within the red walls of the Forbidden City. He was like a prisoner—not an ordinary prisoner but a prisoner in solitary confinement. He had few, if any, boys or girls of his own age to play with. He had to get up early to take his seat on what he considered a stupid throne to receive stupid old men. He was compelled to study ten hours a day the subjects laid down for him by a group of conservative elderly professors who were violently opposed to everything modern or from the Western countries. T'ung Chih wanted to play and live like a boy. He wanted to know about the interesting foreign countries and to know more of some of the things his cousin, Prince Pu Chun, told him about foreigners on the few occasions the young Emperor was allowed to see him. Pu Chun and his brothers were free to go about Peking as they chose. T'ung Chih's four tutors—Li Hung-tsao, Ch'i Chun-tsao, Weng T'ung-ho, and Wo Jen—were all great scholars, among the greatest in China. They were such great scholars that they knew practically nothing about a young boy. They looked on T'ung Chih as an obstinate lad who would not study as he should but always wanted to learn to shoot, hunt, fish, and play. Even Wo Jen, the Mongol, who because of his record as a warrior should have had an influence over the boy, lost his opportunity by insisting that the Emperor learn the classics to enable him to differentiate between a good and a bad official. This made little sense to poor T'ung Chih, who, though an Emperor, wanted most to be a boy.

It is hard to understand how a woman as intelligent as Tz'u Hsi could have understood her own son so little. But it is not hard to understand how a boy living under such unnatural conditions, neglected by his mother, should several years later fall an easy prey to scheming eunuchs and officials who, in an effort to win their way into his good graces, encouraged him to steal out of the palace at every opportunity to visit gambling places, houses of prostitution, and other low forms of entertainment. Emperor T'ung Chih is probably the first of the Ch'ing emperors of whom it can be proven that he made a habit of frequenting such resorts. He visited them often, particularly after the final break with his mother when, in her jealousy, she even interfered in his normal relations with his wife, whom Tz'u Hsi disliked very much.

When Tz'u Hsi first noticed the preference her young son showed for Tz'u An she thought it was nothing serious. She told herself that all she had to do was to show him a little more attention and a son's natural affection for his mother would soon put their relationship on a satisfactory basis. During the New Year's celebration she arranged several parties for him to which she invited a number of young princes and princesses. The entertainments included theatricals and even gambling games. Gambling was then considered a proper amusement for Manchu children.

The young Emperor proved to be a keen gambler. As the New Year's celebrations gave him two weeks of complete freedom from studies and early rising to attend court functions, he enjoyed this very much, and his relations with his mother improved. He seemed to be longing for affection.

Unfortunately, after the holidays, Tz'u Hsi returned to her strenuous official life, and the burdens of state apparently took her entire time. Every few months she would recall her duties as a mother and for several days would be very attentive to her son. But this proved not enough. They gradually drifted further apart. Tz'u Hsi had the same disinclination toward domestic affairs as her son had toward matters of state. She never learned that being a mother was a daily all-time job, not something that could be taken up only occasionally.

Tz'u Hsi had some excuse for her neglect of domestic affairs. The life of a ruler of China was a strenuous occupation, so strenuous that many of the emperors tried to avoid it by resigning. The emperor started his official day at three o'clock in the morning and almost every hour of every day of his life was regulated by the Household Rules of the Ch'ing Dynasty. These rules fixed the hours of his audiences and other official acts, and they were followed without the slightest variation by every Ch'ing ruler from Shun Chih to the end of the reign of Kuang Hsu and the death of Empress Tz'u Hsi.

The following extracts taken from the *Authentic Records and Regulations of the Imperial Household* give some idea of the daily life of an emperor of China. The Emperor was awakened by an official at the first half of the Hour of the Tiger, three o'clock in the morning. He dressed and completed his early "small morning breakfast" by the second Hour of the Tiger, four o'clock, at which time he had to be at the Ch'ien Ch'ing Kung, Palace of Heavenly Purity, to receive, read over, and study the confidential memorials which were handed him in sealed envelopes. These secret memorials were often complaints against some of his officials. Occasionally they included complaints against the Emperor himself. On completion of this work he received his ministers of the Privy Council until the second half of the Hour of the Rabbit (between four and five o'clock in the morning). After this, the Emperor went to the Hall for the Nurture of the Mind, to give interviews to various military and civilian officials.

In the first half of the Hour of the Dragon, seven o'clock in the morning, he had his "large breakfast." He was then given the calling cards of officials and others who were to be presented to him that day. These were small boards of bamboo, painted white and green, with the name of the officials in black characters. After breakfast the Emperor mounted his throne in one of the smaller throne rooms, of which there were several in the Forbidden City, and met the officials and visitors whose calling cards had been accepted. These meetings were strictly private, only the Emperor and the visitor being present. They were confidential meetings between the Emperor and his people. These interviews often went on until twelve o'clock, when the Emperor would retire and partake of what the Chinese, for some unknown reason, called the "evening meal."

At the second Hour of the Ram (one o'clock) the Emperor received his ministers of the Council in the Yang Hsien Tien. What was left of the afternoon after this conference the Emperor was permitted to use for recreation. During the winter months he usually spent this time in discussing history, poetry, literature, painting, or calligraphy, or played chess and other games with the professors of the Han Lin Academy and other friends–not very amusing to a young boy. In the summer months he would go boating or fishing, or putter about among his flowers and goldfish.

This recreation period lasted until the second Hour of the Cock, six o'clock in the afternoon, when the Emperor had his night meal. He usually took this meal with his empress or one of his concubines. At the second half of the Hour of the Dog (between seven and eight in the evening) he often had to receive and study the memorials from the provinces. However, he could do this while the Empress or concubine was still present. At the second half of the Hour of the Pig (ten o'clock in the evening) the Emperor usually had what was called a "night pastry," or light supper, and then retired to bed. No rules were laid down for the next five hours, which seem to have been all the time officially allotted to the Emperor for rest.

The hours for the early-morning meetings were not changed winter or summer. Peking is a northern city on about the latitude of Chicago and with about the same temperature. In winter, when the days are short, the four-o'clock meeting with the Privy Council took place at least three and a half hours before daybreak. There were no electric lights in the palaces and very little heat. The buildings that the Chinese called "warm" had only the floors heated. Foreigners would call them cold, very cold rooms, yet these were the rooms where the Emperor, the Empresses, and all the ministers met every morning during the long northern winters.

These Household Regulations were not rules that were

often broken; they were strictly adhered to. Let the Emperor be late for any one of his appointments and the Board of Censors would deluge him with rebukes, as is shown by thousands of such documents still in the files in the Hall of Records and open to anyone who cares to read them. The only break in the above schedule came on holidays set aside for worship at one of the many national altars or temples, when often a stricter schedule was substituted. The only hours the Emperor could call his own were those between two-thirty in the afternoon until after his night meal—not very appropriate hours for the licentious parties outside Chien Men on which many foreign writers have stated the Emperor spent so much time and money. One would also imagine that the four-o'clock meeting before dawn with his privy councilors must have discouraged any late hours.

The rules were changed slightly from time to time for the benefit of the two coregents. They were then allowed to breakfast at five o'clock. Immediately after breakfast they studied the memorials and met the ministers of the Privy Council. No meetings were omitted or any duties curtailed for the regents. The program was simply retarded two hours, and unless they could shorten some of the meetings these two hours were taken from their afternoon recreation period. But they had one advantage: during the meeting with their ministers they always sat unseen, "behind the curtain." Often during the summer months, when Tz'u Hsi was enjoying her early boat parties on the lakes, only Tz'u An was present at the meetings. They probably did this more often than the records show. It was against regulations but, as we know, Tz'u Hsi often made her own rules. While he was still a young boy the Emperor was required to attend the seven-o'clock meeting. He occupied the throne while the two regents were behind the curtain where they could see but not be seen by the ministers.

The salaries paid the Ch'ing emperors, the two coregents, and every other official—from the Grand Councilor to the lowest concubine—were regulated by the Household Rules. The amount received is clearly shown in the imperial palace payroll records still preserved in the Archives of the National Palace Museum. These show that all the Ch'ing emperors and their officials, up to the latter years of Empress Tz'u Hsi, were rather poorly paid. Certainly every emperor constantly complained about his poverty. None of the Ch'ing emperors were ever accused of graft or other financial irregularities and none apparently died with any considerable fortune. In several reigns some high officials, or more often favorite eunuchs, did acquire huge fortunes, but in most cases this wealth was confiscated at their death. Very often it was the cause of their death.

These palace pay-roll records show that the allowances and salaries were divided into three categories: the Nien Yin, or Yearly Silver Payment; the Yueh Yin, or Monthly Silver Payment; and the Chieh Yin, or Festival Silver Payment. When Tz'u Hsi entered the palace as a low-ranking imperial concubine she received one hundred ounces of silver as Yearly Silver, twenty ounces of silver and one million copper cash monthly as Monthly Silver, and four ounces of gold and four ounces of silver as Festival Silver. This would roughly amount to a little less than four hundred United States dollars a year. In addition to this allowance she received yearly thirty-eight pieces of silk and satin of various kinds, thread, cotton, and other dress materials, also a "rouge, powder, and perfume" allotment, and other incidentals. The rules also specified the kind and quantities of household supplies and the servants to be supplied her.

As the rank of the concubine increased, so did her allowance. When Tz'u Hsi was promoted to the rank of Yi Kuei Fei in the seventh year of Hsien Feng, her Yearly Silver was increased to six hundred ounces, her Monthly Silver to fifty ounces and four million copper cash, and her Festival Silver to eight ounces of gold and eight ounces of silver. This would amount to a total of about one thousand United States dollars a year. All her other allowances were increased proportionately. All the girls received numerous presents from the Emperor and Empress.

When the two Empresses became coregents they each received a basic salary of about $50,000 a year, and in addition many kinds of special allowances, which almost doubled that amount. For each additional honorific title awarded them the salary was increased by double the amount of the Yearly Silver payments, or about $50,000. At Tz'u An's death she had received ten such honorific titles, bringing her yearly allowance to an additional $500,000. Tz'u Hsi lived long enough to enable her to add sixteen such titles or characters to her name (with the additional annual salary of $800,000). On her sixtieth birthday her complete title was Empress, Motherly, Auspicious, Orthodox, Heaven Blessed, Prosperous, All Nourishing, Brightly Manifest, Calm, Sedate, Perfect, Long Lived, Respectful, Reverend, Worshipful, Illustrious, and Exalted. All these sound even more imposing and pleasing to the ear in Chinese, and all are beautifully carved on the tablet at her tomb.

At that time her legitimate income from all sources was almost ten million United States dollars a year—more than double the amount any emperor of China had ever received. From this she had to keep up an enormous establishment which was larger than that any emperor had ever kept. Unfortunately, in her later years her extravagant life, her expensive building projects, particularly the building of her tomb and the new Summer Palace, made her expenses go far beyond even that huge sum. She resorted to numerous means of securing additional funds. Many of these could only be described as plain graft. She accepted presents from persons seeking office. She had her eunuch, Li Lien-ying, act for her in running the Four Big Heng Shops, a company made up of the four guilds of goldsmiths. These were given the monopoly of buying and selling gold and acted as the Empress's agents in receiving payment for appointments to official positions and other forms of graft. This company also collected the Hatamen octroi and other customs duties. The friends of Tz'u Hsi claim that in not one of these transactions did either she or Eunuch Li Lien-ying profit personally. Every dollar so collected was spent on projects for China. They point out that neither the Empress nor the eunuch left fortunes to their families. The relatives of both are without funds today. Much of this may be true, but this part of Tz'u Hsi's life will always remain a blot on her otherwise illustrious control of the Chinese Government.

In looking over the allowances received by Empress Tz'u Hsi from the government, one item keeps constantly reappearing. She always drew ten times as much from the "Rouge and Perfume Account" as Empress Tz'u An or any other women connected with the court. Manchu sources state without the slightest hesitation that Tz'u Hsi used more perfume than other women because she had the "odor of the fox." This was apparently looked upon more as a distinction than a detriment to her charm, as it marked her a true member of the Yehonala clan. While this odor does not seem to have been noticeable to other Manchus, it was apparent to everyone else, including the Chinese.

We have no accurate information on just how strongly the Empress smelled of a fox. No foreigners apparently ever reported this criticism of Tz'u Hsi. If they noticed it they may have thought it another kind of perfume. But the Chinese have a much more sensitive sense of smell than the average foreigner. They also seem to be able to eliminate any odor they do not wish to notice. In traveling in the interior of China I have on a number of occasions had Chinese draw my attention, or attempt to draw my attention, to the sweet fragrance of flowers far beyond the effective range of my nose, especially as we were often at the time standing near one of those open, bad-smelling urinals that one sees so often on the principal streets of their interior cities but the odor of which the Chinese do not seem to object or notice.

This odor of the fox did not in any way reflect on the bathing habits of the good lady. From many reports we learn that she was very fond of her baths. In fact, her doctors on a number of occasions recommended that she bathe less often or at least for shorter periods of time, one of the many recommendations to which she paid not the slightest attention.

Except that they were much more elaborately decorated with glazed tile and terra cotta, the baths in the Forbidden and Imperial cities differed little from the numerous baths in the Tatar and Chinese cities. Some of these latter baths are very old and have always been popular with the Chinese.

The Chinese public bath usually consists of a steam room, where they stay an incredibly long time. After the steam the bather often sits in hot water and drinks hot tea for hours. Few foreigners can stand these baths for any great length of time. Much local gossip and stories are discussed in the baths.

The white-tiled vaulted bath of the Empress Tz'u Hsi still bears her name and was used for years after her death as the strong room for the exhibition of her famous string of pearls and other pieces of state-owned jewels.

By way of digression, let me say that the writer once discussed this peculiarity of Tz'u Hsi at a dinner given by an old Mongol prince formerly of the imperial court. Several members of the imperial clans were present, including relatives of Tz'u Hsi. When the question of the odors of Orientals had been thoroughly discussed from every angle, the Mongol prince turned to me and remarked: "You foreign men have a very bad smell." He made the statement without the slightest intention to be offensive; he was the host and would not under any circumstances have made any statement he thought might have been even slightly impolite. He was simply stating a fact which he assumed everybody knew and which was no more personal than if he had said my skin was white. When I acknowledged that I knew we had an odor that was objectionable to Orientals, he softened his first remark a little by adding: "But your women smell worse." At the time I was sitting between two of his rather plump wives and the room was small and warm. I might have made some pertinent comparisons, but I learned long ago that arguing with other nationals as to which country has the most beautiful women—or, in this case, the strongest-smelling women—seldom tends to improve international relations, which was the object of this particular dinner.

But like all discussions in China, the question of the white man's odor continued for hours. I was amazed to find that all oriental races, and even the blacks of Africa, are apparently agreed that of all the peoples they have ever met white men have the worst odor. Cases were mentioned where young Chinese girls employed by foreign legations as maids to white women of high standing had actually fainted at the early-morning smell of their mistresses. The same story was told of a Hottentot girl similarly employed in Africa in attendance on an Englishwoman of note. I hope these Chinese stories are an exaggeration, but the tellers were unanimous in their opinion that white men smell like grease or bad butter, which to the Oriental is one of the most objectionable of all odors.

The discussion was finally brought to an end by the arrival of the *pièce de résistance* of the meal. I looked down and found in front of me a nice, large, boiled sheep's eye. The eyes of the entire party were turned in my direction. Now a sheep's eye—or at least that particular sheep's eye—is much larger than you would expect a self-respecting sheep to have. To make things worse, the seeing part of the eye was looking directly at me and it had the saddest expression I have ever seen. I knew that if I hesitated even for one moment the good relations I was anxious to cultivate might suffer. My host had given me, the guest, what was considered the finest portion of the meal. I had to eat it with every appearance of relish, which I did. Let me say that I have been a gourmet of well-cooked sheep's eyes ever since.

A domestic tragedy which was to develop into a scandal and embarrassment to Tz'u Hsi took place within the palace. Two serving maids were found murdered. Under ordinary circumstances this would have presented no problem, but these maids were from Tz'u Hsi's own household. They were very young and she had been much attached to them. Even then she would have kept the matter quiet and handled it in her own effective way, but, unfortunately, the news came to the ears of Prince Tun, who saw that it was given publicity. He circulated rumors that the girls were killed because they knew too much about the private life of Tz'u Hsi. Although Prince Tun was a son of Tao Kuang and the brother of Hsien Feng, he heartily disliked Tz'u Hsi and never overlooked an opportunity to make accusations against her.

It is difficult to understand why there were so many serving maids in the palace, as the eunuchs did all the menial work—even acting as hairdressers to the women, as dressmakers, chambermaids, and cooks. Yet there were several hundred maids in the Forbidden City. They had so little to do that they were often called "palace ornaments," which would have been appropriate if only some of them had been ornamental. These girls were drafted for a number of years' service from the families of the Pao Yi, a humble section of the Three Banners of the imperial household, just as the young men of those Banners were drafted for military service. Tz'u Hsi greatly increased the number of maids in the palace as she always liked to have many people around her. She developed an organization of serving maids who were as loyal and almost as helpful to her as spies as her eunuchs were.

But while the maids had no menial work to do, they had two services to perform that probably were unique to China. Whenever the Emperor visited one of his concubines or spent the night with his Empress, one or two of these maids remained in the room with them the entire time to do any little services required. This custom was usual in most higher-class households and was followed in the houses of prostitution—to the embarrassment of many a Western visitor to those resorts.

Another use of these maids was in the Emperor's experimental marriages. There is a detailed account of the trial marriage of Emperor T'ung Chih before his actual marriage to his Empress Aluteh. Why the old women of the palace should have thought that T'ung Chih required an experimental marriage to perfect his ability in that particular duty of a husband is hard to understand. If half the stories of his early visits to prostitutes outside Chien Men are true, he should have been a good teacher himself on that subject to anyone in the Forbidden City. A *shih hun* (to taste marriage) was probably one of the few duties imposed on him which he carried out without making any serious objections.

For the purpose, one or two serving maids would be selected for their gracefulness and cleverness. The shih hun experiments were carried out under the personal direction of the guarding nurse. Curiously, while the Chinese insist on absolute privacy for their religious life, they do not insist on the same privacy for their marital or sex life. The ordinary course for this branch of instruction usually was completed in three periods of experiment and study, but a note at the bottom of the instructions mentioned that if the Emperor should still prove to be unskilled the experiments were to continue until he became expert in technique. Often an emperor became much attached to these experimental wives. If this happened, they were promoted to the positions of imperial concubines, and if they were fortunate enough to give the Emperor a son, they rose even higher in the court. But in any case their position was much improved. They were allowed permanently to wear the "Shang T'ou"—a certain kingfisher-feather ornament —in their hair, which marked them as Ku Niangs and relieved them of doing work of any kind.

It was the hope of every serving maid to become a Ku Niang. But of the many hundreds who entered the palace only a few ever rose above the position of what was practically bondage. They entered the palace at twelve years of age, and at twenty-two were rewarded by the emperor with a sum of money and sent back to their homes. Here they had difficulty in finding husbands, as their experience in the palace with its luxury and easy life poorly prepared them for the duties of wife to a farmer. They also lacked the training as wives which their sisters, who had stayed at home, had received from their mothers. Some of these serving girls returned to their homes in a sorry plight, having been ruined by the palace eunuchs. Although by the operation performed in China the sexual organs of the eunuchs as well as the sex glands had been removed, this did not always remove the sexual desires or the depression resulting from non-fulfillment of this natural instinct. This condition made sexual perverts of some eunuchs, who sometimes attacked the serving maids, whose standing was much lower than theirs. Being unable to satisfy their natural desires, the eunuchs sometimes bit or scratched the girls, attacked them with whips or knives, leaving great scars on their bodies. The girls so marked were usually unable to secure husbands of any kind when they returned to their village, as everyone knew the origin of the scars.

It was soon proved that two sex-crazed eunuchs were responsible for the murder of Tz'u Hsi's young maids. Because of the scandal caused by the maids' deaths Tz'u Hsi received many memorials from the Censors both in Peking and in the provinces, complaining of the power and influence of the eunuchs. These memorials pointed out that by the divine wisdom of the founders of the Ch'ing Dynasty eunuchs had been forbidden to meddle in affairs of state, that she was breaking the Household Rules of the dynasty in allowing eunuchs to influence the Emperor and the government—meaning Tz'u Hsi. They petitioned that all eunuchs who had assumed such powers be banished and that only trustworthy attendants be allowed to serve the Emperor and the coregents.

Tz'u Hsi answered these petitions in detail, agreeing with almost every statement they contained and promising an investigation to remedy the evil. The Chinese called her replies "fine writing on waste paper." The word "waste" is a polite translation of the actual word.

Tz'u Hsi was too dependent on her principal eunuchs to attempt to punish them severely, but she scolded her chief eunuch for allowing such conditions to exist and had the whole system thoroughly investigated. A few eunuchs were executed; others were sent back to their homes. The latter was a severe punishment as, banished from the palace, nothing was left for them except to become beggars. Tz'u Hsi later started a school for the serving maids where they were taught many subjects, including religion and some of the useful occupations they would have learned at home if they had not entered the palace.

2

In 1869 T'ung Chih was seventeen years old, according to the Chinese count. In another year he would be of age. A wife had to be found for him. Both Empresses apparently had the right to choose his wife—Tz'u An as the senior Empress and his legal mother, and Tz'u Hsi as maternal mother. T'ung Chih, the one most concerned, apparently had no rights of any kind in the matter.

Following the usual custom, the governors of the provinces and certain high officials in Peking were asked to submit names of suitable girls. The Board of Selection finally narrowed the list down to seven, called "the Elegant Girls to be submitted to the coregents for the grand selection."

From the beginning Tz'u Hsi favored Aluteh, the daughter of Ch'ung Yi, a professor in the Han Lin Academy and one of the greatest scholars in China. Ch'ung Yi was one of Tz'u Hsi's most loyal supporters and was entirely dominated by her. His daughter Aluteh was also a scholar. She was particularly efficient in making both the finest and the largest Chinese characters—probably the most admired and difficult form of calligraphy in China. In this she was equally efficient with either hand. Aluteh was only fifteen at the time she was recommended as an Elegant Girl.

Tz'u An favored a girl known as Hsun Pin who, although the niece of Aluteh, was three years her senior. Hsun Pin already was a concubine of T'ung Chih and well liked by him. Unfortunately, at the final examination Hsun Pin made the mistake of kowtowing to Tz'u Hsi before she kowtowed to the senior regent, Tz'u An. Because of this serious breach of etiquette Tz'u An conceived a dislike of her and favored Aluteh. Tz'u Hsi, however, thought the concubine had shown great insight in recognizing the greater Empress and promptly dropped Aluteh in favor of Hsun Pin. As neither Empress would again alter her decision they did a most unusual thing: they decided to allow the Emperor to make the final choice. As he was greatly attached to Tz'u An and as Aluteh was very beautiful, he chose her. He expressed his choice by handing Aluteh the gold "Ju Yi," the good-luck scepter which takes the place of an engagement ring in China.

Tz'u Hsi was furious. She regarded it a great humiliation that she, the real mother, had not been able to command the respect of her son in the selection of his wife. To save face she ordered that Hsun Pin should be created a Huei Fei, Imperial Concubine of the First Class, on the same day that Aluteh was created Empress. It was not until later, at the reception for the Grand Wedding, that she realized that in raising Hsun Pin to a Huei Fei she had broken another of the Household Rules by making Hsun Pin, the aunt, inferior in rank to Aluteh, the niece. This was particularly embarrassing to her, as she always prided herself on her perfect knowledge of the Household Rules.

It is generally believed that Tz'u Hsi had a deeper reason

for changing from her first choice of Aluteh than just the mistake in etiquette made by Hsun Pin. Either she had been informed by her spies, or her own instinct warned her, when she saw Aluteh on the day of selection, that this young girl was not the meek, easily controlled maiden she had thought her to be, and that it would be a grave mistake and a distinct menace to her position to have Aluteh as Empress to T'ung Chih. Tz'u Hsi wanted a wife for her son whom she could control as easily as she hoped to be able to control him when he assumed the throne six months later. Aluteh, or Empress Hsiao Cheh as she was called after her marriage, turned out to be one of those brilliant, independent, and courageous women who have appeared so frequently in the history of the Ch'ing Dynasty. She very much resembled Tz'u Hsi at the same age.

The new Empress was a daughter of the Aluteh clan from which she took her name. This was a fierce Mongolian clan that had come to China with the Manchus as one of the Banners. Its members had intermarried so often with the imperial clan that they were considered almost imperial themselves. While Aluteh's father was a great scholar, all the other male members of the family were soldiers. The manner of the death of her four uncles gives a good idea of the courage and determination of her family. When the foreign troops entered Peking in 1900, the four brothers of her father gathered together their families, including the women and children, numbering twenty-seven persons, and had a large pit dug in their own courtyard. All the members of the families seated themselves in the pit, according to rank, clothed in their best garments. They then ordered their servants to bury them alive. They did this rather than submit to the Western soldiers. T'ung Chih's Empress came of a strong and courageous race.

After the selection of Aluteh, the two Empresses issued a joint decree which included the following statement: "It has now been eleven years since Emperor T'ung Chih assumed the Dragon Throne at a very small age and he is now permitted to select a virtuous girl for his consort and to accord him domestic assistance. He has chosen Aluteh, daughter of Ch'ung Yi, to be his Empress and the Imperial Grand Wedding shall be held in the Ninth Moon of the eleventh year of T'ung Chih."

The two Empresses had previously instructed the Board of Rites and the Board of the Imperial Household to order the Imperial Astronomical Observatory to pick out an auspicious day for the marriage, to consult the great Ch'ing Dynasty Ceremonial Records, and to prepare all the various rites and ceremonies for the Imperial Grand Wedding. These included the Delivery of the Betrothal Gifts, the Grand Verification, the Sacrificial Reports, the Preparation and Awarding of the Gold Book of Investiture, the Escorting of the Empress, the Reception Audience, the Congratulatory Reception, and the two Grand Banquets. These ceremonies lasted from the twenty-ninth day of the Tenth Moon of the ninth year of T'ung Chih until the day of the wedding itself, on the third day of the Second Moon of T'ung Chih's reign—nearly eighteen months.

The first ceremony was the Delivery of the Betrothal Gifts. The gifts the Emperor sent to the bride's parents seem strange in view of the fact that Ch'ung Yi was a scholar, but they were in accordance with ancient tradition among the Manchus. The bride's father received among other things twenty horses with proper saddles and harness, ten pack animals carrying twenty complete sets of armor and helmets with a suitable supply of bows and arrows, two hundred ounces of gold, ten thousand ounces of silver, one large jar of pure gold and one of pure silver, one thousand bolts of satin, two hundred bolts of cotton, and numerous other gifts.

A picturesque procession was formed to carry these and the other gifts to the home of the bride. The procession took the longest possible route from the palace to its destination in order to give the people of Peking another pageant, a spectacle they greatly enjoyed and which they expected from their Emperor. Another elaborate procession was provided at the Verification Ceremony when additional presents were sent to the bride's family with the "Imperial Message" which evidently bound the bargain between the Emperor and the bride's family. Two days before the marriage another group of high officials visited the Hall for the Worship of the Ancestors to notify all the Emperor's ancestors and to secure their approval of the forthcoming marriage. A short ceremony with many kowtows was held before each of the tablets of the Ch'ing rulers. As none of the defunct emperors signified any objection, the marriage was considered approved.

On the day before the wedding the ceremony of the investiture of the Gold Book took place. The book was a volume with leaves of pure gold on which were written the family histories of both bride and groom and the details of the wedding. Accompanying this Gold Book was the Gold Seal and the Imperial Message. On the wedding day the Gold Book was taken to the Hall of Ceremony under the protection of the Imperial Guard and many high officials. When this was completed the minister from the Imperial Astronomical Observatory announced that the auspicious hour had come.

A petition was sent to the Emperor asking him to dress in his ceremonial robe and proceed to the Hall of Supreme Harmony. The great bell and the great drum were struck as he entered the hall, accompanied by "Beautiful Music of the Harmonious and Golden Mean." He inspected the Gold Book and examined the Gold Seal. When these were found to be correct an official in a loud voice read the decree from Empress Tz'u An and Empress Tz'u Hsi, ordering the marriage. The Emperor returned to his palace, changed his clothes, and proceeded to the Palace of Maternal Tranquility to pay his respects to the two Empresses and to report to them that all the required ceremonies were now completed according to the Household Rules of the Dynasty and that the Empress-elect was being escorted to the palace. When the two Empresses had signified their approval the Emperor retired to his palace.

The ceremony of escorting the Empress to the palace was the occasion for the most elaborate pageant of the whole wedding. When the delegates bearing the "Staff of the Imperial Message" arrived at the bride's home they again, for about the tenth time, read the decree of the two Empresses and announced again that the day of the wedding had arrived. The wives of all the princes and other high officials who had been appointed to accompany the Empress-elect then asked her please to enter the Phoenix Sedan. This she did, and as she passed through the courtyard her parents and all her relatives bade her farewell, kneeling and kowtowing. She now passed out of their lives and became a member of the imperial family.

To the music of the ever-present band the procession was led by the Imperial Delegation carrying the Gold Book and the Gold Seal in a huge Phoenix Kiosk, which also bore the bride's wedding clothes. After this came the Phoenix Sedan, a detachment of the imperial bodyguard, many sedan chairs carrying court ladies, and hundreds of eunuchs, both mounted and on foot, all elaborately gowned and equipped. The official delegates followed with more of the imperial bodyguard and another band.

Once within the Forbidden City the Empress-elect was taken to the Ch'ien Ch'ing Palace, where the wives of the princes and another group of beautiful ladies of the court assisted her out of her chair. Here she put on the Dragon and Phoenix Robe of Harmony, the Dragon Hood, and was given the Happiness Scepters. After the Phoenix Sedan had been perfumed with Tibetan incense the bride re-entered it and was borne to the palace of the Emperor. He was waiting for her, dressed in Dragon Robes of his rank. Attended by princes and princesses of the imperial blood, the Emperor's closest relatives, the bridal pair proceeded to the nuptial bedroom in the K'ung Ning Palace.

Here the Emperor personally removed the Empress's bridal hood and they seated themselves on the Dragon and Phoenix Bridal Bed. They were served two different kinds of food, symbolic of fertility and long life. The bride and groom toasted each other, each drinking from the other's cup. The court ladies rearranged the hair of the bride from the style of a virgin to that of a married woman. They were then left to consummate the marriage.

While they might be married they were far from through with the marriage ceremonies. The following morning before they could eat a meal they had to proceed to the Altar of Heaven, more than three miles distant, to pay their respects and announce their marriage to Heaven. Later they made the same announcement to their ancestors at the Altar of Earth.

They visited and kowtowed to the God of Married Happiness and to the Kitchen God, after which they returned to the Emperor's palace and had their first meal together, the Feast of the Union. After this meal they visited the Hall of Longevity of the imperial family at Prospect Hill to offer Tibetan incense before the portraits of the Emperor's ancestors and the shrine of his father. They informed Hsien Feng of their marriage and asked his guidance and protection. They were going to need it even sooner than they anticipated.

Within the week after the wedding Aluteh, now known as Empress Hsiao Cheh, clashed with her imperial and imperious mother-in-law. She did not hesitate to stand up to the great Tz'u Hsi and tell her that her name had been accepted by the ancestors and that she was now Empress of China. She reminded Tz'u Hsi that she had entered the palace through the great front gates and not as Tz'u Hsi had done, through the back door as a number-six concubine. Hsiao Cheh was but sixteen years old when she defied the powerful Tz'u Hsi—something that few princes or officials would have dared to do. As the young Empress did this before an audience of several hundred people, it was a bitter experience that Tz'u Hsi was not liable either to forget or forgive. Hsiao Cheh won that argument, but she never won another. She had, as the Chinese call it, "plucked the tiger's whiskers." This was later to cost the beautiful young Empress her life—a rather high price to pay for one hour of triumph.

From that moment Tz'u Hsi did everything she could to cause discord between T'ung Chih and his Empress. She seems to have developed a dislike for her son that was almost as violent as her hatred of Hsiao Cheh. There was a sinister motive for her acts; she was fully aware that if an heir were born of the strong-willed Hsiao Cheh, the latter would from that day become Empress Mother and Tz'u Hsi's rival. In the event of the Emperor's death, which everyone knew was a possibility, as he was always in frail health, Hsiao Cheh would be Empress Dowager and Tz'u Hsi would be relegated to a position not much above that of an imperial concubine, with neither power nor prestige. This she was determined to prevent at any cost.

In the meantime the Emperor had become very fond of his new wife. He was pleased to find that not only was she the most beautiful woman in his court, but her education exceeded even his own. She knew the *Four Books*, the *Five Classics*, as well as the poetry of the T'ang Dynasty, and was familiar with the essays of the old classic writers. He also admired her skill in calligraphy and in other branches of painting. The eunuchs who had been ordered to spy on the young pair reported to Tz'u Hsi that the Emperor spent only one or two days a month with the imperial concubines; all the other nights he slept with the new Empress.

Tz'u Hsi summoned Hsiao Cheh to her palace and lectured her severely. She accused her of using improper coquetry to induce the Emperor to sleep with her so often, thus ruining his health. There is no record of Hsiao Cheh's retorts to her mother-in-law, but they were probably what any high-spirited, quick-tempered daughter-in-law might say at such a time on such a subject. Whatever it was, Tz'u Hsi never repeated the lecture but she did summon the Emperor and forbade him to visit his Empress so often. She commanded him to pay more attention to Huei Fei.

To insure T'ung Chih's obedience to this command Tz'u Hsi stationed a number of eunuchs at the entrance of Hsiao Cheh's palace. She instructed them that whenever the Emperor should attempt to enter they were to fall on their knees and beg him not to do so, as his mother, Empress Tz'u Hsi, had given orders for him to visit Concubine Huei Fei. The Emperor knew that his mother's eunuchs were capable of forcibly preventing him from entering the Empress's palace. Though enraged at this interference with his private life he dared not disobey his "Sacred Mother," regardless of how he felt about his wife.

From then on he lived alone in the Yang Hsin Tien Palace. He would not visit the Empress, Huei Fei, nor any of his other concubines. He was young and living an unnatural life for a newly married man. Under such conditions he fell easy victim to unscrupulous and vicious eunuchs and minor officials, who hoped to gain his good will by helping him find pleasures elsewhere. At first he indulged in indecent intimacies with young eunuchs. Soon he began to spend his leisure hours in visits to houses of ill fame in the Chinese city. At first he always returned to the palace in the evenings, but later he began to stay out all night and was often late for his four-o'clock morning meetings with his ministers.

This led to investigations. Prince Kung soon started looking for his nephew in winehouses, theaters, and places of prostitution. Usually he found him in the House of the Fourth Matron, a famous house of ill fame in the Chinese city. This was reported to Tz'u Hsi, but she refused to do anything to correct or punish the young man. This led to the accusation that Tz'u Hsi was actually assisting, through her eunuchs, in ruining her son's health. It was openly said that she now hated both the Emperor and the Empress and considered them a menace to the dynasty and the country, that she was willing to risk her son's life, if necessary, rather than permit him to produce an heir to the throne.

Although she always claimed that she did this and her later acts to save the Ch'ing Dynasty, it is clear that her appetite for power had increased to such abnormal proportions that it ruled her as absolutely as she attempted to rule her son and her daughter-in-law.

At this time, when Tz'u Hsi's relations with her coregent, her son and his Empress, and with some of the imperial princes were at the lowest ebb, the Emperor came of age. Arrangements had to be made for the coregents to hand the control of the government over to him. Usually such an event called for many ceremonies, pageants, parades, and celebrations. But it was generally felt both within the court and throughout the country that the people had little reason to celebrate the coming of age and the assumption of power of Emperor T'ung Chih. Tales of his debauchery had been widely spread by Tz'u Hsi's eunuchs and others.

Prince Kung, as the Emperor's nearest male relative and the senior imperial prince, petitioned the coregents that no large national celebrations be held because of the unsettled condition of the country.

The ending of the first regency and the transfer of power to the Emperor were effected by the simple issuance of three decrees. The first, issued by the coregents, praised themselves for exercising great prudence in the interests of the Emperor and empire. In the second the coregents turned over the power to the Emperor "with the hope that Emperor T'ung Chih will continue to reverence the great God and gain the love of his ancestors," and calling on all imperial princes and ministers to show their loyalty to the empire and assist the Emperor. The third decree was issued by the Emperor. In it he stated that "thanks to the graciousness of the two Empress coregents we have been able to devote our time to acquiring knowledge in a composed and unperturbed manner."

Everybody knew that the fine sentiments expressed in the three decrees were again nothing but "fine writing on waste paper."

With the termination of the regency, Tz'u Hsi became Empress Dowager and was freed from the slightly restraining influence of Tz'u An. But on the same day Emperor T'ung Chih issued the first decree in his own name. In this decree he stated: "Having been entrusted with the ponderous mission by the late Emperor Hsien Feng, our father, we ascended the throne when only six years of age. On account of our small age we entrusted the management of state affairs to Empress Tz'u An and Empress Tz'u Hsi, who have been kindly acting for us as coregents for eleven years. . . ."

The Emperor knew that as Empress Dowager his mother would have even more strict and effective control over his actions than she had as coregent. He knew that he would be allowed to carry out only the formalities of government. He would have to attend all the early meetings of the ministers and follow the ordered daily activities of an emperor of the Ch'ing Dynasty. He would have to carry out the sacrificial and other formal ceremonies. In addition he would be required to continue with his studies. But his mother would continue to treat him as a little boy. She would make all the decisions and all the government appointments for him. She would probably also persist in regulating his private life. Under these circumstances, being an emperor did not offer much to a lad of eighteen with even as little ambition as he had.

The Emperor, encouraged by his courageous Hsiao Cheh, made a desperate attempt to break away from the control of his mother. He refused to submit state papers and other documents to Tz'u Hsi for her inspection and approval. She countered by ordering all state papers sent directly to her. He remembered how much Tz'u Hsi used to like the old Yuan Ming Yuan, which was destroyed by the British and French armies. He started to rebuild these buildings in the hope she might move out there again. But Tz'u Hsi had other plans and ordered Prince Kung to have all work at the Yuan Ming Yuan stopped. For this the Emperor dismissed Prince Kung and his brother from all their positions and honors, as Tz'u Hsi herself had done a few years before. Tz'u Hsi commanded him to restore both princes to their former positions and then ordered him to add a few more honors just to show who was running things. This the Emperor was forced to do.

His mother again began to interfere in T'ung Chih's relations with his wife by once more stationing her eunuchs at the door of Hsiao Cheh's palace. The young Emperor and Empress had now learned that Tz'u Hsi was not to be opposed and that only by complete submission to her will could they live within the Forbidden City in any degree of peace or comfort.

To his mother T'ung Chih continued to be as undutiful and as disrespectful as he dared, and he returned to his dissolute ways.

3

The complete domination of the young Emperor by his mother undoubtedly created in him a sense of inferiority that was largely responsible for his dislike of all meetings with his ministers. He felt that they looked on him as a weak child. This made him bitter. But deep down in his mind there was still a strong reverence and respect for his official position of

Emperor. The tradition of a long line of strong ancestors was too deep-rooted to be easily broken.

While T'ung Chih detested most of his duties there was one that he treated with respect and reverence. This was officiating at the great sacrificial ceremonies. At these he was the Son of Heaven and leader of his people. No one could dictate to him or interfere with him in any way, not even Tz'u Hsi.

Fortunately for T'ung Chih's self-esteem there were many such ceremonies, including the various sacrifices at the Temple and Altar of Heaven, the Altar of Earth, the Imperial Ancestors, and the many special patrons of the dynasty. There were also numerous other small sacrifices which the Emperor had to make on special occasions, such as drought, flood, famine, war, or other national calamities. While most of T'ung Chih's predecessors had made it a practice to send an imperial prince to officiate in their stead at the medium or small sacrifices, he usually and gladly performed them in person.

The most important sacrifice of the entire year was the Ta Ssu Yuan Ch'iu, Grand Sacrifice of the Altar of Heaven. This was held twice a year.

The more impressive of the two was that of the Winter Solstice. The origin of the Winter Solstice sacrifice in China goes back further than the similar druid celebration in early Britain. It goes back to the very beginning of the Chinese people. In the first Winter Solstice sacrifice of which there is record, before the fourteenth century B.C., the Emperor clearly defined and accepted responsibility for the acts and errors of his people. The occasion was a great drought. When it was suggested that a human sacrifice was necessary to appease the wrath of the gods the Emperor declared: "If a man is demanded as a sacrifice let the Emperor be that man." On that occasion the Emperor fasted, purified himself, and rode in a common cart to a grove where, under the open sky and before his people, he publicly prayed to Heaven, acknowledging his sins, taking upon himself the entire blame for the anger of the gods, and asking that the whole punishment be placed on him and not on the people. There is no record of what punishment Heaven placed on the Emperor, but it is known that on that day he established a custom for all future sacrifices at the Winter Solstice.

No foreigner has ever witnessed an emperor of China officiating at this important ceremony, but there exists a very complete record of the first Sacrifice of the Winter Solstice in which Emperor T'ung Chih officiated after he assumed control of the government. Because the human body, even of an emperor, is considered unclean, T'ung Chih had to observe a three-day abstinence period before he could act in the capacity of high priest at this important ceremony. To purify his body the Emperor had to spend the first two days of this period in the Chai Kung, Abstinence Palace, a lonely place located in the southeastern part of the Forbidden City, far from any other palace. Here he bathed and changed his clothes often, refrained from drinking wine and from the use of tobacco or opium. He could eat no flesh of animal, fowl, fish, or such strong-flavored foods as onions, garlic, leeks, pepper, or other seasonings. He had to refrain from all contact and sexual relations with his Empress and other women, give up all games and other pleasures; nor could he take the life of any living thing.

T'ung Chih spent the third day of the abstinence period in the Palace of Abstinence, which was in the southwest corner of the grounds of the Temple of Heaven. This was an even more desolate and lonely place than the palace of the same name in the Forbidden City. This period was devoted to the purification of his thoughts and desires. During these twenty-four hours the Emperor was supposed to review all the events of his reign during the past year, especially his mistakes, which he wrote down on paper especially prepared for this purpose. This T'ung Chih later read aloud to the people, after which the paper was burned with the sacrifice, the smoke carrying the record of his sins to Heaven. An eyewitness has told the writer that at his first sacrifice, when T'ung Chih repeated the traditional words, "Whatever guilt is found in my people let the punishment rest on me, for I alone am guilty," great tears streamed down his face. He was only eighteen years old at the time. This incident suggested to many who saw it that T'ung Chih might have been a good man and a noble emperor if the circumstances of his early life had been different.

On the completion of the second day of his abstinence period, at the Hour of the Tiger, T'ung Chih left the Chai Kung and proceeded to the Palace of Heavenly Purity. Here, after being properly robed in his Dragon Coat and his famous Nine Dragon hat covered with pearls and precious stones, he entered his ceremonial chair and was carried through the Gate of Supreme Harmony to join the Grand Procession that was to accompany him to the grounds of the Temple of Heaven.

This procession to the Winter Solstice Sacrifice was the greatest pageant of the year in Peking, a city where every funeral, every wedding, and every holiday is made an excuse for a colorful spectacle. As it was midwinter, darkness lay over the city at that hour, but thousands of huge, gay-colored lanterns carried by the marchers lighted the way. Every chair, every animal, and every person was garbed in the brightest hues procurable. There were hundreds of flags of every shape, size, and design. All this revealed by the lanterns' light made a riot of color that could not be equaled in any other country in the world.

The procession was made up of six sections. The first of these was led by four "Tao Hsiang," large elephants draped with bright-colored blankets. These were followed by five more elephants bearing gold-colored harness and huge saddles carrying the "Treasury Vases." After the elephants came numerous officials, some mounted and some in chairs, a number of two-wheeled carriages—one, for some unknown reason, drawn by an elephant, the others by six horses each. Carefully spaced in each section of the procession were hundreds of large colored horn lanterns carried by men in brilliant uniforms.

Immediately following the elephants was a twenty-four-piece band of horns of every size and description. About the middle of the procession marched another band of a hundred musicians playing bass drums, cymbals, gongs, flutes, reed instruments, metal and even wooden horns, hand bells, and instruments unknown to the Western world.

The second section consisted of men carrying the ritual weapons, banners, and flags and accompanied by military officers, civilians, and religious leaders. The third section included men carrying banners and canopies. In the fourth section were men carrying decorative fans—small fans, large fans, fans of every shape and size. The fifth section was formed by horses carrying the domestic furniture and paraphernalia necessary for the comfort of the Emperor and his guests. The sixth and final section was the most colorful of all. It included hundreds of huge embroidery-covered chairs and palanquins bearing the imperial princes, other members of the imperial household, and high officials.

Each was accompanied by a bodyguard carrying not military weapons but incense burners and other means of protection against spiritual enemies. In the center of this group was the Imperial Palanquin of the Emperor, covered with gold cloth and carried on the shoulders of thirty-six chair bearers. This palanquin was more than eleven feet in height and in design resembled a miniature palace. It was attended by a number of eunuchs whose sole duty seemed to be to steady the palanquin. It was accompanied by a bodyguard armed with bows and arrows, leopard-tail spears, and other ancient arms carried only as ceremonial weapons.

On arrival at the Chao Heng Men, the Emperor alighted from his palanquin and walked to the Temple of Heaven. His first duty was to burn incense and kowtow before the spirit tablets of all the past emperors of his dynasty. He then entered the Palace of Abstinence for the remaining twenty-four hours of his three-day fast.

The Temple of Heaven, the Altar of Heaven, and the supporting buildings form a group second only to the buildings and palaces of the Forbidden City in magnificence and dignity. The main building of this group is the Hall of Heaven, a stately structure standing high on a circular platform supported by three terraces, all of the purest white marble, elegantly carved. The building itself is circular in form, the entire structure supported by large wooden columns with cornices highly decorated in the usual Chinese designs. The glory of the building is the great three-terraced roof of beautiful glazed blue tiles. The building, the carved marble balustrades that protect each of the marble terraces, the approach and the supporting buildings are all so beautifully proportioned that the size of this temple is not at first apparent. In design it can be compared only with the Taj Mahal. Many authorities believe that in its simplicity, its beautiful proportions, its pure design and brilliant coloring it excels even that famous building.

The Altar of Heaven stands alone in quiet, magnificent dignity in the center of a huge area bounded by four high red walls. It is built of the purest white marble, round in shape to signify that heaven is round, as the square Altar of Earth signifies that the earth is square. The Altar of Heaven also consists of three terraces, each encompassed by a beautifully carved marble balustrade. The first terrace has a diameter of two hundred and ten feet; the second, one hundred and fifty feet, and the top terrace, which forms the platform for the Ceremony of Sacrifice, has a diameter of ninety feet. This altar and all the other structures of this group were built by Yung Lo, the great Ming emperor who built the earliest of the beautiful buildings in Peking. But the Altar of Heaven was not just an architect's dream created in marble; it was the work of many architects, astronomers, and astrologers. Every detail in its design and almost every stone in the structure is a symbol of some tradition or legend much of the meaning of which was lost centuries ago.

The present altar is a survival of the early primitive altars on which each year at the Winter Solstice the emperors of more than four thousand years ago offered sacrifice and made public acknowledgment of their dependence on the one God—the God of Heaven. Before this God they acknowledged their sins and begged forgiveness and guidance for the coming year.

The Altar of Heaven had become more elaborate and the ceremony of the sacrifice more ostentatious and magnificent with the passing of time. But the original idea proclaimed in China one thousand years before Abraham left Ur of the Chaldees, that there is one God over and above all emperors and all peoples—a God who dwells not in temples built by man but who is everywhere, invisible but seeing and knowing all things—that idea had prevailed and was acknowledged at every celebration of the Winter Solstice. This idea still lives in the minds of the Chinese people and is acknowledged by every Chinese, be he a Buddhist, Confucian, Mohammedan, or whatever else. The Chinese acknowledged that destiny had made the reigning Emperor of China the Son of Heaven and the sole representative of God on earth. This made the Emperor, as the Son of Heaven, responsible for all the sins of the people. He became the "sin bearer of his people." This doctrine was preached in the towns and cities of Palestine seventeen hundred years after it was first proclaimed in China by an early emperor of the Shang Dynasty.

In addition to the annual Winter and Summer Solstices sacrifices were also offered at the Temple of Heaven on the occasion of the enthronement of a new emperor, the birthday or wedding of an emperor, or the birth of an heir. Services were also held when the coffin of an emperor was taken from the city to the imperial tomb, to celebrate the triumphal return of a victorious army, or whenever an emperor decided he had something of importance to report or to petition Heaven for, or merely whenever the Emperor felt that a big parade was advisable.

There are many other altars in Peking in addition to the Altar of Heaven. The principal ones are the Altar of Harvests, in the western section of the Forbidden City, apparently a private altar of the Emperor; the square Altar of Earth; the Temple or Altar of the Moon, where the Harvest Moon Festival is held on the day of the autumn equinox; and the altar in the grounds of the Temple of Agriculture. There are no temples for the worship of the Supreme Being, as the Chinese have always held the belief that no building could hold God, who can be worshiped only under the broad blue canopy of heaven.

During the twenty-four hours the Emperor spent in the Palace of Abstinence, the officials of the Department of Ceremonial Rites made the preparations at the Altar of Heaven. They first erected in the very center of the altar a large tent—the tent of the Great God of the Heavens. This was round and of yellow silk draped with heaven-blue satin. In it was placed the gold Dragon Throne of the Emperor. The throne faced south, and in front of the throne was the sacrificial offerings, consisting of the annual message of the Emperor, fruit, wine, jade, rolls of silk, as well as the best products of the land, all of which were later burned as sacrifice. In front of the tent was exhibited the carcass of a whole ox, the finest young ox that could be obtained. Five square tents of the same color as the main tent were placed on either side of it. Each of these tents had a throne, furniture, and offerings similar to those in the main tent, except that the square tents also held the tablets of former emperors. On each of the two lower terraces were erected six additional square tents of the same color. These contained the spirit tablets of the sun god, the star gods, the moon god, the gods of thunder, rain, wind, and clouds, and various offerings to these deities.

The two bands which had taken part in the procession were stationed below the lowest terrace. In front of the altar were two groups of dancing boys, each consisting of sixty-four. The first group was dressed in ancient uniforms of brilliant colors and each boy carried a shield and battle-ax. Each boy of the second or civilian group carried a long yellow pheasant feather in his left hand and a three-holed flute in his right hand.

At four o'clock in the morning of the third day of abstinence, the Emperor, wearing his sacrificial garments, entered his Jade Palanquin at the Palace of Abstinence and proceeded to the altar, accompanied by his ministers and one hundred and thirty-two of the Imperial Guard carrying large horn lanterns and various incense burners. During this procession to the altar the drum in the drum tower and the bell in the bell tower, though more than six miles away, were each struck forty-nine times, announcing to the city the arrival of the Son of Heaven at the altar. At the south steps to the altar the Emperor alighted from the Jade Palanquin and after a short rest in a yellow draped tent mounted the steps and took his place on the throne in the Great Tent.

This was the signal for both bands to strike up and for the lighting of the great fire under the ox and the other sacrifices. While the ox was being consumed the Emperor walked to the various square tents, knelt, made his obeisances before the many ancestral tablets, and offered appropriate sacrifices of jade, silk, and other articles.

On the Emperor's return to the First Terrace he poured wine into the golden goblets and, kneeling, made libations to the spirits of the past emperors. While the Emperor was still kneeling, the music stopped and he read his annual message to the Supreme Great God of Heaven. This message was then put on the fire of the great sacrifice.

The Emperor rose and walked to the Second Terrace. The music started again and the boys began their dances. The Emperor returned to the First Terrace and repeated the previous ritual before the tablets of the elements. The music and dancing continued until the Emperor entered his palanquin and returned to the Forbidden City.

T'ung Chih derived the greatest satisfaction from the performance of these religious rites. As he was carried back to his palace and his problems, he undoubtedly felt a warm glow of pleasure in the fact that though Tz'u Hsi might rule the empire and him, she could not be the Son of Heaven.

4

The coming of age of Emperor T'ung Chih had brought forward for immediate solution a problem that the Chinese government had been consistently avoiding for half a century. This was the question of the kowtow and whether representatives of foreign governments might be presented to the Emperor without performing this obeisance.

The kowtow—kneeling and touching the ground with the forehead—had been required of all persons received by the Emperor since the beginning of the Chinese Empire. It was considered a sign of homage, submission, and worship. It also had a practical value in protecting the Emperor from possible harm, as a kneeling person was in a rather poor position to attempt assassination.

The foreign representatives stoutly refused to kowtow. They offered to pay the Emperor the same form of respect they gave their own rulers. This did not satisfy the Manchus, who claimed that what was proper or adequate for a petty Western ruler was hardly adequate for the Emperor of China, who was the Son of Heaven and Emperor of all the world—or such parts as were of any importance. As Son of Heaven he was both Emperor and representative of the God of Heaven. As such, one of the Censors suggested, the foreign representatives should pay the same respect to the Son of Heaven as they gave to their representative of Heaven, the Pope. As this would call for kissing the hand or foot of the Emperor, the suggestion was not popular with the foreign envoys.

When the Treaty of 1860 allowed representatives of foreign powers to reside in Peking, the Manchu Government was able to postpone the question of presentation of these ministers to the Emperor as well as the kowtow because at that time the Emperor was a mere child. When the Emperor became of age and assumed the throne on February 23, 1873, the envoys of Russia, Great Britain, the United States, Holland, and Japan immediately requested an audience. The ministers had been sitting in Peking twelve long years waiting to be presented. With the exception of Prince Kung, they had met only a few minor officials of the Foreign Office. Now they made their request a demand and the Manchu Government could find no sufficient reason for any further postponement of the troublesome question.

As was usual, when the government was faced with such problems, memorials poured in on the Emperor from every part of the country. The contents of some of these give an insight into the feelings of the Chinese educated class toward foreigners. One scholar argued that the question of whether the foreign envoys should kowtow to the Emperor was really of too small importance to cause any bother or excitement. He pointed out that the foreign barbarians knew nothing about the meaning of good manners, ceremony, and duty, the relations between a sovereign and his people, between father and son, husband and wife, and an older and younger brother; yet the Chinese were demanding that they conform to the five principles of conduct and duty. He advanced the view that one might as well bring in a number of horses, pigs, and other animals and expect them to follow the proper procedure of good manners toward educated people.

Another Censor mentioned that China had many treaties, containing many thousands of words, with the governments of the barbarians, and that in not one of them were mentioned reverence toward parents, the cultivation of good manners, respect for the eight virtues, or the cardinal principles of the Chinese nation. All that the foreigners were interested in were material profits. For them to kowtow to the Emperor would add no dignity or luster to the Emperor.

Another Censor who had been greatly amused by the skin-tight trousers worn by the British and French army officers declared it was useless to ask them to kowtow, as they could not do so without first removing their trousers, which would not add to the dignity of the occasion.

Notwithstanding all the advice, Tz'u Hsi realized that China could delay no longer on this question. She ended further discussion by ordering Prince Kung to make the necessary arrangements for the Emperor to receive the foreign envoys without the kowtow.

Prince Kung carried out these orders. The Emperor announced he would receive the foreign envoys on Sunday, June 29. But the envoys had several objections to the decree announcing this decision. They objected to the declaration that "the foreign ministers had humbly begged and implored an audience with the Emperor." The decree described the foreign ministers in the same terms used to describe the representatives of states dependent on China. These and a number of other words in the decrees which the envoys considered offensive to their dignity were finally altered to everybody's satisfaction. Then came questions of procedure and the examination of the letters of credence, but, finally, after many conferences, everything was completed for the audience.

The foreign envoys met at six o'clock on Sunday morning at the nearby French cathedral. They wore full-dress uniforms, many of them very elaborate and colorful, heavily loaded with gold braid and decorations. They were to find that the Emperor and his officials were dressed in the plainest dark-colored gowns, with no ornament or decorations of any kind.

Now came a series of delays, probably intentional. The palace chairs finally arrived at the cathedral and the representatives were carried into the grounds of the Imperial City, not into the Forbidden City. They entered by the Fu Hua Men, left their chairs at this gate, and walked to the Shih Ying Palace. Before entering the palace the party was entertained in a large tent that had been erected to serve as a waiting room. Here there was another delay of an hour and a half, waiting for the Emperor to arrive. It was reported he could not be found, as he had not yet returned from one of his late parties outside Ch'ien Men. The feelings and dignity of the Western ministers were ruffled not a little by the announcement that the Japanese representative, being an ambassador and outranking all the other foreign ministers, would be received first and alone.

The ministers entered by the western of the three entrance doors to one of the most elaborate throne rooms in Peking. This was the one already described as used by the Emperor when receiving the princes of Mongolia and other rulers of dependent states. Its use on this occasion was not entirely a coincidence. The Emperor was seated on a rather modest throne, facing south. He must have been a fine-looking young man at that time, as his appearance made a rather good impression on the foreign envoys, even in such annoying circumstances. They approached the throne. The Russian minister, being *doyen* of the corps, read the prepared address. It was translated by Prince Kung. When the address was completed the foreign ministers laid their credentials on a low table before the Emperor. The Emperor spoke a few words in Manchu to Prince Kung, who kowtowed to the Emperor and then informed the ministers that the Emperor accepted their letters of credence and that he expressed a hope that their respective rulers were in good health. The Emperor also expressed the hope that foreign affairs might all be arranged satisfactorily between the ministers and the Chinese Foreign Office. This carried the suggestion that no further audiences with the Emperor would be necessary. This closed the audience, which had lasted not more than fifteen minutes. A rather poor show and reward for the many years of waiting.

But it did one thing: it solved the question of the kowtow. Never again would it even be suggested that any foreign representative kowtow to an emperor of China. It also provided a fine spectacle to the thousands of Chinese who watched the foreign envoys pass by in their gorgeous uniforms. It was well that the ministers understood little Chinese, or their feelings might have been hurt by the frank and humorous comments of the spectators. The American representative's high silk hat and long-tailed black evening coat bore too striking a resemblance to a big black crow to escape the notice and wit of the Chinese street crowds.

5

It is rather difficult to understand the life of Empress Tz'u Hsi during the short period Emperor T'ung Chih was head of the government.

To outward appearance it looked as if she was pleased at being relieved from the duties of state. She spent much of her time with her flowers, her silkworms, dogs, and birds. She was particularly fond of an unusual parrot which, if half the stories told about it are true, was a wonderful linguist. It must also have been a wise old bird, as it repeated at opportune moments the most flattering things about the Empress, who apparently loved flattery whether from man or bird. Tz'u Hsi claimed all the credit for teaching the parrot to talk. She used the common Chinese method of placing the bird before a large mirror, then having a man behind the mirror talk to it. The parrot, seeing its image in the mirror and hearing the voice, thinks that this is another bird doing the talking and tries to outdo it.

Tz'u Hsi was also fond of a very unpleasant, smelly mongrel dog she called Chiang (Ginger), which showed great intuition in detecting and biting any person Tz'u Hsi did not like. It is odd that she preferred this nasty little cur to the many beautiful well-bred Pekingese in her kennels. Ginger is well known in history as biting some of the most prominent Chinese men and women of the time.

Though apparently she had turned domestic, she had not really given up the management of the empire and the palace. Every official knew she was controlling the Emperor and the government even more completely than she had done during the first regency. Through her eunuchs she knew everything that was going on in the Forbidden City. The Emperor was aware of this. While at this time the Emperor dutifully attended every meeting with the ministers and officials until the noon hour, he took no real interest in the government.

Tz'u Hsi's hatred of Empress Hsiao Cheh continued to grow as she realized more fully what an intelligent and strong-willed daughter-in-law she had acquired. She was more determined than ever that Hsiao Cheh should not become the mother of the next emperor. To keep Hsiao Cheh from her husband Tz'u Hsi made her virtually a prisoner, announcing that she was too young to fulfill the intimate part of the marriage contract. The young Emperor, who could at times be as stubborn as his mother, retaliated by again absolutely refusing to live with Huei Fei as his mother directed. Tz'u Hsi had no objection to Concubine Huei Fei becoming the mother of the heir to the throne, as she had found she could easily control her. Supposedly the Emperor had sensed this plan, which explains his repudiation of Huei Fei of whom, formerly, he was very fond.

At first T'ung Chih found some amusement in theatricals, even acting in some of the plays. In this way he came in contact with Wang Er-jung, a eunuch of more than seventy years of age who had a good reputation, as he had attended the Emperor's father when a boy. Prince Kung thought he would be a good, safe man to look after the young Emperor. But, unfortunately, Wang had become an opium addict and this took so much of his time that he turned the young boy over to the care of his assistants. Among them were four handsome young eunuchs who had been trained as "Floral Girls," eunuchs who took the part of girls on the stage. They acted in an effeminate manner, both on and off the stage, especially the younger one, Li Ch'ang-fu, who made a particularly good-looking girl. The Emperor became fond of these four eunuchs and soon had them moved to his palace where, dressed and painted as young girls, they played the part of concubines. The Emperor's character was rapidly deteriorating.

As there were few secrets in the Forbidden City, such a fine piece of gossip soon became known all over Peking. The Emperor's two tutors, who should have been his guardians also, did nothing to check this unsavory affair and were afraid to report it to Tz'u Hsi. The Emperor's uncle, however, did discuss it with her. Tz'u Hsi must have known through her spies what was going on but she did nothing to correct her son. Prince Kung finally expelled the four male concubines from the Forbidden City and was so incensed that he almost had old Eunuch Wang executed. Only the latter's age and early association with the Emperor's father saved his life.

After the closing of this disgraceful chapter in the young Emperor's life, his better instincts seemed temporarily to revive. He listened to his uncle's advice and took no offense at the latter's interference with his habits or life. He spent his spare time during the next few months innocently wandering about the streets of the Tatar city north of Prospect Hill. This was a very interesting section of Peking at that time, especially the small towns or suburbs that had grown up just outside the city gates. As customs duty, or *likin,* was charged on all goods passing through the gates, these little towns were centers of a black market where farm produce could be bought cheaper than in the city. There also sprang up a kind of black market in places of entertainment. Indecent plays were put on and brothels flourished that would not have been allowed within the walls of the Tatar city.

This was particularly true outside the Ch'ien Men. The guards at the city gates soon came to know the young Emperor, but, as many former emperors of the Ch'ing Dynasty had also visited such places, they did not think the visits of T'ung Chih unusual. Except for making the usual report required of them they did nothing about it.

It was not long before T'ung Chih began to hire mule carts to visit places far from the Forbidden City where he was not known. One evening while having a meal in a restaurant outside the Ch'ien Men he heard a very beautiful voice singing some of his favorite songs. The Emperor had inherited exceptional musical ability from his mother. The singer was T'ung Chih's superior in voice and in accompanying himself on the three-stringed violin.

The Emperor called for the singer and found him a very attractive young man named Wang Ch'ing-chi. He was a student who had come up from one of the provinces for the imperial examinations but had failed to pass. He was proficient in classical literature, poetry, music, and painting, and also at chess and other games. Refusing to go back to his native province as a failure, he had been living the attractive life of a vagabond, gaining his livelihood by singing in restaurants.

T'ung Chih took a great liking to this carefree, happy young man. In a short time he had him appointed to a good position in the Han Lin Academy under his father-in-law and brought him into the palace as a tutor. At first Wang had a good influence on the young Emperor, but the vagabond in him soon asserted itself and the two began planning a more adventurous life. As Wang knew well every restaurant, theater, and house of ill fame in or about Peking, he was just the man the Emperor was looking for. They were soon having large parties outside the city gates, and T'ung Chih again visited brothels, this time of a much higher class and more exclusive than he would have been able to find without an experienced guide.

While T'ung Chih had been formerly looked on by the other imperial princes as rather a dull bore and they would have little to do with him, the Emperor had now progressed beyond them in his knowledge of the vicious life of the city. It was not long before Tsai Cheng, eldest son of Prince Kung, was joining T'ung Chih and Wang Ch'ing-chi in their revels outside the Tatar city. When this came to the attention of Prince Kung, he immediately locked up his son. That cured him. Unfortunately, he could not use the same forceful measures with the Emperor, but he did what he could.

Whenever it was reported to him that the Emperor was on one of his parties Prince Kung would get into his mule cart and start hunting for his imperial nephew. His cart soon became a familiar object in parts of the city Prince Kung would never have visited on any other errand. He had little difficulty in finding the Emperor, as the latter was now known to all the police and was usually found in the Yu Shun brothel. Curiously, the Emperor's respect for his older relatives, especially his uncle, was so ingrained in him that he did not openly resent Prince Kung's interference with his private life and always obediently returned with him to the Forbidden

City. Prince Kung had two reasons for watching over the Emperor so carefully. He appears really to have liked the young man, and he was anxious to save the Ch'ing Dynasty and his own family from disgrace if possible.

But as his Sixth Uncle, Prince Kung, was spoiling too many of his pleasures, the Emperor decided to conceal the places he visited in the future. He started visiting disguised brothels in the West City, a section that was patronized only by the imperial princes and sons of the more important families. In this he made a grave mistake. As long as he visited the more professional places that were run for the middle class and were, therefore, supervised by the police, he was comparatively free of the dangers of disease. He caught no disease until be began visiting the supposedly higher-class brothels which were run secretly and were not supervised.

In the West City he came in contact with a woman who was to become well known in Peking. This was Ch'en Ch'i Nai Nai, or Grandmother Ch'en, at that time a woman seventy-four years old, whose house was at Nan Ying Fang. If T'ung Chih had met this woman earlier in his life he might never have contracted the disease which ultimately caused his death.

This woman immediately guessed who her new client was. She was a motherly old woman, knew the story of T'ung Chih's life, and was very sympathetic toward him. She took the Emperor to her home and explained in detail the behind-the-scene secrets of brothels and the danger he, the Emperor, ran in catching a venereal disease which might end his life. She urged the Emperor to stop visiting ordinary brothels. If he would do so she offered to make her home a secret, safe, and comfortable rendezvous for his exclusive use.

It may be unreasonable to believe that she did not have a selfish motive in making such an arrangement. She undoubtedly knew that if she should find a young girl for the Emperor whom he liked, he might later take her into the palace as a concubine. He accepted her offer. The girl selected for him was one of her granddaughters, and she became pregnant. But Grandmother Ch'en's plan came too late: the Emperor had already contracted a venereal disease.

In the twelfth year of the reign of Kuang Hsu, as Prince

Ch'un, one of T'ung Chih's uncles, and Eunuch Li Lien-ying were reviewing the Imperial Chinese Navy at Taku, a twelve-year-old boy was presented to the prince as the son of the late Emperor T'ung Chih. When Prince Ch'un heard the story and examined the boy he believed the report. He wept bitter tears over what, as he said, might have been if Fate had taken just a slightly different turn. He saw that this descendant of the Ch'ings was amply provided for.

The story was soon brought to Peking, and Grandmother Ch'en was much discussed and given an honorable place in the history of Emperor T'ung Chih. The Chinese people are reasonable and broad-minded in such matters.

6

While Emperor T'ung Chih was living alone in the Yang Hsin Tien Hall and spending so much of his time in brothels his Empress, Hsiao Cheh, was having a difficult time. Tz'u Hsi had her constantly watched by her eunuchs and made her wait on her practically as a serving girl. In this Tz'u Hsi was within her legal rights as a mother-in-law.

Tz'u Hsi was very fond of theatricals and, especially as she grew older, in those that were just a trifle off color. At the performance of one of these plays Hsiao Cheh turned her head away and would not look at a particularly obscene incident. This infuriated Tz'u Hsi, who publicly accused the young Empress of attempting to show herself more refined than her mother-in-law. Some of Hsiao Cheh's friends advised her to be more affectionate to Tz'u Hsi, but Hsiao Cheh, proud and haughty, replied she would show the Empress all due respect, as it was her duty to do, but she would not be more friendly with Tz'u Hsi as she, Hsiao Cheh, had been received by heaven, earth, and the ancestors as Empress of China and so would not humiliate herself before Tz'u Hsi. This was reported to Tz'u Hsi and embittered her even more against her daughter-in-law.

It is probable that neither Tz'u Hsi nor Hsiao Cheh realized that the Emperor was suffering from syphilis. When Tz'u Hsi next visited the Emperor she was shocked to see him suffering from open sores. She cursed Hsiao Cheh for not taking better care of the Emperor. Hsiao Cheh reminded her that she herself had put a ban on the Emperor visiting her and that the ban was still being enforced by her eunuchs.

Tz'u Hsi had no answer to this, as she knew it was true. But, as in all emergencies, Tz'u Hsi acted promptly. She summoned the best doctors in Peking and from the provinces. However, they could do little to relieve the Emperor's condition. She called together the ministers and informed them of the Emperor's state of health. The ministers begged her to take over the government again with Tz'u An as coregent until the Emperor recovered. As this was her own plan she graciously acquiesced.

A decree was issued by Tz'u Hsi in the name of the Emperor which included the following explanation: "We have had the good fortune to contract smallpox and during my sickness Empress Tz'u An and Empress Tz'u Hsi have, after much urging, accepted the responsibility of carrying on the affairs of state for me until my recovery. For their abundant kindness and care for our person we are deeply grateful and hereby confer on them additional honors and titles to show in this way our gratitude toward them." Here was more "fine talk on waste paper." The Emperor of China was dying and the second regency, which was to last for twelve years, was inaugurated.

Tz'u Hsi is often accused of having caused the death of her son. Without doubt her neglect and her behavior toward him and his Empress were the most important contributing causes of his contracting the disease, but it is equally evident that when Tz'u Hsi once realized her son was actually dying her mother love asserted itself, and she did everything possible to save him.

The realization that her husband was dying shocked Hsiao Cheh. Defying Tz'u Hsi and all her edicts, she stayed night and day with her Emperor. At one time T'ung Chih was apparently recovering but had a relapse. Great carbuncles broke out on his body, one particularly large one appeared on the back of his neck. They oozed much pus and gave off a very disagreeable odor. Nonetheless, Hsiao Cheh herself bathed him and attended to his needs. Knowing that he was dying and realizing the ability and courage of his Empress, T'ung Chih, like his father before him, secretly wrote a decree in his own handwriting and had the proper seals affixed to make it legal and binding. In this he appointed Hsiao Cheh sole regent after his death.

This was promptly reported to Tz'u Hsi by her eunuchs, who were in constant attendance on the Emperor. Tz'u Hsi suddenly appeared in the room of the dying Emperor and demanded that the decree be handed over to her. The Emperor, who was always a coward in her presence, even when a well man, did not have the courage to refuse. He handed over the decree. Tz'u Hsi read it and burned it in the flame of one of the large candles at the foot of his bed.

While we do not know the exact contents of this decree, the mildest guesses are that it banished Tz'u Hsi to the "Cold Chambers," meaning solitary confinement in some distant palace. Others claim it actually called for her death. Whatever it was, it so infuriated her that she cursed both the young Empress and the Emperor. She slapped Hsiao Cheh, and the huge rings on her hands cut the young Empress's face until it bled profusely. The eunuchs in attendance could not interfere in any way.

Tz'u An, who had just arrived at the death chamber, fainted when she saw Tz'u Hsi's cruel treatment of Hsiao Cheh and the Emperor. But Hsiao Cheh did not faint. She rose from her kneeling position and cursed her mother-in-law in return. She told Tz'u Hsi that if she had been unfaithful to her husband Tz'u Hsi could order her to commit suicide, but that it was not within her rights to strike her. She challenged her to attempt to do it again.

With Tz'u An lying unconscious, his own Empress with severe cuts on her face and covered with blood, and Tz'u Hsi in a fury, all this was far too much for the dying Emperor. He fainted and never recovered consciousness.

T'ung Chih left no heir, and as far as was known had not designated his successor, as he had the right to do. According to the Household Rules of the Ch'ing Dynasty, the procedure to be followed under such conditions was for Empress Hsiao

Cheh to adopt an heir to her husband to succeed him on the Dragon Throne and to carry out the proper sacrifice at his grave and before the ancestral tablets. The Household Rules also clearly stated that such an heir and successor to the throne must be of the generation succeeding that of the late Emperor. No emperor of the same generation could occupy the throne.

There was one imperial prince who fitted all these requirements. He was Prince P'u K'an, son of Prince Tsai Chih, the elder brother of Emperor Hsien Feng. Prince P'u K'an was about twenty-two years old and had a very good reputation.

This arrangement would have made Hsiao Cheh mother of the adopted son and so Empress Dowager of China, relegating Tz'u Hsi to the position of Grand Empress Dowager, a position of great respect but without the slightest power in the government. This Tz'u Hsi was determined should not happen if she had to break every rule of the Ch'ing Dynasty and every law in China to prevent it.

As usual in a state emergency, Tz'u Hsi was the only one who had a definite plan and who could act immediately. She called together all the princes and other members of the imperial family and the ministers, numbering more than a hundred persons. This was a gathering far too large to be controlled by any one prince or unorganized faction.

The two coregents presided at the meeting, though Tz'u Hsi was actually in command. The two thrones were placed in the center of the hall where Tz'u Hsi could watch every person present. When the princes and officials entered they found the two Empresses seated on their thrones with handkerchiefs over their faces, weeping bitterly.

Tz'u An was the first to speak. She said: "The Emperor is dead and has left no son. Who should be brought into the palace and be adopted as a son to the late Emperor? Let everyone state their views, truthfully and without restrictions, as the situation is desperate. Let us all please help."

As the nobles and princes were very familiar with the inner affairs of the court, and as none of them dared offend either of the coregents, they wisely bowed their heads and said nothing.

Tz'u Hsi took advantage of this pause and in a very solemn

tone said: "I desire that Tsai T'ien, the eldest son of Prince Ch'un, be the adopted son and heir to the Emperor Hsien Feng and be the successor to Emperor T'ung Chih." This child was her nephew, the son of her sister Phoenix.

Everyone present knew that this was not in accordance with the Household Rules, but only one man had the courage to say so. He was Huang Yu, an attaché to the Southern Study. He cried out in a loud voice: "I invite the Empress coregents to regard more highly the Rules of the Imperial Ancestors, and to select as an heir a man who has reached his majority in age and who is a wise man in affairs of state."

All the officials present trembled at this courageous statement. They feared Tz'u Hsi would be greatly enraged, but the Empress only asked in a mild voice who the speaker was. In a loud voice Huang Yu answered: "It is your humble minister, Huang Yu."

Again, and quietly, Tz'u Hsi said she did not favor the choice of a grown man as Emperor. She cited the example of Dorgon, who had chosen a child to be the first Ch'ing Emperor. She said she believed that a youthful person should be chosen so that he could be properly educated for the great position he would occupy. Then in a very stern voice she cried: "Prince Ch'un, have you heard?"

Hearing his name called so loudly by the great Empress, poor weak Prince Ch'un was thrown into such a state of embarrassment and confusion that he meekly uttered the single word: "*Cha*," which means "I have heard and I will follow."

When he realized what he had done in agreeing that his son should be heir to Hsien Feng and future Emperor of China, he knew he had made one of the gravest mistakes of his life. Losing his only son would deprive him of a son to carry on the genealogical line of his family. Worse still, being the father of the Emperor in addition to Tz'u Hsi's brother-in-law he had not the slightest doubt would subject him to the persecution and tyranny of Tz'u Hsi for the rest of his life. He had spent most of his time during the previous ten years avoiding Tz'u Hsi, a thing he knew he could not do as father of the Emperor. He made one great effort to escape from his mistake. He rushed over to Tz'u Hsi, fell on the floor and kowtowed, begging her to make another choice. When she refused, Prince Ch'un was so grieved that he fainted. Tz'u Hsi calmly ordered her eunuchs to carry him out of the room. The matter was closed. Tsai T'ien would be the next Emperor of China.

7

What the princes and ministers probably did not know, but were soon to find out, was that Tz'u Hsi had taken every precaution to insure their agreement with her decision. She had had Jung Lu surround the building they were meeting in with his soldiers, the Imperial Guard. All the gates were manned against anyone leaving or entering the hall. Tz'u Hsi left nothing to chance or careless planning.

Tz'u An felt that she had been both ignored and deceived by her coregent, as Tz'u Hsi had failed to propose the name of Prince P'u K'an, whom they had agreed upon before the meeting. She protested to Tz'u Hsi, at first in a mild, subdued voice; later the argument grew heated. It was not long before the two Empresses were shouting at each other at the top of their voices, to the entertainment of all the members of the court, who had retired to an adjoining room. As usual, Tz'u Hsi overruled and outshouted her coregent.

It was unfortunate that the two persons who had the courage to oppose Tz'u Hsi were not present at this conference. Tz'u Hsi took no chances. She had called the meeting at the very hour that Hsiao Cheh, as wife, and Prince Kung, as senior uncle, had to spend praying at the coffin of the late Emperor. There is little doubt that if Hsiao Cheh had been present she would have fought hard to have Prince P'u K'an adopted as her son and the son of the late Emperor. This would have been in strict accordance with the Household Rules of the dynasty. In this she would probably have had the support of Prince Kung. Together they might have been able to influence the other imperial princes who, without a leader, lacked the courage to oppose Tz'u Hsi's scheme, however much they objected to it. But Tz'u Hsi was extremely clever and had made her plans too carefully to let any possible interference occur.

While she kept the princes and others in useless discussions at the meeting, Tz'u Hsi secretly sent Jung Lu with a strong guard and accompanied by a number of the princes whom she knew she could trust to the home of Prince Ch'un to bring his son, Tsai T'ien, the future Emperor, to the Yang Hsin Hall.

Little Tsai T'ien was only four years old at the time. He was a well-brought-up child and care had been taken to see that his hours of sleep were guarded. Every precaution was used to see that he was never disturbed. But he was awakened this night by the arrival of his father, Prince Ch'un, and the large, noisy military guard which was to escort him to the palace.

Tz'u Hsi had kept her plans so secret that she had not told even her sister Phoenix of her intentions. When Phoenix learned that Tz'u Hsi wished to adopt her only son and make him Emperor, she was terribly upset and broke into tears. She had feared her older sister since childhood and particularly after she became Empress. She realized that if Tz'u Hsi adopted little Tsai T'ien as her son it would not only deprive her of her own child but it would give her sister even more power over her than she formerly had. She also realized that if Tz'u Hsi had no love for her own son she would have still less affection for an adopted son. Phoenix knew well the unhappy life T'ung Chih led as Emperor, and she did not want her son to have a similar fate.

At first she absolutely refused to part with the child. She refused to listen to the arguments of the princes, who tried to point out to her the great honor it would be to have her child Emperor of China, and that really it made little difference whether he grew up in the palace or in her own home. They warned her that if she refused she would make an enemy of her all-powerful sister. They argued from the Hour of the Pig (ten o'clock in the evening) until the Hour of the Ox (three o'clock in the morning), and still Phoenix refused. Finally, Jung Lu knelt on the floor before her and Prince Ch'un and said: "My dear Husband of Second Sister (Jung Lu was married to a cousin of Tz'u Hsi), unless you let your son go this night we will all have to die here."

At this plea the unhappy parents finally gave their consent.

It was then found that Tz'u Hsi even had the proper clothes already prepared for little Tsai T'ien. This seems to show that her plans were made long before her own son died. These garments had been brought by Jung Lu. The child was dressed in them and taken back to the Yang Hsin Hall in the Imperial Yellow Chair, preceded by the long and imposing procession.

The night was one of the worst Peking had known for years —very cold, and a great dust cloud covered the city. Peking was having one of its rare but famous yellow—or as the Chinese call them, red—snowstorms, the snow being colored by the yellow dust from the Gobi Desert. Both father and mother looked on this storm as a bad omen for their son. If Prince Ch'un and his wife could have foreseen the future and the unhappiness that was to come to their child they probably would have wished him dead that night rather than Emperor of China.

During all the long hours the imperial delegation had spent at the home of Prince Ch'un, Tz'u Hsi and the assembly waited not very patiently at the Yang Hsin Hall.

When Tz'u Hsi was told that the future Emperor of China had arrived, she ordered him brought in. She found the child asleep. She picked him up and said: "My child, just for your sake I have already worn out my heart." Which shows that she was clever enough to convince even herself that she was personally making a great sacrifice in putting her nephew on the throne.

She carried the child in her arms, entered a warm chair, and was carried to the Ch'ang Ch'un Palace, where shortly after three o'clock in the morning on the thirteenth day of January 1875 Tsai T'ien was proclaimed Emperor of China and the ninth ruler of the Ch'ing Dynasty. He was given the name Kuang Hsu, meaning Glorious Succession, to strengthen the idea that he was a direct descendant of the Ch'ing emperors.

When the death of T'ung Chih and the appointment of Tsai T'ien were announced by a number of decrees the following day, thousands of memorials began to pour in from all parts of China. All condemned the violation of the Household Rules and the appointment of an infant as Emperor when the legal and proper choice was a young man of good character and mature age. Some of the memorials pointed out that the new Emperor was a sickly child and would probably not live to assume control of the government. Most of the memorials were directed against Tz'u Hsi and condemned her actions in the strongest terms. They predicted that great calamities would be the result, both to her and to the empire, for so openly defying the will of Heaven.

To these rebukes Tz'u Hsi said nothing. She rode out the storm without retreating one inch from her position.

Emperor T'ung Chih had died at the age of nineteen, after a reign of thirteen years, though he had been actual ruler for only two years. Of all the Ch'ing emperors, the son of the great Tz'u Hsi must be rated as the weakest, most depraved, and with the least feeling of responsibility. He was the natural result of his environment and his mother's neglect.

Unfortunately, Tz'u Hsi did not realize that the failure of T'ung Chih was her failure. She proceeded to make many of the same mistakes with the new Emperor. Kuang Hsu was of somewhat stouter fiber than his cousin, T'ung Chih, yet Tz'u Hsi was to succeed in making his reign also a failure.

Emperor T'ung Chih entered the Dragon Chariot and ascended to the celestial regions at the Hour of the Cock (six in the afternoon), on the fifth day of the Twelfth Moon of the thirteenth year of his reign. At the Hour of the Dragon (eight o'clock in the morning), on the following day, his body was put in the Sedan of Good Auspices and carried to the Palace of Heavenly Purity, where it lay in state until the minor encoffining and all the ceremonies and sacrifices were completed. After it was permanently encoffined it was carried to the Hall of the Observation of the Virtuous in the northwestern corner of Prospect Hill, where it lay until the funeral four years later.

Tz'u Hsi was very pleased that all her plans had been so successful. Except for the Censors, whom she was never able to control, there were only two important persons, Empress Hsiao Cheh and Yu K'o-tu, who dared express even the slightest opposition to her.

In addition to being a very outspoken young woman, Hsiao Cheh now became a more serious menace. She was with child. If this child were a son he would be the legal heir to the late Emperor T'ung Chih. With Kuang Hsu's title to the throne under violent criticism, this might bring complications that even Tz'u Hsi would find difficult to solve. Tz'u Hsi determined to rid herself of this menace.

But she also knew that her reputation could hardly stand another scandal. Hsiao Cheh would have to be removed in some way that would bring as little suspicion on her as possible. She decided to work through Ch'ung Yi, the father of Hsiao Cheh. She had always been able to handle him without difficulty.

She summoned Ch'ung Yi to her palace. She pointed out to the father how worried she was over his daughter, how she had always tried to protect her, but that she was now threatened with disasters that even the Empress did not know how to cope with. She told Ch'ung Yi that his daughter was with child, and how unfortunate it would be for both his daughter and the child if she should give birth to a son now that the Council had put another Emperor on the throne. It would require the deposition of Emperor Kuang Hsu. Even she, Tz'u Hsi, did not have the power or courage to do such a thing. She also suggested that as T'ung Chih had actually died of a horrible disease the unborn child would also have that disease. This would bring sorrow to the mother and to her entire family. With tears in her eyes she begged Ch'ung Yi to help her find some way to save his daughter from all the unhappiness that loomed ahead of her.

The father understood exactly what Tz'u Hsi meant. He told her he would carefully consider the matter and report to her. Tz'u Hsi then summoned Hsiao Cheh to her presence. She pointed out to Hsiao Cheh the difficult position she was in, and repeated all the things she had told Hsiao Cheh's father. She also reminded her how their great ancestress, Empress Hsiao Lieh, the mother of Dorgon, had gained fame by committing suicide and following her lord and Emperor into the next world when she was faced with somewhat similar difficulties. The young Empress said nothing, but she fully understood the threat implied in Tz'u Hsi's suggestion.

When Ch'ung Yi returned to his home he found a note from his daughter, begging him to come to her immediately, as she urgently needed his help and advice. The family of Ch'ung Yi was a fierce, courageous Mongol family whose sons and daughters never hesitated to kill or commit suicide when such a course seemed to them the right solution of a difficulty. As we mentioned before, the four brothers of Ch'ung Yi, together with their entire families, committed suicide in 1900, rather than surrender to the foreign armies. Ch'ung Yi himself was later to commit suicide. The severe measures he was to suggest to his daughter were to them neither unfatherly nor unusual.

Over the usual ceremonial tea, the father and daughter calmly discussed the situation. Their final unspoken decision was that Hsiao Cheh should commit suicide in order that she and her unborn child could accompany T'ung Chih into the celestial regions. But with so many eunuchs listening Ch'ung Yi could not give his daughter his advice openly. So with his finger he made the Chinese character for death on the inside bottom of the teacup he was using.

Hsiao Cheh read, understood, and gave a sign that she would obey.

Meanwhile Tz'u An was greatly worried over Hsiao Cheh. She visited her at the first opportunity and said: "My child, I am ashamed at myself that I have been a party to the great wrong that has been done you, but have no fear, as long as I live I will protect you."

Hsiao Cheh fell to her knees and thanked Tz'u An, saying: "Happiness has not been destined for me and I have caused you to worry about me. Please leave me and worry no more. I am too unworthy even to serve you." As she rose from the floor, she appeared cheerful.

From this Tz'u An knew as plainly as if she had been told that Hsiao Cheh intended to leave this world. In tears she said: "My child, are even you going to desert me?"

Tz'u An immediately reported to Tz'u Hsi to ask her assistance. She was amazed to find how calmly Tz'u Hsi took the news and she immediately suspected Tz'u Hsi had planned it that way.

Hsiao Cheh refused to take food. Tz'u An sent the best doctors to her, but though they tried to feed her forcibly she continued to refuse to eat. On the seventy-fourth day after the death of T'ung Chih, Hsiao Cheh deliberately committed suicide by what the Chinese called "eating gold." Actually, she swallowed mercury. Her death was publicly announced to be owing to a long illness brought on by grief over the loss of her husband, but this announcement only increased the stories that Tz'u Hsi had poisoned the young Empress.[1]

[1] Years later, when all of us in Peking were shocked by the news that Hsiao Cheh's tomb had been opened and robbed, it was learned that the vandals evidently recalled the report that the Empress had "eaten gold." They dissected the body in a vain effort to recover the gold.

6. THE WEST VERSUS THE EAST

Tz'u Hsi was well pleased that her plans had worked out so successfully. However, much of this satisfaction was lessened when she realized that while she had been so busily engaged with her domestic affairs the problem of China's relations with the foreign powers was gradually becoming more grave. This would later develop into a threat that would not only undo all she believed she had accomplished for the Ch'ing Dynasty, but would threaten her rule and her life.

To understand China's foreign relations we must go back to the very time when Empress Tz'u Hsi assumed control of the government at the beginning of the first regency. At that time—the year 1861—the Tai Ping rebellion was at its height. The Tai Pings were firmly established with Nanking as their capital. It looked very dark for the regency.

But Tz'u Hsi's usual good luck held. On July 1, 1864, Hung Hsiu-ch'uan, supreme leader and founder of the Tai Ping rebellion, committed suicide, and on July 19 the city of Nanking was captured by the imperial troops under General Tseng Kuo-ch'uan. This marked the turning point of the rebellion and of the fortunes of the coregents.

Tz'u Hsi was overjoyed. She was not overmodest in her claim for a considerable share of the credit for the successful termination of the war, owing to her recommendation of General Tseng Kuo-fan as commander in chief of the imperial armies operating against the rebels. This credit she justly deserved.

There has always been considerable speculation as to how Tz'u Hsi came to know and recommend Tseng Kuo-fan to Emperor Hsien Feng. He was a native of Hunan and at the time he received his appointment was little known in Peking. The general opinion is that while her father was military Tao T'ai in Wuhu she heard some of the many stories circulated at that time in the Yangtze Valley about the unusual success Tseng Kuo-fan, a Chinese general, was having in fighting the Tai Ping rebels in his province with local Chinese militia. In this Tseng Kuo-fan was greatly assisted by his younger brother, Tseng Kuo-ch'uan, who raised and commanded the famous Hunan Braves, a Chinese army that deserves most of the credit for the final capture of Nanking.

In these battles Tseng Kuo-ch'uan and the imperial armies first encountered the explosive shells, mines, and other modern artillery which had been furnished the Tai Ping rebels by the Western nations.

When offered the assistance of the Ever Victorious Army of General Charles Gordon, Tseng Kuo-ch'uan refused the offer, stating that he preferred to depend on his Hunan Braves. He was finally able to surround Nanking and capture the city. Foreign writers give much of the credit, some of them all the credit, for the capture of Nanking to General Gordon. The facts are that his army was never a part of either of the two Chinese armies which actually captured the city. However, Gordon's ability as a military engineer was without doubt of great value in the capture of Soochow.

In refusing to allow the Ever Victorious Army to become a part of his force or that of his brother, or to allow it to accompany any Chinese army west of Nanking, General Tseng Kuo-fan stated that while it might be justifiable to allow foreign officers to assist in the defense of Shanghai, or Ningpo, where they were actually defending their own interests, he did not approve using them as mercenaries to fight in other parts of China. He also pointed out that part of the Ever Victorious Army had deserted and was at that time fighting with the Tai Ping rebels, that General Gordon himself had fought against the imperial armies of China only a short time before. He further pointed out that all the modern artillery and most of the other munitions being used against the imperial armies by the Tai Ping rebels had been furnished them by the Western nations who now wanted to assist the imperial armies. Curiously, he also accused the foreigners in the Ever Victorious Army of unnecessary cruelty against prisoners and too much looting of civilians, the same accusations the foreigners made against the Chinese.

Tz'u Hsi gave General Tseng Kuo-fan every honor and every title she could bestow upon him. She tried to have him transferred to Peking but he insisted that his services were required in Nanking for several months after the capture of the city. Two years later he was made governor general of Chihli province and became a member of the Imperial Government.

Although he was only fifty-seven years old when he became governor, Tz'u Hsi always looked on him as an old man—a wise old man—an attitude which he seems to have encouraged. There are records of a number of conversations between them in which he talked to her as a father, pointed out her mistakes, and persuaded her to do things no younger man would have dared even discuss with her. She recognized his exceptional foresight and his ability in selecting and training men for important positions. He brought a number of young men to Tz'u Hsi's attention who later became important in her government. Among these were Li Hung-chang and Pieng Yu-lin.

It was also Tseng Kuo-fan who persuaded Tz'u Hsi to send young Chinese abroad to study in foreign universities. The first group left China in the summer of 1872. Among them were T'ang Shao-i, later to become Premier of China and known to many Americans as a great friend of ex-President Herbert Hoover, Ts'ai T'ing-kan (the only Chinese name many foreigners could remember), Yung Kwai, and others who were to become important officials.

These students had their headquarters in Hartford, Connecticut. They were not so successful as they should have been because Tz'u Hsi followed her usual plan of trying to balance the two extremes and sent Jung Hung, a modernist, and Ch'en Lan-pin, an extreme conservative, to supervise their education in America. Ch'en Lan-pin wanted to keep the students from absorbing too many American customs and Jung Hung favored as many American ideas and customs as possible.

When these young men returned to China they would have been much more influential if they had not become quite so pro-American. The elder Chinese soon got tired of being told by young boys how far behind the times they were.

But one thing these students did do—they introduced an entirely new type of Chinese to the American people. The students were not kept together in America, but were sent to various schools. The result was they became very lonesome and homesick. As Ts'ai T'ing-kan often mentioned in telling of those early days in America, "he believed some of the boys would have actually died of homesickness if it had not been for a number of those big-hearted, kindly old New England boardinghouse keepers, who took them in and mothered them as they would have cared for their own." As long as any of that group of Chinese lived, they never tired of praising those fine women, many of whom were richly rewarded when the Chinese students became able to do so. One or two of these women were invited and even made the trip to China to see their Chinese "boys" again. They were probably the best missionaries of good will America ever sent to the East.

On the death of Tseng Kuo-fan on March 12, 1872, he was succeeded in the confidence of Tz'u Hsi by his pupil, Li Hung-chang.

Li Hung-chang first came into prominence during the Tai Ping rebellion when, like Tseng Kuo-fan, he raised local Chinese military forces to fight the rebels. Li Hung-chang was recommended by Tseng Kuo-fan as his successor to several important positions, particularly as commander of military affairs in Shantung province and later as governor of Chihli province. He held this and other positions, such as Grand Secretary and Grand Tutor of the Emperor, which kept him in Chihli province for the next twenty-five years. As Grand Tutor of the Emperor he came in direct contact with Tz'u Hsi and the Imperial Government. He was greatly respected by the many foreigners who came to know him, particularly on his trip around the world. Curiously, foreigners came to respect practically all the Chinese they knew well. It was the

Chinese officials they had no opportunity of meeting whom they condemned. This suggests that if they had known the others better they would have had a different opinion of them also.

Li Hung-chang's first important experience as a negotiator came in the Formosa affair with Japan, a difficulty caused by the murder of some Loo-Choo sailors by Formosans. While the resulting treaty did temporarily avert war with Japan, it cannot be called a success. China had to pay an indemnity, and the treaty unfortunately described the Loo-Choo islanders as "people belonging to Japan." Japan took this as sufficient proof that China renounced any claim to the islands and promptly annexed them. Li Hung-chang was also of great assistance to General Tseng Kuo-fan in "the Tientsin Affair."

This Tientsin Affair was the most important of many attacks by the Chinese on foreign missionaries as a result of the Treaty of 1860 which ended the Arrow War.

The treaty allowed missionaries to buy property and carry on their work in every part of China under the protection of the foreign powers. Immediately there was a rush of missionaries to China that was not unlike the gold rush to California or Alaska. Several different orders of the Roman Catholic Church, practically all the Protestant denominations, and even individual missionaries representing no one except themselves rushed to China to save the souls of the heathen Chinese. They built churches, schools, and hospitals in many parts of the country, often with a very scant knowledge of China and even less of the existing religions they were attacking.

There were many very fine men and women among those early missionaries who, without the slightest doubt, came to China for the sole purpose of doing good. But they believed the Chinese could be helped only by being turned into Christians. The Chinese criticized Christianity with an equal lack of knowledge of its teachings. All that the average educated Chinese and the officials knew of Christianity was that it was being forced on their country by military power, and that it was undermining their family life and their ancient customs.

Ten years after the Treaty of 1860 the whole of China was deeply resentful of this rush of missionaries to every part of the country. The Roman Catholic Church was more active than the Protestants at first and came in for most of the animosity. The signs of this resentment were so evident in many parts of China that the foreign powers should have been warned. But they were not. The most violent, but not the first, outbreak against foreign missionaries occurred in Tientsin in 1870, shortly before the marriage of the young Emperor and Hsiao Cheh.

Soon after Tientsin was opened to foreign residence by the Treaty of 1860 the Jesuits built a cathedral in Tientsin and the Sisters of Mercy built an orphanage and school.

Certainly no one who has ever seen these gentle sisters going about their work so quietly in China would ever accuse them of planning anything but kindness. But their institution at first attracted very few Chinese orphans; so the sisters, with the best of intentions but with little worldly wisdom, offered a reward of two dollars to anyone who would bring an orphan to them. This had the desired result: they soon had a deluge of Chinese babies. But, unfortunately, this offer also started a wave of kidnaping. Naturally this was resented in a country where the people love their children as the Chinese do. To make things worse, an epidemic broke out in the orphanage and many of the babies died. In an effort to find the cause of the epidemic autopsies were held and certain organs were removed for further study.

All this was duly retold by the Chinese servants of the orphanage to their friends in the city as thrilling gossip. The stories were soon exaggerated beyond all reason.

Among other things the Chinese believed that the foreigners were using the eyes and the hearts of the children to make medicine as their own doctors used these organs of animals. Chinese opened graves of some children recently buried by the orphanage and found bodies that lacked certain organs. It is easy to imagine the amount of resentment these unfortunate misunderstandings caused in Tientsin. Mobs appeared in many parts of the city and threatened the lives of all foreigners.

One of the stories which I thoroughly believed when I

landed in China and which is generally thought to be true even today in foreign countries is that girl babies are not wanted and that many Chinese people destroy their girl babies.

Most of the Chinese people are Buddhist. While Buddhism does not prohibit all killing, as does its present religion Hinduism, or Brahmanism, it does influence the Chinese people against unnecessary killing. You have only to see how difficult it is to persuade a Chinese woman to destroy an aged or diseased pet cat or dog to realize how absurd it is to believe that a Chinese woman, with her great love for children, would consent to the killing of her own daughter.

The suggestion that the Chinese destroy many of their girl babies usually refers to the poorer classes. With the desire for large families so strong among the more prosperous classes and their willingness to adopt any homeless child that is found, any Chinese family with more children than it can support can get twenty-five dollars or more for any child they want to part with. I have yet to see any Chinese who would destroy anything for which he could get twenty-five dollars.

While stopping with missionary or other foreign families in the interior of China I usually brought up this question. I found that opinion was about equally divided. Those who believed that the Chinese did destroy many of their girl babies claimed that babies were thrown over the city walls. Some offered to show me if I would get up early some morning. I always accepted such offers and wasted many hours of good early-morning sleep walking around city walls. But it never seemed to be a good morning for girl babies. I never saw one that had been thrown over the city wall.

But I have seen babies being buried under rather suspicious circumstances in Peking. Less than a year ago I was walking along the banks of a small stream, it was in fact an open sewer but bore the name of the Jade Canal. Here I was astonished to see a neighbor of mine, a rickshaw boy I had known for twenty or more years, digging a grave near the canal. I knew they had had a girl baby a few days before; I also knew that the family already had more children than they could support. I was sure I had my first case of infant killing. When, as diplomatically as I could, I asked the cause of the death of the child the father knew what I meant. He was greatly incensed and told me to look into his courtyard if I thought such a thing of him. There I saw the mother and the whole family crying; they had been crying the entire night. The poor mother did not want to part with her child even after it was dead. I felt so ashamed that I avoided that family for weeks.

I am not suggesting that Chinese people never destroy newborn children, probably some do, as in other lands, but I am suggesting that it cannot be a common custom in China or I would have been able to have found at least one case in the many years I have lived there. In discussing this with a foreign doctor who had been in China twenty years, he suggested that the destruction of babies was greatest in the countries that had the most illegitimate children. If this is true, China would undoubtedly be at or near the bottom of any such list.

Custom, which is stronger than law in China, has made and enforces some rather rigid rules for the purchase or adoption of children. When adopted, the child has all the privileges of the other children in the family. When only purchased, and not adopted, custom demands that such a child be well cared for, given the same primary education as the other children, and a proper marriage be arranged for it. If the child is a girl, she must be given a two-hundred-dollar wedding present.

I stayed for some time with a wealthy Chinese family in Changtu. This family had fifteen children of their own and had six purchased children. They all attended the private school of the family and played together. The only way I could tell the purchased children from the others was because they were usually better looking. They had been chosen; the family had no choice with their own children—they had to keep what the gods sent them.

While I was stopping with this family the oldest of the purchased children was married to a young official. She was a beautiful girl of about eighteen. The marriage was practically the same as they would have given to one of their own daughters. The young man she married was the son of a fairly good family.

The Jesuits were also accused of forcing young men into their employment by actually kidnaping them. Although there is in existence the sworn statement of a young Chinese claiming he was kidnaped and another sworn statement of a man who claimed he did the kidnaping, there must have been some mistake in this accusation. For the five dollars they were supposed to have offered for the young men it was unnecessary for them to resort to kidnaping, since they could have hired the man's service for this amount at that time. The secrecy maintained by the Catholic Church of everything that occurred behind their high walls added to the suspicions of the Chinese. As one native described it, the Catholic compound appeared more forbidden to outsiders than the Forbidden City of Peking.

In Tientsin the French were particularly unpopular, as the French Government had recently converted a famous Confucian temple into a consulate. French Sisters of Mercy had also come under suspicion because of their annoying habit of baptizing dying Chinese children wherever they could find them, regardless of whether the parents of the children were Christian or not.

This was regrettable, as at the time Empress Tz'u Hsi was carrying out a policy of appeasement toward all foreigners. She sent her most-trusted and least anti-foreign official, Ch'ung Hou as commissioner with full powers to settle the affair. Unfortunately, the French in Tientsin had in Monsieur Fontanier a very impetuous consul. Previous to the arrival of the commissioner, the Chinese had laid their complaints before the consul, who disputed the truth of their charges. An angry discussion followed, but it seems to have been agreed that an inspection should be made of the Catholic Mission premises. Evidently this did not calm the aroused feelings of the people.

Soon after the arrival of Commissioner Ch'ung Hou in Tientsin, Monsieur Fontanier was attacked by a mob in front of the commissioner's yamen. The commissioner sent assistance to the consul and brought him into the yamen. He was astonished to find the French consul armed with two pistols in his belt and a foreigner who accompanied him armed with a sword.

When the consul saw the commissioner, whom he knew, he lost his temper, rushed at him, fired a shot from his pistol, and challenged him to a duel. He was disarmed and taken into the commissioner's office. The commissioner tried to quiet him and asked him to remain, as the crowd outside was still threatening, but Monsieur Fontanier refused to stay and rushed out of the yamen.

Outside he met Magistrate Liu Chieh who, with a small police force, was trying to control the mob. When Monsieur Fontanier saw Magistrate Liu he fired at him, missed, but killed one of his assistants. At this the mob got out of control. They killed Monsieur Fontanier, set fire to the cathedral and the orphanage of the Sisters of Charity, and also destroyed a Protestant chapel. During the rioting the mob killed ten Sisters of Mercy, two Catholic priests, the French consul, five other French men and women, two Russians (probably mistaken for French), and thirty-five Chinese Christians who were employed in the orphanage.

Fortunately for China the French were at that time engaged in the Franco-Prussian War, which was not going well for them; consequently they could take no drastic action against the Chinese. Otherwise Empress Tz'u Hsi would probably have had a war with France on her hands. Tseng Kuo-fan, governor of Chihli province, in which Tientsin is located, had only recently settled a somewhat similar incident in Yangchow, where a Chinese mob had destroyed the buildings of the China Inland Mission, a British Protestant missionary society. He met Count de Rochechouart, the French chargé d'affaires, and, after many discussions, in which every foreigner in Tientsin apparently wanted to take part, a settlement was finally arranged. Sixteen of the mob were convicted of murder and were beheaded in the presence of the foreign consuls and most of the foreign population of Tientsin. Commissioner Ch'ung Hou was required to make a journey to France personally to apologize to the French President.

Although a treaty settled the Tientsin incident, it did nothing to settle the greater problem of the missionary in China. Some of the remarks and suggestions made during the negotiations tended to intensify the feeling against foreigners. For instance, the French and one other power insisted that the district magistrate and the city mayor of Tientsin be executed. This Tseng Kuo-fan absolutely refused to do without a proper trial of the two officials. As the French did not want a public trial, which would have brought out certain facts they did not want on record, the lives of the two officials were saved.

One of the leading Protestant missionaries, although Protestants were not involved in the negotiations, suggested that the French postpone a settlement of the affair until they could assemble a fleet and completely destroy the suburb of Tientsin where the massacre and atrocities occurred. This suggestion was given wide publicity and added considerably to the feelings against the Christian religion and its missionaries in China.

After completion of the negotiations with the French, Tseng Kuo-fan had a long discussion with Empress Tz'u Hsi on the entire missionary problem. Governor Tseng was one of the wise and farseeing advisers surrounding the Empress at that time. He was also one of the most trusted. He pointed out to the Empress that of all the problems facing China the missionary problem was the most dangerous. The missionaries were not only undermining the old customs and traditions of the country but also opposing government officials. If Chinese mobs continued to attack missionaries, as they had done at Tientsin, it would without doubt lead ultimately to war with the Western nations. When asked for his suggestions he proposed to the Empress that the government draw up regulations governing the work of missionaries in China and submit these to the foreign powers.

This suggestion was adopted. A few months after the Tientsin affair China sent a communiqué to the foreign legations, pointing out the threatening situation developing throughout China against missionaries. The communiqué suggested that the foreign powers restrain the zeal displayed by certain of their Christian workers and recommended that missionaries cease interfering with the courts of China in legal affairs in which Chinese Christians were involved. They accompanied this suggestion with a proposed series of regulations consisting of eight articles. The following is a translation from the Chinese of a somewhat brief summary of these articles:

ARTICLE I Christian missionaries should not act covertly but should notify the Chinese authorities when they establish an orphanage. As the Chinese have ample orphanages throughout the country for their people, the Christian orphanages, in order to end evil rumors, should admit only the children of Christian converts. The orphanages should be open to supervision by the Chinese authorities.

ARTICLE II In order to observe the proprieties, no Chinese woman should be allowed to enter churches when men are present. Nor should foreign women engage in the propagation of religion.

ARTICLE III Christian missionaries should not constitute themselves into a privileged class but should conform to the laws and customs of China. They should not act as officials nor should they attempt to withdraw their converts from the jurisdiction of Chinese courts.

ARTICLE IV If a foreigner should kill a man, he should be judged and punished according to the laws of his country. If a Chinese convert should kill a man, he should be judged and punished according to the Chinese law, and missionaries in such cases should not attempt to interfere with the Chinese authorities in an effort to protect the convert.

ARTICLE V Passports of missionaries traveling in the interior of China should clearly bear the name of the province and prefecture where they intend to reside. Missionaries should not transfer their passports to others or otherwise make improper use of them to hide their whereabouts. Missionaries should not smuggle through the Chinese customs contraband or articles on which duty should be paid.

ARTICLE VI Missionaries of Christian churches should not take evil characters into their religion nor protect such characters when they declare themselves Christian. The Chinese authorities will furnish the missionaries with the character of any person they take into their religion.

ARTICLE VII Missionaries must observe the customs of China when they visit a Chinese official and must not unceremoniously enter the yamen of the officials without first securing permission so as not to bring confusion and disorder into the affairs of the officials. Missionaries must not assume official privileges.

ARTICLE VIII If a missionary wishes to purchase property on which to build a church or other building he should first proceed to the local authority to find who is the real owner of the property. The missionary must not make unjust claims for the restoration of any property that at one time belonged to the missionary, regardless of the injustice to the Chinese who honestly bought and paid for the property.

The most enlightening thing about these regulations was that the Chinese Government considered it necessary to ask for them. It suggests that some of the missionaries in their zeal must have used questionable methods in their attempt to gain converts.

No attempt was made in these proposed regulations in any way to dictate or interfere with missionaries in their strictly religious work; they were an effort to regulate or control the missionary when he went beyond the teaching of his religion.

Hundreds of memorials were sent to the court in Peking by officials from the provinces demanding protection from missionaries. The most common complaint was that some of the missionaries, taking the position that extraterritoriality gave them immunity from arrest or even restraint from any Chinese police or other official, would brush the guards aside and march unannounced into the presence of the mayor or *hsien* magistrate, usually to demand the release of some Chinese Christian convert whom the authorities had under arrest. In a country where even entering an ordinary home and particularly the office of an official is always accompanied by a dignified exchange of cards and other formalities, such action by the foreigners was sometimes rather upsetting to the enforcement of the law in the community.

This show of force by the foreigner undoubtedly often increased the importance of the foreigner among the lower classes. Especially as he could protect his converts from punishment by the magistrate it made him almost a god. But it did little to improve his reputation with the educated or upper classes.

The early Christian missionary work of Schall, Ricci, Verbiest, and the Nestorian teachers had been accepted by Chinese and Manchus. They had enjoyed the friendship and respect of emperors and imperial princes. After the Treaty of 1860 the Christian converts were largely of the lowest class. Chinese officials, especially in the provinces, repeatedly made the claim that criminals were often protected from just punishment for their crimes by the foreign missionary, which was hardly intended under extraterritoriality.

With the exception of Article II and possibly Article VI, none of the articles seem to be particularly unreasonable, but the French Government absolutely refused to discuss them. The other foreign governments paid little attention to them at first. Later they accepted most of them in principle but objected to them in detail, which is the diplomatic way of avoiding action. The result was that the number of missionaries increased and conditions continued to get worse. Attacks on missionaries became more numerous until the final outbreak in 1900. All of this might have been avoided if the Western powers and the missionaries had met this honest effort of the Chinese Government to find a solution to the problem.

The foreign powers took the same attitude and followed the same "do-nothing" policy in the Chinese Government's effort to improve the conditions of the coolie trade in South China, which was also causing mob attacks on foreigners. This coolie trade was probably the most disgraceful and most inhumane of all the incidents between the Western powers and China. Like the opium trade, this trade in coolies was also illegal, as the laws of China had for centuries prohibited the emigration of Chinese to foreign countries.

The need for cheap labor in Cuba, in the United States, in the plantations of the West Indies, the gold fields of Australia and Africa, made the shipment of Chinese coolies to these countries a very large and profitable business. In theory, the laborers were to be paid four dollars a month and were to be volunteers; but when coolies did not volunteer in sufficient numbers they were procured by other means, usually by kidnaping. In a short time this kidnaping became so serious that in some southern coast cities no Chinese could appear on the street, even in daytime, without danger of being kidnaped and carried off a prisoner to be sold to one of the coolie agents at so much a head. As many as five or six foreign ships would be lying offshore at a time to receive the coolies brought to them. Once aboard such a ship they were carried away and were usually never heard from again. As the ships and the buyers of the coolies were protected by the foreign governments, the mobs were further aroused against all foreigners.

The Chinese Government attempted to arrive at some agreement with the foreign powers for the control of this trade. The Chinese also wanted some record of the coolies taken from China and to secure for them some protection while working in the foreign countries.

The British Government did make an attempt to put this business on a more humane basis. They established an emigration house to handle the sending of coolies to the West Indies. This worked satisfactorily for a short time, but the British soon found they had little control over their own nationals and none over the citizens of other countries engaged in this profitable trade. So they gave up the emigration house and the trade continued, regardless of the protests of the Chinese Government and the threats from Chinese mobs.

The burning of the ship *Don Juan* within a few miles of Hong Kong, in which more than five hundred Chinese coolies lost their lives, finally brought this inhumane trade to the attention of the whole world. It forced the interested Western governments to sign an agreement in March 1866, but the agreement was not ratified by the French Government until two years later. It was then sent to China but never put into effect by the interested powers. The coolie trade continued as long as there was a demand for cheap labor from China.

The failure of the Chinese Government to secure any satisfactory agreements in dealing with the representatives of the foreign powers had one good result: it convinced the Chinese that they had to have their own representatives in foreign capitals to deal directly with the governments of those lands.

Feeling that their position had been misrepresented abroad, they wanted some person, as Prince Kung expressed it, to tell the whole world of the many difficulties of China and of her sincere desire to be friendly and progressive.

For this important mission the Chinese Government did a most unusual thing. It appointed a foreigner, Anson Burlingame, an American who had been minister in Peking for six years. He was given rank of Minister Plenipotentiary and Envoy Extraordinary with powers to represent the government of China in the principal capitals of the Western nations.

The Burlingame Mission, which included a number of prominent Chinese, left Shanghai in February 1868. The President of the United States, Andrew Johnson, received the mission and a banquet was tendered the visitors by the city of New York. In his speech at this banquet Mr. Burlingame said: "The East which men have sought since the days of Alexander the Great now seeks the West. China, emerging from the mists of time, suddenly appears at your gates and confronts you by its representatives here tonight. What have you to say to her? She comes with no menace but with the great doctrine of Confucius, uttered two thousand three hundred years ago: 'Do not unto others what you would not have others do unto you.' Will you not respond with the more positive doctrine of Christianity: 'We will do unto others what we would have others do unto us'? China tells you that she is willing to enter into relations with you according to your international law, that she is willing to take its obligations and privileges. China asks you to forget your ancient prejudices, to abandon your assumptions of superiority, and to submit your questions to her as she proposes to submit her questions to you, to the arbitration of reason. China wishes no war but she asks of you not to interfere in her internal affairs. She asks you not to send her religious teachers who are incompetent men. She asks you to respect the neutrality of her waters and the integrity of her territory. She asks to be left free to unfold herself in that form of civilization of which she is most capable. She asks you to give to those treaties which were exacted under the pressure of war a generous and Christian construction."

This speech outlined the new policy of China toward the Western world. It had been discussed and approved in substance by the highest officials of the Chinese government before Mr. Burlingame left China. It received a fairly good reception in America from all except the missionaries, who thought it advocated a restriction of their work in China.

In England both the mission and the suggestions in Mr. Burlingame's speech received a less cordial reception. Foreign Minister Lord Clarendon replied to the speech in a long letter to Mr. Burlingame in which he outlined British policy in China. The letter satisfied neither Mr. Burlingame nor the British merchants, who still wanted what they called a "strong policy toward China," backed up, if necessary, by military force. They wanted the existing treaties carried out without change, and they wanted full protection of British subjects residing in China. The letter ended with the usual pledge of friendly feelings toward China—something which no one knew better than the Chinese meant nothing.

The Burlingame Mission visited several other European capitals without any apparent results. Mr. Burlingame and his suite received their most cordial reception in Russia, which, being a semi-oriental country, always understood the Chinese and enjoyed better relations with them than any other Western nation. Unfortunately Mr. Burlingame died in Russia before anything definite was accomplished.

The Chinese looked on the Burlingame Mission on which they had put such high hopes as a failure. They had made what they thought was a very cordial gesture to the Western nations and it had not been reciprocated. Race prejudice and greed for trade and territory had triumphed again. If Burlingame had lived, his greatest value to China probably would have been his influence on China, not on the Western powers.

The French continued to push their penetration and conquest of Indo-China. In 1874, in spite of their beautiful speeches of friendship to the Burlingame Mission, they attacked and forced the King of Annam to transfer his allegiance from China to France. The French Government refused even to discuss the question of Indo-China with the Chinese, claiming it concerned only France and the King of Annam.

The British took over a part of Burma, another country owing allegiance to China. They sent a large expedition into northern Burma, Szechuan, Yunnan, and Kweichow, maintaining it was to study trade conditions, but the Chinese were very suspicious when they found that the expedition was composed largely of military officers and troops. The murder on the Szechuan-Burma border of A. R. Margary, a fine young man who joined the expedition as Chinese interpreter, brought this affair to the knowledge of the people of England.

The Japanese, not to be left behind in the scramble for Chinese territory, started to create trouble in Korea which finally resulted in Korea being taken over by Japan. The Russians were using the same tactics on the Mongolian-Siberian border. Chinese officials had every reason to believe that the Burlingame Mission and their gesture of asking for the friendship of the Western nations and fair treatment was a failure.

Unfortunately this failure was the last attempt of China or the Western powers to stop the growth of misunderstanding and prejudice between the East and the West.

7. THE SECOND REGENCY

When Emperor Kuang Hsu was brought into the palace he was a small, sickly child of four. He cried for days after leaving his mother and begged to be taken home. His mother had spoiled him by putting no restraint of any kind on what he did and what he ate.

Tz'u Hsi realized that she had neglected her own son as a child and was determined to give more attention to her adopted son, the new Emperor. At first she went to the opposite extreme and gave him too much personal attention. She decreased the number of attendants on the young boy from forty servants to two nurses and a reasonable number of eunuchs. She improved his meals with the result that he soon became a strong, healthy young boy.

When she found that he had an unreasonable fear of thunder and other loud noises, she moved him into her own bedroom, where he slept for many years. Regardless of how busy she might be, whenever there was a thunderstorm Tz'u Hsi either went herself to the young boy or had a eunuch go to him. She ordered the eunuchs to beat drums and gongs to drown out as much of the noise of the thunder as possible. When the storms occurred at night she would take the small boy into bed with her.

At six, when he had been in the palace two years, he was started on his studies. Tz'u Hsi searched all China for the best tutors she could find. He was instructed in horsemanship and archery by two Manchu princes. In the preliminary examination which was given him to measure his intelligence the tutors were surprised to find that already he was proficient in the writing of simple characters. To their further astonishment they found that he could recite many passages from the *Four Books,* having been personally taught by Tz'u Hsi for more than a year. Tz'u Hsi was at this time showing an entirely new phase of her many-sided character.

Having passed the intelligence test with high marks, the small boy was started on his formal studies. Even an Emperor had to go through the formality of the commencement ceremony required of all boys beginning their school life. Kuang Hsu had to pay due homage and respect to each of his tutors. The first Chinese character he was taught was the character for wealth. Beneath this character the Emperor was required to write many times "I do not like this character nor what it stands for because if an Emperor seeks wealth the people will be poor."

When eleven years of age the Emperor dumfounded his tutors by remarking that the T'ang Dynasty was ruined through the elevation of the eunuchs. "Am I not right, Old Teacher?"

The tutors knew that the young Emperor was referring to the influence of Eunuch Li Lien-ying and so did not know what to answer, but they all marveled at the intelligence of their young pupil. In the seventeenth year of his reign he had a teacher brought into the palace to teach him the English language, and other teachers to instruct him in chemistry, Western science, modern military subjects, and Western governments' systems.

Unlike other Ch'ing emperors and princes, Kuang Hsu cared little for the theater and such amusements. He gave all his spare time to his studies, becoming one of the best-educated men in the imperial court. The *coup d'état* which he attempted in 1898 was no sudden fancy of an uneducated boy as many have described it.

Several small incidents in his early life show another side of his character. When he was seven years old there had been no snow for the three winter months when snow is much needed by the farmers. The Emperor spent three days praying at the Round Temple of Supreme Deity. When a heavy snowstorm did come the Emperor stood bareheaded in the snow and without heavy clothes. Seeing this, Tz'u Hsi shouted at him: "All your clothes and shoes are getting wet. Hurry and come in." He dropped to his knees in the snow and replied: "The Imperial Mother has pity on my clothes and shoes, but are we having pity on the poor people who will have no food today?"

On another occasion, when there was a severe drought, the Emperor, then ten years old, prayed daily for ten days but still there was no rain. Famine threatened the country and the Emperor forbade the eating of any meat in the palace. Finding that the imperial tutors were still eating meat, he stamped his foot and said: "The gods have not given us rain and all the crops are dry and withered, the farmers are worried, and the imperial family is living on vegetables. How can you teach anybody anything if you do as you are now doing?"

He issued a decree putting himself, every prince, official, and tutor on a strict vegetable diet until the gods gave the land rain.

Kuang Hsu might have become one of the great emperors of China if he had been successful in 1898 in breaking the hold Tz'u Hsi had on him and on the government.

But even with every personal attention on the part of Tz'u Hsi, she was never able to gain the young Emperor's complete confidence or affection to the extent that Tz'u An was able to do without any apparent effort. Tz'u An really understood children. She always spoke in a mild and gentle manner, never lost her temper, and was never abusive to anyone.

Tz'u Hsi often lost her temper, at which times she spoke in a very loud and harsh voice and in an insulting manner. She terrorized people by staring at them with eyes that seemed to snap fire. At other times she would curse them, more in the manner of a man than a woman. While she never acted in this way toward the Emperor, or at least not in his younger years, he often saw her treat others in this manner. His attitude toward Tz'u Hsi was one more of respect and fear than of love. This did not escape her.

The young Emperor also early developed an inferiority complex when in the Empress's presence. While his physicians recognized the cause, they dared not speak of it to Tz'u

Hsi but diagnosed his timidity as owing to the physical weakness of his childhood. This defect of character was to show itself in many disastrous ways in his later life.

With her sister Phoenix's son established on the Dragon Throne, the Empress extended more favors to other members of her family. Both her brothers, now dukes, bought palaces in Ta Ts'ao Ch'ang, a very select neighborhood. Their mother, now known as Lady Hwei, lived with them, happy in the knowledge that all her dreams had come true even beyond her fondest hopes. A very fortunate and proud woman was Lady Hwei. Her home was one of the finest palaces of Peking. She knew it was a permanent home this time. Did she sometimes wish that her careless, selfish, not too courageous husband were with her to share the family's good fortune?

During this period Tz'u Hsi also appeared to have changed her attitude toward Tz'u An. She was actually cultivating the latter's friendship and good will. Apparently their quarrel at the time Kuang Hsu was named Emperor and the many memorials from the Censors on that question worried Tz'u Hsi more than she cared to acknowledge. She wanted peace in her official family and started with Tz'u An.

To achieve this Tz'u Hsi did a remarkable thing at a time when Tz'u An was ill and the court doctors did not seem able to cure her. After a few weeks, as Tz'u An was not getting better, she stopped taking the medicine prescribed by the doctors and took instead a brew prepared by Tz'u Hsi. In a few days she was cured. She noticed that Tz'u Hsi had a bandage of white cloth on her left arm and asked about it. Tz'u Hsi answered that three days before she had cut a piece of flesh from her arm and boiled it with the ginseng that she gave Tz'u An to drink. It was this concoction that made Tz'u An well. Tz'u An wept when she realized what Tz'u Hsi had done and told her: "It is quite out of my imagination what a good woman you are."

It was not unknown for Chinese women to cut off pieces of their own flesh to make medicines for relatives they loved.

But this happy relationship between the two Empresses did not last long. They again quarreled over the honors to be paid to their respective deceased fathers. Both had been posthumously awarded the highest titles they were entitled to. This meant that Tz'u Hsi's father, as the father of a concubine, was awarded a lower title than Tz'u An's father, as the father of an empress. When Tz'u Hsi asked Tz'u An to agree that each receive an equal title Tz'u An refused.

In the quarrel that ensued Tz'u An told Tz'u Hsi that if she had not been brought into the palace as a concubine her father would have had no title of any kind and would be no better than a corrupt criminal who had died in jail. This so enraged Tz'u Hsi that she pleaded sick and would not attend the meetings with ministers for several days. Their quarrels were becoming more frequent, and in spite of Tz'u Hsi's efforts to placate Tz'u An their friendship was drawing to a close.

The rumor was allowed to circulate that even the robust health and strong constitution of Tz'u Hsi could not stand the heavy load she was carrying in managing the government. Soon after her violent quarrel with Tz'u An, she temporarily withdrew from public life. Tz'u An received daily reports on her condition, and as there was no apparent improvement in the health of the coregent she, on her own responsibility, issued a decree instructing the governors of the provinces to send their best doctors to Peking for a consultation. Some of Tz'u Hsi's critics suggested at that time that Tz'u An suspected Tz'u Hsi was not really ill and took this method of not only finding out for herself, but of informing the court in a way to which Tz'u Hsi could not openly object.

Two clever women were here opposed to each other. Tz'u Hsi understood and was furious. At first she refused to see the doctors. She claimed she was entirely satisfied with her own physician. But the doctors had come a long way and made a report anyway, ordering complete rest for Tz'u Hsi. Tz'u Hsi had to obey. She was temporarily relieved of her duties and Tz'u An ruled as sole regent.

Tz'u An saw little of Tz'u Hsi during this period and such calls as she did make were formal, carefully arranged official visits. But as Tz'u Hsi's health apparently did not improve, Tz'u An's conscience began to trouble her. She began to fear her quarrels with Tz'u Hsi and her attitude were the cause of the latter's illness. This was brought forcibly to her attention at a meeting of the Privy Council on the tenth day of the Third Month of the following year, when a memorial from one of the Censors was read, asking about the health of Tz'u Hsi.

As soon as the meeting was over, and not waiting for her breakfast, Tz'u An went directly to the palace of Tz'u Hsi. She was not expected at such an early hour—about five-thirty in the morning. Here occurred one of those curious, almost insignificant accidents which sometimes change the course of history. Instead of announcing the arrival of Tz'u An, as he should have done, the eunuch in charge, caught off guard, took her directly to the bedroom of the Empress. Catching Tz'u Hsi entirely unprepared, Tz'u An evidently saw several things she was never intended to see.

Tz'u An tried to indicate that she had noticed nothing out of the ordinary and might have succeeded if she had not committed a serious error. Tz'u An still had in her possession the decree mentioned earlier which Emperor Hsien Feng had given her, ordering the removal and death of Tz'u Hsi at any time she threatened Tz'u An or became a danger to the state. Tz'u An now decided to use this decree, not to destroy Tz'u Hsi, but to win back her friendship and co-operation.

She pointed out to Tz'u Hsi that they had been friends since girlhood; that while they had had some quarrels they had also worked together successfully through many troublous years. She then showed Tz'u Hsi the decree, pointing out that although she had had it all these years, she had never had the slightest intention of using it. Then Tz'u An burned the decree over one of the large candles at the head of Tz'u Hsi's bed.

Tz'u Hsi was too stunned to speak as she realized the danger that had been hanging over her head all these years, but she appeared very grateful to Tz'u An.

It did not take Tz'u Hsi long to come to two conclusions: first, she was convinced Tz'u An had seen more than the latter pretended to have seen; second, with the evidence against her which Tz'u An now had she did not need the decree. It was perfectly safe for her to burn it. Tz'u Hsi realized that her innermost secrets could be forced out of her maids and eunuchs and that this was all that would be necessary to have her removed from power. This was too great a weapon to be left in any woman's hands, however friendly she might appear to be. Tz'u Hsi judged Tz'u An by her own standards and how she herself would have acted under similar circumstances.

A few hours after her surprise visit Tz'u An received a present of steamed rice cakes from Tz'u Hsi. These were her favorite pastries, and she ate them without the slightest suspicion. By eight o'clock that night Tz'u An was dead.

It was now Tz'u Hsi's turn to make some grave mistakes that were to point the finger of suspicion directly at her. She either overlooked or deliberately failed to notify the next of kin that Tz'u An was ill, nor did she later notify them that the Empress was dead.

Tz'u An's closest relative was her brother Kuang K'eh, whose wife was the sister of Prince Tun, the fifth younger brother of the late Emperor Hsien Feng. Prince Tun was the one brother of Hsien Feng who never became friendly with Tz'u Hsi, and his feelings were shared by his sister, the wife of Kuang K'eh.

In order to keep a close watch on everything Tz'u Hsi did, Prince Tun had also done a little spy planting. By a clever ruse he had planted a very young eunuch named Ma Wen-fu in the palace of Tz'u An. Tz'u An used him to send messages out of the palace and he had opportunities for meeting both Prince Tun and his brother-in-law, Kuang K'eh. He told Prince Tun and Kuang K'eh that Tz'u Hsi had sent some steamed rice cakes to Tz'u An on the morning of the latter's visit to Tz'u Hsi.

When the wife of Kuang K'eh heard about the rice cakes, she immediately suspected the danger to Tz'u An. She rushed to the palace. Although as the wife of a high official she had the right of entry at any time, she was not allowed to pass through the outer gate. When asked why, she was told this was by orders of Tz'u Hsi. This greatly increased her fears.

When she reported to her husband he also realized his sister's danger. As soon as the gates were opened next morning to allow the ministers to enter for their four-o'clock conference, Kuang K'eh rushed in with them. He found all the inmates of the palace in mourning and his sister dead.

Though he knew the penalty might be death, Kuang K'eh broke into the meeting of the Privy Council without announcement or ceremony and demanded to see the body of Tz'u An. But Tz'u Hsi had already given her orders and his request was refused. When Kuang K'eh tried to find the little eunuch Ma Wen-fu he was told that he had been flogged to death that morning for stealing. Someone had effectively closed the mouth of the one witness who knew most about the death of Tz'u An.

The ministers of the Privy Council adjourned their meeting and went directly to the Chung Ts'ueh Palace to perform their ceremonial duties before the remains of Tz'u An. They were amazed to find Tz'u Hsi, whom they had been told was very ill, calmly sitting on a chair, apparently in perfect health. They could not understand how Tz'u An, who had shown not the slightest sign of being ill just twenty-four hours before, was now dead, and Tz'u Hsi, who had been reputedly ill at that time, was now in good health. But Tz'u Hsi was ready with one of her pretty explanations. She told the ministers: "Because I have been unwell for nearly a year, Empress Tz'u An has been overworking and made herself sick. Now she has left me and gone ahead to the Great Beyond. I am deeply distressed. Please look on her face for the last time." The last words have always been interpreted to mean that the ministers could see for themselves that Tz'u An had not been strangled or stabbed. Tz'u Hsi's insistence on this only made the officials more suspicious.

Even Tz'u Hsi's friends acknowledged she made many mistakes the day following Tz'u An's death. She should not have forbidden the wife of Kuang K'eh to see Tz'u An the night she died. Neither should she have forbidden Tz'u An's brother from making the usual sacrifices before her coffin. The flogging of the small eunuch Ma Wen-fu was also a mistake. All these things contributed to make people even more suspicious. Her actions in this entire affair gave every evidence of a hurriedly concocted plot, not her usual well-thought-out planning. It was generally known that Tz'u An ate steamed rice cakes a few hours before she was taken violently ill, that these cakes were sent her by Tz'u Hsi, and that Tz'u Hsi often personally cooked these unusual small cakes. Tz'u An's manner of death gave every evidence of arsenic poisoning.

This naturally raises the question: What did Tz'u An see on that unannounced early-morning visit to the palace of Tz'u Hsi? This question was discussed from a thousand angles by all classes in gossip-loving Peking and later by all China for many years to come. One theory was that Tz'u An saw unmistakable evidence that a man had spent the night in Tz'u Hsi's apartment. Another was that Tz'u An saw a newborn baby—proof that Tz'u Hsi's long seclusion had been a ruse to hide the fact that she was pregnant, and that she had just become a mother. All these were but rumors; the public was never able to obtain any proof of what actually happened that morning. The secret was well kept for years.

Two incidents gave strength to these rumors. When the two famous physicians, Hsueh Fu-ch'en and Wong Shou-chang, arrived in Peking shortly after the death of Tz'u An, and were taken to see Tz'u Hsi, who still kept to her private apartments and was known to be far from well. She did not want to see these physicians but could not very well refuse, as they were sent to her palace by Jung Lu. After a long examination the two doctors stated that the Empress was suffering from "steaming of the bones" and recommended that she be put on a milk diet. As cow's milk was considered unclean by the Chinese, the physicians recommended human milk, and a number of healthy Chinese women were brought into the palace to provide the milk. To avoid contact with any vessels, the Empress took the milk direct from the nurses' breasts.

Naturally all this finally reached the ears of the court and in addition later furnished a fine topic for gossip to the crowds in the teahouses. They immediately recalled that "steaming of the bones" was known to the common people as "milk leg," a common disease of women following childbirth. They also naturally thought that the women taken into the palace were to furnish milk for a newborn child. It never occurred to them that the milk could be for the Empress. Many theories were advanced as to who was the father of the Empress's child.

The mystery—one of many hidden in the Forbidden City—remained unsolved until long after most of the persons involved were dead. Details of this mystery became known only a few years ago.

To understand what actually happened in the privacy of Tz'u Hsi's palace in the Forbidden City one must go back a full year and a half before Tz'u Hsi's retirement and look in on Eunuch Li Lien-ying as he sat one evening in his well-furnished quarters. Li Lien-ying was much troubled. He had a difficult problem to solve. A few months after the funeral of Emperor Hsien Feng, Li had noticed there was something wrong with Tz'u Hsi. He knew the Empress better than any other person and he watched over her as a father. To him she was almost a goddess. He knew that Tz'u Hsi had always been very energetic and hardworking, but now she was restless, could not sleep, and was unhappy. He saw her attempt to obtain enjoyment out of the theater, lately choosing risqué and unconventional plays, out of the cultivation of her flowers, her silkworms, her goldfish, her singing crickets, and her dogs. However, she quickly lost interest in all of these in turn.

Although Li Lien-ying was the head eunuch and one of the most powerful men in the Forbidden City, he still had to do a service for the Empress that seemingly was below the dignity of his position but which Tz'u Hsi believed no one else could do so well. This was to massage her. This had been one of his duties since the stay at Jehol. After the death of T'ung Chih, when the responsibilities of rule fell again on Tz'u Hsi—now forty years old—Li had to massage her almost daily, usually late in the evening before she retired. She had become so accustomed to Eunuch Li that she gradually lost all embarrassment in his presence and Li often massaged her while she was lying on her bed, dressed only in the scantiest clothing. Li soon noticed that she obtained more pleasure from these treatments than just relief from physical weariness. Li was no psychologist; it is doubtful whether he had ever heard of the word. But if he did not know much about women in general, he did know more than anyone else about his Empress. He realized that Tz'u Hsi had not been leading a normal sex life since the death of Hsien Feng nearly fourteen years earlier. It was rather a shock to him when he realized that although a great Empress his mistress was also just a woman with all a woman's weaknesses.

He also realized that it was just a matter of time before this condition would result in a scandal of some kind—a scandal that would bring a lot of trouble to somebody. Most probably that somebody would be Li Lien-ying. He knew that even with the friendship of Tz'u Hsi his life could be snuffed out as easily as the life of the equally powerful eunuch, An Teh-hai, had been. In any scandal, Li's very intimacy with the Empress would constitute his greatest danger. He was a man of more caution than courage, so he pleaded illness and tried to resign from the palace. This was denied him by Tz'u Hsi in such strong language that he never again tried to resign.

However, if not a courageous man, he was a very resourceful one, as he had to be in his position. After weeks of thought he finally formulated a plan that he hoped would save both himself and the Empress. He decided that the safety of both depended upon satisfying the sex demands of his mistress in some way. For this purpose he knew he must find a man who could be absolutely trusted and one who could be freely admitted into the palace without arousing suspicion. He must also be a man attractive to the Empress, as the success of the whole scheme depended on her never knowing that it had been planned.

Li knew that none of the actors that the Empress had shown an interest in at times would do. The actor belonged to the lowest class in the social scale and no excuse could be invented that would allow an actor frequent access to the Empress's apartments. Neither would Jung Lu, her most intimate friend, serve for this purpose, as he was then absent from Peking—having been banished by the Empress herself in a rage after catching him in an affair with one of her ladies in waiting. Even had he been near at hand and his relations with the Empress on a satisfactory basis, and although his position as commander of the Imperial Guard gave him the privilege of visiting the Forbidden City at any time, he was already under suspicion of being too intimate with the Empress and was, therefore, closely spied on by her enemies.

Just when Li despaired of finding a suitable lover for Tz'u Hsi, Fate furnished him with one. He was a young man who, because of his failure in the imperial examinations and low way of earning his living, was hiding his identity under the name of Yao Pao-sheng. Yao was from the provinces and had passed all the examinations up to the finals. Like the young man who had become Emperor Hsien Feng's boon companion, this one, too, was making a poor living by singing and telling stories in the restaurants outside Ch'ien Men. This was a usual occupation for students while waiting the three years until the next examination. Although Yao was rough in his manners and poorly dressed, Li took him to his apartments in the Forbidden City. He placed him under older eunuchs to teach him court etiquette. He had him fed and properly dressed and soon even Li was astonished by the change in his appearance. Li then had him study medicine for a few months under another friend. Li was doing a thorough job.

Soon after Yao Pao-sheng was ready for presentation to the Empress, Tz'u Hsi became ill. The court physician, Fan Shou-hsing, was called in and prescribed for her. He was considered the best physician in China, but, being an old man and extremely unattractive in appearance, Tz'u Hsi disliked him and would not take his medicine. He was the opportunity Li Lien-ying had been waiting for. He presented Yao Pao-sheng, now Dr. Yao, to the Empress. After going through all the formalities, Yao was finally allowed to feel her pulse. His diagnosis and suggestions pleased the Empress, in fact she was pleased with both the diagnosis and the handsome young doctor.

When the Board of Imperial Physicians heard of Dr. Yao, they protested to the Empress, pointing out that the young and unknown physician was not of sufficient rank to treat such a great personage as the Empress. She immediately solved this difficulty by giving Dr. Yao a rank above them all. Dr. Yao became a permanent official in the palace with the privilege of entering or leaving the palace at any time.

It was not long before Dr. Yao and Tz'u Hsi were spending far more time together than his professional duties seemed to warrant. It was rumored that he was helping his patient by reading the classics to her. Later he read love stories, as lovers are prone to do. He knew many interesting tales and the off-color stories that circulated in the restaurants of the city, which amused the Empress very much. Li Lien-ying's scheme was working out as he had planned; in fact, it worked out too well. Tz'u Hsi became pregnant.

This was hardly a part of the plan, but nothing could be done about it. Fortunately for Tz'u Hsi this occurred shortly after the second regency and when things in the Ch'ing court were running more smoothly than they had for years. When her secret could no longer be kept from prying eyes, Tz'u Hsi took to her bed. The decree was issued announcing that she was too ill to attend the meetings of the Council, and that Tz'u An would take charge of all government affairs until her recovery.

Tz'u An called often on her coregent at the beginning of the latter's illness, but her visits became less frequent when Tz'u Hsi, afraid of the sharp instincts of Tz'u An, took measures to discourage her. All palaces in the Forbidden City were surrounded by high walls, giving absolute privacy to each palace. Notwithstanding this privacy, however, rumors soon began to circulate that Tz'u Hsi was giving rather late and sometimes boisterous parties and was having very fine dinners for a sick woman. It was said that the guests at these parties consisted of the Empress, her new doctor, Eunuch Li Lien-ying, and his sister Lady Li, who evidently had been taken into the secret. The general opinion fostered by Li Lien-ying was that Tz'u Hsi was feigning illness in order to have a long rest from responsibility. Li Lien-ying had laid his plans carefully, so carefully that no one guessed the secret of what Tz'u An saw on that unfortunate early-morning surprise visit. Tz'u An did not live long enough to tell anyone what she had seen.

With the birth of the child, a boy, Li Lien-ying had another serious problem on his hands. It was no longer safe to have the doctor remain in Peking to hang like a sword over Li's and the Empress's heads. Curiously enough Yao was not killed. Perhaps the Empress really loved him. At all events, she protected him, giving him sufficient money to return to his native province. Li added a few grim warnings that were sufficiently convincing to persuade Yao to keep his lips sealed. But threats were probably not necessary, as Yao appears to have been a rather decent man. He insisted on taking his son with him and the child was smuggled out of the Forbidden City by Li Lien-ying's sister. The child was kept in the White Cloud Temple for a few days and then taken by his father to his native home, where Dr. Yao resumed his proper name and continued the practice of medicine. Somewhere in China a son of the great Empress probably lives today, perhaps unaware of his imperial parentage.

Again the gods had protected Tz'u Hsi. If her secret had become known nothing could have prevented her banishment to the "cold palace." Yao Pao-sheng was a Chinese and, broad-minded as the Manchus were in most things, when it came to the reputation of their Empress and the purity of their Manchu blood, the Household Rules would have made no exception. Not even for an empress as powerful as Tz'u Hsi.

Tz'u Hsi unwisely showed her recently developed hatred toward Tz'u An even after the latter's death. She refused to wear the usual mourning and to do homage before the Empress's coffin, stating: "She was but an empress regent as I am. Why should I kowtow to her now that she is dead?" She also refused to accompany the funeral procession to the city gates as was required of emperor and empresses in such cases. The boy Emperor performed this ceremony alone. All this was noted by the public and created an unfavorable impression. The Chinese repeated an old proverb: "Enmity should not be carried beyond the grave, regardless of how profound the hatred before death."

Immediately on the completion of the sacrifices before the coffin of the former coregent, Tz'u Hsi issued a decree in which she stated: "At the order of the Emperor I have reluctantly assumed the sole regency and will in the future attend to the affairs of state."

Soon everyone noticed that Tz'u Hsi emerged from her retirement a different person. Tz'u Hsi, the sole regent, was a very different person from Tz'u Hsi the coregent. She no longer requested ministers to do anything. She now ordered them in no uncertain terms—and they obeyed.

But there were a few people she could not control. The

Censors continued to criticize her, regardless of her threats. The brother of Tz'u An continued to stand at the gates of the palace and to cry in a loud voice, demanding justice for the death of Tz'u An. He was especially loud and fluent in his demands whenever Tz'u Hsi or her ministers passed through the gates, but no one dared to silence him. As a Manchu clansman he was within his rights to stand at the gates and demand justice. Even the Empress could not stop him. He kept up his protests and his pleas until finally his mind failed and he died insane.

Among the many protests made to Tz'u Hsi, only one caused her serious concern. This came from the humble little Manchu secretary, Wu K'o-tu, who had presumed to raise an objection because she had not followed tradition and appointed an heir to Emperor T'ung Chih. He wrote a final memorial and in the traditional manner committed suicide before the grave of Emperor T'ung Chih and Empress Hsiao Cheh. By this courageous act Wu K'o-tu focused the attention of the whole nation and the world on the gravity of the situation, and he did it in a way that was irrefutable and final.

Tz'u Hsi realized the seriousness of the suicide of Wu K'o-tu. Like rulers of other countries under similar circumstances, she arranged a series of great pageants to keep the officials busy and take the minds of the people off the unfortunate affair. The great sacrifices of the Winter and Summer Solstices at the Temple of Heaven, the sacrifices at the Temple of Agriculture, the Altars of Earth, and other sacrifices were carried out more elaborately than usual. In all these the child Emperor, Kuang Hsu, performed the ritual. In addition, Tz'u Hsi turned the entire North Sea Palace area into a fair, a village fair on a large scale, the profits from which were to be distributed among the poor. Perhaps she recalled the enjoyment she had as a girl in these gatherings. She ordered all shops, tradesmen, restaurants, and places of entertainment to prepare elaborate and highly decorated booths and exhibits. The fair was to continue for a whole week–longer, if weather interfered.

The Empress and all the court dressed themselves as peasants or laborers, carried shopping baskets, and discarded all signs of rank. The imperial eunuchs acted as salesmen and as barkers for side shows. Naturally, no one was fooled by the disguises. Whenever the Empress and the other members of the court bought anything they were charged ten times the usual price, but no one minded. As Tz'u Hsi well knew, it was a cheap price to pay for popularity.

The Empress and the court entered gaily into the spirit of the fair. They spent every afternoon and evening in the grounds, visiting each show, restaurant, and almost every shop, and enjoyed themselves as did the general public. Tz'u Hsi and the others of the court wore humble dress to be in keeping with the spirit of the fair, not to hide their identity. It is remarkable that they evidently had not the slightest fear of assassination or even annoyance—which is in sharp contrast to the position of the royal families of Europe, or even the President of the United States, who never appear in public without ample guards. No fewer than five attempts were made on the life of the beloved and well-guarded Queen Victoria.

This fair did much to clear the atmosphere of Peking and the surrounding country of the suspicion, rumors, and dissatisfaction caused by the events of the preceding year. It was such a success that it was continued annually for many years.

2

The time was fast approaching when the young Emperor would have to be provided with an Empress and the usual Elegant Girls. A decree was issued commanding the registration of the daughters of suitable age of the military and civil officials as candidates. The registration was open for six months and the selection was to be made by Tz'u Hsi.

Unexpectedly, and at great loss of face to her, with the exception of the two daughters of Kuei Hsiang, the Empress's own younger brother, not one candidate registered. In other words, no Manchu girl in all China—except the two nieces of Tz'u Hsi, who probably had no choice in the matter—wanted to become Empress of China. Everyone knew too well the treatment Tz'u Hsi had given T'ung Chih's Empress Hsiao Cheh, and the suspicions regarding the latter's suicide. No family wanted its daughters to be exposed to the same fate. This was probably the first time in history that there were no candidates for the highest position open to any woman in China.

This was a great insult to the dignity of Tz'u Hsi and to the Ch'ing Dynasty. She did not give the girls an opportunity to refuse a second time, and in her next decree she designated the daughters of certain high officials and made their registration compulsory. The eight Elegant Girls finally selected included the two daughters of Kuei Hsiang. The elder of these girls Tz'u Hsi was determined should be chosen Empress. Unfortunately, they were both extremely unattractive, particularly the elder sister. Knowing that both would probably be rejected by the Emperor if he were given the opportunity to do so, Tz'u Hsi forestalled such a possibility by putting her nieces at the top of the list. She also carefully arranged the names of the other six girls in the order she wanted them placed as concubines.

On the morning of the inspection the Elegant Girls were taken to the Great Hall which had been especially decorated for the occasion. Tz'u Hsi was seated on the throne. The Emperor was on her left, and behind the Empress stood the wives of the imperial princes, dukes, and high-ranking officials. Eunuch Li Lien-ying stood close to the Empress to carry out her orders.

Each candidate had her name written on a small board of fir wood, with her age, the origin of the family, and the official ranks of her father and mother, grandfather and grandmother, and great-grandfather and great-grandmother. As their names were called, each of the girls walked past Tz'u Hsi and the Emperor several times. After the candidates had been carefully inspected, Tz'u Hsi took the Good Luck Scepter, handed it to the Emperor, and instructed him to make his choice. The Emperor replied: "The selection of the future Empress is of such great importance that the Imperial Father (he always addressed the Empress as Imperial Father on formal occasions) should make the selection, as your son and minister does not dare to make the decision himself."

Tz'u Hsi again urged him to make his own selection. Taking the Empress at her word, he thanked her and was about to give the scepter to the daughter of Teh Hsing, the prettiest girl in the group, when Tz'u Hsi called out sharply: "Emperor! Emperor!"

He turned and found the Empress pointing to her niece, the eldest daughter of Kuei Hsiang.

The young Emperor completely lost his head, as he always did when commanded by Tz'u Hsi, and thrust the scepter at the daughter of Kuei Hsiang. Tz'u Hsi was very angry at the rudeness shown by the Emperor to her niece, who was also his own cousin, but not half so angry as the Emperor in being forced to choose the wrong girl as his Empress.

Never again was Tz'u Hsi to have his confidence. On this occasion was planted the seed that was to grow and develop into the *coup d'état* of 1898, with all its disastrous results.

After choosing her niece to be Empress, Tz'u Hsi continued to choose the concubines. Aware of the Emperor's preference for the beautiful daughter of Teh Hsing, and fearing this would make her niece's position difficult, she passed over this girl and selected the two daughters of Ch'ang Hsu as imperial concubines. The beautiful girl favored by the Emperor calmly returned to her home, bathed, and then strangled herself, as she felt that having been handed the golden scepter by the Emperor she had been made his wife and was now divorced—a disgrace that only her death could remove.

Once again Tz'u Hsi showed that while she was a good judge of men and seldom made a mistake in selecting her male officials, she was a poor judge of women. In choosing the second daughter of Ch'ang Hsu as one of the two imperial concubines she again selected a young girl who, though she was low in rank, was not afraid to oppose her on occasion. This girl, the younger daughter of Ch'ang Hsu, became known as the Pearl Concubine, and proved to be one of the strongest advocates of the reform movement which was to threaten the life of Tz'u Hsi.

Her sister, known as the Lustrous Concubine, was a rather plump, good-natured young woman who became popular with the Emperor and the whole court. Both girls were exceptionally intelligent. Lustrous Concubine is still remembered for her books of poetry and her beautiful Chinese paintings. Pearl Concubine was more interested in political science, foreign history, geography, and the systems of foreign governments. She became of great assistance to Emperor Kuang Hsu in his later plans for China. All the sons of Ch'ang Hsu were noted scholars, particularly Chih Juei, the eldest. The father must have been a very progressive man. He employed the best tutors in China for his sons and, against all custom and local prejudice, he had allowed his two daughters to study with their brothers. This made the Pearl Concubine one of the best-educated girls of her time in China.

The wedding of Kuang Hsu was similar to that of Emperor T'ung Chih and all the other weddings of Ch'ing emperors, excepting that it was more elaborate, the presents were more numerous and most costly, the processions longer and gayer, and it cost more than any previous wedding in the country's history. It also turned out to be the last great wedding of an emperor of China. The wedding of P'u Yi, the last emperor, was to be a relatively simple affair.

Kuang Hsu's wedding was supposed to cost five million ounces of silver. It ultimately cost twenty-one million ounces of silver and more than one hundred thousand ounces of gold—about $15,000,000. The young Emperor must have thought this a great deal to pay for a girl he did not want and whom he never learned to like. Some of the heavy expense was owing to the fact that the huge Gate of Supreme Harmony was entirely destroyed by fire six weeks before the wedding. This was considered a bad omen. As the gate was a necessary part of the marriage ceremony, Chinese workmen built an entire new gate—the duplicate in size, design, and decoration of the original, but of temporary materials. When Tz'u Hsi was shown the new gate she said: "Very good. It looks as if the T'ai Ho Men had never been destroyed." The building and decorating of that immense gate in such a short time are still mentioned as great feats in construction.

Tz'u Hsi personally supervised every detail of the wedding ceremony. She was very pleased at everything—as she well might be, as it was all according to her plan. She was marrying a most unattractive but docile niece to her nephew, the Emperor of China. She was confident she would have no such nonsense with her as she had had with the wife she had chosen for her son.

At eleven o'clock in the evening of the twenty-sixth day of the First Moon the future Empress was brought through the new Gate of Supreme Harmony and through the seven other great gates to the Palace of Earthly Tranquility. Here she was met by the Emperor, Tz'u Hsi, the two imperial concubines, and members of the court. The actual ceremony, like all weddings in China, was a simple declaration before witnesses and the ancestral tablets that each partner took the other as husband or wife.

Emperor Kuang Hsu had become of age. Tz'u Hsi should have handed over the control of the government to him at that time, but this she had been reluctant to do. At the request of a number of memorials sent in by persons who wished to please her, she had allowed herself to be persuaded to retain power for a few years longer. As this raised increasing opposition throughout the provinces and as no good reasons could be advanced for Tz'u Hsi to continue to retain control of the government after Emperor Kuang Hsu's wedding, she made the gesture of giving up the regency at this time.

Tz'u Hsi was now fifty-five years of age, and had been in power for more than thirty years. She retired to her luxurious Summer Palace, which had been recently completed, and tried to convey the impression that she intended to give up all government cares and live a life of ease and privacy. However, it soon became evident that while she did give up the regency and the early-morning meetings with the ministers, as well as certain other outward signs of rulership, she had not the slightest intention of giving up any part of her actual control over the government. In place of the regency, Tz'u Hsi was persuaded to accept a "tutelage" which actually gave her even more authority over the Emperor than she had had as regent.

At a meeting of all the ministers and imperial princes she made a long address to the Emperor in which she pointed out the great care she had taken of him since that night when he entered the palace at the age of four, how she let him sleep in her bed when he was afraid, how she had personally looked after the food he had eaten and the clothes he had worn, how she had taught him the *Four Books* of Confucius, and how she had labored day and night for the welfare of the nation and the prolongation of the dynasty. "Now that you are about to take over the affairs of the nation, you must remember all these things," she concluded.

The Emperor fell to his knees and promised to remember the debt he owed Tz'u Hsi. She also made him promise he would not dismiss any officials she had appointed or make new appointments without her knowledge, and to consult her before making any important decisions. The kneeling Emperor replied: "Your son and minister shall not use his own arbitrary judgment and shall most decidedly ask for instructions from his Imperial Father."

Tz'u Hsi then turned to the ministers and princes and asked: "Have you all heard what Emperor Kuang Hsu has promised on his bended knees?" They answered: "Cha [We have heard and it shall be done]." Tz'u Hsi saw to it that all this was made legal by issuing the proper decrees.

In this way the weak Kuang put the halter around his own neck. He had been brought up in such awe of Tz'u Hsi that he could never oppose her when face to face.

3

In carrying out this well-planned program, Tz'u Hsi thought she had made her position unassailable and free from all danger. Instead, the next decade was to be probably the most dangerous period of her reign.

The very completeness of her plan to retain hold on the government and her humiliating treatment of the Emperor did much toward bringing on the reform movement that ended in the coup d'état of 1898. This was planned to remove Tz'u Hsi completely from all government affairs, either to the "cold palace" or even to kill her if necessary. It failed only because of the inexperience of Emperor Kuang Hsu and the traitorous act of one of the officials he trusted.

When Kuang Hsu was a small boy and Tz'u Hsi was closely supervising his education, he had suggested that he wanted to study the English language so that he could read foreign books and study the geography, history, and systems of government of Western countries. This pleased Tz'u Hsi very much. She looked on it as evidence of the superior intelligence of her nephew. Later suitable teachers for all these subjects were found, and the young man proved to be a very apt student. The Empress herself showed considerable interest at this time in foreign ideas and in foreign inventions. She called in Li Hung-chang, her one friend who had been in foreign countries, and questioned him for hours. He told her of an enterprising Western salesman who wanted to sell railways to China and who had offered to give the Emperor a miniature railway as a present to show him how a modern railway was operated. The train was large enough for each coach to carry two passengers. Li Hung-chang suggested that the Empress accept this offer. She did so willingly and ordered the railway built along the west shore of the three lakes in the Imperial City, passing close to her new residence in the Sea Palace area.

She could hardly wait for the opening day when she, the Emperor, and a few of her friends were to take the first ride. A Chinese engineer had been carefully instructed in the operation of the train. He was most anxious to make a good showing in the presence of the Emperor and Empress, so he built a great fire in the engine. So fierce was the fire that it caused steam to escape continuously from the safety valve. Not being well versed in the use of the safety valve and thinking that it was a great waste to have so much of his good steam escaping, the engineer closed the safety valve. The not unnatural result was that a few hours before the arrival of the imperial family the boiler exploded and blew both the engine and engineer clear out of the Imperial City.

While this incident somewhat lessened the Empress's enthusiasm for steam engines, and probably delayed the introduction of railways into China for several years, it did not stop the operation of the miniature train. The Empress ordered it operated by man power for several years. Nor did it influence her against other Western inventions. The Empress also had electric lights secretly installed in her new Winter Palace and later in the Summer Palace. Many foreign musical instruments, including organs, were found in the palaces, particularly in the quarters of Tz'u Hsi and the concubines, by the foreign troops when they entered and looted the imperial palaces in 1900.

Tz'u Hsi had further talks with Li Hung-chang about foreign countries and foreign governments. This seems to confirm the opinion that while Tz'u Hsi was even more strongly anti-foreign than when she entered the palace, she was not opposed to the introduction of such foreign ideas as she and her ministers thought would be of value to China. She later opposed the reform movement of Kuang Hsu and K'ang Yu-wei not so much because she objected to the reforms (many of them she later put in force herself) but because she believed some of the reforms endangered the dynasty and her own position.

To all outward appearances the domestic relations between Tz'u Hsi and her adopted son the Emperor were cordial during the first few months after his assumption of power.

In the thirteenth year of Emperor Kuang Hsu's reign the new Palace of the Dancing Phoenix, which Tz'u Hsi built in the Sea Palace area of the Imperial City, was completed. To celebrate this, she arranged for the greatest display of fireworks probably ever given in any country up to that time. The celebration lasted an entire month. During the day huge pageants and many theatricals were produced on the eastern shore of the lake with the rock gardens and red walls of the Forbidden City as a background. This was viewed largely from the imperial barges and the boats on the lakes. In the evening the entire eastern shore of the two lakes was used for the main display of fireworks—huge archways of colored lights, illuminated displays of every description, and thousands of lights of every color were distributed throughout the Sea Palace area. This was a fete the whole city could enjoy.

The invited audience consisted of the imperial family, all the imperial princes and leading Manchu families, the families of all the government officials, and many officials from the provinces. They were seated at banquet tables on the porticoes of the palaces on the western shore or at tables scattered throughout the grounds, whence they could see the fireworks reflected in the still water of the lakes.

The expense of this exhibition was enormous, far exceeding all estimates or amounts thought possible or appropriate for the object of the celebration. As one Chinese general dryly commented: "It cost as much as a military campaign."

The expense was so severely criticized by the Censors and the officials from the provinces that Tz'u Hsi never attempted to repeat the performance. It was also many years before she again had anything really worth celebrating in such an elaborate manner.

Tz'u Hsi was enjoying life in her new palace, with the boating parties, picnics, visits to the many old temples and palaces of past emperors in the neighborhood, and especially the many theatricals and other forms of entertainment she arranged.

But in one thing her self-esteem was not complete. While she had become the absolute ruler of China she had never been accepted as a social equal by the wives of the old Manchu families of the Aisin Gioro clan. These women, many of them older than Tz'u Hsi, were wives of imperial princes and looked on her as an upstart. They knew and she knew that there were many generations of her family which were not important while these old families were blue-blooded without a break to the origin of the Manchu race. While Tz'u Hsi could make or degrade these families politically, she could not break down the invisible social barriers they had built up in the centuries to protect themselves.

This situation galled Tz'u Hsi. She knew the value of these fences as well as anyone. She used them freely herself when she needed them, but she resented them when they shut her out.

As her next move Tz'u Hsi tore down completely one of the fences that surrounded the Manchu upper classes. China had no caste system, unless one could so call the privileges given to scholars. There was no position except that of Emperor that most boys could not at that time dream of someday occupying if they had the ability to pass the imperial examinations. The same was true of young girls, if they possessed the beauty and brains to attract the attention of an emperor, prince, or official. But while they had no rigid caste system in China, the people were divided into nine groups—headed by the scholars, officials and soldiers, and followed in order by farmers, artisans, merchants and bankers, astrologers and fortunetellers, physicians, harlots, and last of all actors. The actor's son was barred by his birth from the imperial examinations. An actor could not address an emperor, prince, or high official in ordinary clothes. He could do so only in the costume of the role he personified on the stage, and then he was considered as that character, not as himself. To break this rule meant death.

It was this very high fence that Tz'u Hsi chose first to tear down. Not that she objected to that particular fence more than any other, but because it restricted her most in the things she wanted to do. She had also heard rumors that a number of young and neglected wives of her inner circle had not troubled to try to break down that fence, but had occasionally jumped over it for a few hours of illicit pleasure with certain actors.

Because of Tz'u Hsi's fondness for the stage she was well acquainted with all the prominent actors of the time. No popular performer missed an opportunity to play before her in the theaters of the Imperial City. The first actor whose name became connected with Tz'u Hsi was Yang Yueh-lou. He was a fine-looking man. Being an excellent athlete and possessed of a strong face, he took only the parts of heroes and warriors. His name was linked with those of a number of young women of the old Manchu families.

The next actor to be singled out by Tz'u Hsi was Hou Chunshan, who specialized in playing the parts of Flower Girls. He was very successful in portraying the motions of amorous women even to the most minute detail. He was often commanded to play before Tz'u Hsi in her private theater and even in her palace. At that time he was only nineteen years old. He looked like a beautiful girl and had the manners and carriage of a most tantalizing and frivolous woman. He tried to escape from Tz'u Hsi's too-marked attention by feigning illness. When she ordered him to play on her private stage, ill or not, Hou mysteriously disappeared from Peking. He was thinking of his own safety.

He was followed in the not-too-welcome attentions of Tz'u Hsi by Chao Chua-chi, probably the most sought-after actor of that time. Chao Chua-chi was popular for two reasons: without doubt he was a great actor, but he also sang and portrayed parts in a play known as *The Falling Lotus Flowers.* All the songs were based on the love episodes of young girls craving passion, or of young married women missing their absent husbands too much. It takes little imagination to see why such actors and such songs were banned by good society, and also why the publicity resulting from the ban made them popular. Tz'u Hsi shocked all the imperial household by having Chao Chua-chi and his troupe perform often in her palace.

Chao Chua-chi was followed by another actor, Chao Hsing-ch'uan. He openly accepted all honors and gifts from Tz'u Hsi and even bragged publicly about his influence with the Empress. His professional name was "Puffed Hair Chao," a name known to almost every man, woman, and child in Peking. He was a Manchu and seems to have come from a good family. He was also known as "the most beautiful woman in Peking." A dramatic critic of the time described him as follows: "The reason Puffed Hair Chao is so passionately sought after by young women of the wealthy and good families is that besides being handsome he is extremely expressive in acting the parts of lewd women craving love and is able to depict to perfection the tantalizing walk of mischievous young maidens. His eyes are filled with such devilish seductiveness that even the most demure and self-respecting young woman develops a desire for sexual excitement."

Naturally Tz'u Hsi had to have Puffed Hair Chao perform in the Imperial Theater, regardless of the criticisms and protests of the older imperial princes. After his first performance she was as openly stage-struck over Puffed Hair Chao as the most foolish young woman who have been clandestinely trying to meet him. She loaded him with gifts, at first following the rule of presenting the gifts on the stage. Later, she invited the actor to her palace and personally handed them to him. In defiance of all rules of etiquette, she even allowed him to eat in her presence.

At this time Peking had a long rainy spell. The imperial theaters were flooded and, as Tz'u Hsi could not leave the palace, she took advantage of this to have Puffed Hair Chao perform in her private apartments in the Lo Shou T'ang.

Such a thing was a gross violation of all the rules of good form at court. According to the Ch'ing Household Rules, the actor who rashly accepted such favors should have been decapitated. The entire household, and especially the brothers of Emperor Hsien Feng, were indignant at this flagrant misbehavior of Tz'u Hsi.

But of all the imperial princes only Prince Tun had the courage to voice his protests to Tz'u Hsi herself, and he evidently required a little artificial stimulant to give him the necessary courage.

After a huge meal with much wine, at which the princes discussed their sister-in-law's indiscretions with Puffed Hair Chao, Prince Tun decided to face her in her palace. He reached the private quarters of the Empress while Actor Chao was giving one of his lewd performances. Evidently the part he was playing required the actor to be dressed only in his trousers, leaving the upper part of his body bare. Prince Tun, who was now thoroughly intoxicated, listened outside the door to the performance. When it ended, he tore off his gown and shirt and, clad only in his trousers, marched into the Empress's room and sang the same songs Chao had been singing.

When the prince openly accused the Empress of having illicit relations with the actor, she calmly replied that he was drunk and did not know what he was saying. She ordered her eunuchs to throw him out, which they did—probably to their own enjoyment.

That settled the affair as far as Tz'u Hsi was concerned, but unfortunately not for Actor Puffed Hair Chao. A few days later Puffed Hair Chao joined the fast-increasing ranks of missing actors.

In addition to the Palace of the Dancing Phoenix Empress Tz'u Hsi had built at enormous cost her Summer Palace some fifteen miles from Peking where she could retire during the months of hot weather and whenever she felt a need for privacy.

Whenever she was in residence there, the Emperor dutifully made from two to three long journeys weekly to pay his respects to his Imperial Father and to present reports. When the Empress visited the Forbidden City the Emperor met her and welcomed her on bended knees at the entrance to the palace. In all this formality the Emperor was most punctilious in following the exact letter of the old customs of respect and obedience due an aged mother and an Empress. But it was only the lull before the storm.

The Emperor was determined to carry out certain reforms in the government and customs of the country. In this he was supported by the Pearl Concubine and by what was then known as the Southern party. For some years the court had been dividing itself into two groups. These were the Northern party (the conservative group) or Tz'u Hsi's party, known as the Old Mother party, and the Southern party of the reform group, called the Young Emperor's party. This division grew rapidly after the retirement of Tz'u Hsi to the Summer Palace and soon involved even the Grand Council.

Weng T'ung-ho, the leader of the Young Emperor's party, at that time occupied the high position of Grand Secretary. He had been a tutor of the Emperor and without doubt greatly influenced him in his plans for reform. Unfortunately Prince Kung died at the very time when his wise counsel and influence over his nephew, the Emperor, were most needed. If he had lived he probably would have been able to reconcile the views of Tz'u Hsi and the Emperor and there would have been no split and no coup d'état. Both the Emperor and Tz'u Hsi personally visited Prince Kung's sickbed a number of times and both sincerely mourned his death. On this occasion Tz'u Hsi issued one of her finest decrees in which she recalled their long friendship and gave Prince Kung full credit for all his unselfish assistance to her.

One of the greatest, though also perhaps the most unfortunate, services Weng T'ung-ho did for the Emperor was to bring K'ang Yu-wei to his attention, telling the Emperor that

K'ang had ten times his own ability. This seemingly exaggerated praise was probably true. K'ang Yu-wei became the Emperor's most influential and trusted adviser and Tz'u Hsi's most hated opponent. He was the very man the Emperor had been seeking for a long time.

The influence of K'ang Yu-wei soon became evident. Within a few days the Emperor inaugurated what is known as the Hundred Days of Reform. His first reform decree advocated that European studies be added to the canons of the sages. This struck at the imperial examinations. In a succeeding decree the Emperor advocated foreign travel and foreign education even for the imperial princes.

While Tz'u Hsi did not object to these decrees, the older Manchus vigorously opposed them. They claimed that the decrees favored foreign ideas and struck at the very fundamentals of the old customs of China. They repeated a very apt old Chinese proverb: "In converting barbarians to Chinese ideas we must not let China be converted by the barbarians."

The Emperor followed up with a perfect stream of decrees, each advocating some new reform. He even recommended the cutting off of all queues. Among other things, he abolished the imperial examinations, and attempted to reform the Manchu Imperial Guard of Peking. In this he was hitting at Jung Lu, one of his strongest opponents. He forgot his promises to Tz'u Hsi and dismissed a number of her appointees. He ordered every large city to publish official gazettes and to allow freedom of the press. He started naval colleges and laid the foundation for a modern Chinese navy. He ordered the translation of many foreign scientific books, built new roads, and suggested that the Manchus leave crowded Peking, settle in the provinces, and enter trade and business.

Throughout this rain of decrees Tz'u Hsi remained silent. But, to make her own position more secure, she took the precaution of putting Jung Lu on the Grand Council. She also kept her spy system in good order and without doubt knew everything that was being planned by the Emperor and his Reform party.

But the old Manchus did not remain silent or inactive. They organized against the Emperor, even though many of them had formerly opposed Tz'u Hsi. They sent a huge delegation to the Summer Palace to petition her to return to Peking and again take over active and effective control of the government. They claimed that the young Emperor was ruining the country and endangering the Ch'ing Dynasty. To all this she turned a deaf ear, knowing that the time to act had not yet come. She waited in the secrecy of her Summer Palace until the Emperor and his party had further weakened their position with the influential families.

At this point K'ang Yu-wei, who saw the storm coming, entirely mistook the strength and ability of Tz'u Hsi. He continued to prejudice the Emperor against her, pointing out that she was endangering the financial position of the nation by her extravagant expenditures in the construction of her tomb and further additions to her Summer Palace. This was true. He now openly advocated that for the safety of his reforms and the future of China the Emperor should surround the Summer Palace, take Tz'u Hsi prisoner, and banish her to one of the islands in the Nan Hai.

In effect, K'ang Yu-wei asked that the young Emperor, without experience, without one powerful friend in the army, and with few supporters in Peking—as his reforms had estranged every Manchu family—should challenge the power of the experienced Tz'u Hsi with her host of friends in every important position in the capital and in the provinces. A courageous but unwise plan framed by two rash young men.

At this time Jung Lu was back in Tz'u Hsi's good graces and was Viceroy of Chihli. This was one of the important positions Tz'u Hsi always reserved for a loyal friend. As Viceroy he was in supreme command of all the troops of the province, including the new foreign-trained army commanded by Yuan Shih-k'ai.

Yuan Shih-k'ai was at that time about forty years old and a friend and follower of Li Hung-chang, another loyal supporter of Tz'u Hsi.

The Emperor and K'ang Yu-wei knew that both Jung Lu and Li Hung-chang would, without the slightest doubt, remain loyal to Tz'u Hsi. But Yuan Shih-k'ai was at that time not very popular with either Tz'u Hsi or with the public because his failure as resident general in Korea was blamed for the recent war with Japan and the loss of Korea. The Emperor had had a number of talks with Yuan Shih-k'ai, who assured him that he favored the Emperor's reform movement and praised him as a courageous and far-seeing ruler. This led the Emperor to believe that Yuan Shih-k'ai would support him. The Emperor was either a very courageous or a very foolish young man to risk his future and possibly his life on such a flimsy supposition. He placed trust in a man who later was disloyal to and deserted every friend and every cause with which he was associated.

Kuang Hsu had two other meetings with Yuan Shih-k'ai. The first in the Summer Palace. At this meeting the Emperor explained to Yuan Shih-k'ai his plans for carrying out the reforms outlined in his various decrees. Yuan Shih-k'ai appeared to be favorably impressed with the Emperor's plans. The Emperor then went further and told him of his plans to create a large modern army, intimating that he would like to have Yuan Shih-k'ai as commander of this force. Yuan Shih-k'ai professed his complete and absolute loyalty to the Emperor.

At the completion of this interview, Tz'u Hsi sent for the Emperor and questioned him closely about his talk with Yuan Shih-k'ai. Her intuition and spying eunuchs had evidently warned her that their talk was not entirely on army reform, as the Emperor had assured her. She professed complete accord with the Emperor's plan to create a modern army. At this meeting Tz'u Hsi accused the Emperor's friend, K'ang Yu-wei, of spreading damaging rumors about her and of advocating reforms that were dangerous to the dynasty. Evidently she was not fully aware of the plot against her, but she demanded that K'ang Yu-wei be arrested. The Emperor warned his friend that he could no longer protect him and gave him time to escape from the city before, in obedience to Tz'u Hsi's command, he issued the decree ordering his arrest.

A few days later Yuan Shih-k'ai had his final meeting with Kuang Hsu. This meeting was held in the private palace of the Empress in Peking, where he thought he was safe from the ears of the Empress's spies. Without further investigation and evidently with none of the careful planning that such an undertaking required to be successful, especially against such a shrewd opponent as Tz'u Hsi, the Emperor boldly told Yuan Shih-k'ai of his plan to arrest and execute Jung Lu (Yuan Shih-k'ai's superior officer) and to seize the Empress Dowager at her home in the Summer Palace.

He asked Yuan Shih-k'ai if he would be loyal to him and carry out this plan with his force of foreign-trained troops. Yuan Shih-k'ai, on bended knees, assured the Emperor of his loyalty and promised faithful obedience to the plan.

Kuang Hsu then rashly gave Yuan Shih-k'ai two decrees, one authorizing him to execute Jung Lu, the other ordering the seizure of Tz'u Hsi, thereby placing in Yuan Shih-k'ai's hands undeniable evidence of the entire plot.

With the exception of the two leaders of the Southern party, the Emperor had no supporters in the government. He had only the word of Yuan Shih-k'ai, a Chinese as yet untried in his professed loyalty to the Ch'ing Emperor. It is doubtful whether even if Yuan Shih-k'ai had been loyal, and his troops had obeyed him against Tz'u Hsi, he possessed sufficient military strength to succeed against the Imperial Guards and the army in Peking, both organizations intensely loyal to the Empress and Jung Lu.

But Yuan Shih-k'ai was not loyal to his promise or to his Emperor. He went directly from his meeting with the Emperor to Tientsin, where he was closeted for hours with Jung Lu. He told Jung Lu the Emperor's entire plan—how the Emperor had given him the official order to kill him. This he showed Jung Lu. Jung Lu calmly stated that he was not astonished at the plan of the foolish young Emperor, but he was amazed at his ability to fool the Venerable Ancestor even temporarily.

Jung Lu left for Peking within an hour after the meeting with Yuan Shih-k'ai and arrived in the capital at ten o'clock that evening. Without ceremony he went directly to Tz'u Hsi's palace in the Imperial City. He found the Empress neither unduly surprised nor worried over his disclosures. But she lost no further time. She called together her loyal officials and certain of the imperial princes. They fell to their knees and begged her to resume the reins of government in order to save the country and the Ch'ing Dynasty. This was all the authority she required—or wanted. Characteristically, she acted quickly, and though it was now long past midnight she ordered all the guards in the palace replaced by Jung Lu's men.

When the Emperor left his palace at four o'clock in the morning for his meeting with the ministers, he was arrested and lodged in the Ocean Terrace. This was a beautiful little palace on an island in the Nan Hai—a palace, not a prison. He was to remain there a virtual prisoner until the flight from Peking in 1900. On his return, he chose to take up his residence there again, and there he remained until his death eight years later.

At first the Pearl Concubine was allowed to stay with the Emperor to spare him from further discomforts. One day she foolishly reminded Tz'u Hsi that Kuang Hsu was the lawful Ch'ing Emperor and that even she could not set aside the Mandate of Heaven and arrest him. The Empress's reply that she had arrested him appeared to be sufficient to quiet the Pearl Concubine. But Tz'u Hsi emphasized her point by removing the Pearl Concubine from the Ocean Terrace and replacing her with the young Empress, whom she could trust to keep a close watch on all the Emperor's movements. The beautiful Pearl Concubine, the only woman the Emperor apparently ever loved and whom he was never to see again, was imprisoned in a small but charming palace just to the west of the large palace she had occupied as an imperial concubine. She was allowed to see no one, but she poured out her love for her Emperor in a large number of letters. None of these ever reached him—Tz'u Hsi saw to that—but some of them reached the writer while at work on this book. She wrote many of her letters under a large flowering apple tree which is still the first tree in all the Forbidden City to bloom. Attendants tell visitors that the ghost of the beautiful Pearl Concubine still lives in the palace and is often seen in the spring, seated under the blossoming boughs writing her love letters to the Emperor. Today the Pearl Concubine is a national heroine, as one of China's early reformers.

All Tz'u Hsi's actions were made legal by a decree issued by her in the name of the Emperor, in which he was made to state: "The country is now passing through a serious crisis beyond my poor ability to cope with. So, fearing for the future of our country, and realizing my duty to our ancestors, I have besought Her Majesty to condescend once more to administer the affairs of government. She has graciously honored us by voluntarily giving up her life of ease which she has so deservedly earned and to condescend once more to administer the government. I command all the princes and the ministers to join me in performing the proper obeisance before our Imperial Mother."

Empress Tz'u Hsi took the first opportunity to visit Kuang Hsu in his palace prison. It is well for the Empress's reputation that there is no record of that meeting, but it is known that she cursed the Emperor so long and so loudly that even her own eunuchs were frightened. Cursing in China is not profanity, but it casts such serious reflections on the victim's ancestors and his own origin that it usually has the hoped-for effect.

The Emperor was informed that he would not be executed as, she said, he so richly deserved. At least not at this time. It was through no kindness of heart that Tz'u Hsi did not execute the Emperor. Had she done so she would have been compelled to appoint a successor to him—a prince who might menace her authority. In the imprisoned Kuang Hsu she had an emperor who was absolutely under her control. In her generosity, Tz'u Hsi announced, she would allow him to retain his throne, but he would be kept a prisoner and she would handle all government affairs. He would be allowed to see no one. However, for company, Tz'u Hsi would graciously allow his Empress, her niece, to visit him. This probably was one of the bitterest punishments, as the Emperor disliked his Empress very much. In addition to being unpleasing in appearance, she had an extremely sharp tongue, was overbearing in her attitude, and made no effort to conceal the fact that she was not an affectionate wife but an agent for her aunt. The Emperor's eunuchs were replaced by eunuchs from Tz'u Hsi's household.

It is not hard to imagine the feelings of the ambitious young Emperor, twenty-eight years old, as he sat alone in his palace prison and recalled the events of the short time he was actually in control of the government. He had made a desperate effort to carry through his plans for a modern China to enable her to take her proper place among the great nations of the world. He had gambled all on one throw of the dice, and he had failed miserably. He saw all his reforms swept away, all his friends either killed or banished from Peking. He was a prisoner in almost solitary confinement. Most of all, he missed his beautiful Pearl Concubine, who, he knew, was also a prisoner and treated even more severely than he was.

For all this he blamed one man—Yuan Shih-k'ai. And rightly. The Emperor never blamed Jung Lu for his predicament, though Jung Lu was the actual officer who had arrested him. He said once: "Because I tried to kill Jung Lu, Jung Lu had a perfect right to act as he did. But not Yuan Shih-k'ai, who gave me his sworn word to support me."

8. THE BOXER UPRISING

From the very day that Empress Tz'u Hsi first seized control of the Manchu Empire she had been the target for a steady barrage of petitions from the Censors and from the people of China.

The right to petition and to criticize their rulers, even the Emperor, was one of the oldest rights of the Chinese people. No ruler, not even Tz'u Hsi, who broke so many traditions, attempted in any way to curtail or ignore this ancient privilege. Many of the petitions were suggestions for changes in the laws or criticism of a local magistrate. Most of the former rulers had encouraged the petitions, as they gave the Emperor a direct insight into the condition and mind of his people. The majority of the petitions addressed to Empress Tz'u Hsi were criticisms of Empress Tz'u Hsi.

But after the criticisms of her daring overthrow of tradition in placing Kuang Hsu on the Dragon Throne had died down, there were several noticeable changes in the petitions. First, they so increased in number that, as one Chinese stated, they could not be answered or even counted. But Tz'u Hsi continued to read and in some cases to reply to as many as she could. As the petitions increased in numbers they changed in tone. They ceased to criticize Tz'u Hsi—which must have astonished and pleased her. The appeals to the Empress were becoming almost entirely criticisms of the foreigners living in China.

Tz'u Hsi saw something in these petitions that evidently no one else saw. Her instinct and her knowledge of the Chinese people warned her that a real danger was threatening the country, herself, and her dynasty. This was no local affair like the Tientsin massacre; it was a whole nation being aroused. The sleeping dragon had begun to stir. No one knew better than Tz'u Hsi that once the great dragon of China really became aroused no one, nothing, not even the Empress herself, could control it. It might destroy everything.

Tz'u Hsi was faced with a problem she did not know how to solve. She could not convince her associates that it even existed. On this problem her instincts and desires were on one side, her good judgment on the other. She undoubtedly hated the foreigner for what he had done to China as sincerely as the most extreme fanatic. She, too, wanted every foreigner out of China if only this could be accomplished without risk to the dynasty. Being of two minds, she did what she could to halt this anti-foreign movement. She issued a decree in the name of the Emperor in which she ordered all Chinese officials to get better acquainted and to visit more often the missionaries living in their neighborhood. To offset the frequent complaint of missionaries that they could not see Chinese officials of rank, she stated that Christian bishops were to be considered of equal rank with a governor and could demand audience with such an official. Christian ministers of lesser rank could demand audience with Chinese officials of similar standing.

The decree also stated that the Emperor dismissed the charge that the teachings of missionaries incited people to rebellion. Not because this was not true; he thought that even missionaries would agree that it was true. But he believed if the teachings of the missionaries did tend to create rebellion against conditions that were bad or hampered the formation of a modern China that such efforts should be encouraged.

This certainly was a broad-minded policy and seems an earnest attempt on Tz'u Hsi's part to avoid trouble between the Chinese people and the missionaries.

But Empress Tz'u Hsi soon realized that all the decrees and mandates she could issue could not stop the dragon from moving. The petitions continued to pour in, and in ever-greater numbers. They came from two distinct classes. Those from the officials and the educated class were against the acts of the foreign governments. The petitions from the lower classes were against the acts of individual foreigners and especially missionaries.

Since the Treaty of Nanking the foreign powers had united and increased their pressure on China until they had forced the government to open practically every Chinese port to foreign trade and residence. In many of these open ports they had demanded and had received what was called foreign concessions or sections of the cities entirely under foreign control. In cities such as Shanghai these foreign concessions became large separate cities. Although the concessions were in fact under Chinese sovereignty, the foreign powers installed their own police and their own courts and forbade the Chinese the right to own property within the settlements.

In addition to these concessions the foreign governments had seized and the Chinese Government had lost complete control of large areas of Chinese territory—even whole provinces. The French had taken Indo-China; the British, Burma and Weihaiwei (they already had Hong Kong); the Japanese, Korea, Formosa, and a number of other islands. The Russians seized Port Arthur, Darien, and with their railways practically all Manchuria. The Germans seized Kiaochow Bay and the port of Tsingtao, using as a pretext for this annexation the murder of two German missionaries. All this totaled a comparatively large part of the Manchu Empire. Even this did not satisfy the foreign powers; they openly discussed the partition of all China among themselves. Naturally the officials and educated classes were much worried over the future of their country.

Although most of this was not understood by the great mass of the Chinese people living in the interior provinces, they had grievances, many grievances, of their own. They were the same grievances that had led to the Tientsin massacre but magnified a hundred or more times, and with a few new ones added.

The grievances of the Chinese against the missionaries are best told by an incident reported to me by one of the fine old missionaries who had lived practically his entire life in China. This is not an isolated case but one typical of scores of similar stories told me by men who actually witnessed the events described.

A Chinese named Wang, living in a small Chinese city, suddenly became converted and joined the local Christian church. Some time later Wang laid claim to the property of his neighbor Chang, alleging that he had bought the property from Chang's father who had recently died. Chang took the case to the local magistrate, who upheld his claim, as all the people in the neighborhood knew it was his family property and that Wang's papers were false.

Wang then visited his missionary friend. He asked the missionary to give him his visiting card to show the magistrate that he was a Christian and a friend of the missionary. The missionary gave Wang his card but, despite this, the magistrate refused again to turn Chang's property over to Wang.

In response to Wang's appeals, the missionary made a personal call on the magistrate. Instead of sending in his card and waiting in the waiting room, with a cup or two of tea, as is customary and as all other callers would have done, the missionary brushed aside the guards and noisily marched directly into the magistrate's private office—an almost unbelievable breach of etiquette.

The magistrate told the missionary that Wang and all his brothers were well-known criminals. The court had a long list of their crimes, which the magistrate attempted to show the missionary. He also attempted to show him the record of the Chang family, who had owned the disputed property for ten or more generations and were known by all the citizens of the town as honest, hard-working citizens. The magistrate reminded the missionary that the Chinese Government had offered to supply all missionaries with the records of their converts before these last were accepted by the churches.

The missionary brushed all this aside with the statement that all that was in the past and, consequently, irrelevant, as Wang had become a Christian, joined his church, and was, therefore, an honest man. He claimed that the magistrate was discriminating against Wang because he was a Christian, which was against the Tientsin Treaty. He demanded that Wang be given the property immediately.

When the magistrate still refused to make Chang's property over to the ex-criminal, the missionary reported his version of the affair to his consul. The consul passed it on to the ambassador or minister who, in turn, sent it on to the Chinese Foreign Office. The foreign minister, knowing nothing of the case but knowing well his instructions from Empress Tz'u Hsi that he was to do nothing that would offend the foreign governments, after delaying it as long as he could, sent word to the magistrate to decide the case in favor of Wang. Wang got the property and in gratitude gave a large contribution to the local church.

This case became the talk of the countryside. It aroused considerable indignation among the local people, who have a strong love for justice. It probably meant several more petitions to Tz'u Hsi. But above all else it pointed out to Chinese of shady character another material advantage to becoming a Christian.

As these conditions continued to multiply, a feeling grew up among the great mass of the Chinese people that their government was unable to solve this problem for them or give them protection.

As a result, innumerable secret societies sprang up all over China with the one object of driving the foreigner and everything foreign out of the country. Most of these were gradually absorbed by an organization called "Boxers" by the foreigners. The Boxers were a revival of a semi-religious society founded about the year 1700. At that time they were known as the I Ho Ch'uan, or Society of Harmonious Fists.

Foreigners first began to get uneasy over the revival of the society during the summer of 1899. The Boxers declared it their intention to remove the foreign poison from the hearts of the people of China and to restore the old religion, the old freedom, and the old way of living that the Chinese had developed through the centuries. This appealed to almost every man and woman in China.

To strengthen their hold on the people the Boxers claimed that their society was not organized by man but was heavenly commanded and that all true Boxers would be protected by divine Providence.

Tz'u Hsi could scarcely have believed the stories that the Boxers were immune to the bullets of foreign guns, even after the demonstration given her in the Forbidden City. At this demonstration a number of Boxers were lined up against the wall while the guns—old muzzle-loaders—were carefully loaded in her presence. The powder was put in the guns, well wadded, and lead bullets added. After many flourishes of the guns, the soldiers took aim and fired at the Boxers. Without doubt some of the load from the guns did hit the men and was seen to drop to the ground, but the men were unhurt. This experiment was not only shown before Tz'u Hsi, but before many other persons, many times, in many parts of China. It won many to the Boxers' cause.

The only plausible explanation ever given for the "miracle" was that when the lead bullets were placed in the guns no wadding was added, so that in flourishing the guns about before firing—always a part of the demonstration—the lead bullets were allowed to drop from the muzzles. Thus only the paper wadding hit the men. These demonstrations convinced many people that the Boxers were protected by the gods and could not be killed by foreign guns.

They cleverly chose for their slogan "Free China from all foreigners and uphold the Ch'ing Dynasty." Movements of this kind usually originate among the lowest classes, but the Society of Harmonious Fists appealed to all classes. Many of the imperial princes and some of the best-educated men in China openly declared themselves to be Boxers.

The Boxer movement first started in Shantung province which, as the home of Confucius, is the spiritual heart of China. Here hostility against the foreigner was probably stronger than in any other North China province, owing to the seizure of Kiaochow Bay by the Germans and the occupation of Weihaiwei by the British. The movement in this province also received the active support of Yu Hsien, governor of Shantung, whose son became one of the Boxer leaders.

As Tz'u Hsi feared that the activities of Governor Yu Hsien might bring on trouble with the foreign governments, she transferred him to Peking. There he became a less conspicuous but exceedingly effective leader of the Boxer movement and greatly influenced Tz'u Hsi.

Yuan Shih-k'ai was sent to Shantung to succeed Yu Hsien, with orders to restrain the people from any outbreaks of violence. This Yuan Shih-k'ai was willing to do as he, with his two friends Jung Lu and Li Hung-chang, knew that the Boxers could not succeed against the military might of the combined foreign powers and would only bring greater calamities, possibly even the division of China.

This legend of the invulnerability of the Boxers to foreign bullets was something he knew he had to dispel. To accomplish this he invited a number of Boxer leaders to dine with him. He questioned them about their claims to invulnerability and listened gravely while they boasted of this. At the completion of their story he asked them to line up along the wall and give a demonstration with his soldiers.

This time the rifles were properly loaded and properly aimed, with the result that Yuan Shih-k'ai exploded the myth and removed all the Boxer leaders at the banquet in one volley.

The Boxers' only explanation for this unfortunate affair was that these men were not true Boxers and that they were killed because they lacked sufficient faith.

The movement continued to grow, and it began to be dangerous for any Chinese to work for or even be seen with a foreigner.

A proclamation appeared in Chihli ordering all Christian churches to be converted into "Immortal Halls" or Boxer Halls within one week. Failing this, the buildings would be torn down or burned.

While events were rapidly reaching a climax in the provinces, Peking remained outwardly calm. Eleven countries had established legations in the capital. These ministers, with the British Commissioner of Customs, formed the governing body of the foreign population of Peking. None of them had much to do except attend picnics, dinners, races, and other social affairs. Politics was their main topic of conversation.

Even as late as May 1900 the Boxers were considered by foreign diplomats as more or less something of a joke and were rather welcomed, as providing another topic to argue over at the weekly meetings of the diplomatic body. Only the French minister, as protector of the missionary work of the Roman Catholic Church, was annoying in his prophecies of danger and in his demands for more foreign troops to be ordered to Peking.

The foreign representatives allowed matters to drift, unmindful of conditions which were to burst into actual fighting in only two months' time. They did order a few extra guards from the men of war lying off Taku, but they refused to see an emergency. In the early part of June armed Boxers appeared openly on the streets of Peking. Their hair was tied up in red cloth, they wore red ribbons on their wrists and ankles, and a great red sash around the waist.

Chinese servants soon began asking their foreign masters for leave to visit their native homes outside Peking. To old hands in China this is a sure sign that trouble is brewing. Trains to Tientsin were running late and with less frequency. Foreigners, even members of legations, were threatened on the streets of Peking. But still the foreign ministers continued to cable to their governments that Peking was secure, that even if the Boxers did rebel, the people in the capital would be safe. It was typical that the burning of the buildings of the foreign race track outside Peking did more to rouse the foreign diplomats than the massacre of thousands of Chinese Christians in the provinces.

On June 12 an incident occurred which showed how completely the foreigners misunderstood their position in China. The German minister, Baron von Ketteler, noticed a Boxer in full uniform driving down Legation Street, sitting on the shaft of a cart, and calmly sharpening a knife on the sole of his shoe. The good baron decided to show his resentment toward all Boxers and this one in particular. Instead of calling a policeman, he took his cane, gave the Boxer a thorough thrashing, then dragged him to his legation and handed him over to the German guard. The baron evidently forgot that he was in China, not in Germany. Later in the day three other Boxers were found in the Chinese post office close to the legations. They were driven out with whips by the legation staff.

By the middle of June the Boxers had begun to attack and burn the homes of Chinese Christians in the capital, starting large fires both in the Chinese city and the Tatar city. Still the foreign ministers seemed undecided what united action to take. The Boxers followed up by destroying the homes of foreigners. On June 15 Austrian and German legation guards opened fire with a machine gun on a group of what they hoped were Boxers. One of the French cathedrals was set afire and a mixed group of foreign volunteers rescued a number of Chinese Christians. No one could guess how many of these had been butchered before the arrival of the relief column.

Even in the face of all this the foreign legations failed to adopt a common policy toward the Chinese Government or even a united front for defense. However, each of the larger legations began to construct separate and often unrelated barricades. The Germans took over that part of the city wall nearest to their legation and from that position fired on anyone who looked like a Boxer. This was condemned by the other legations.

At first the ministers objected to allowing any Chinese Christians into the legation area, claiming this would entail danger. But as rescue parties and missionaries continued to bring in Chinese Christians the large group of buildings of Prince Su's palace was turned over for their use. Without the aid later given by these Chinese Christians in building defense barricades, filling sandbags, and even in fighting, the legation area could probably not have been successfully defended.

On June 19 the Chinese Foreign Office sent an identical communication to each of the foreign ministers in Peking stating that Admiral Seymour, commander of the Allied Forces, had started landing troops on Chinese soil without permission from the government and had threatened to attack the Taku forts if the Chinese interfered with him. As the Chinese Government considered this action a declaration of war on China, the foreign ministers were notified that they must leave Peking within twenty-four hours and return to their respective countries. The communication further stated that a Chinese escort would be provided for their protection. Nothing was mentioned about the future of the remaining hundreds of foreign men, women, and children or the thousands of Chinese Christians.

All the ministers, except Baron von Ketteler, agreed to leave the following day, provided the Chinese Government furnished the necessary transportation. When the foreigners in Peking heard of this decision they informed the ministers that even if they were included in the flight from Peking they would prefer to stay and die fighting behind their barricades rather than be massacred en route to the coast. And to their undying glory the missionaries stated that under no conditions would they desert the Chinese Christians, who undoubtedly would all be massacred if the foreigners left them unprotected.

It was later learned that only the presence of the foreign ministers in the legation area prevented Jung Lu and other Chinese leaders from allowing the use of the imperial artillery and troops in an all-out attack that undoubtedly would have wiped out every foreigner and Chinese Christian in Peking. It was not from any love of the foreign ministers that Jung Lu kept his army from destroying them. He had discussed this possibility with Tz'u Hsi. But they feared that if the representatives of the governments and rulers of foreign countries were killed, the foreign nations would probably insist on the execution of an equal number of persons of equal rank from the Manchu Government and this list might include the Emperor, Tz'u Hsi, and assuredly Jung Lu.

Baron von Ketteler would not agree to the ministers leaving Peking, and they could not very well leave without him and his guards. The baron finally broke up the long meeting of the ministers by announcing that he had an appointment with the Chinese Foreign Office that morning and intended keeping it, regardless of all the Boxers in China. The ministers and his own associates tried to persuade him not to take the risk of appearing on the streets at such a time, but he disregarded them and set off for the Foreign Office. The ministers gave him authority to negotiate for them, but none volunteered to accompany him.

The German minister dressed in full uniform and rode in his official red-and-green chair. He was accompanied by his secretary and interpreter, Mr. Cordes. He started north on Hatamen Street toward the Foreign Office, which was less than a mile from the German legation. He refused a guard but did take one German dragoon as escort. In a few minutes the dragoon returned to the legation, bloody and at a mad gallop, with the news that the German minister had been killed. The secretary, seriously wounded, had been carried away by the mob.

It took only a few minutes for the German guard to organize and march, grim-faced and with fixed bayonets, to the scene of the attack. But the minister's body, the wounded secretary, the minister's chair, and every trace of the happening had disappeared. The street was entirely deserted. The minister's body was never found. One of the Boxer leaders later claimed he tanned the baron's skin and used it to cover his saddle.

This tragedy settled all arguments. The ministers unanimously decided to give up the idea of retreating. They made arrangements for the defense of the legation quarter, believing that it would be a fight to the finish and, if defeated, every foreign man, woman, and child would be massacred. All foreigners and every Chinese Christian who could be reached were brought into the legation area—all except courageous Bishop Favier, who, with a few French and Italian guards, was determined to defend the Pei T'ang, the Northern Cathedral. The defense of this cathedral with such a small force, entirely cut off from the legations, is one of the most courageous and outstanding events of the missionary movement in China.

There are many diaries written by men and women giving a day-by-day account of the siege of the Peking legations. They show that among the defenders were many courageous men and women, many who were unselfish and who shared everything they had. Others were rank cowards, hoarders, and even thieves. One white man deserted and gave valuable information of the weakness of the defense force to the Chinese.

Fortunately he spoke only to Jung Lu who, as we know, did not want the ministers massacred.

Most of the writers give praise to the Chinese Christians, although here, too, there were many who lacked courage. Chinese servants who were not Christians but who from a strong sense of loyalty decided to stay with their masters and share their fate justly received the highest praise in many of these diaries. Most, if not all, of the diaries condemn the ministers, with the exception of Baron von Ketteler, the American minister, and, to a lesser extent, Monsieur Pichon, the French minister. One curious thing is noticeable in the diaries: the writers usually condemn their own officials more than those of the other countries.

On June 21 the siege began in earnest. It continued until August 14, when a Sikh soldier cautiously poked his bearded head above the wall of the open sewer passing in front of the British legation. In a short time the British grounds were crowded with Sikhs. The troops of the allied armies had entered Peking. The siege was over. The first duty of the Allies was to relieve Bishop Favier and his brave little group of priests, nuns, and a few guards, who had withstood almost incessant savage attacks. In a later conversation Jung Lu told the bishop that if the latter ever wanted to give up being a missionary he would gladly commission him a general.

So much has been written about the siege of Peking and Tientsin that one need not take time to repeat the events of those fifty-four days. With the entrance of foreign troops into the capital looting began again. But first the Forbidden City had to be captured.

It was found that this city, which looked too beautiful to be a fortress, was in reality a strong citadel. With wide moats, enormously thick walls, and fortified gates, it was almost impregnable. If the Chinese regular army had attempted to defend the Forbidden City as vigorously as the foreigners defended the flimsy defenses of the legation area, it would have taken the Allies many weeks to capture it even with their modern cannon. But the Chinese defended it only long enough to give the Emperor, Empress Tz'u Hsi, and the court time to escape through the North Gate. Wisely they had no desire for their beautiful Forbidden City to be shelled and destroyed.

No estimate has ever been made of the loot taken from Peking, but it must have been one of the richest cities ever plundered. The Japanese, knowing the city better than the others, seized the Board of Revenue, capturing an enormous amount of silver. Sidewalk stalls run by foreign soldiers for the sale of loot sprang up in many parts of the city. Unfortunately, the soldiers wanted only silver or something they could use in purchases. They often wantonly destroyed fine porcelains, paintings, and other works of art worth many times what they carried off. Many of the finest Chinese pieces in the museums and homes of Europe and America today came from the loot of Peking.

Probably the most shocking and cold-blooded massacre of foreigners occurred in Taiyuan Fu.

Soon after the notorious Yu Hsien was transferred from Peking to be governor of Shansi province, he asked for a complete list of all foreign missionaries in Taiyuan Fu. He gave as reason his intention to send the foreigners safely to the coast. When he had all the names he ordered all the missionaries to his yamen. No sooner had they entered the courtyard than he let in the Boxers, who promptly slaughtered the thirty-three men, women, and children, reportedly with the governor looking on and encouraging the massacre. Later that day twelve Roman Catholic priests were murdered in somewhat the same manner.

Innumerable protests and suggestions, especially from mission societies and the families of those killed, poured into the foreign offices of the different countries, demanding that the Chinese be justly punished for these crimes. Some of the suggestions demanded that Empress Tz'u Hsi be executed. Others suggested that the Emperor, all the imperial princes whose names were known to the writers, as well as other officials with all their followers, should also be put to death. As one writer said, this should be done so that the blood of the innocent American women and children would cease to cry for vengeance on their bloody savage murderers. Nearly all asked for huge indemnities. Some demanded that China be divided up among the foreign powers. Others wanted foreign troops to remain indefinitely in China. Still others recommended that it be put in the treaty that the Chinese cease binding the feet of their women, that they cut off their queues, that the pensions of Manchus be stopped, that the Manchus be driven from the throne, and that no Manchu be allowed to hold office. A few writers suggested that curbs be put on missionaries.

2

The question naturally arises: What were Tz'u Hsi, the Emperor, the imperial princes, Jung Lu, Li Hung-chang, Yuan Shih-k'ai, Yu Hsien, and the other members of the court doing and thinking during the fifty-four days of the siege?

Empress Tz'u Hsi chose this seemingly inappropriate time to attempt to pluck a thorn out of her side which had been there since the *coup d'état* of 1898. She decided to use the Boxers to rid herself of Emperor Kuang Hsu. Her right-about-face in policy was owing to the foreign nations' attempts to deal directly with the Emperor. If these attempts succeeded, Tz'u Hsi knew it would endanger if not terminate her own power and prestige. Kuang Hsu not only hated his Imperial Father but had given every evidence of being in favor of the reforms the foreigners were demanding. As long as Kuang Hsu was Emperor he constituted a distinct danger. Tz'u Hsi now determined to force his abdication and to substitute for him another boy Emperor, making herself regent for the third time.

On the twenty-fifth day of the last Chinese month of the year 1899 she called together the grand secretaries, the presidents of the boards, and the imperial princes, and announced her intention of changing the occupant of the throne. She gave as her reason that the present Emperor had not shown her due respect or gratitude for the many favors she had done him and that he had even contrived a plot to kill her. She also reminded the assembly that at the time the Emperor was placed on the throne there were many dissenting voices in the provinces because T'ung Chih had no heir. She now wished to correct this undesirable situation. She informed them she had decided that P'u Chun, the eldest son of Prince Tuan, was to receive the "Great Succession." This was her decision. All she wanted from the Council were suggestions as to how the present Emperor should be treated after his abdication.

Grand Secretary Hsu T'ung suggested that Tz'u Hsi confer on Kuang Hsu the title Duke of Confused Virtue—a title used by a deposed emperor in the Sung Dynasty. This suggestion was approved by the Empress.

Another secretary, a Chinese named Sun Chia-nai, had the courage to object to the proposal to depose the present Emperor. He said if this plan was carried out it would certainly cause rebellion in the southern provinces. The Empress turned on him angrily, reminded him that he was a Chinese, did not understand the Ch'ing Household Rules, and had no right to interfere in matters of interest only to Manchus. She soon found, however, that Sun Chia-nai was right. When her decision reached the provinces, so many protests poured in from governors and army leaders she was glad to accept a compromise recommended by Jung Lu. For the time being she named Prince Tuan's son heir apparent but not Emperor. It is curious that Jung Lu, whom Emperor Kuang Hsu had once ordered killed, should have been the latter's strongest defender at this time. It speaks well for Jung Lu that he was willing to forget personal enmity for what he thought was the good of the country. This forbearance is the more remarkable because the wife of Prince Tuan was his daughter and the child P'u Chun his grandson.

Tz'u Hsi's attitude toward the Boxers changed several times. At first, when many of the imperial princes and other Manchus joined the Society of Harmonious Fists, she called them "society bandits." However, after the demonstration of invulnerability to foreign bullets, her attitude changed considerably.

Knowing Tz'u Hsi's desire to remove Kuang Hsu from the throne and of the opposition of Jung Lu, Li Hung-chang, and a number of ministers toward them, the Boxers issued the following declaration: "If peaceful years are desired there must be removed from this world one dragon, two tigers, and thirteen sheep." This referred to the Emperor, Jung Lu, Li Hung-chang, and the thirteen ministers who seemed to favor the foreign nations.

It was at this point that the Boxers, believing that Empress Tz'u Hsi was in sympathy with them, made a grave mistake —the mistake of forcibly entering the sacred palace grounds in an attempt to seize the Emperor and the other officials on their death list.

The time chosen was when the Emperor was meeting with his council. At the entry of the armed mob the Emperor, officials, attendants, and even the guards, sought refuge in another part of the maze of palaces. Empress Tz'u Hsi heard the commotion and demanded to know what was disturbing the sacred quietness of the Forbidden City. She was told that several thousand Kansu Boxers had invaded the palaces in search of the Emperor.

Regardless of her own plans for getting rid of the Emperor, Tz'u Hsi would brook no such violation of the traditions surrounding the Ch'ing emperors. She stepped out into the great courtyard and faced the invaders.

There she stood—a little woman not more than five feet tall, and weighing scarcely a hundred pounds. She was nearly sixty-five years old. For almost half a century she had dominated China—ruled one fifth of all the peoples in the world. There she stood—alone except for her always-faithful friend, Eunuch Li Lien-ying.

Although she knew the mob was made up of murderers, bandits, and looters, she did not flinch. She defied them and cursed them until they halted scarcely fifty feet from her, but close enough for them to see something they had never before seen in the face of a woman. She cursed them until they were glad to sneak back whence they came, never again to have the courage to meet the righteous anger of such a woman.

The gods must have protected Tz'u Hsi that day.

3

This attack on the palace caused a further change in Tz'u Hsi's attitude toward the Boxers. She now began to fear them.

But she still wanted to use them, if possible, to rid herself of the Emperor and to drive the foreigners out of China without involving the use of government troops, which would have fastened the guilt on her. It later developed that Tz'u Hsi finally realized the danger to herself if the ministers and other foreigners were driven out or killed by regular government troops. But she still entertained the sly idea that if this were done by an irresponsible mob and she later arrested and executed the leaders and members of that mob in sufficient numbers, she could divert suspicion from herself and the government and still win her end.

To further this plan and, as she said, to throw dust into the eyes of the foreign ministers, she issued a number of decrees in which she ordered the governors of the provinces to see that the Boxers and other such societies be curbed and Chinese Christians protected. One decree stated: "It is to be reiterated that the common people and Chinese Christians are both subjects of the empire and are both deserving of the same protection, and that when they are brought before local officials the cases should be heard and judged fairly, basing the decisions on what is right and what is wrong and not on whether they are Christians or not Christians. Let this be obeyed."

What could be fairer? Nothing, except that another decree was secretly sent at the same time to the same governors ordering them to destroy all foreigners and Chinese Christians. This was the famous decree in which the word "destroy" was changed to "protect" by Kuan Ch'ang and Hsu Chung-ch'ing before the decree left Peking. The two courageous ministers who made this alteration were executed immediately their action was discovered.

When hostilities finally broke out in Peking, Tz'u Hsi, acting on her own and quite counter to international usage, sent cables directly to the President of France, the President of the United States, to Queen Victoria, the Tsar of Russia, and the Emperor of Japan. All these cables were personal messages from Tz'u Hsi and were cleverly worded to start dissensions among the Allies, which she hoped she might be able to turn to her advantage later when the final treaty would be made.

The cable to Queen Victoria was of considerable length. It thanked Great Britain for having (she hoped) no idea of territorial aggrandizement, but only a desire to promote trade between the two countries. It cleverly pointed out that 70 or 80 per cent of all the foreign trade of China was done with England, and all this trade was now stopped by the horrors of war. It asked Queen Victoria to consider how disastrous and fatal it would be to her trade if by any conceivable combination of circumstances the independence of China should be lost or certain powers possessed themselves of large parts of Chinese territory. The cable requested Great Britain to act as mediator for China in all negotiations.

The message to the Tsar of Russia was equally clever. It recalled that the two countries had enjoyed two hundred and fifty years of unbroken good relations and a friendship which was always more cordial than that existing between China and any other country. It went on to point out the difficulties the Chinese Government was now experiencing in Peking and the disturbances caused by rebels, and expressed Tz'u Hsi's great concern that no harm come to the foreign ministers and the legations. She closed the message with the following appeal: "Among all the powers none has enjoyed such friendly relations with China as Russia. And now that China has incurred the enmity of the foreign powers by circumstances beyond her control, I must rely upon your country to act as peacemaker on our behalf. I now make an earnest and sincere appeal to Your Majesty, begging that you will come forward as arbitrator."

To the Japanese Emperor she sent the following cable: "The empires of Japan and China hang together as the lips and the teeth, and the relations between our two empires have always been sympathetic. At the present time it appears to us that the European countries and our Asiatic civilizations are opposed to each other, so everything depends on our two Asiatic empires standing firmly together at this juncture. The earth-hungry powers of the West have their tigerish eyes of greed fixed in our direction and certainly will not confine their attentions to China. If our empire is broken up your country will not be able to maintain its independence. We should disregard all trifling causes of discord between us and act as comrade nations. We rely on Your Majesty to come forward as arbitrator in our behalf."

The cable to the President of the United States and the one to the President of France were along the same lines. Like the other messages, both asked the President of each country to act as arbitrator.

A little study will show the subtlety of these cables. Each one emphasized the one thing each of the foreign countries was most interested in. Each ruler thought the appeal was made directly and exclusively to him and to his nation. These were but the beginning of actual offers made to the different countries during the peace-treaty negotiations. No, Tz'u Hsi was not idle or wasting her time in pleasure during the siege of the legations as many foreigners thought.

In addition to her international problems at this time, and during the siege of Peking's legation quarter, Tz'u Hsi had one serious domestic affair that almost succeeded in wrecking her plans.

It seems that when she drove the Boxer mob out of the palace area that did not end the incident. Nor did the postponement of the dethronement of Emperor Kuang Hsu please the Boxer leaders, especially Prince Tuan, father of P'u Chun, the heir apparent. The Boxers made one more attempt to persuade Tz'u Hsi to place P'u Chun on the throne without delay. They met with Tz'u Hsi and together they sent two prominent Boxer leaders to Jung Lu with two proposed decrees for his consideration and decision. The decrees advocated the immediate dethronement of the Emperor.

It was a bitter cold night and the Boxers found Jung Lu comfortably seated in a large chair near a good fire. He was annoyed at being disturbed at so late an hour. He read the decrees, then he tore them up and threw them into the fire. The Boxers protested this lack of respect toward them and reminded him that the decrees were from the Old Buddha. They asked him what message they should take back to her. He replied that he did not care what they told her. If the Venerable Ancestor felt offended and wanted to punish him, let her cut off his head. That was a matter between him and the Venerable Ancestor, and was no concern of theirs. He left them to make of that whatever they wished, and stumped off to bed.

Next morning Jung Lu presented himself before Tz'u Hsi. He prostrated himself and told the Empress: "The Emperor has done nothing against virtue and he is praised by all the foreign ministers as a wise and talented ruler. If you at this time carry out the Boxer proposal to dethrone him all the reputation you have built up for so many years will vanish into nothing. Moreover, after you have lived ten thousand years (after death), how can you face the departed spirits of Emperor Hsien Feng and your son, Emperor T'ung Chih?" Both Tz'u Hsi and Jung Lu were weeping by this time, and the Empress said repeatedly: "What you have said is right." Jung Lu knew his Venerable Ancestor. And the Venerable Ancestor knew a friend whose counsel she could trust.

This brought both Jung Lu and Tz'u Hsi into direct opposition to Prince Tuan and many of the imperial princes, the Grand Council, and other Boxer leaders.

The Boxers now decided to oust both the Emperor and Tz'u Hsi. During the fighting in Peking and taking advantage of the absence of Tz'u Hsi from the Forbidden City (she was then at the new Summer Palace), Prince Tuan took control of all vital political and military affairs. He started issuing decrees in her name and that of the Emperor. But though an imperial prince, Prince Tuan was only a partially educated man; the Chinese describe him as rude and devoid of common sense. As he dared not consult with the proper persons regarding his decrees, they were badly worded and full of wrongly used characters. When the decrees were delivered to Tz'u Hsi at the Summer Palace it is doubtful which made her more angry—the effrontery of decrees in her name or the attempt to pass off such badly worded decrees as coming from her. She started immediately for Peking and boldly faced Prince Tuan and the other Boxer leaders.

It was not until she was actually in the Forbidden City that she realized she had walked into a trap. She found all her eunuchs dressed in the bright red uniform of the Boxers. Two similar uniforms had been prepared for her. They were of red cloud pattern silk, embroidered with a dragon design and the symbol for water. Tz'u Hsi agreed to let her eunuchs wear any uniform the Boxers wanted them to wear, but she absolutely refused to let anyone dictate to her what she was to wear. She lost control of her temper and told Prince Tuan: "Dig up the bones of your deceased father and put the red garments on *him*. Then I will also put them on." Prince Tuan realized he had gone too far and did not press her further. But the Boxer leaders were in control of the government and they informed Tz'u Hsi she was to do as they directed. If she would not issue the decrees they ordered they declared that they would issue them in her name. They also told her that the court and all the people in Peking were under their orders, and there was no way for her or anyone else to escape. Li Lien-ying and the other faithful eunuchs were under arrest.

By now Tz'u Hsi had her temper once more under control and her mind was functioning with its habitual swiftness. She quietly agreed to everything. But secretly she dispatched one of her young eunuchs to Jung Lu, asking him to send several of his regiments to the Summer Palace. She told the conspirators that as her presence was not required, since they were doing so well in Peking, she would retire and await their pleasure at the Summer Palace. The Boxers did not want her in Peking to interfere with their plans. Consequently they willingly agreed to this proposal, but took the precaution of sending their own guard with her.

When Tz'u Hsi and the Boxer guard reached the Summer Palace they found Jung Lu already there with four of his best regiments. The Boxers were disarmed. Jung Lu and his troops marched immediately on Peking and took over the Forbidden City and the Imperial City without firing a shot. The Boxers had hardly expected and were not prepared for any such quick and decisive action.

The Empress was now in complete control again, a much wiser woman than she had been a few days before.

The attempt by Prince Tuan and the Boxer leaders to take over the Chinese Government and to use Tz'u Hsi as a tool against the foreigners had many reactions. It stopped all further wavering by the Empress and definitely turned her against the Boxers and their leaders. While she remained as anti-foreign as before, she never again believed that the Boxers could be trusted or that they could ever drive the foreigners out of China. She saw plainly for the first time that Jung Lu, Li Hung-chang, Yuan Shih-k'ai, and their friends were right in advising her that it would be a great calamity to China, to herself, and to the Ch'ing Dynasty if the foreigners in the legation quarter were killed. This, without doubt, saved the legations from attack by the imperial artillery and regular armies. She instructed the Foreign Office to arrange the armistice that so puzzled the foreigners. She also sent carloads of fruit and vegetables to the women and children in the legation area.

The southern provinces did not openly join the Boxer movement. This may seem extraordinary, as the southern Chinese are usually the first to rebel against any grievances, but there were several reasons why they remained inactive at this time. At the beginning the revolt was against the government. Later it ostensibly came out in support of the government and of the Ch'ing Dynasty in order to secure the help of certain Ch'ing princes. Although the southern ports had suffered more than any other part of China from foreign sailors and soldiers, missionary work was not then so highly organized as in North China, and it was against the missionary that the chief attack of the Boxers was directed. The southern provinces had not yet recovered from the Tai Ping rebellion, and so were slow in joining any new movement.

But probably one of the most important reasons why the southern provinces took no part in the uprising was a joint message sent by Jung Lu and Yuan Shih-k'ai to the governors, telling them that the Boxers could not succeed against the combined Western countries and advising them not to join the Boxer movement, as it would only bring ruin to their provinces and to China.

4

When the foreign troops entered Peking on August 14 the Empress felt it was unwise to remain longer in the capital.

For herself she would have stayed throughout the foreign occupation—she never lacked courage—but she knew that if she and the Emperor remained the Allies would insist on negotiating only with the Emperor. She knew how unpopular she was at that time with the governments of all the foreign countries and that they would not resist this opportunity to set her aside.

Tz'u Hsi called an emergency meeting of the Grand Council on the evening of August 14. She told them of her plans to leave Peking with the Emperor and a small suite on the following morning and asked their advice on the most suitable city in which to set up the temporary government of China. They all agreed that she should go first to Taiyuan Fu. If necessary, she should later remove to Sian Fu, an ancient capital of China in Shansi province, beyond any possibility of capture by the foreign armies.

The next morning the Empress arose at the first Hour of the Tiger. She dressed herself in the blue cotton clothes worn by peasant women and had her hair dressed in Chinese style. Her only remark was: "Who would have ever thought it would come to this?" But, true to her nature, she wasted little time in regrets. She had much to do. All the concubines were summoned and told that for the present they would have to remain in the Forbidden City. The Pearl Concubine had been released from her prison and presented herself with the others. At sight of the Empress she threw herself on her knees and begged that she and the Emperor be allowed to remain in Peking. Tz'u Hsi replied that such a proposal was impossible, the Emperor had to go with her. But every time the Empress stood still for a minute the Pearl Concubine would throw herself again at her feet with the same plea. This became not only very annoying to the Empress but also delayed her hurried preparations to get away from Peking.

What happened at this point is much disputed. Some of the persons present have reported that the Empress in her annoyance exclaimed: "Cannot someone get rid of this person for me? Why doesn't someone throw her down a well?" not thinking that her eunuchs might take her at her word. Others claimed that the Empress deliberately ordered the eunuchs to rid her of the Pearl Concubine. Whichever story is true makes little difference now. Two eunuchs did throw the Pearl Concubine head first down a beautifully carved deep well near by.

When the Emperor heard of this he was almost overcome by his grief; but he was soon brought out of his weeping by a sharp order from the Empress to get into one of the carts and draw the curtains so no one could see him.

After she had all the carts loaded to her satisfaction, Tz'u Hsi took a seat on the shaft of her cart where peasant women usually sat and ordered the cartmen to whip up their mules. She instructed them that if any foreign devils stopped them on the way they were to say nothing but leave all the talking to her. She had planned to say that they were simple country people fleeing from the terrible Boxers. In such an emergency Tz'u Hsi was always at her best. She was the only Chinese leader who did not lose her head the day the foreign troops entered Peking.

With all the eunuchs, concubines, and officials of the court prostrate on the ground, the carts started off. They passed through the north gate of the palace, the Gate of Military Prowess. A few officials followed at a distance, but otherwise the carts were unprotected. They left Peking by the Teh Sheng Men, the Gate of Victory, just a few hours before Japanese troops—"the Hairy Dwarfs," as the Empress called them—entered the city by the same gate.

They reached the Summer Palace by eight o'clock. There the farm carts became the "Sacred Chariots of Their Majesties" and were welcomed as such, even though it was hard to convince soldiers and attendants that the two bedraggled, dusty, and begrimed persons who alighted were the Son of Heaven and the Old Buddha.

Four of the imperial princes, a number of officials and secretaries representing the various boards now joined the party. Also about one thousand of the troops of General Ma Yu-k'un and an equal number of the Heavenly Tiger Bannermen of Prince Chuan arrived as bodyguard. A fast messenger from Jung Lu brought news that he was rallying the Chinese troops, also the sad news that many of the old Manchu families were committing mass suicide rather than face the foreign soldiers who had started looting the palaces and the city of Peking. After giving a few orders about burying the treasure that she had to leave behind and without taking further rest, Tz'u Hsi ordered the carts to start for Kalgan. They chose this rather unusual route through Chihli and Shansi provinces to Taiyuan Fu, as this was considered safer from foreign pursuit, although a much more difficult and uncomfortable road to travel.

The party traveled the whole day with so little to eat that they were glad to accept the wheat cakes and beans offered them by country people. Fourteen hours after the carts had left the Forbidden City they arrived at the small town of Kuanshih, thirty miles from Peking. It is difficult to understand how an old woman such as Tz'u Hsi, unaccustomed to hardship, could spend so many hours and travel so far in an uncomfortable Peking cart, but she did. And she was ready to start again at four o'clock the following morning.

At Kuanshih a Chinese merchant named Li gave them what food he could spare and a small building in which to spend the night. But they had to sleep rolled up in their blankets on a hard brick *kang*, like ordinary country folk. He also provided them with one mule litter, which Tz'u Hsi used until she was able to get a more comfortable chair at Huailai, which they reached the following day. At one stop they could find no sleeping accommodations of any kind and Tz'u Hsi and the Emperor sat on a bench supporting each other back to back the entire night. The imperial party was shocked to find that every village through which they passed had been looted and destroyed by the Boxers. Tz'u Hsi made few complaints at the hardships she had to endure. This kept the others from complaining. She seemed to be standing the trip much better than any other member of the party. Old Eunuch Li Lien-ying was at her side constantly, doing what he could to help her.

At Huailai she was given a banquet by Wu Yung, the local magistrate. Here she had some of the delicacies to which she had been accustomed in Peking. But, more important, Wu Yung provided both Empress and the Emperor with garments befitting their rank. After a day's rest, good food, and dressed in proper clothing, Tz'u Hsi again turned her attention to her official duties. Wang Wen-shao caught up with them at Huai-lai and gave her further news of Peking—all of it bad. Many more of their friends and officials, including Yu Lu, Viceroy of Chihli, had committed suicide.

The Empress called together her few advisers, all the government that was left of the Manchu Empire, to discuss further plans or, rather, as usual, to approve the plans she had made. She sent Prince Ch'ing back to Peking to start peace negotiations with the foreigners. She instructed him to follow a policy similar to the one Prince Kung had followed so successfully against the French and British in 1860. He was to join Li Hung-chang, and together they were to discuss every point at great length even for days, so as to wear out the patience of the foreigners. They were to do everything possible to take advantage of the rivalries of the foreign nations and to get them quarreling among themselves, especially the British, Russians, and French. Li Hung-chang was to discuss reforms with the Americans and convince them that China would carry out these reforms with the help of the United States as soon as the government could return to Peking. The quick mind of Tz'u Hsi was evidently working again.

It is remarkable that during all these days of hardship, danger, and extremely difficult traveling she kept her good nature. One of the attendants said that she was much better natured on this trip than when she was surrounded with all the luxury of the Forbidden City. At times when the Emperor and imperial princes saw how low their fortunes had fallen they despaired of ever being able to save China and the dynasty, but the old Empress never doubted for a minute. She was confident that China and the dynasty would be saved and that she was the one person to do it. She said stoutly that the gods had protected her too many years to desert her now.

To encourage the others she began to point out to them the beauties of the country through which they were passing. She reminded the Emperor that this was the farthest he had ever been from Peking, that he should take advantage of the opportunity to learn more about his country. She asked one of the princes if it was not good to get away from the city and to breathe the good air of Shansi province.

The Empress and her party reached Taiyuan Fu on September 10. Here they had every reason to expect accommodations befitting their needs and their rank, as Taiyuan Fu was an important city, the capital of one of the largest and wealthiest provinces of China. Here the Empress planned to set up her temporary government. But first she had to deal with Governor Yu Hsien. Yu Hsien had been influential in aiding the Boxer uprising in Shantung when he was governor of that province. In Peking he had been one of the most important Boxer leaders and the one who probably had most influenced Tz'u Hsi in their favor.

The governor also remembered all these things and naturally was somewhat apprehensive over the meeting with the Old Buddha–a meeting he would gladly have avoided had he been able to do so. But he did rather take her by surprise by greeting her some distance from the city. When the Empress first saw him he was on his knees by the roadside. She ordered him to approach and in no mild tone reminded him of all his promises in Peking and blamed him for the fall of the capital and all their misfortunes. He answered her by offering her his life. He also explained that the failure of the Boxers was owing to the fact that they had lost faith, had disobeyed their officers, and had aroused the wrath of the gods by plundering and murdering innocent Chinese who were not Christians. Before she could answer him he reminded her of the good work he had done in ridding all Shansi province of foreigners and Chinese Christians. As he expressed it: "I caught them all in a net and allowed none to escape."

The Empress said nothing further beyond asking the governor to accompany them. She could not resist keeping him in suspense regarding the punishment he would receive. When she reached the governor's yamen she found that he had vacated it for her use and had refurnished it with imperial furniture from the museum. Her quarters at the yamen proved almost as comfortable as her palace in Peking.

The governor had a banquet prepared for them and before the banquet he and his soldiers acted out the massacre of the missionaries that had taken place in the very courtyard of the yamen the Empress and her suite were then occupying. It is hard to understand how a woman, so kindly in many ways, could listen to the horrible details of the massacre of those innocent men, women, and children, yet she did. She questioned the governor minutely whenever the details were not clear to her. Both Tz'u Hsi and Yu Hsien must have hated the white man very much.

The Empress dismissed Yu Hsien from his position as governor but explained to him that it was only to throw dust in the eyes of the foreigners. She warned him of his danger from the foreigners by telling him: "The price of coffins is getting cheaper." She was a good prophet, as Yu Hsien's name later headed the list of Boxer officials the Allies demanded be executed under the peace treaty.

The Empress was soon joined by Jung Lu. He brought more news of the looting of Peking and the suicide of more of her friends, including Ch'ung Ch'i, the father of the young Empress of T'ung Chih, who had committed suicide at her father's suggestion. Tz'u Hsi knew him as a good man and mourned his death. She told Jung Lu that so many of her friends had committed suicide since the capture of Peking that she felt almost alone; that he and she would now have to do the work of ten persons to save China and the Ch'ing Dynasty. She ordered as many members of the Grand Council and other officials as were alive to join her at Taiyuan Fu. Wang Wen-shao, Lu Ch'uan-lin, and a number of the imperial princes were with her. Emperor Kuang Hsu was given more freedom and an opportunity to perform more of the duties connected with his office. Slowly the Manchu Government began to function again.

But soon reports reached Taiyuan Fu that the Allies, especially the Germans, were organizing a punitive expedition to send to Shansi to capture Governor Yu Hsien and to avenge the massacre of the missionaries in that city. Tz'u Hsi decided to leave Taiyuan Fu at once. She ordered her court to start for Sian Fu the following day. It never took her long to make up her mind or to act on any move she decided upon.

The journey to Sian Fu was made in the style and dignity

befitting the Emperor and Empress. Their days of hardship were over. Sian Fu was one of the oldest cities in China but not so attractive or comfortable as Taiyuan Fu. There, the imperial family occupied the governor's yamen. Sian Fu had once been the capital of China and it had many buildings suitable for officials. A large room was decorated and furnished as a throne room, adjoining rooms were used as antechambers, waiting rooms, and small audience chambers. The throne was of yellow lacquer and decorated like the throne in Peking. All the buildings were newly painted and lacquered and looked gay and bright. It was the Peking court in miniature.

The imperial household was also operated along the same lines as in Peking except that it was now on a much more economical basis, as the governor of Shansi took charge of all expenditures. He was an interesting old man and amused Tz'u Hsi very much. When she mentioned that he had cut their household expenses 90 per cent, he replied that even that could still be cut to advantage. It was not long before revenues from the provinces began to pour into Sian Fu and the financial difficulties of the government were solved.

While in Taiyuan Fu the Empress was prevailed upon by Viceroy Tuan Fang to allow him to give her a birthday dinner. He must not serve anything except roast duck, roast pig, Shou T'ao, and Shao Mien (longevity peaches and longevity noodles). When at this dinner Tz'u Hsi saw the Emperor, the Empress, and the other younger members of her court laugh and enjoy themselves for the first time since they had left Peking, she realized that even though they were all in exile they must not drop all the amusement and celebrations to which they had been accustomed. To cure their homesickness and keep up the morale of her court she must give the young people more pleasures. Perhaps Tz'u Hsi wanted a few herself.

She ordered the Emperor to assume his proper position and celebrate all the festivals as if they were in Peking. The first celebration was the Festival of the Coming Spring. In Peking a bull of a certain breed was always sacrificed at this celebration. As it was impossible to bring such a bull from Peking they had an artist draw the likeness of the bull, complete with nimbus. This was duly sacrificed. The only drawback was that the painted bull provided no meat for the feast that followed.

They next celebrated the coming of the new year with a week of theatricals, feasts, and gambling. This was followed by the Lantern Festival on the fifteenth day of the First Moon. On the fifth day of the Fifth Moon the Dragon Boat Festival was celebrated complete with "tsung tzu" and cakes of the Five Poisonous Reptiles (snake, lizard, toad, centipede, and scorpion). The likeness of one of these was on each cake and they were served with mulberries and cherries. The Sacrifice to the Moon on the fifteenth day of the Eighth Moon was also celebrated but was somewhat curtailed, as everyone was busy packing for the return to Peking. All this time the court was showing one of the peculiar characteristics of the Chinese people—the ability to enjoy life even when suffering the greatest grief and tragedy.

A little incident occurred in Sian Fu which showed that Tz'u Hsi, despite her dignity, her power, and at times her hardness, was really a woman at heart, with a woman's desire to possess and wear beautiful things and all a woman's vanity and love for the admiration of men and other women. Jung Lu, who evidently knew this, brought the Empress a wonderful robe as a present from Peking. It was of pink satin embroidered all over with white plum blossoms interspersed with huge butterflies in all the colors of the rainbow. To add to the dazzling effect, all the stamens of the flowers and the markings on the butterfly wings were set in small pearls and jade.

Tz'u Hsi was extremely pleased with the robe but she realized it was just a little too dazzling and gay for a woman of her position and age. Yet she wanted very much to wear it and would have donned it without a moment's hesitation if it had not been for one person. That person was Princess Jung Shou, an imperial princess of the bluest blood. Tz'u Hsi had admired her very much but had always stood in awe of her, as the princess never missed an opportunity to show Tz'u Hsi that she considered herself superior by birth. She was quick to criticize any little social error Tz'u Hsi might make. Tz'u Hsi might be the undisputed dictator of the government, but Princess Jung Shou was the undisputed dictator of fashion and all social rules. Tz'u Hsi wanted to secure Princess Jung Shou's approval of her new robe. According to the Household Rules, Empress Tz'u Hsi could wear only garments of bright yellow, blue, or reddish purple, but with the princess's approval there would be nobody to object to her wearing the beautiful pink robe Jung Lu had selected for her.

One day when they were having a friendly chat the Empress, in the most casual way, asked the princess her opinion of the design of embroidery work she could recommend for a pink robe. The princess evidently had heard about the new pink robe and replied: "Yesterday in a silk shop I saw a piece of dress material of beautiful pink satin on which were embroidered white plum blossoms and many five-colored butterflies. The stamens of the flowers and the butterfly wings were of pearl and jade. I wished to buy this for you, Venerable Ancestor, but I dared not buy it, as according to the Household Rules of our ancestors you cannot wear it." As the princess had exactly described Tz'u Hsi's new robe, the Empress knew she was opposed by as subtle a piece of sarcasm as she herself could have coined. With one last hope she asked: "Could I not wear it in the privacy of my palace? When I hold court I could take it off. Would not that be proper?"

The princess remarked: "I hear that the banks of the Yellow River have again overflowed and thousands of our people are homeless and without food and clothing. We should economize so as to be able to give relief to the unfortunate sufferers." Tz'u Hsi knew then that she would never secure the princess's approval to wear her beautiful present from Jung Lu.

Yuan Shih-k'ai heard about Jung Lu's gift to Tz'u Hsi; everyone at court had heard of it. Although Yuan Shih-k'ai was an underling of Jung Lu and owed his position to him, he was continuously trying to undermine him. He took advantage of the robe incident to present the Empress with another more expensive garment of even greater brilliancy. It was of bright yellow satin embroidered with pink tree peonies, a color the Empress could wear. It was also accompanied by a shoulder cape made of more than three thousand real pearls —a very costly present. This Tz'u Hsi found waiting for her on her return to Peking.

She accepted it with much pleasure and Yuan Shih-k'ai soon received the position he was seeking. The Venerable Ancestor never hesitated to accept the most expensive personal presents from her officials.

Tz'u Hsi was very busy in Sian Fu. She insisted on being informed of every detail of the peace negotiations as these were being carried on in Peking. Neither Prince Ch'ing nor Li Hung-chang could make any important decision without her approval. This wasted much time, but that was one of the things she had planned as, she said, delay made the foreign representatives impatient and gave them time to quarrel among themselves. A preliminary agreement was finally completed. It was sent to Sian Fu and, after a week's discussion and careful study by Tz'u Hsi, was finally accepted and signed by the Emperor. The detailed terms of the treaty took many more months to complete. But with the conclusion of the preliminary agreement the court knew its long exile was nearly over. The Empress was very pleased with herself, as she now felt that with the peace treaty she had saved China and the dynasty.

On the twenty-fourth day of the Eighth Moon (October 20), 1901, Tz'u Hsi, the Emperor, and the court left Sian Fu to return to Peking. They traveled by leisurely stages and in a style befitting their rank. Their first important stop was Honan Fu, another old capital of China. They made a long stay at Kaifeng Fu, waiting for the final signing of the peace treaty. Here the Empress was much saddened by the report of the death of Li Hung-chang, one of her most talented and trusted advisers and the principal negotiator of the treaty. With his death she realized that while she had protected him for his part in the Chinese-Japanese war she had never sufficiently honored him for his many services to her and to China. She tried to make up for this by erecting two shrines to his memory, one in Peking and the other in his native city.

But Tz'u Hsi never let grief interfere long with her plans.

At Kaifeng Fu she celebrated both the signing of the treaty and her sixty-sixth birthday with a number of magnificent theatrical entertainments, bringing to Kaifeng Fu the most noted actors in all China. She also issued a decree adding posthumous honors to Li Hung-chang and publicly thanking Prince Ch'ing, Yuan Shih-k'ai, and others for their assistance in concluding the terms with the Allies. She particularly thanked and praised Jung Lu for his wise advice to her during the entire Boxer uprising, mentioning that it was he who had always advised her against the Boxers. Everybody was in an excellent mood as they started again for Peking.

The journey from Kaifeng Fu northward was made as pleasant as possible for the imperial court. Every foot of the highway for the two hundred and fifty miles between Kaifeng Fu and Chengting Fu was swept smooth, every stone removed, and the entire surface covered with yellow sand. At the approach to large towns and cities the road was carefully swept again and no foot was allowed to touch it until after the passage of the imperial procession. It was more like a triumphal progress than the return of exiles.

The imperial entourage had grown considerably. It now consisted of Empress Tz'u Hsi, the Emperor and his Empress (the niece of Tz'u Hsi), the Lustrous Concubine Chin Fei (sister of the unfortunate Pearl Concubine), about seventy-five ladies in waiting, and the usual number of imperial princes. In addition to all these there were the many eunuchs and personal servants. Tz'u Hsi, the Emperor and his Empress traveled in the large imperial palanquins, the princesses in imperial yellow chairs, and the Lustrous Concubine in a green chair with yellow borders. The other ladies rode in Peking carts, usually two to a cart. Most of the eunuchs and other retainers traveled on horseback, as did many of the imperial princes, although a few preferred mule litters. All princes had their own retinue ranging from twenty-five to one hundred retainers. A large body of cavalry accompanied the court the entire distance.

In addition to all these there were innumerable carts carrying Tz'u Hsi's personal baggage, the many presents she had received from the governors of provinces and other officials, and the personal cooking utensils and household articles used on the journey. It took a considerable number of carts to carry the large quantity of bullion that had been sent the government from the provinces during their stay in Sian Fu. With the additional carts carrying the baggage of the princes, officials, and other members of the court, together with the commissariat, the procession was several miles in length. It provided a wonderful spectacle for the villages and cities through which they passed.

But one can well imagine the confusion such a procession caused when it arrived and tried to find accommodations for a three-day stay at the small city of Chengting Fu, a city already filled by officials and their retinues waiting to welcome the imperial family. When they arrived, on January 1, the weather was bitter cold.

Tz'u Hsi was in particularly good spirits on her arrival in Chengting Fu. Personal discomforts never seemed to affect her good nature. Here she met many old friends who had come from Peking to welcome her back to Chihli province. She issued a number of decrees, including one which announced that the Emperor would receive the foreign envoys in the Great Throne Room in the Forbidden City immediately on his return to Peking—a concession the emperors of China had always refused in the past. She also announced that she would personally receive the ministers' wives, and that she looked forward to this. While this was probably far from the truth, it did indicate a desire on her part to cultivate more friendly relations between the Chinese court and the representatives of the foreign governments. The decrees showed not a different woman but the same woman with a different policy. Although she continued to hate foreigners until her death, she now tried to appease the barbarians, as she realized they would always remain in China.

She also held out the olive branch to some of her former enemies among her own people. She conferred posthumous honors on the Pearl Concubine. In the decree, in addition to praising her virtue and courage, Tz'u Hsi calmly stated: "This admirable young woman, when she found she could not catch up with the court after its departure from Peking, chose to commit suicide rather than witness the destruction and pollution of the imperial shrines"—a fine-sounding statement that did not deceive anyone. Tz'u Hsi continued to stand condemned for the death of the Pearl Concubine.

Chengting Fu was at that time the southern terminus of the railroad being built from Peking to Hankow. Tz'u Hsi proposed using the railroad for the remainder of her journey back to the capital. The Belgian officials put at her disposal a special train with a luxuriously appointed drawing-room car for the Empress and almost equally fine cars for the Emperor and other members of the imperial family.

The Empress was as enthusiastic and eager over her first ride on a real steam railway as any child. She supervised the loading of her personal things and most of the other baggage on the three trains that preceded the imperial train. She evidently did not entirely trust foreign trains and ordered that the baggage trains must not proceed to Peking ahead of her but must stop at each important station until her train could catch up with them.

On the day of departure she arrived at the station at seven o'clock although the train was not to leave until nine-thirty. She again inspected every part of the train, as did the Lustrous Concubine, who proved to be a most lively young woman. Both asked questions of everybody, looked into the locomotive, and discussed the operation of the train with the engineer. All the women of the imperial court, including Tz'u Hsi, were dressed in their gayest clothes and they greatly impressed the foreigners who witnessed the departure of the train. When the train finally pulled out of the station, Tz'u Hsi stood on the platform of the rear coach waving her hand at everyone, foreigners and Chinese alike.

When she was told that the legations had issued an order forbidding all foreign nationals to be on the streets through which she would pass when entering the city, she issued a decree canceling that order. Her train arrived at a temporary station that had been built for the occasion near the southern entrance to the Chinese city of Peking. The original station had been destroyed by the Boxers. Here the train was met by almost every official in Peking and Chihli province. Huge pavilions had been built for the reception that followed the arrival of the train. A special enclosure had been prepared for foreigners which gave them a good view of the imperial family. The Empress was accompanied by the Emperor, the young Empress, and a number of the ladies in waiting, and, as always, by Eunuch Li Lien-ying. She personally thanked the foreign staff of the railroad for the fine accommodations they had arranged for her and for her comfortable journey. She was very pleased at returning to her old home and familiar surroundings. She had been an exile for eighteen months.

When the reception was finally over, Tz'u Hsi entered her huge imperial palanquin and, following imperial custom, entered Peking by the Yung-ting Men, leading directly to the Forbidden City. The Emperor had gone on ahead and welcomed the Empress on his knees at every gate. Tz'u Hsi was accompanied by her suite, the imperial princes and officials, all in their gayest gowns and riding in brightly colored chairs, making one of the most brilliant pageants ever witnessed by foreigners in China. Did Tz'u Hsi compare the triumphal return with her ignominous flight through the North Gate eighteen months before?

One memorable incident occurred at Ch'ien Men. At this gate that is flanked by two little temples with their yellow-tiled roofs—each temple not more than thirty feet square—the Empress, according to custom, alighted from her palanquin to give thanks for her safe return. She evidently did not realize until that moment that the city wall was crowded with foreign troops and civilians watching her entry into the city. For the first time men and, worst of all, foreign men looked down on an Emperor or Empress of China. She took one upward glance, and surprise showed for an instant on her face. But only for an instant. She curtsied in the Chinese fashion to the staring but silent crowds and entered the small imperial temple at the right of the entrance. A few minutes later she returned to her chair as though it was quite the usual thing to be stared at from above by foreigners.

Not a sound was heard, hardly a person moved while the little Empress, looking much smaller from the height above, with the bright face and sparkling eyes, paid her respects to her ancestors and thanked them for bringing her safely back to the capital.

Much had been done by her servants to collect as many of the Empress's personal effects as could be found or bought from looters, and her palace was restored as nearly as possible to its former grandeur. The Empress missed many of her most precious possessions, but no one ever heard her complain or utter one word of regret over her losses. She realized that she had passed through another great crisis, probably the greatest of her life, successfully and safely. Her personal losses were small indeed to what might have occurred. The only loss she did complain of was the loss of so many of her old friends, who had either been killed or had committed suicide during the looting of Peking.

Her first act on reaching her palace was to dig up the treasure and personal articles which she had hurriedly buried in her courtyard before fleeing from Peking. Evidently she was worried over the possibility of their being gone. When she found the hoard intact, she commented dryly: "Anyone but a foreigner would have found my things." She then made an inspection of the other palaces and was shocked to find how many had been burned and how thoroughly others had been looted.

While it was true that China was forced to pay a large indemnity to repay the foreigners for their losses in China and to pay the Allies for the expenses of the campaign, it was not too burdensome. The foreigners did demand the lives of a number of Boxer leaders and of a few imperial princes who were invited to commit suicide. But with the exception of two, or at most three, Tz'u Hsi would have executed these men anyway for misleading her. In all, only one hundred and fifty offenders were punished, most of them by banishment or forms of degradation. China had to send an imperial prince to Germany and another to Japan to apologize personally to the emperors of those countries for the killing of their representatives in China. The only trouble this gave Tz'u Hsi was in choosing which imperial prince to send, as they all wanted to make the trip.

One foreign demand was that the official imperial examinations be suspended for five years in forty-five cities where foreigners had been massacred or subjected to cruel treatment. This caused the old Empress to smile, as she had already decided to abolish the examinations for the entire country.

The honor of the five courageous officials who had been executed for opposing Tz'u Hsi in her support of the Boxers was restored by imperial decrees.

Probably the one thing in the peace settlement that hurt the pride of the Chinese most was the establishment of the legation quarter within the Tatar city of Peking—another city within a city. It was directly at the main entrance to the Forbidden City. The quarter was made into fortresses by surrounding it on the remaining three sides with a high wall complete with loopholes for both rifle and cannon. A wide glacis clear of all buildings separated the area from the Tatar city. The quarter was under the exclusive control of the foreign governments. Chinese, other than servants and employees of the legation administration, were not allowed either to live or own property within this area. The streets were patrolled by legation police. No armed Chinese was allowed to enter this quarter, making it a foreign city within the city of Peking. In this area the foreign governments built their legations. They also allowed the construction of a limited number of foreign banks, a few foreign-owned shops and clubs, and two hotels. The Chinese later came to object very strongly to the way in which the legation area was administered, as it sometimes became the asylum for certain Chinese officials and other persons wanted by the Chinese Government and courts of justice.

The most serious complaint of the Chinese against the peace treaty or protocol of 1900, as it came to be known, was that the cause of the war was never mentioned. Nor was the slightest attempt made to remove the causes of friction between the Chinese and the foreigners. The Chinese prophesied another Boxer uprising within fifty years. They were true prophets. Another uprising did come—forty-eight years later. This time it is called the Communist uprising.

The Manchu and Chinese negotiators and Empress Tz'u Hsi understood that although they had lost the war to the foreigners and had suffered much in prestige and from the acts of the foreign troops, they had outwitted the foreign diplomats in the negotiations of the peace treaty. Without doubt the personal cables Tz'u Hsi sent the rulers of each of the foreign powers and which were cabled back to the respective representatives in China did much to influence the ministers, especially the British, French, and American. Best results probably came from the sly suggestions of the negotiators to each of the foreign powers that if they were not too unfriendly and gave a little assistance to the government at this time it would help their nationals to secure concessions later.

The reforms Tz'u Hsi announced as early as January 1901 also made a favorable impression on the foreigners. To the Russians the Chinese suggested more railways in Manchuria. To the Germans the same in Shantung. The British and Americans were to get both railways and mining concessions in the Yangtze Valley. The French were interested in Yunnan and Szechuan provinces. Many of these schemes were later realized, but their principal value to the Chinese at this time was to influence the foreign plenipotentiaries at the peace conference.

Li Hung-chang and Prince Ch'ing signed the protocol for China. Exactly two months later Li Hung-chang died. With his death China lost one of her most enlightened statesmen and his passing was greatly mourned by Tz'u Hsi, the Emperor, and the entire court.

5

Tz'u Hsi was among the first of any Manchu or Chinese officials fully to recognize the necessity of a radical change in the policy and attitude of the Chinese Government toward the Western nations. The failure of the Boxer uprising and the occupation and looting of Peking by the foreign troops was a bitter lesson, and one she never forgot.

She was now convinced that the foreigner was in China to stay. With that conclusion reached, it did not take her long to decide that it would be wise for her to make friends with and, if possible, use the foreign nations to her advantage. In discussing this program with Prince Ch'ing she never showed the slightest doubt of her ability to achieve both of these objectives. While she recognized their military strength, she still doubted the ability and genius of the foreigners. Some of the results she obtained during the next few years point to the belief that her estimation of the ability of foreign diplomats was not far from correct.

To carry out her plan she knew that she must do two things: she must educate her own people to become more friendly to foreigners and she must remove the foreigners' distrust of her. Remembering the high praise given Emperor Kuang Hsu by all the foreign government representatives and the foreign press for his proposed reforms in 1898, she determined to follow his example and inaugurate reforms, even to granting the Chinese people a constitution.

Her advisers cautioned her to move carefully and slowly, but Tz'u Hsi was never one to follow advice of that kind. While still at Sian Fu she issued, in the name of the Emperor, the first of her famous Four Edicts. As there was no one in Sian Fu half so capable as herself in framing such laws, she is given all the credit by modern scholars not only for the clever arguments, the keen intelligence, the statesmanship and grasp of the international situation shown in the decrees, but also for the beautiful language in which they are written. Many Chinese scholars did not agree with the substance of the decrees, but all admired them as equal in scholarship to any ever issued during the Ch'ing Dynasty.

All Four Edicts were well received in every part of China. Even the people of Canton and the southern province, who seldom praised anything that came from the Manchu court, were enthusiastic over the new foreign policy. Without doubt this rather universal praise from so many unexpected sources pleased Tz'u Hsi very much and encouraged her to go further than she had first intended.

The unexpected pleasure she got from entertaining and becoming acquainted with more of the women of the diplomatic corps in Peking also had the same effect on her social activities. Not only did she receive some of these women at formal state affairs, but several were invited to private parties.

She also did an unusual thing in commissioning Miss Katherine Carl, a talented American artist, to paint her portrait, and even consented that the portrait be sent to the St. Louis Exposition and later given to the people of the United States. Miss Carl enjoyed an intimacy with Tz'u Hsi for many months that would have been utterly impossible a few years before. She described the Empress: "She is small, not quite five feet tall, with exquisitely dainty hands and feet, narrow, high-bred face, and a long chin of the type generally called strong. Her eyes have so kindly a look, her face shines with so sweet an expression she seems beautiful. She has a sweet dignity, charming manners, and a lovable nature; there is a look in her eyes of patient resignation that is almost pathetic."

It is apparent that while Tz'u Hsi was doing a fine job in educating her own people she, a woman more than sixty-six years old, was doing an even better job in educating herself regarding foreigners and was enjoying it. The only open opposition to her program came from the old Manchu families, who thought she was ruining the dynasty, and from foreigners who would not believe in the sincerity of her plans for reform.

In one decree she announced: "Due to improper appointments by us the dynasty which had existed for two hundred and fifty years was endangered for no good reason. In the course of the massacres and the siege of the legations many Christians and other good people were killed, as fire often destroys jade as well as common stones. The foreign envoys were also victimized as the fish in a moat are harmed when the city wall is burned. When we ponder over these things a pain comes to our heart because we realize that we have done a shameful thing to neighboring countries and committed a sin against our children. Our regret knows no bounds. Bitterly have we reproached ourselves with the thought that for the past twenty years abuses have been steadily increasing while we have postponed their correction until the country was imperiled."

The Chinese ironically call the Four Edicts of Tz'u Hsi her Penitential Decrees, knowing well that Tz'u Hsi was probably never penitent about anything in all her life. In these decrees she first took some blame on herself, but she did not in any way overdo this self-condemnation.

The Household Rules of the dynasty had always been looked on as something that could not be altered and had to be followed without question and to the letter. As we know, Tz'u Hsi had often used these rules to her own advantage. Now she attempted to reverse her position. She used the writings of Confucius to prove that when any condition had run its natural course it was succeeded by another. That while there were certain things that must remain unchanged, such as the relations between sovereign and people, between father and son, man and wife, and the five great moral obligations, there were other matters in which there could be no objection to change.

After Tz'u Hsi's return to Peking she found that officials both in the capital and in the provinces had not taken her decrees very seriously. They thought she was just amusing herself by again throwing dust in the eyes of the foreigners and so played safe by ignoring the suggested changes. They were rudely shaken out of this belief. A decree issued soon after Tz'u Hsi's return thanked the gods for bringing her back safely, then declared that the Emperor was fully determined to put into force all the reforms necessary to deliver the empire from its present weak state.

This and following decrees specified certain reforms that could not be delayed. She suggested the abolition of one of the oldest and most closely followed Manchu rules by recommending that, in the interests of a united country, Manchus and Chinese intermarry. She prohibited foot-binding among Chinese. Both Manchus and Chinese were advised to send sons abroad, particularly to America and Great Britain, to be educated at the expense of the Chinese Government. She also declared her intention to abolish the imperial examinations, as in her opinion no satisfactory system of modern education could be adopted as long as these examinations existed. She abolished all medieval forms of punishment and torture to force confessions from prisoners. She did this as she realized that China would have to have her laws, punishments, courts, and police more in line with those of foreign countries if

China were ever to rid herself of extraterritoriality and have foreigners submit to Chinese courts.

She next sent a commission under Prince Tsai Tseh to Europe to study Western systems of government. This commission returned in 1905 with the recommendation that China adopt a constitution. Tz'u Hsi agreed, and in another cleverly worded decree announced that China would be given a constitution as soon as the country could be prepared for the changes this would involve.

It takes only a casual study of the reforms suggested by Tz'u Hsi in her numerous edicts and decrees to realize how much more important, more practical, and better planned her program of reform was than that attempted by Emperor Kuang Hsu and K'ang Yu-wei during the Hundred Days of Reform of 1898.

6

While Tz'u Hsi was preparing her own people for the changes in government she intended to carry out she was also making every effort to improve her relations with the foreign representatives in Peking. As mentioned before, she ordered a special enclosure prepared so foreigners could watch the arrival of the court in Peking. A few days later six of the foreign ministers presented their credentials to the Emperor. On this occasion the foreign ministers were allowed to enter the Forbidden City through the main entrance. After the ceremony they were received for the first time by Tz'u Hsi.

On January 27 the entire diplomatic corps was formally received by the Emperor and Tz'u Hsi. This was a historic occasion. After many years of waiting the ministers of the Western nations finally stood before the Manchu Emperor in the Great Throne Room and not in the inferior throne room intended for Mongol and other dependent nations.

They made the most of the occasion. They came dressed in their most brilliant and ornate uniforms and wearing every decoration they possessed.

Unfortunately, they had one problem—the weather was cold, below freezing, and the throne room was not heated. The question was should they wear their greatcoats and be comfortable but hide their beautiful uniforms? Or should they risk pneumonia but be presented in all their glory? For the honor of their countries, and to their undying credit, they chose the latter.

Some of the ministers presented a fine appearance. The diplomatic uniform of the representative of one of the Scandinavian countries was cream-colored, trimmed with gold. This particular representative was some inches more than six feet tall. He rather stole the show and was the talk of the Chinese in Peking for weeks.

This reception was followed by many others given by Tz'u Hsi to the ladies of the diplomatic corps in her effort to develop better relations with the foreigners. But attendance at these receptions by the foreign ladies was severely criticized in many quarters, especially by the missionaries and by those who were not invited. Commenting on this, the wife of one of the foreign representatives wrote: "There was sharp and bitter criticism of our acceptance of the imperial invitations. Individual bitterness still has its poison and would keep the breach open and even widen it if possible, but wisdom seeks to close the breach. Pressing the thorns of sorrow and revenge deeper into our hearts will not lessen the sting of the horrible past nor permit us to rest in peace."

Critics said they could not see how foreign women could shake the hand of a woman which, they claimed, was stained with the blood of innocent children. Others put it more mildly by asking how American and European women could associate on friendly terms with a woman who so recently supported a scheme to massacre the entire foreign population of Peking. Still others criticized the American minister's wife because she referred to Tz'u Hsi as "My friend, the Empress Tz'u Hsi." Evidently the women of the Christian nations were not ready to accept the olive branch held out by the Empress, a woman described by them as a heathen. While many foreigners were massacred and inhumanly treated by the Chinese during the Boxer uprising, the Chinese suffered many times the losses of foreigners. It is probable that Tz'u Hsi had more relatives and members of her family and more of her friends killed by the

Boxers than all the foreigners put together. She and her friends blamed the foreigners for their losses just as the foreigners blamed the Chinese, yet the heathen seemed to be more willing than the Christian to forgive and forget.

Two little incidents occurred at these receptions for foreign women that are of interest. At the first reception Tz'u Hsi, who did not understand foreign languages and much like a deaf person was liable to be suspicious of what she did not understand, thought she noticed her guests smiling and making fun of some of her finest curios. She told one of her ladies that she could not stop the foreign women from criticizing her possessions but they would never again have the opportunity to do this. Later receptions were held in a foreign-style building furnished with inferior foreign furniture, as she could get no other in China. The result was that the Empress was frequently accused by foreigners of having very bad taste.

The Empress was also rather annoyed at a certain foreign missionary who always came to the receptions to act as interpreter. Her Chinese was excellent and she was a fine, well-educated woman, but the Empress preferred to use her own interpreters, as she had two young Manchu princesses who spoke excellent English and French. This foreign woman came so often that it finally annoyed Tz'u Hsi very much. She still was not fond of missionaries, either men or women. She and her ladies in waiting discussed this difficulty in an effort to find some remedy without hurting the lady's feelings. They decided that if on the next visit of the foreign interpreter the Empress told her: "We are all so glad to see you here so often," even a foreigner would know this meant she was coming too often. However, the missionary thought this meant that the Empress was very pleased that she came so often, and from that time never missed a reception at the palace.

Soon after her return to Peking Tz'u Hsi suffered a great personal loss in the death of Jung Lu. When Jung Lu alighted from the train on their arrival in the capital from Sian Fu it was noticed that he seemed a sick man. While the same age as Tz'u Hsi, he now appeared to be ten or fifteen years her senior. He died April 11, 1903.

Shortly before his death he dictated a valedictory memorial to Tz'u Hsi in which he referred to himself as "your slave, Jung Lu." He recalled their many years together since they first entered the palace and the numerous honors she had bestowed on him. He reminded her of his services at the time of the Su Shun conspiracy and how by her great wisdom and strength she was able to defeat the conspirators. He thanked her for making him minister of the imperial household, which allowed him to be in constant attendance on her. He next mentioned his assistance to her at the time Emperor T'ung Chih mounted the Dragon Throne, also later, when he died, and Emperor Kuang Hsu was placed on the throne. He slyly reminded the Empress of the time she banished him from the court because of his indiscretion with one of her ladies in waiting. He ended his memorial by telling her he was at the point of death and that with his last breath he entreated her vigorously to continue her program of reforms so that China could take her rightful place among the great nations of the world. He advised her to watch carefully the appointment of men to official positions, to set an example by reducing her own expenses, and suggested that she follow the custom of Emperor Ch'ien Lung and visit regularly various parts of the country to learn the truth about the condition of her subjects.

Tz'u Hsi greatly grieved over the death of Jung Lu; following receipt of his valedictory memorial and the report of his death she saw no one for an entire day. In addition to a mandate in which she recalled the many incidents of their work together she described him as a most patriotic and loyal servant who alone had stood firmly and fearlessly against the Boxer leaders. She had kept Jung Lu in some important position close to the throne from the time of the Su Shun conspiracy. He repaid her trust by remaining absolutely loyal to her every minute of his life. He undoubtedly saved her life on three occasions, and there is little doubt that without him Tz'u Hsi would never have attained her unchallenged position, and no one realized this more than she did. She gave him every position and honor within her power. When he died he was both Grand Secretary and Grand Councilor, next to the Emperor the highest positions within the Chinese Empire. It later became known that she had promised him that one of his grandsons should be made Emperor of China—a promise she was to keep.

The death of Jung Lu again revived the many discussions regarding the intimate relations between him and the Empress. There are a number of little clues that reveal the intimate relationship that existed between them. For instance, on three separate occasions he rushed into the private apartments of Tz'u Hsi in the middle of the night without previous notification or invitation. This suggests that he was familiar with her apartments and it is significant that the eunuchs and guards allowed him to pass into her bedroom without challenge or delay. It indicates that he had done that very thing before and that the guards knew he would be welcome. Ordinarily no man, not even the son of the Empress, would have been allowed to enter her private apartments without first being announced by the guard and orders given to let him pass.

In reviewing the long lives of these two interesting persons it appears very evident that the relations between them were more intimate than even their friends would acknowledge during their lifetimes. But Jung Lu was no libertine. He was sincere in his affections. It is also clear that Jung Lu, although friend and lover, never aroused in Tz'u Hsi the grand passion. No man could have done that because her grand passion was not sexual, it was ambition. Both were intelligent, hard-working people. Both devoted their lives to achieving certain objectives, and both succeeded. To both, personal relations were secondary to the main aims of their lives.

The question naturally is asked: What about the Empress's affairs with Dr. Yao Pao-sheng and later with the actors? These affairs tend to prove rather than disprove the case of Jung Lu. It was during Jung Lu's several years' absence from Peking that the affairs with Dr. Yao and the actors took place, suggesting that it was the absence of Jung Lu that probably was the main cause of all of them. No further indiscretions of this nature by Tz'u Hsi were even hinted at after his return to Peking. All in all, the evidence supporting the theory that Tz'u Hsi and Jung Lu were more than just friends is now too strong for even the supporters of both families to continue to deny the possibility of the truth of this theory.

During the flight from Peking and the months spent in Taiyuan Fu, Sian Fu, and their journey back to Peking, the relations between Emperor Kuang Hsu and Tz'u Hsi seemed to be cordial. Owing to the lack of proper accommodations they were forced to live in comparatively close proximity. The Empress had given up all thought of replacing him by another prince more amenable to her will. She knew that to attempt this would ruin her position with the foreigners. The enemies of the Empress claim that on the court's return to Peking she again imprisoned the Emperor in the Ocean Terrace. But the generally accepted theory is that the Emperor himself was stubborn and deliberately refused to live in any other palace. He chose to live in the Han Yuan Tien in the South Sea Palace area, in the same building that had been his prison before the flight to Sian Fu. He also insisted on signing all his poems and private papers "Ch'en Ch'uan Chung"—Minister Ch'uan Chung—as he claimed he was no longer Emperor. Tz'u Hsi was the Emperor. This attitude annoyed Tz'u Hsi more than an attempt on his part to assume power would have done.

As the Emperor's attitude soon became known to the entire court it probably was the most effective method of protest he could have adopted, although he continued to take orders from the Empress. His first official act was to pay a formal call on Tz'u Hsi and the ancient Grand Dowager Imperial Concubine Li, a concubine of Hsien Feng. He also officiated at the sacrifices at the Altar of Heaven and was very punctilious in his religious duties as the Son of Heaven. He attended the meetings of his ministers. Here, during this period, Tz'u Hsi treated him with considerable respect, frequently asked for his opinion, and addressed him as Imperial Father. But the Emperor, although dutiful and quiet, remained stubborn. This was unfortunate, as he could have assisted Tz'u Hsi in her reform movement which he himself had, in fact, attempted to inaugurate.

In the meantime she spent much of her time in building

and rebuilding many of the palaces in the Forbidden City and Sea Palace area and at the Summer Palace, which had been destroyed. The German General von Waldersee is accused of burning a fine palace late one night just because he felt like celebrating and wanted to see a big fire. Tz'u Hsi was apparently as fond of architecture and constructing large buildings as any of the Ming emperors, and she soon had several palaces under construction in the city. At the Summer Palace she not only replaced those burned but added a number of new and important buildings. She made frequent visits to the Tung Ling, ninety miles east of Peking, to supervise the construction of her expensive tomb—no easy or comfortable journey in a palanquin. It is remarkable how a woman of her age could have been so active and so keenly interested in so many matters.

The years following Tz'u Hsi's return to Peking from Sian Fu were probably the happiest of her life. Her position was now secure. She had finally won the respect and loyalty of her people. Her domestic problems were solved. Chinese wits said that foreign cannon were good missionaries, since they had converted Tz'u Hsi to a policy of good neighborliness. Others claimed it was the long talks she had with Jung Lu and some of the officials from the provinces, who had a broad view of international affairs, which changed her attitude toward foreigners and Western ideas of government. Whatever it was, the Tz'u Hsi who returned from Sian Fu was a different ruler from the Tz'u Hsi who had fled from Peking.

If it was only a change in attitude then she was a very good actress, as she convinced almost every foreigner who came in contact with her that she was a kindly old woman friendly to everyone. She now made many journeys to and from the Summer Palace by the canal, which at that time connected the Peking lakes with the lake at the Summer Palace. At such times a number of foreigners would collect on the banks of the canal just outside the city to watch the Empress's magnificent boat, oared by more than a score of rowers, glide by. The Empress always was interested in these crowds and whenever she saw a foreigner she knew she would wave her hand, even as she did on the streets of Peking. This familiarity shocked the old Manchu families, who considered it most undignified behavior for an empress.

Tz'u Hsi was equally interested in her own people. She often had her chair stop on the street to watch people at their daily work. She was particularly interested in the food of the poorer classes, probably remembering her own early and occasionally hungry days. She insisted on inspecting the community kitchens from which the poorer classes received most of their food. On several occasions she discussed and compared the food of the Chinese people and of Americans with Miss Carl.

She had a two-storied building called the T'iao Yuan Chai built on the north side of the Summer Palace grounds. From the balcony of this building she could see the little village and the road just outside the wall. She would sit for hours on this balcony watching the people below her passing up and down the road. They were mostly farmers, small tradesmen, with an occasional monk from a nearby temple, or just sightseers visiting the Jade Fountain and the Western Hills. When asked by her ladies why she spent so much time on that balcony when from other seats she could feed her eyes on the beautiful lakes and hills, she replied that the most interesting sight in the world was the common people of China. She was becoming the mother of her people.

Tz'u Hsi was particularly fond of the rice-planting songs of the peasants. The words of many of these songs are rather vulgar and contain obscene passages which bar them from being sung in the Peking theaters. In the spring it has long been the custom for the people of Peking and the nearby rural districts to make pilgrimages to the Temple of the Goddess of Azure Clouds on the summit of the Mystic Peak, Miao Feng Shan. Performances are given at the temple and consist of singing and dancing the old folk songs, including the old rice-planting songs. It was the custom that on the return of the pilgrims they had to perform at any place they passed through and were asked to stop.

Tz'u Hsi was eager to hear these songs and so used to arrange to have the pilgrims perform just outside the north wall of the Summer Palace, close to the T'iao Yuan Chai. The pilgrims were given tea and pastries from her own kitchens. She enjoyed these exhibitions so much that she again broke all rules and in following years invited them to give their performance inside the Summer Palace. This imperial interest increased the popularity of the festival so much that many young people of the best Manchu and Chinese families began to join the pilgrimages and to take part in the performances before Tz'u Hsi. The attention Tz'u Hsi paid to the affairs of the common people soon became known to the people of Peking. They were discussed in the teashops of the city and did much to spread her reputation as the Venerable Ancestor with the interests of her people at heart.

Tz'u Hsi continued to meet foreigners often, especially foreign women. She even invited some of the women to small private luncheons and picnics where they reported that she seemed to enjoy herself as much or more than any of them. Miss Carl took many meals with the Empress and her ladies while working on her portrait. When Miss Carl was present the old Empress had the food served in individual portions to each guest, instead of following the usual Chinese custom of serving the food in large bowls from which guests helped themselves.

All this seemed to indicate an entirely different person from the woman of the three regencies. Out of the quick-tempered, revengeful woman there had emerged one who, though she blamed the foreigner for all her burned palaces, looted treasures, and the death of her friends, was making every effort to forgive and forget. In this she was unlike the foreigner who insisted on keeping fresh the conspicuously painted sign on a section of the bullet-pocked wall of the British legation: *Lest We Forget*. Perhaps the writer who described Tz'u Hsi as not one person but several persons in one came nearer the truth than those who called her a kind-hearted old lady, or the others who named her a Jezebel and a murderer.

During Tz'u Hsi's early life, and up to the time of her flight to Sian Fu, she was a very superstitious woman. She never made a journey or did any other important act without first consulting one of the imperial astrologers or soothsayers. Superstition is a very difficult thing to rid oneself of, especially as a person gets older. But Tz'u Hsi did so. After her return to Peking she proceeded to defy every taboo, curse, and prediction of the Imperial Board of Astrologers. This so worried her associates, who thought she was getting dangerously unconventional, that they ordered Chang Shih-hsiang, the most noted Chinese geomancer, physiognomist, and astrologer, to come to Peking. He greatly amused Tz'u Hsi. She took him with her on one of her visits to the tomb she was building for herself. Astrologer Chang recommended certain changes in the location of some of the buildings and predicted that if the changes were not made the tomb would be desecrated and robbed within fifty years of her death. Tz'u Hsi laughed at him and ordered the opposite to what he recommended. Strangely enough, the old astrologer was proven right—her tomb was robbed twice within twenty years of her death.

She again defied Astrologer Chang and broke one of the strongest taboos of the Manchus by insisting on visiting the Chi Hsiang So—the Good Luck Ground of Ten Thousand Years—where her coffin was stored in the imperial palace. Emperor Kuang Hsu, his Empress, the imperial concubines, the princes, and her ministers all knelt down and begged her not to defy the gods, but she only smiled and said: "I do not believe that looking at my coffin will make me die. If it does, what do one or two days earlier matter?" She entered not once but many times. Later, when she died suddenly, the people recalled the old superstition and shook their heads.

Her flouting of the old superstitions and taboos was shown particularly in her changed attitude toward death. Previously she had refused to have the word "death" mentioned in her presence, especially in connection with the word "sheep," as she had been born in the Year of the Ram. She was extremely fond of the characters for longevity. She inserted it in the names of all the palaces she built or lived in. She had it woven or embroidered in all her garments. She claimed that if the word "longevity" was used to name anything and everything connected with her she would live to a very old age. Though she dreaded death, it looked as though some kind of magic had been worked in her case, as she appeared to be possessed of eternal youth. Almost every foreign woman who saw her at close quarters when she was nearing seventy would not believe her to be more than thirty years old.

This is not unusual, as few foreigners can guess correctly a Chinese woman's age. But Tz'u Hsi also gave the same impression of youth to the Chinese, who claimed the Taoist priest, Kao Jen-t'ung, had given her the herb of ten thousand years. But her ladies in waiting credited her youthful appearance entirely to the care she took of her beautiful skin and the nourishing food she always ate. Miss Carl described her as one of the best-groomed women in the world. She was careful in the use of cosmetics and made the most of those she used. Once a foreign friend recommended a particularly good skin food and sent Tz'u Hsi a few bottles of it. When she had the labels translated she found that the manufacturer ordered the user to shake the bottle well before using. Tz'u Hsi said no foreigner was going to order her what to do, and she used the lotion without shaking the bottle.

After her return to Peking, Tz'u Hsi seemed to enjoy shocking the ladies of her court by continuously joking about and even defying death. This was particularly so when arrangements were made for the celebration of her seventieth birthday. Her ministers wanted to make this an elaborate celebration, as they had held no celebration for her sixtieth birthday because the country was at war with Japan at the time. At first Tz'u Hsi refused to have a celebration of any kind, but when it was pointed out to her that the people would be very disappointed, she allowed what she termed an "austere" celebration. This eventually turned out to be one of the most elaborate celebrations of her life.

The ceremonies were held at the new Summer Palace. As Tz'u Hsi was particularly fond of chrysanthemums, two hundred pots of rare white and purple chrysanthemums were especially grown for the celebration. Each plant was three feet high and each blossom measured six inches or more in diameter. Chrysanthemums were also used to line both sides of the path from the P'ai Yun Gate to the P'ai Yun Hall. They were also placed on the marble stairways and arranged in the courtyards to form the Chinese characters for Ten Thousand Years of Happiness. A thirteen-story pagoda was built of bamboo and covered with chrysanthemums, as were the buildings and the hills, giving the impression of mountains of flowers.

At a given signal, when Tz'u Hsi's chair was passing, thousands of brightly colored birds were released from cages. They broke into song as they fluttered around the courtyard and buildings. All this, together with the wind bells on the eaves of the buildings and the soft music of hidden orchestras, was very pleasing both to the ears and the eyes. The celebrations were continued at night with lantern and flower pageants on the Summer Palace lake. If Tz'u Hsi had consulted Astrologer Chang he might have told her that this was the last great birthday celebration she would ever enjoy on this earth. But the astrologer did not feel very friendly toward Tz'u Hsi, as she had played a number of tricks on him by sending him eunuchs and officials in disguise and with false birth characters. Even though he had seen through the ruse and the disguise in almost every case, Tz'u Hsi's lack of respect did not please the important soothsayer.

Tz'u Hsi took up the opium habit at this time. She smoked a specially prepared opium three times daily, having her first pipe at her early rising hour of four o'clock in the morning, the second after her noon meal, and the third before retiring. This gave her the relaxation she required because, as her physician said, "She was wringing the juices of her brain dry in arduous work." She never became an addict but used opium in a way that most probably was beneficial to her after her vitality and mental powers began to decline. She certainly would have been amused if anyone had told her that in smoking opium she was doing anything immoral or even injurious.

The Russo-Japanese War caused her considerable worry. Like all Manchus and Chinese, her sympathies were with Japan, and she did everything possible to assist that nation and still remain technically neutral. She encouraged Chinese to volunteer for the Japanese Army. Young Chinese and Manchus, under Chang Tso-lin, gave valuable services as irregular troops against the Russians. They were so effective that the Russian Government protested and Tz'u Hsi was obliged to declare them outlaws, but she continued secretly to give them all the support and assistance they required. While this declaration by the Chinese Government did not hamper Chang Tso-lin in any way, it did brand him, one of the greatest Chinese of modern times, as an outlaw—regardless of his later accomplishments in keeping order for many years in one of the most turbulent parts of China. His enemies appreciated him far more than those who should have been his friends. The Japanese won the Russo-Japanese War but it turned out to be no gain to China, only a change of powers controlling Manchuria.

The Japanese took over all the concessions, rights, and possessions formerly held by the Russians in Manchuria south of Chang-chun and proved even worse tenants than the Russians had been.

9. THE OLD BUDDHA

Although Emperor Kuang Hsu stubbornly insisted in living in the Ocean Terrace after his return from Peking he was no longer closely confined as prisoner. Outwardly he always paid the greatest respect to Tz'u Hsi. He usually addressed her as Venerable Ancestor, a title she preferred in her later years, as it suggested she was starting a new family line–which she was not. As she was still regent or tutor, she occupied the highest place at all audiences, but when they dined together the Emperor occupied the place of honor. He is described by Miss Carl, who saw him on a number of occasions, as a small, slightly built young man of rather darker complexion than the average Manchu. He had a well-shaped head, high forehead, large brown eyes, good-sized nose and mouth. There was little charm or magnetism, but his general appearance suggested reserve strength. Miss Carl saw no evidence of any feeling of animosity toward Tz'u Hsi. The Emperor treated her with great formality. They seemed friendly toward each other and acted much as one would expect a mother and son to act under similar circumstances. He completely ignored the many pretty girls in Tz'u Hsi's entourage.

Like a number of his ancestors, he showed great interest in mechanical instruments, especially clocks. He liked to take them apart but was not always able to get them to run again. The Empress told Miss Carl that she hid her best clocks when he was expected in her palace. This does not indicate any such arrogant treatment of Kuang Hsu that so many writers mention. Like most mothers, she never thoroughly realized that Kuang Hsu was actually a grown man.

At audiences during this period the Empress often asked his opinion and tried to give the impression that her decisions were their joint opinion. During these last years she never publicly rebuked him but she did punish him or attempt to teach him in rather subtle ways. He was much delighted one day to receive an invitation to accompany her to a theater. When the play was announced he found it to be the *T'ien Lei Fao*, or *Retribution of Heavenly Thunder*. The play depicted how a boy called Chang Chi-pao, in spite of the kindness of his foster parents, had, through his unfilial acts, caused their suicide and how the gods in turn destroyed Chang Chi-pao by heavenly thunder. The Emperor knew he was not going to like that play. It was too evident why it was chosen by the Empress, even if she had not asked him: "Do you understand why Chang Chi-pao was killed by heavenly thunder?" The Emperor replied: "Because he was not filial." Tz'u Hsi smiled and said: "Everything will be all right if you just understand that."

In one of the plays Tz'u Hsi attended she was astonished to see an old friend of her earlier life, the actor Yang Hsiao-lo, taking the leading part. She had thought him dead years ago when he disappeared from Peking because of her too-persistent interest in him. Actor Yang was to cause one more scandal in the court before he again disappeared. As on the former occasion, this was not entirely his fault. It seems that, as his father before him, he possessed some exceedingly strong attraction for women, although he was far too rough in appearance to be called a handsome man. But the women flocked to him. It was not long before many of the young widows and other ladies from the court were openly pursuing Actor Yang. They usually arranged to meet him at one of the foreign-operated hotels in the legation quarter. Although this scandalous action of the young Manchu women was reported to Tz'u Hsi, she took no steps to stop it. She had never worried much about the morals of her court. She said she had enough trouble looking after the women when they were in the Forbidden City to bother about what they did outside its walls.

By the Fifth Moon of that year the weather had become very hot. Tz'u Hsi would eat only cold and raw foods, and the dysentery from which she occasionally suffered returned.

She became irritable and restive. She retired to the Summer Palace and later moved into the Western Hills to the Fragrant Hall in the Hunting Park where it was cooler. At this time, when she was really a sick woman, she had an attack of conscience. Ten years before, on the advice of Prince Kung and P'u Wei, Tz'u Hsi had issued a decree prohibiting the use of opium in China. The rules for the suppression of the opium evil were drafted by Tz'u Hsi herself. She gave all officials who smoked opium ten years to cure themselves of the habit. At the end of these ten years all opium users were to be examined and if they still had the habit they were to be dismissed from office. The ten-year period was now up and she ordered the required action taken.

In the meantime Tz'u Hsi had herself become a smoker of opium and during her sickness had been using it in increasing quantities. It was the one thing that gave her some relief. Against the advice of her physician and her friends she now obeyed the new law and gave up opium entirely. She did it abruptly, without the usual gradual cure. This so affected her health that her physician and friends were much worried and advised her to take at least a little opium until she had regained her health. When they continued to urge her, she showed them a yellow paper on which she was preparing a new decree which stated "Those who urge others to smoke opium shall be penalized in the same manner as those who have been convicted of having poisoned people with opium. . . ." This silenced her friends; they knew that she intended to live by her own rules even if they killed her.

But, sick or not, she continued to hold meetings with her ministers, at first in the palace, then in her bedroom, and finally lying in bed wrapped in a huge quilt. When the Emperor failed to make his regular long journey to the Western Hills to report, pay his respects, and to inquire about her condition, she was told by the eunuchs that the Emperor, "The Ten Thousand Year Lord" as they called him, had caught a slight cold and did not get up that morning. Even the eunuch whom she sent personally to inquire about his condition brought back the same report. For some reason they were all afraid to tell Tz'u Hsi that the Emperor was probably much more seriously ill than she was. She sent back word commanding the Emperor to take better care of himself.

Tz'u Hsi improved considerably after she moved to the Western Hills. She was soon spending most of her time sitting on the open portico in front of her bedroom. She was now living in a palace almost at the top of the hill from which she could see the surrounding country and on clear days the walls of Peking. Her greatest interest at this time seemed to be in the history and governments of Western countries. She had many of her envoys who had lived in foreign countries visit her and tell her of the people and the countries of Europe and America. On a number of occasions an old Chinese scholar visited and told her of the many things he had learned in his studies abroad. This man who, on account of his long hair, unkempt queue, and careless way of dressing, appeared to be a very old man, was well versed not only in the classics of China, but also had a number of degrees from universities of Europe and America. Although a Chinese, he was a stanch supporter of the Manchus and was equally anti-foreign. He probably never told Tz'u Hsi that it was he who wrote many or most of the war songs that the Boxer armies had used, cleverly fitting them to the tunes of hymns the missionaries had taught their Chinese converts.

He amused the Empress very much with his tales, most of them against the white man, whom he learned to dislike during his years abroad. In the course of one of their talks he told Tz'u Hsi that although the Christian nations preached peace and love to all men they did not practice this, as they were the most warlike and the greatest killers of all peoples in the world. During their entire history the Christian nations were either fighting one another or conquering some heathen country, usually claiming that they were doing this to keep the peace or in the name of their religion. All inventions for killing people in large numbers were made in these Christian countries. They had taken the Chinese explosive powder used for centuries to celebrate happy events and within one year had put it into a gun with which to kill people. Whenever a country accepted their religion it, too, became warlike, disturbances broke out, and wars were started, as had happened in China.

But the Empress's rather pleasant days and many discussions in the Western Hills were suddenly interrupted by a curious phenomenon that occurred at this time. About nine o'clock in the evening of the twenty-first day of the Seventh Moon, Tz'u Hsi and a few friends were sitting on the open terrace. It was a clear, cloudless night, and the stars appeared particularly large and bright. Suddenly a huge comet or other heavenly body appeared in the northwestern sky, traveling at great speed across the heavens, and disappeared over the southeastern horizon. Tz'u Hsi described it as having the size and brightness of the moon and with a long tail shaped like a broom, fully five or seven miles in length. The comet passed immediately in front of the Empress and her party and appeared to them very close. It was accompanied by a noisy rush of wind that caused the tiles on the roofs of buildings to shake.

This comet made a tremendous impression on Tz'u Hsi. Almost every word—good and bad—had at one time or another been used to describe her, but now she spoke of herself in a way that had never been used before in connection with her—she was frightened. So frightened that she was temporarily cured of her illness. And also cured of her disregard for superstitions. She was certain that the comet was a warning of some kind directed to her, and she immediately sent for the imperial astrologer. The officials and princes had long wanted Tz'u Hsi to leave the Western Hills and return to the city. The astrologer, who knew perfectly well what the comet was, advised her to return to Peking immediately, intimating that her recovery would be unfavorably influenced by the comet if she remained in the Western Hills. Tz'u Hsi packed up and returned the following day to the safety of the Forbidden City.

On her arrival she received word that the Dalai Lama of Tibet had accepted her invitation to visit the Ch'ing court and that he had already left Lhasa. This pleased Tz'u Hsi very much. In addition to the political importance of the Dalai Lama's visit to China she considered him a man of great virtue who, as a Buddhist saint, possessed mystic influences which she believed could cure her illness. She started immediately to make elaborate plans for his reception at the Summer Palace. During his stay in Peking he lodged at the Lama Temple.

The Dalai Lama was an interesting man. His name was Awonglopusang Tabukebuke Chiamutso, which was abbreviated in the Ch'ing court to Awanglosanchiatso. This did not help much, as it still remained overlong compared with the monosyllabic names of the Chinese. At the time of his visit to Peking he was thirty-three years old and was regarded as the thirteenth reincarnation of Avalokiteshvara. He was one of the two lamas who ruled Tibet. His associate was called the Panshen Lama. As the reincarnation of Nirmanakaya, the latter was the senior lama, but as the Dalai Lama occupied Lhasa he was the political head of the government and known as the Glorious King. The Panshen Lama was known as the Glorious Teacher and was the religious head of the government.

Buddhism was introduced into Tibet about A.D. 630 by Srong Tsan Gampo who, as head of the Lhasa government, entered into diplomatic relations with Emperor T'ai Tsung of the T'ang Dynasty of China. The favorite of his two wives was Wen Ch'eng, a Chinese princess who is worshiped by the Tibetans under the name of Glorious Mother. The Mongols call her the Virgin Goddess, and she is the famous Kwan Yin, Goddess of Mercy, of the Chinese, one of the most revered deities in China. Several paintings of Empress Tz'u Hsi show her dressed as Kwan Yin, a costume she was very fond of wearing.

The visit of the Dalai Lama at this time caused a minor political problem. Tz'u Hsi had invited him against the advice of many of her officials, who saw dire calamity in having the Living Buddha, their own Old Buddha, and the Son of Heaven all in Peking at the same time. Tibet was a vassal state of China and the Dalai Lama was the senior of the two ruling lamas of Tibet.

On his arrival he was received by the Emperor. After kowtowing he was invited to sit beside the Emperor in order to restore his dignity, somewhat impaired by the kowtow. But the Living Buddha and Tibetans who accompanied him objected most to the requirement that he also kowtow to Tz'u Hsi, as they said that notwithstanding her position she was but a woman. But kowtow he did, after which he was appeased by an elaborate banquet, one of the most elaborate he had ever attended.

At this banquet the Tibetans gave one of their mystic religious dances with incantations from their holy scriptures. This so pleased Tz'u Hsi that she granted the Dalai Lama the title of the Faithful and Obedient Supporter of Creation. She also made him high priest of all the Buddhas of the world. She gave orders that he was to have an increase of 10,000 taels to his yearly grant, thoughtfully adding that this was to be paid by the government of the neighboring province of Szechuan and not by the national treasury. The Dalai Lama gave Tz'u Hsi many presents and promised to pray regularly for her health, prosperity, and long life.

She required these prayers sooner than anyone believed she would. The Emperor, Tz'u Hsi, and all the Chinese participants became very ill immediately following the banquet. Tz'u Hsi was unconscious for some time. It was partly her old complaint, dysentery, a very plebeian disease which is no respecter of persons. When the Dalai Lama heard of her illness he immediately prepared a Buddhist tonic called the "Goddess of Mercy Rice of Nutrition and Life," which contained many of the medicines famous in Tibet. He administered it to Tz'u Hsi with solemn Buddhist rites. It had phenomenal results. The Empress seemingly was cured in a few hours.

Tz'u Hsi did not underestimate the importance of the Dalai Lama when she invited him to Peking. The British Government for some time had been negotiating with the Tibetans in an effort to secure a foothold in western Tibet as they had in Burma. This Tz'u Hsi was determined to prevent if she could. After Tz'u Hsi had entertained the Dalai Lama and his Tibetan companions for several weeks, they returned home firm friends of China. The British threat to Tibet was removed for the time being.

While Tz'u Hsi revived quickly with the help of the potent medicine of the Dalai Lama and her strong will, which some said could defy death itself, the medicine had no such effect on the Emperor. He continued to get worse. No one dared report the Emperor's serious condition to Tz'u Hsi, as he had pleaded sickness so many times that she always flew into a rage whenever the servants reported him ill. Not realizing the gravity of his present illness she ordered him to attend the two banquets she gave on successive nights to the Dalai Lama in the Pavilion of Purple Light. Tz'u Hsi refused to attend either banquet because she did not want to show the Dalai Lama that she was still ill and, as she said, "like a weak woman." The Emperor had to be carried to the banquets in what the Chinese call a soft chair. He managed to sit through both feasts, but after the last he had to be supported back to the Han Yuan Tien Hall at the Ocean Terrace. He never again left his palace alive.

Those in immediate attendance on Tz'u Hsi and the Emperor now feared that both were dying. But the Empress seemed to hold death at bay and continued to meet her ministers. She endured her pains in silence and kept her suffering from the notice of the court, or thought she did. She still talked in a loud voice and, as one of her attendants said, her ruggedness and stubbornness were alarming and past all understanding.

Not so with Emperor Kuang Hsu. He saw no one. His only attendant was an old eunuch named Wang An, more than seventy years of age, who had served and watched over the Emperor since he was born. It was this eunuch who several times during the Emperor's imprisonment had kept him from committing suicide by reminding him that he was the successor of a great line of Ch'ing emperors and so could not take that easy way out of his troubles. As Emperor, he had to remain and accept what the gods had ordained so that when the Old Buddha died he would be able to take his rightful place as the ruler of China. If he committed suicide, what excuse could he give his ancestors for deserting his place and duties when he met them in the celestial regions? Eunuch

Wang An asked. There seemed no answer to that, so the Emperor lived on.

During the last days of his life he continually called on the Empress, crying "Huang Ah Ma [Imperial Father, help me]." To Wang An he said many times: "I hate myself for having been born such a bitter-fated Emperor, to become a solitary ghost after my death." Wang An always answered him: "As long as there is Wang An, your old serf, you shall not be a solitary ghost." By this the eunuch intimated that the Emperor would not go alone into the next world as he, Wang An, would accompany him on that journey.

A few days before the death of the Emperor the old eunuch stood at a palace window and openly shouted insults to Li Lien-ying in an effort to so anger the chief eunuch that he would come across the drawbridge to the Ocean Terrace to punish him. The scheme worked. Eunuch Li did defy the Empress Tz'u Hsi and came to the palace of the Emperor, but not in anger. When he saw the condition of Kuang Hsu he fell on his knees and in tears he said: "Oh, Emperor, it was not because your humble serf had no conscience that he did not visit you before. Your Empress and the imperial concubines have themselves turned unfaithful and unworthy of your favors and have themselves neglected you and ordered us to do the same. That there should be a profound hostility between you and Empress Tz'u Hsi is the will of Heaven and no human can alter or control it. But Empress Tz'u is now dying, and if the Emperor will but take care of his dragon body for ten days, your humble serf, Li Lien-ying, will bring the master to the Yuan Hsien Hall and you will take over complete control of the government. Then let your humble serf, Li Lien-ying, receive the punishment of lingering death and he will not complain." The Emperor replied sadly: "I shall not have such good fortune as to live and do as you suggest."

From that time Li saw to it that the Emperor received a continuous supply of the best fruits and choice foods from the imperial kitchens. Some of Li's many enemies claimed that he visited the Emperor at that time only because he thought the Emperor would outlive Tz'u Hsi and so wanted to curry favor with him. The truth no one will ever know, but there is proof that Li was sincere in his talk with the Emperor. Eunuch Li was a very tired old man at the time and knew that he had only a few more years to enjoy any power he might gain. He always said he wanted to retire to the farm he owned north of Peking.

While the Emperor was dying in his beautiful palace prison alone and neglected by all except his faithful eunuch, Tz'u Hsi was also dying in her richly furnished palace only a few hundred yards away. But she was neither alone nor forgotten. She was surrounded by a group of imperial concubines, princes and princesses, dukes and officials, who ministered to her slightest whim and presented her with every delicacy to be found in Peking or all China. The Emperor was apparently dying of neglect, overwork while ill, malnutrition, and because his mind could not surmount his problems. Tz'u Hsi kept from dying by the greatest care and by a mind that defied even death itself. The Emperor in his loneliness wrote four lines on his bedroom wall with his finger dipped in soot from his charcoal stove. In these four lines he cried out: "Though the affection between a son and his mother has been severed beyond repair (referring to Tz'u Hsi and himself), why should not my wife come to see me even though there is no love? And why does not my younger brother look on me for a minute?"

The brother he referred to was Prince Ch'un. This prince was a weak young man who was so afraid of his aunt, Tz'u Hsi, that he feared to ask permission to visit his brother. He made one attempt to do this without permission but Tz'u Hsi's eunuchs would not allow him to cross the bridge leading to the Ocean Terrace.

When he told Empress Hsiao Ting of the Emperor's condition she boldly visited her husband without asking permission of Tz'u Hsi. When the Emperor's physician and Hsiao Ting finally convinced Tz'u Hsi that the Emperor was dying, she ordered Prince Ch'un to go immediately to his brother. At the Emperor's bedside Prince Ch'un fell at his feet and cried bitterly. The Emperor, showing complete composure, said to the prince: "I have occupied the Dragon Throne for thirty-four years. I have no son. The Fifth Lord [his brother] must make haste and ask the Grand Sacred Mother Empress to select and adopt a son and heir to carry on the dynasty." Fearing that if he said more it might get his brother into trouble, he pointed a finger to the mattress on his bed to show the miserable way he was living and said: "Remember this."

When Prince Ch'un reported this conversation to Tz'u Hsi she seemed to realize for the first time that the Emperor was actually dying. She cried out several times: "Tsai T'ien, Tsai T'ien," and fainted. (Tsai T'ien was the personal name of Kuang Hsu.) The imperial physician gave her a herbal medicine but she could not be revived until after midnight. It was believed that the real reason why Tz'u Hsi fainted was because she suddenly realized that her death and the death of the Emperor, whenever they occurred, would probably mean the end of the dynasty, a catastrophe for which she would be entirely to blame. Her spirit, therefore, would have no honor when she faced her ancestors in the Great Beyond. But even in the condition she was in at that time, when she knew she was dying and needed every extra hour she could get, she refused to take opium as recommended by her physician. Opium derivatives were given her with her medicine without her knowledge. These, together with her strong will, soon revived her.

True to her nature, she lost no further time in regrets. She called an immediate meeting of the Imperial Presence, which included the princes, dukes, and grand ministers, to select an heir for the dying Emperor. She was carried to this meeting in the Fo Chao Lou, sitting on a throne with crossed legs like a Buddhist monk, her indomitable will triumphing over pain. Again she asked for no opinions but announced to the assembly that she had decided on P'u Yi, one of the sons of Tsai Feng, Prince Ch'un, as the next emperor. She ordered him brought immediately into the palace. As Prince P'u Yi was the grandson of Jung Lu, she was fulfilling her promise to him to place one of his descendants on the throne of China. P'u Yi was also the nephew of Emperor Kuang Hsu and a brother of the child who had once been designated heir apparent. None of the princes or the other Manchu members of the council dared object to this decision, but, again, two Chinese members of the Privy Council did object strenuously. They both kowtowed to Tz'u Hsi and said: "Now that the revolutionists are humming like so many bees outside, if a child emperor be placed on the Dragon Throne and the Old Buddha should come to the unutterable [death], who would be available to handle the rehabilitation? The Old Buddha must be requested to name an adult as Emperor." Tz'u Hsi replied as she had on a previous occasion: "This is something that concerns only our own family. What right have ministers who are Chinese and not of our family to make any assertion?"

She was the old imperious Empress Tz'u Hsi again. She ended all argument by ordering Prince Ch'un to return to his home and bring his son to the assembly.

Although not greatly pleased at the prospect of having his son made Emperor, he obeyed. When he reached his home he found his wife with the young boy, healthy, fair, and fat. In her terror of Tz'u Hsi the mother tried to run away with the child. But the prince caught her and brought both back, saying: "When it comes as an order from Empress Tz'u Hsi, who can resist?"

When the old Seventh Concubine Fu Chin, the mother of Prince Ch'un and grandmother of P'u Yi, heard the quarreling she ordered both husband and wife to her room to tell her what was causing so much commotion. While the wife explained to her mother-in-law, Prince Ch'un seized his son, ran to his sedan chair, and took him to the palace. P'u Yi's mother was another woman who did not want her son to be Emperor of China. And old Seventh Concubine Fu Chin was another of those courageous Manchu women. She was a devout Buddhist who read her scriptures and chanted her prayers daily, and ordinarily never allowed a wicked word to pass her lips, but when she saw her favorite grandson snatched away and taken to the palace to be made Emperor, she walked to the balcony of her room and before the crowd, which had by now assembled in the courtyard, she stamped her foot and, pointing in the direction of the imperial palace, cursed loudly: "That woman has ruined my son [Emperor Kuang Hsu], and now plans to ruin my grandson. That wicked woman has indeed become entangled with our family with vicious affinities for two generations. The gods have no power. If this were not so, why have they let that she devil do so much mischief?"

When Prince Ch'un arrived at the palace with his son he found that the effect of the opium had worn off and Tz'u Hsi had again become so ill that she had retired to her bed. He handed the boy to Empress Hsiao Ting, wife of the Emperor and future Empress Dowager, with the words: "I am handing you this child whom I have snatched from his mother." As he said this, his eyes filled with tears. Empress Hsiao Ting replied: "Fifth Lord, please keep your mind at ease. I will never treat him wrongly." He was taken to the bedside of Tz'u Hsi, who put her hand on his head and said: "My child, you have great luck. You are destined to a greatness greater than that of your uncle." In this she proved herself to be a poor prophet, for P'u Yi has since been driven three times from a throne and is now a prisoner of the Russians somewhere in Siberia.

Tz'u Hsi reminded those present that when P'u Yi was born, on midnight of the fourteenth day of the First Month of the thirty-fourth year of the reign of Kuang Hsu, a great flame appeared above the roof of the palace of his parents. It was so bright that the whole sky in the northwestern part of Peking appeared blood red. It remained for some time and looked so much like a conflagration that the city fire department rushed to the palace of Prince Ch'un, where they found no fire but were told the glow in the sky was made by the gods to announce the birth of a great son to an old Manchu family. Tz'u Hsi declared this a good omen and said P'u Yi was the reincarnation of the Fire Dragon and had been dispatched by the gods to rescue China from her difficulties.

While the court was appointing a new heir apparent and Kuang Hsu was being given an adopted son and heir, no one troubled to find out what actually was happening at Ocean Terrace. The Emperor was evidently entirely forgotten. At daybreak of the following morning, when a servant carried the usual morning pastries to the Emperor, he found old Eunuch Wang An dead outside the Emperor's door. The servant knocked repeatedly but got no response. He reported his fear that the Emperor was too weak to reply. When this became known at the Fo Chao Lou there was a great commotion. Empress Hsiao Ting courageously woke Tz'u Hsi and kneeling on the floor said: "Please let the Imperial Father [Tz'u Hsi] have pity on this bitter-fated child and allow her to go to the Ocean Terrace to wait on her husband, the Emperor." Tz'u Hsi, who also now became alarmed, muttered: "I certainly have not refused to let you go. All this trouble is your fault, not mine, because of the disharmony between husband and wife. Let anyone who wants to go go."

At this Empress Hsiao Ting, accompanied by more than a dozen of the imperial princes and princesses, rushed to the Ocean Terrace. They broke open the doors of the Emperor's room. They found it in a terrible condition. The paper windows had blown out, the ceiling was covered with spider webs, and a cold, piercing wind blew across the room. Empress Hsiao Ting pushed aside the curtains surrounding the bed and called, "Ten Thousand Year Lord." Receiving no answer, Prince Ch'un lifted the quilt. The Emperor was dead. He had been dead for several hours. The Son of Heaven and his faithful eunuch had passed into the Great Beyond together.

When the news of the death of the Emperor became known, the soldiers guarding the Ocean Terrace knelt on the shore of the lake and wept as did the servants and the eunuchs of the entire sea area, and even the princes and princesses. Tz'u Hsi had seen with somewhat of a shock the eagerness with which Hsiao Ting and the princes and princesses left her to rush to the Ocean Terrace. Now she saw clearly the mistake she had made in her treatment of the Emperor when she heard the weeping and saw the sorrow of all the people in the palaces at the announcement of his death. The final blow came when her devoted Li Lien-ying appeared before her with reddened eyes. When she realized then that in all the court she was the only person hostile to the Emperor she also wept and said over and over: "I have made many mistakes. I have made many mistakes."

The next few hours were the last hours of Tz'u Hsi's life. One person who was at the bedside of the Empress the entire time wrote: "The Empress Tz'u Hsi had become very angry with herself and she felt deeply distressed. She now realized that one empress regent (Tz'u An), two emperors (T'ung Chih and Kuang Hsu), one empress (Hsiao Cheh), one imperial concubine (the Pearl Concubine), and two other young girls who were to become concubines, had lost their lives through acts of hers. As she pondered over and occasionally mentioned these things she began to fear the heavenly retribution for all her misdeeds. The seventy-four-year-old woman became so agitated that she fainted again."

Eunuch Li Lien-ying rushed to the Ocean Terrace with the news that Empress Tz'u Hsi was dying. Empress Hsiao Ting and the others who were still at the bedside of the dead Emperor returned to the bedroom of Tz'u Hsi. The dying Empress now gave her final orders: that P'u Yi should become the adopted son and heir to both Emperor Kuang Hsu and his predecessor, T'ung Chih, thus restoring the family line and providing a successor to both emperors. The mother of the Emperor should be made Empress Dowager, and the father Prince Regent to direct the affairs of state until P'u Yi became of age. She called on all present to support the regent and the new Emperor. When the princes and officials fell on their knees and said: "Let the Old Buddha please quiet herself and recover from her illness," she smiled and said: "No, I have sinned enough. I will die." She pointed a finger at her niece, Empress Hsiao Ting, and said to the four grand councilors: "I have nothing more to tell you, but remember these my last words–never again make a woman regent and ruler of China."

Thus died the great Tz'u Hsi, surrounded by many of the greatest princes and high officials of the land, in the most luxurious palace to be found in any country. Thus died the little girl who as Green Jade was born amid poverty and who largely, by her own efforts, became the greatest ruler of her people–some believe the greatest woman ruler in history. Many of those present at her bedside that early November morning believed and said that Tz'u Hsi died not because she had to die, or because her time had come, but because she herself decided to die. She was now very tired and longed this time not for her Summer Palace but for rest and peace, surrounded by the things she loved, in the great tomb she had built for herself in the solitude and quietness of the Tung Ling.

While Tz'u Hsi did not believe that her reign had been successful, the people of China, the great Ch'ing princes, the officials, and most of the foreigners who had come to know her and her work, all these believed that her life had been a success—a success even beyond the dreams of Soothsayer Fu. Her constant aim had been to assure the continuance of the Ch'ing Dynasty. In this she succeeded as long as she was alive. Her strength was revealed by the speed with which the dynasty fell after her guiding hand was removed.

2

Previous to the death of Emperor K'ang Hsi the Manchus cremated the remains of their emperors, princes, and important persons, and placed their ashes in porcelain jars for burial. In the time of Emperor K'ang Hsu, the Ch'ing Dynasty adopted the burial custom of the earlier Ming emperors. They encoffined the bodies and entombed them in huge, strong, and extravagantly built tombs. The cost of the construction of the coffins, the amount of jewels and treasures buried with the remains, and the size and cost of the construction of the tombs increased with each succeeding emperor until the climax of expenditure was reached with the tomb of Empress Tz'u Hsi. Although, as an empress, she was not entitled to any such expenditure as she authorized for her tomb, she spent untold millions and much of her time during the last twenty or more years of her life in building a tomb that probably exceeded even the burial vaults of the Pharaohs in cost, size, and treasures.

Of the tomb itself little need be said. It was of the same plan and style as the other imperial tombs except that it was even larger, more elaborate, and built at much greater expense than the famous Ming tomb of Yung Lo. Greater care was taken to see that it was both burglar- and waterproof. She made many visits to the Tung Ling during the last years of her life and if anything did not suit her she ordered changes in the construction, regardless of the cost. As she had rare taste and ideas of proportion the result was a tomb of good design and great magnificence.

While the tomb differed little in outward appearance from the other tombs of the Ch'ing and Ming emperors, her coffin differed greatly. It really consisted of two coffins, one within the other. The smaller coffin was made of "Gold Thread Fragrant Cedar Wood"—deliciously scented wood that lasts almost indefinitely when kept fairly dry. This inner coffin was a huge affair, in design somewhat like a Chinese temple. It was lacquered on the inside in pale yellow, then upholstered in bright yellow satin embroidered with the dragon and phoenix designs. A "treasure bed" of the same material and design as the upholstering was placed inside the coffin. The body rested on this. Lining the inner sides of the inner coffin were rows of shelves on which were placed treasures of every description, including the rarest and most expensive jades of every color, antique bronzes, gold and silver objects, fine porcelains, and precious jewels. The space under the treasure bed, which was usually filled with charcoal and rare incense, in Tz'u Hsi's coffin was filled to capacity with pearls mixed with the powder of white and purple sandalwood, ligaloes wood, camphor, musk, and other sweet-smelling materials. This was supposed to keep the body from decomposing, and to preserve its flesh color.

The outer surface of the inner coffin was heavily lacquered and carved in the Endless Swastika on which was superimposed an ornamentation of peonies. There are two traditional types of the peony design: one, the "positive," was used only for emperors; the other, the "negative," was used for empresses. Characteristically, Tz'u Hsi chose the positive design to adorn her coffin.

The outer, or Gold Coffin, was similar in design and was lined with the same material and in the same manner as the inner coffin. The exterior was covered with three layers of heavy gold leaf, which gave it the appearance of being solid gold. It was twelve and a half feet in length, five feet wide, and seven feet high. After the inner coffin with the body was in place and everything sealed, the entire surface of the outer coffin was lacquered every other day until forty-seven layers of transparent lacquer had been applied, giving it a very rich-looking surface. When thoroughly dried, a satin covering, embroidered with golden dragons, was draped over it. Here was truly a coffin worthy of the great Empress of one fifth of the world's people.

As extravagant as the tomb and the two coffins were, the greatest expense was lavished on the garments in which her body was clothed, and on the several mattresses and quilts on which it was placed within the inner coffin. For a description of these one can quote an inventory that was made at the time by the eunuch who supervised the encoffining of the body of Tz'u Hsi. Describing the garments and jewels he wrote: "The most attractive among these was the pearl jacket worn next to the skin and the pearl shoes, the toe of which was a huge night-illuminating pearl. Next to these were the Pearl Dragon Robe. The robe was of yellow satin with the dragon interspersed with small characters for Buddha and longevity embroidered in gold. The eyes and the scales of the dragon were made of large pearls and the characters for Buddha and longevity were made of circles of smaller pearls with one large pearl in the center of each. The Dragon Audience Skirt was a hundred pleated skirt embroidered with golden dragons, the eyes made of large pearls. The Pearl Dragon Coat was a sleeveless affair, much like a waistcoat, and was made of yellow satin embroidered in designs of clouds, sea waves, and dragons, with the eyes also of pearls.

"In addition to these, there were Seven Wonders, not found in any Ming or Ch'ing grave or in any other country. Two of these consisted of long strings of amber beads, which were hung obliquely on the breast, making a cross. The third was another necklace made of one hundred and eight huge Sungari pearls with an equal number of precious stones of different colors. The fourth was the phoenix headdress made of one hundred and twenty-eight lesser pearls, eight cat's-eyes, eight pure gold phoenixes, and numbers of other jewels. The fifth was the famous pair of white jade bracelets with encased dragons. These were the purest white jade. When held to the light each had a black object inside which looked like a dragon. When the bracelet was moved slightly it appeared as if the dragon actually moved. These bracelets were well known and were considered almost priceless. The sixth wonder was the equally famous Precious Pearl Hand Beads, which consisted of eighteen pearls, all of uniform size and color, but which when placed in the dark gave out a stream of light. The seventh wonder was the Sun and Moon Pearls, which consisted of one round pearl embraced within a crescent-shaped pearl. This was placed in the mouth of Empress Tz'u Hsi. These Seven Wonders were the greatest of all the treasures of the Ch'ings.

"The mattresses and quilt inside the inner coffin were all exquisite products of the silk industry of China. The body of the Empress was laid on three mattresses. The first was of velvet lined with satin. The second was a yellow satin mattress embroidered with dragons and clouds, and the third another nine-dragon yellow mattress filled with cocoon silk. A large number of bolts of silk of various colors were placed over the body and used to fill in the space between the body and the walls of the inner coffin. Over all this were placed a number of silk quilts of various colors, in which were woven in gold thread passages from the Buddhist scriptures in the original Sanskrit."

This enormous gold coffin, filled with priceless treasures, jewels, and other valuable works of art worth millions of dollars, was left in the underground chamber at the imperial Eastern Tombs in lonely country, ninety miles from the nearest city and guarded only by a few old eunuchs. As all this was known to everyone in China, is it any wonder that as soon as Empress Tz'u Hsi was buried many minds started to devise schemes to rob the tomb of its treasures?

The sudden death of the Emperor, according to the official records, occurred at the First House of the Tiger on the twentieth day of the Tenth Moon of the thirty-fourth year of Kuang Hsu's reign. The appointment of Prince P'u Yi as heir and successor of the Emperor, his confirmation as Emperor and the death of Tz'u Hsi all took place within thirty hours and raised many problems requiring immediate decisions. This threw a tremendous load onto the shoulders of a group of men who had for so many years had all their decisions made for them. For the next few days the government of China was like a ship that during a storm not only lost its rudder but its helmsman, captain, compass, and sailing orders all at the same time.

Again it was a woman, another of those remarkable Manchu princesses, who first regained her composure. She was Hsiao Ting, the new Empress Dowager. Taking the Imperial Exalted Concubine Chin Fei, the young Emperor, and the Prince Regent with her, she went to the Ocean Terrace. After paying proper respects to the late Emperor, the Minor Encoffining Ceremony was performed. At the Major Encoffining Ceremony, which took place at three o'clock the same afternoon, the Empress Dowager and Imperial Concubine Chin Fei cut off some of their hair, wrapped it in the proper paper, and put the package in the right hand of the dead Emperor. The tip of the queue of the boy Emperor, similarly wrapped, was put in the left hand of the Emperor. The coffin was then taken to the Ch'ien Ch'ing Kung.

The Minor Encoffining Ceremony for Empress Tz'u Hsi was performed at the Hour of the Snake (ten o'clock in the morning), and the Major Encoffining at the Hour of the Cock (six o'clock in the afternoon of the same day). Tz'u Hsi's coffin was then placed in the front hall of the Fo Chao Lou. Two groups were appointed, one for the Emperor and one for Tz'u Hsi, composed of imperial princes, their wives, other princesses, and high officials to wear official mourning and perform the mourning ceremonies. These consisted of loud weeping and wailing at each of the two coffins for one hundred days. In addition to the numerous family sacrificial ceremonies held by the Prince Regent, the Emperor, the Empress Dowager, and certain imperial princes, there were large Buddhist prayer meetings for the chanting of the Sutras held simultaneously at the Chun Cheng Tien in the imperial palace, the Lama temple of Yung Hou Kung, the Kuan Teh Hall at Prospect Hill, and in the former residence of the Emperor at the Ocean Terrace. These meetings were conducted by numerous Taoist, Lama, and Buddhist priests.

Ceremonies were also held in all Lama, Taoist, and Buddhist temples and Chinese Christian churches throughout China.

In addition to the above-mentioned religious services, the whole nation was put under severe restrictions. On the twenty-fourth day of the same moon a decree was issued by the Prince Regent which read as follows: "Beginning from the twenty-fourth day of the Tenth Moon and for one hundred days all civil and military officials in the entire country shall wear mourning and the officials and the people shall not shave their heads. No weddings, no musical concerts, or theatricals shall be performed during this period." In addition it was commanded that no wife or concubine must become pregnant.

Any child conceived during this period would, when born, be declared a "black baby"—illegitimate. The second character in the child's name must in some way include the radical for dog, thus proclaiming to the world for the remainder of his life that his parents had transgressed against the law of mourning continence.

As separate services were held for the Emperor and Tz'u Hsi the one-hundred-day mourning period was one of almost constant ceremonies. Not all of these were gloomy. All were colorful and all provided spectacles for the people of Peking and the numerous visitors to the city. This was particularly true of the Dragon Boat and Ghost Festival.

The Ghost Festival is a very old institution in China and is held on the day on which the spirits of the dead are believed to be delivered from purgatory by Buddhist prayer ceremonies. The great event of the day is the burning of the Doctrine Boat on which are enshrined the spirit tablets of the deceased persons. As the Ghost Festival was the last great ceremony to be held before the coffins were carried to their final resting places, the Prince Regent planned to make the festival of such magnificence that the people would forget their recent criticism that the government and imperial family had been rather miserly with some of the celebrations. At first the festival was planned only for the Empress Tz'u Hsi, but so many friends of the deceased Emperor, especially Chang Chih-tung, protested that the Emperor be given a festival of equal magnificence, that the Prince Regent decided to make this particular Ghost Festival a joint celebration, thus shrewdly saving the expense of two ceremonies.

The Doctrine Boat was a very large and ornamental float, one hundred and sixty-eight feet in length and more than twenty-three feet high. It was constructed largely of paper or papier-mâché mounted on a framework of wood and kaoliang stalks. On the bow was a large golden dragon head, more than ten feet across. On the stern was a huge demon of the same size, with a ferocious face and brandishing a three-pronged halberd. The sides of the boat were painted with a design of waves superimposed with lotus flowers. The boat was fully manned with paper sailors dressed in typical white silk jackets and trousers, with black satin boots and straw hats. The approach to the main part of the superstructure of the boat was through a three-arched, five-colored *pai lou* leading to a building which was a copy of two halls at the Summer Palace. These paper palaces were complete in every detail, including the furniture and decorations. All the imperial cortege on the deck of the boat and in the palaces, all the civil and military officials, the Buddhist images, the serving maids, eunuchs, and cooks in the galley were lifesize paper dolls. Many of the papier-mâché images of important persons were portraits. All were dressed in silk and satin.

The imperial flag flew from the top of the high mast of the boat. This flag was a square, boxlike affair that resembled the cooking pot used in the army in ancient times. On the crossbar below the flag were hung the banners of the Empress Tz'u Hsi and the Emperor. The decorated float was on exhibition to the public for five days. On the fifth day it and everything connected with it were burned in a mighty conflagration.

The one-hundred-day mourning period finally came to an end, and as all the sacrifices, ceremonies, and other festivals had been completed, a decree was issued stating that the funeral of Tz'u Hsi was to be held on the twenty-seventh day of the Ninth Moon and the funeral of Emperor Kuang Hsu on the fifth day of the Tenth Moon. On these days the respective coffins would leave Peking for the imperial tombs.

Those days before the funeral of the Emperor the Prince

Regent, the boy Emperor, the Empress Dowager, and all the princes, princesses, and officials of the mourning cortege performed the farewell rites before the coffin. Two days later the ministers of the various foreign countries paid their last respects to the late Emperor in the Kuan Hall in the Prospect Hill enclosure.

At an early hour next morning the coffin was placed on a catafalque heavily draped with yellow silk and borne outside the gate by thirty-two men. There the coffin was placed on a larger catafalque with eighty bearers. The Prince Regent led the funeral procession on foot, with the little Emperor in his arms.

At the Fu Ch'eng Men, the Empress Dowager Lung Yu and her ladies waited on their knees by the roadside for the funeral procession to arrive. On the arrival of the catafalque the Empress Dowager and the young Emperor offered libations and did the ceremonial wailing and performed the last rites. They remained on their knees until the catafalque, now carried by sixty shifts of one hundred and twenty-eight men each, passed by and proceeded directly to the Western Tombs accompanied by a small number of princes, dukes, high officials, and eunuchs. As the tomb for the Emperor was not completed the coffin was placed in a nearby temple to await later entombment.

But the Emperor's funeral made but a poor show after the more elaborate obsequies accorded the Empress Tz'u Hsi. As one Chinese observer remarked, the final funeral procession for the Emperor had but one yellow parasol and one sixteen-man sedan chair, compared with the hundreds of these that had accompanied the funeral procession of Tz'u Hsi. But there was one thing about his funeral that would probably have pleased Kuang Hsu very much: he was being buried in the Western Tombs, as far from the grave of Tz'u Hsi in the Eastern Tombs as was possible and still be buried in an imperial tomb of the Ch'ing Dynasty.

Kuang Hsu was destined to lie undisturbed in his grave. The comparatively poor treasures that were buried with him did not tempt robbers to disturb his last sleep.

The magnificence of Empress Tz'u Hsi's entombment was the talk of Peking for weeks—which no doubt is as she herself would have had it.

On the twenty-third day of the Ninth Moon the Prince Regent, the boy Emperor, the Empress Dowager, the princes and princesses, dukes and officials, performed the farewell rites before the coffin. Two days later the ministers of the various foreign countries paid their respects. At four o'clock on the morning of the funeral the immense coffin, draped in yellow, was carried on a small catafalque from the Huang Chi Hall, while the Prince Regent, carrying the young Emperor, walked before it to lead the way to the Tung Hua Men. Outside this gate the catafalque was changed to one carried by eighty men. This was again changed outside the Ch'ao Yang Men to the Wan Tzu Kuan, requiring one hundred and twenty-eight men. There were sixty shifts of these carriers, making a total of seven thousand, six hundred men required to carry China's last Empress the ninety miles to the Tung Ling.

All along the route crowds gathered to enjoy the show and to pay their final homage to the woman whose power had seemed greater than death. The watchers saw a small and very tired-looking old man who trotted alongside the catafalque, endeavoring to steady the swaying coffin with his uplifted hand. Grief as well as experience had etched his face with innumerable lines. From the start of the funeral procession for as long as it remained in sight he was seen running beside the great Empress's bier. It was Eunuch Li Lien-ying, attempting to render the last service he could give to the person he loved most.

Empress Tz'u Hsi had never known peace in her life, or was she to enjoy it long after death. Barely twenty years after her entombment covetous men, attracted by the enormous wealth she had attempted to take with her, broke into her tomb and disturbed the peace she had striven so hard to insure.

The tomb, and especially the underground vault containing the coffins of Tz'u Hsi, had been designed with great skill and carefully and solidly constructed under the supervision of Prince Kung, Jung Lu, and even the Empress herself. The walls and roof of the vault were of tremendous thickness and strength, supposedly strong enough to defy any attempts to break open the vault. But the Chinese and Manchu builders evidently overlooked one thing: it never occurred to them that the vault might be entered from below. The floor of the vault was not made of sufficient strength or thickness. The robbers, army engineers who had learned their science in foreign schools, tunneled from below and with modern tools and explosives broke through the floor of the tomb.

The robbers plundered the grave of all its treasures, which some persons have estimated at a value of more than $750,000,000. It might be said that in robbing the tomb of its treasure the robbers caused no material loss to the wealth of the world. If such things have a value, they were worth far more in the thieves' market than hidden forever on the body of Empress Tz'u Hsi. The treasures soon found their way to the markets of Asia, Europe, and America. Many of them are now giving pleasure in museums and private homes to those who love beautiful works of art.

But in looting the grave the robbers desecrated the body of the Empress. They stripped it of all its jeweled robes and left it lying naked beside the empty coffin, in danger of being attacked and devoured by hungry dogs. The body was later recovered by a few faithful eunuchs who, at the risk of their lives, did what they could to protect all that remained of their Empress.

When the ex-Emperor P'u Yi heard of this vandalism, although himself an exile living in poverty and driven from his home by the soldiers of the "Christian General," he sent a few of his attendants who, with faithful eunuchs living in the neighborhood, gave the remains of Tz'u Hsi as respectful and decent reinterment as in their poverty they could afford.

The Empress Tz'u Hsi now sleeps in her great lacquered coffin, but with none of the precious and beautiful things she loved so deeply and had hoped to have with her forever. She is no longer robed in her famous pearl-covered garments. Nor does she rest on richly ornamented silken mattresses and quilts. She wears the plain, unadorned dress of a Manchu woman, no better than and very similar to what she wore in the long-ago days when the fulfillment of Soothsayer Fu's prophecy concerning her seemed no more than a fantastic dream.

INDEX

DOLPHIN BOOKS AND DOLPHIN MASTERS

The bold face **M** indicates a Dolphin Master. Dolphin Masters are Dolphin Books in the editions of greatest importance to the teacher and student. In selecting the Dolphin Masters, the editors have taken particular pains to choose copies of the most significant edition (usually the first) by obtaining original books or their facsimiles or by having reproductions made of library copies of particularly rare editions. Facsimiles of original title pages and other appropriate material from the first edition are included in many Masters.

FICTION

JANE EYRE Charlotte Brontë	C5
THE SCARLET LETTER Nathaniel Hawthorne	C7
KIDNAPPED Robert Louis Stevenson	C8
THE RISE OF SILAS LAPHAM William Dean Howells	C9
UNCLE TOM'S CABIN Harriet Beecher Stowe **M**	C13
THE PRAIRIE James Fenimore Cooper	C14
THE PICTURE OF DORIAN GRAY Oscar Wilde	C15
THE WAY OF ALL FLESH Samuel Butler	C16
THE RED AND THE BLACK Stendhal	C17
PERE GORIOT Honoré de Balzac	C18
MADAME BOVARY Gustave Flaubert	C19
THE VICAR OF WAKEFIELD Oliver Goldsmith	C20
THE MILL ON THE FLOSS George Eliot	C21
JUDE THE OBSCURE Thomas Hardy	C22
MANON LESCAUT Abbé Prévost	C29
IVANHOE Sir Walter Scott	C31
A TALE OF TWO CITIES Charles Dickens	C32
NORTHANGER ABBEY and PERSUASION Jane Austen **M**	C34
THE MOONSTONE Wilkie Collins	C35
FRANKENSTEIN Mary Shelley	C44
THREE MEN IN A BOAT Jerome K. Jerome	C46
TALES OF THE GROTESQUE AND ARABESQUE Edgar Allan Poe **M**	C50
HIS MONKEY WIFE John Collier	C53
LOOKING BACKWARD (2000–1887) Edward Bellamy	C55
MOLL FLANDERS Daniel Defoe	C56
BARCHESTER TOWERS Anthony Trollope	C57
CRANFORD E. C. Gaskell	C60
THE RED BADGE OF COURAGE Stephen Crane	C61
ADAM BEDE George Eliot	C62
JOSEPH ANDREWS Henry Fielding	C63
A CHRISTMAS CAROL Charles Dickens	C65
VILLETTE Charlotte Brontë	C66
MOBY DICK Herman Melville	C70
TREASURE ISLAND Robert Louis Stevenson	C72
PRIDE AND PREJUDICE Jane Austen	C74
FAR FROM THE MADDING CROWD Thomas Hardy	C75
THE LOG OF A COWBOY Andy Adams	C77
BLACK BEAUTY Anna Sewell	C78
GULLIVER'S TRAVELS Jonathan Swift	C86

A HAZARD OF NEW FORTUNES William Dean Howells C88
QUENTIN DURWARD Sir Walter Scott C89
ALICE'S ADVENTURES UNDERGROUND and ALICE'S ADVENTURES IN WONDERLAND Lewis Carroll M C94
THE ADVENTURES OF HUCKLEBERRY FINN Mark Twain C98
ROBINSON CRUSOE Daniel Defoe C103
TRISTRAM SHANDY Laurence Sterne C104
BURIED ALIVE Arnold Bennett C105
WUTHERING HEIGHTS Emily Brontë C107
PORTRAIT OF A MAN WITH RED HAIR Hugh Walpole C108
THE MARBLE FAUN Nathaniel Hawthorne C110
AUTOCRAT OF THE BREAKFAST TABLE Oliver Wendell Holmes C111
MANSFIELD PARK Jane Austen C113
HARD TIMES Charles Dickens C114
THE DAMNATION OF THERON WARE Harold Frederic C116
THE RETURN OF THE NATIVE Thomas Hardy C119
THE EXPEDITION OF HUMPHRY CLINKER Tobias Smollett C120
THE HISTORY OF HENRY ESMOND, ESQ. William Makepeace Thackeray C121
EVELINA Fanny Burney C123
THE DAY OF THE TRIFFIDS John Wyndham C130
THE PRIVATE PAPERS OF HENRY RYECROFT George Gissing C131
THE ADVENTURES OF TOM SAWYER Mark Twain C133
THE WARDEN Anthony Trollope C134
TRILBY George du Maurier C135
TESS OF THE D'URBERVILLES Thomas Hardy C138
NEW GRUB STREET George Gissing C139
RODERICK RANDOM Tobias Smollett C140
DAVID HARUM Edward Noyes Westcott C146
EUGENIE GRANDET Honoré de Balzac C147
THE HOUSE OF THE SEVEN GABLES Nathaniel Hawthorne C148
EMMA Jane Austen C149
SILAS MARNER George Eliot C151
RESURRECTION Leo Tolstoy C152
THE MAYOR OF CASTERBRIDGE Thomas Hardy C153
ELSIE VENNER Oliver Wendell Holmes C154
SISTER CARRIE Theodore Dreiser C160
TWENTY THOUSAND LEAGUES UNDER THE SEA Jules Verne C167
AROUND THE WORLD IN EIGHTY DAYS Jules Verne C168
THE PATHFINDER James Fenimore Cooper C173
SENSE AND SENSIBILITY Jane Austen C174
BEN-HUR Lew Wallace C175
GREAT EXPECTATIONS Charles Dickens C181
OLIVER TWIST Charles Dickens C182
OMOO Herman Melville C183
KING SOLOMON'S MINES H. Rider Haggard C188
THE FANCHER TRAIN Amelia Bean C197
THE SKETCHBOOK OF GEOFFREY CRAYON, GENT. Washington Irving M C206
THE SPY James Fenimore Cooper C207
NANA Emile Zola C208
SHE H. Rider Haggard C210
THE LAST OF THE MOHICANS James Fenimore Cooper C211

POETRY AND DRAMA

THE DIVINE COMEDY OF DANTE ALIGHIERI: THE INFERNO
Translated by Henry Wadsworth Longfellow M — C1
LEAVES OF GRASS Walt Whitman M — C3
LYRICAL BALLADS William Wordsworth and
Samuel Taylor Coleridge M — C4
POEMS OF KEATS AND SHELLEY (1820) M — C11
INVITATION TO POETRY Lloyd Frankenberg — C24
archy and mehitabel don marquis — C26
RUBAIYAT OF OMAR KHAYYAM Edward FitzGerald, translator — C28
SHAKESPEARE'S SONNETS M — C33
THE GOLDEN TREASURY OF ENGLISH SONGS AND LYRICS
Francis Turner Palgrave M — C45
THE DRAMATIC WORKS OF SHERIDAN
Richard Brinsley Sheridan M — C47
THE DIVINE COMEDY OF DANTE ALIGHIERI: PURGATORIO
Translated by Henry Wadsworth Longfellow M — C51
THE DIVINE COMEDY OF DANTE ALIGHIERI: PARADISO
Translated by Henry Wadsworth Longfellow M — C52
DON JUAN Lord Byron — C64
PARADISE LOST John Milton — C73
MEN AND WOMEN Robert Browning — C136
THE PLAYS OF OSCAR WILDE Oscar Wilde — C137
H. M. S. PINAFORE, AND SIX OTHER SAVOY OPERAS
W. S. Gilbert — C155
THE MIKADO, AND FIVE OTHER SAVOY OPERAS
W. S. Gilbert — C158
IDYLLS OF THE KING Alfred, Lord Tennyson — C165
EIGHT DRAMAS OF CALDERON
Edward FitzGerald, translator M — C169
PLEASURE DOME Lloyd Frankenberg — C190
SIBYLLINE LEAVES Samuel Taylor Coleridge M — C195
SONNETS FROM THE PORTUGUESE AND OTHER POEMS
Elizabeth Barrett Browning — C209

HISTORY AND BIOGRAPHY

THE BERNAL DIAZ CHRONICLES
Albert Idell, editor and translator — C25
OUR FRIEND JAMES JOYCE Mary and Padraic Colum — C27
GIANTS OF GEOLOGY Carroll Lane and Mildred Adams Fenton — C36
MR. LINCOLN'S ARMY Bruce Catton — C37
BATTLES THAT CHANGED HISTORY Fletcher Pratt — C38
TEACHER Helen Keller — C39
THE LIFE OF CHARLOTTE BRONTE E. C. Gaskell M — C48
COMMON SENSE and THE CRISIS Thomas Paine M — C49
THE FOUR GEORGES William Makepeace Thackeray — C54
TWO YEARS BEFORE THE MAST R. H. Dana — C76
SEA FIGHTS AND SHIPWRECKS Hanson W. Baldwin — C84
THE AUTOBIOGRAPHY OF BENJAMIN FRANKLIN M — C87
LIVES OF THE POETS [Cowley to Prior] Samuel Johnson — C91
LIVES OF THE POETS [Congreve to Gray] Samuel Johnson — C92
THE MAN WHO KILLED LINCOLN Philip Van Doren Stern — C101
LIFE OF NELSON Robert Southey — C112
THE LIFE OF SIR ARTHUR CONAN DOYLE John Dickson Carr — C117
TONGUE OF THE PROPHETS Robert St. John — C118
AN AUTOBIOGRAPHY Anthony Trollope — C128

AUTOBIOGRAPHY OF BENVENUTO CELLINI Benvenuto Cellini C129
THE PELOPONNESIAN WAR Thucydides C150
VENERABLE ANCESTOR Harry Hussey C157
BENT'S FORT David Lavender C159
BALBOA OF DARIEN Kathleen Romoli C162
THE CONQUEST OF PERU William H. Prescott C166
EXPERIMENT IN REBELLION Clifford Dowdey C171
THE AUTOBIOGRAPHY OF JOHN STUART MILL
John Stuart Mill C179

PHILOSOPHY AND RELIGION

WALDEN Henry David Thoreau C10
THE REPUBLIC AND OTHER WORKS Plato C12
THE LIFE OF JESUS Ernest Renan C59
THE MEDITATIONS OF MARCUS AURELIUS
Translated by George Long C68
THE VARIETIES OF RELIGIOUS EXPERIENCE William James C71
ON THE NATURE OF THINGS Lucretius
Translated by H. A. J. Munro C80
THE RATIONALISTS Descartes, Spinoza, Leibniz C82
THE EMPIRICISTS Locke, Berkeley, Hume C109
THE SECRET SAYINGS OF JESUS
Robert M. Grant with David Noel Freedman C163

ESSAYS AND LETTERS

THE CONDUCT OF LIFE Ralph Waldo Emerson M C2
THE ESSAYS OF ELIA and THE LAST ESSAYS OF ELIA
Charles Lamb M C6
LECTURES ON THE ENGLISH COMIC WRITERS
William Hazlitt M C30
HAWTHORNE Henry James C58
THE ESSAYS OF FRANCIS BACON C67
THE SPIRIT OF THE AGE William Hazlitt C79
ON HEROES AND HERO-WORSHIP and REPRESENTATIVE MEN
Thomas Carlyle and Ralph Waldo Emerson C83
LIFE IN MEXICO Frances Calderón de la Barca C93
THE NATURAL HISTORY OF SELBORNE Gilbert White C96
CONFESSIONS OF AN ENGLISH OPIUM-EATER and SUSPIRIA
DE PROFUNDIS Thomas De Quincey M C97
THE COMPLETE ANGLER Izaak Walton C102
THE NEXT MILLION YEARS C. G. Darwin C106
AN ALMANAC OF LIBERTY William O. Douglas C115
LETTERS FROM AN AMERICAN FARMER
J. H. St. John Crèvecoeur C164
FABIAN ESSAYS IN SOCIALISM Edited by G. B. Shaw C170

MYSTERY

BLACK PLUMES Margery Allingham C41
THE MAN IN THE GREEN HAT Manning Coles C42
THE BELL IN THE FOG John Stephen Strange C43
THE PEOPLE AGAINST O'HARA Eleazar Lipsky C122
A STUDY IN SCARLET & THE SIGN OF FOUR
Sir Arthur Conan Doyle C124

ADVENTURES OF SHERLOCK HOLMES
Sir Arthur Conan Doyle C125
MEMOIRS OF SHERLOCK HOLMES Sir Arthur Conan Doyle C126
THE HOUND OF THE BASKERVILLES
Sir Arthur Conan Doyle C127
POOR HARRIET Elizabeth Fenwick C185
THE WHISPER IN THE GLOOM Nicholas Blake C186
THE LADY AND HER DOCTOR Evelyn Piper C187
A HERO FOR LEANDA Andrew Garve C189

MISCELLANEOUS

A HANDBOOK TO MARRIAGE Theodor Bovet C23
SEX AND FAMILY IN THE BIBLE AND THE MIDDLE EAST
Raphael Patai C40
THE EXECUTIVE LIFE Editors of FORTUNE C69
ZAPOTEC Helen Augur C81
CONVERSATIONS WITH TOSCANINI B. H. Haggin C85
AMERICAN WAYS OF LIFE George R. Stewart C90
THE ABC OF CHILD CARE Allan Fromme, Ph.D. C95
THE AGE OF FABLE Thomas Bulfinch C132
THE LIFE AND DEATH OF CELLS Joseph G. Hoffman C156
MARRIAGE EAST AND WEST David and Vera Mace C161
THE ORIGIN OF SPECIES Charles Darwin C172
PRIMITIVE PEOPLES TODAY Edward Weyer, Jr. C200

DOLPHIN REFERENCE SERIES

POEMS TO REMEMBER John Kieran, editor C99
100 GREAT OPERAS AND THEIR STORIES Henry W. Simon C100
THE FAMILY HANDBOOK OF HOME NURSING AND MEDICAL
CARE I. J. Rossman, M.D. and Doris R. Schwartz, R.N. C141
THE COMPLETE BOOK OF CHESS TACTICS Fred Reinfeld C143
THESAURUS OF ANECDOTES Edmund Fuller C191

DOLPHIN HANDBOOK SERIES

THE FINE ART OF MIXING DRINKS David A. Embury C177
HOW TO SAY A FEW WORDS David Guy Powers C178
HOW TO BE A CONSISTENT WINNER IN THE MOST POPULAR
CARD GAMES John R. Crawford C180
COOKING WITH A FRENCH TOUCH Gerald Maurois C184
BEER AND GOOD FOOD Myra Waldo C196
CREATIVE COOKING Nicholas Roosevelt C213
A NEW WAY TO BETTER ENGLISH Rudolf Flesch C214
IT'S EASY TO INCREASE YOUR VOCABULARY William Morris C215

ANCHOR BOOKS

ADAMS, HENRY A Henry Adams Reader A177
——— Mont-Saint-Michel and Chartres A166
ALAIN-FOURNIER, HENRI The Wanderer A14
ALBRIGHT, W. F. From the Stone Age to Christianity A100
ALLPORT, GORDON W. The Nature of Prejudice A149
ANDRADE, E. N. DA C. An Approach to Modern Physics A111
——— Sir Isaac Newton A151
ARENDT, HANNAH The Human Condition A182
ARISTOPHANES Five Comedies A57
ARON, RAYMOND On War A171
AUDEN, W. H.; GREENBERG, NOAH; KALLMAN, CHESTER An Elizabethan Song Book A56
AUERBACH, ERICH Mimesis A107
BARK, WILLIAM CARROLL Origins of the Medieval World A190
BARTH, KARL Community, State and Church A221
BARZUN, JACQUES Darwin, Marx, Wagner A127
——— Teacher in America A25
BATE, WALTER JACKSON Prefaces to Criticism A165
BAUDELAIRE, CHARLES The Mirror of Art A84
BEDIER, JOSEPH The Romance of Tristan and Iseult A2
BEERBOHM, MAX A Selection from "Around Theatres" A226
BEETHOVEN Letters, Journals and Conversations A206
BENTLEY, ERIC (Ed.) The Classic Theatre I: Six Italian Plays A155a
——— The Classic Theatre II: Five German Plays A155b
——— The Classic Theatre III: Six Spanish Plays A155c
BENTLEY, ERIC (Ed.) The Modern Theatre I, II, III, IV, V, VI A48a, A48b, A48c, A48d, A48e, A48f
——— From the American Drama (The Modern Theatre IV) A48d
BERENSON, BERNARD Aesthetics and History A36
BERGSON, HENRI "Laughter" in Comedy A87
——— Matter and Memory A172
——— The Two Sources of Morality and Religion A28
BISHOP, AMASA Project Sherwood, A202
BLACKMUR, R. P. Form and Value in Modern Poetry A96
BRENNER, CHARLES An Elementary Textbook of Psychoanalysis A102
BROGAN, D. W. Politics in America, A198
BROOKS, VAN WYCK America's Coming of Age A129
BURCKHARDT, JACOB The Age of Constantine the Great A65
BURTT, EDWIN ARTHUR The Metaphysical Foundations of Modern Science A41
BUTTERFIELD, HERBERT and OTHERS A Short History of Science A180
CABLE, GEORGE W. Creoles and Cajuns A179
——— The Negro Question A144
CASSIRER, ERNST An Essay on Man A3
CASTIGLIONE, BALDESAR The Book of the Courtier A186
CHAPMAN, JOHN JAY The Selected Writings of John Jay Chapman A161
CHASE, RICHARD The American Novel and Its Tradition A116
CHEKHOV, ANTON Peasants and Other Stories A66
CLARK, KENNETH The Nude A168
COLETTE My Mother's House and The Vagabond A62
CONANT, JAMES B. Modern Science and Modern Man A10
CONNOLLY, CYRIL Enemies of Promise and Other Essays, A194
CONRAD, JOSEPH Chance A113
——— A Mirror of the Sea and A Personal Record A207
——— The Rescue, A199
——— The Secret Agent A8
——— The Shadow-Line and Two Other Tales A178
——— Tales of Heroes and History A228

CONRAD, JOSEPH Victory A106
———— Youth: A Narrative and Two Other Stories A173
COULANGES, FUSTEL DE The Ancient City A76
CRANE, HART The Complete Poems of Hart Crane A128
CROMBIE, A. C. Medieval and Early Modern Science: I, II A167a, A167b
DANTZIG, TOBIAS Number, the Language of Science A67
DICKINSON, EMILY Selected Poems and Letters A192
DIDEROT, DENIS Rameau's Nephew and Other Works A61
DOLLARD, JOHN Caste and Class in a Southern Town A95
DOSTOEVSKY, FYODOR Three Short Novels A193
DOUGHTY, C. M. Travels in Arabia Deserta A50
DUMAS, ALEXANDRE Adventures in Spain A211
DUPEE, F. W. Henry James A68
EDEL, LEON Literary Biography A188
FERGUSSON, FRANCIS The Human Image in Dramatic Literature A124
———— The Idea of a Theatre A4
FINCH, JAMES K. The Story of Engineering A214
FLORES, ANGEL (Ed.) An Anthology of French Poetry A134
———— An Anthology of German Poetry A197
———— Nineteenth Century French Tales A217
———— Nineteenth Century German Tales A184
FLORNOY, BERTRAND The World of the Inca A137
FORTUNE, EDITORS OF The Exploding Metropolis A146
FRANKFORT, HENRI The Birth of Civilization in the Near East A89
FREUD, SIGMUND Civilization and Its Discontents A130
———— The Future of an Illusion A99
———— A General Selection from the Works of A115
———— The Origins of Psychoanalysis A112
FRY, ROGER Transformations A77
GALILEO Discoveries and Opinions A94
GARNETT, DAVID Pocahontas A157
GASTER, T. H. The Dead Sea Scriptures in English Translation A92
GOFFMAN, ERVING The Presentation of Self in Everyday Life A174
GOGOL, NICOLAI Tales of Good and Evil A120
GONCOURT, EDMOND and JULES DE The Goncourt Journals A158
GOYA, FRANCISCO DE The Disasters of War AA1
GRANVILLE-BARKER, H. and HARRISON, G. B. A Companion to Shakespeare Studies, A191
GRAVES, ROBERT Good-Bye to All That A123
———— The Poems of Robert Graves—Chosen by Himself A139
GREEN, HENRY Loving A18
HADAS, MOSES (Ed.) A History of Rome A78
————(Ed) The Stoic Philosophy of Seneca A148
————(Trans.) Three Greek Romances A21
HAGGIN, B. H. The Listener's Musical Companion A183
HAHN, WALTER F. and NEFF, JOHN C. American Strategy for the Nuclear Age A224
HALL, ROBERT A. JR. Linguistics and Your Language A201
HANDLIN, OSCAR Race and Nationality in American Life A110
HENDERSON, HAROLD An Introduction to Haiku A150
HERBERG, WILL Four Existentialist Theologians A141
———— Protestant, Catholic, Jew A195
HOLT, ELIZABETH GILMORE A Documentary History of Art: I, II A114a, A114b
HUIZINGA, J. The Waning of the Middle Ages A42
IBSEN, HENRIK Brand A215
———— When We Dead Awaken and Three Other Plays A215b
JAMES, HENRY The Ambassadors A154
———— The Awkward Age A138
———— In the Cage and Other Tales A131
———— Selected Letters, A204
———— What Maisie Knew A43
JARRELL, RANDALL (Ed.) The Anchor Book of Stories A145

JASPERS, KARL Man in the Modern Age A101
JESPERSEN, OTTO Growth and Structure of the English Language A46
JEWETT, SARAH ORNE The Country of the Pointed Firs A26
JONES, ERNEST Hamlet and Oedipus A31
JUNG, C. G. Psyche and Symbol A136
KAFKA, FRANZ Amerika A49
KAUFMANN, WALTER From Shakespeare to Existentialism A213
KAZIN, ALFRED On Native Grounds A69
KEATS, JOHN Selected Letters A70
KIERKEGAARD, SOREN Either/Or, I, II A181a, A181b
——— Fear and Trembling and The Sickness Unto Death A30
——— Selections from the Writings of Kierkegaard A210
KISSINGER, HENRY Nuclear Weapons and Foreign Policy A152
KITTO, H. D. F. Greek Tragedy A38
KRAMER, SAMUEL NOAH History Begins at Sumer A175
LASKY, MELVIN J. (Ed.) The Anchor Review: Number One A64, Number Two A109
LAWRENCE, D. H. Sea and Sardinia and Selections from Twilight in Italy A39
——— Studies in Classic American Literature A5
LEAVIS, F. R. The Great Tradition A40
LERMONTOV, MIHAIL A Hero of Our Time A133
LEWIS, D. B. WYNDHAM François Villon A147
LEWIS, W. H. The Splendid Century A122
LUBELL, SAMUEL The Future of American Politics A71
LYNN, Kenneth S. The Comic Tradition in America A187
MALINOWSKI, BRONISLAW Magic, Science and Religion A23
MARX, KARL and ENGELS, FRIEDRICH Basic Writings on Politics and Philosophy A185
MATTINGLY, HAROLD Roman Imperial Civilisation A160
MAURIAC, FRANCOIS Thérèse A79
MELVILLE, HERMAN Redburn: His First Voyage A118
MEREDITH, GEORGE "An Essay on Comedy" in Comedy A87
MEYERHOFF, HANS (Ed.) The Philosophy of History in Our Time A164
MILLER, PERRY (Ed.) The American Puritans: Their Prose and Poetry A80
———(Ed.) The American Transcendentalists: Their Prose and Poetry A119
MONTAIGNE, MICHEL DE The Complete Essays, Vols. I, II, III A227a, A227b, A227c
MURASAKI, LADY The Tale of Genji A55
——— The Tale of Genji, Part II A176
MURRAY, GILBERT Five Stages of Greek Religion A51
MURRAY, MARGARET The God of the Witches A212
NEALE, J. E. Queen Elizabeth I A105
NEHRU, JAWAHARLAL Discovery of India, A200
NIETZSCHE, FRIEDRICH The Birth of Tragedy and The Genealogy of Morals A81
ORTEGA Y GASSET, JOSE The Dehumanization of Art A72
ORWELL, GEORGE A Collection of Essays A29
PANOFSKY, ERWIN Meaning in the Visual Arts A59
PEIRCE, CHARLES S. Values in a Universe of Chance A126
PETERSEN, WILLIAM (Ed.) American Social Patterns A86
PIERSON, GEORGE W. and LUNT, DUDLEY C. Tocqueville in America A189
PIRENNE, HENRI A History of Europe: I, II A156a, A156b
——— Medieval Cities A82
POLYA, G. How to Solve It A93
POWER, EILEEN Medieval People A32
PRAZ, MARIO The Flaming Heart A132
PROUST, MARCEL Pleasures and Days and Other Writings A97
RAHV, PHILIP Discovery of Europe A208

RIESMAN, DAVID Constraint and Variety in American Education A1[illegible]
——— The Lonely Crowd A16
——— Selected Essays from Individualism Reconsidered A58
RILKE, RAINER MARIA Selected Letters A223
ROUGEMONT, DENIS DE Love in the Western World A121
ROURKE, CONSTANCE American Humor A12
RUSSELL, BERTRAND Mysticism and Logic A104
SANTAYANA, GEORGE Character and Opinion in the United States A7[illegible]
——— Three Philosophical Poets A17
SCHRODINGER, ERWIN What Is Life? A88
SCOTT, GEOFFREY The Architecture of Humanism A33
SHAW, BERNARD Shaw on Music A53
SHERRINGTON, SIR CHARLES Man on His Nature A15
SIGERIST, HENRY E. The Great Doctors A140
SNOW, C. P. The Masters: A Novel A162
STEEGMULLER, FRANCIS The Grand Mademoiselle A205
STENDHAL The Charterhouse of Parma A1
——— Five Short Novels of Stendhal A153
——— On Love A103
STRINDBERG, AUGUST Six Plays A54
——— Five Plays A219
SUZUKI, D. T. Zen Buddhism A90
SYPHER, WYLIE (Ed.) Comedy A87
——— Four Stages of Renaissance Style A45
TAYLOR, A. E. Socrates A9
TITCHMARSH, E. C. Mathematics for the General Reader A169
TOCQUEVILLE, ALEXIS DE The European Revolution and the Correspondence with Gobineau A163
——— The Old Regime and the French Revolution A60
TOKLAS, ALICE B. The Alice B. Toklas Cook Book A196
TRAVERSI, D. A. An Approach to Shakespeare A74
TRELAWNEY, E. J. The Last Days of Shelley and Byron A225
TREVELYAN, G. M. History of England I, II, III A22a, A22b, A22c
TRILLING, LIONEL The Liberal Imagination A13
——— The Middle of the Journey A98
TROTSKY, LEON The Russian Revolution A170
TSAO HSUEH-CHIN Dream of the Red Chamber A159
TURGENEV, IVAN Selected Tales A203
TURNER, W. J. Mozart: The Man and His Works A24
VAN DOREN, MARK Shakespeare A11
VERGA, GIOVANNI The House by the Medlar Tree A47
VIDICH, ARTHUR J. and BENSMAN, JOSEPH Small Town in Mass Society A216
VIRGIL The Aeneid A20
WADDELL, HELEN The Wandering Scholars A63
WALEY, ARTHUR Three Ways of Thought in Ancient China A75
WESTON, JESSIE From Ritual to Romance A125
WHYTE, WILLIAM H., JR. The Organization Man A117
WIENER, NORBERT The Human Use of Human Beings A34
WILDER, THORNTON Heaven's My Destination A209
WILLEY, BASIL The Seventeenth Century Background A19
WILLIAMS, RAYMOND Culture and Society 1780–1950 A220
WILSON, EDMUND Eight Essays A37
——— A Literary Chronicle: 1920–1950 A85

——— A Piece of My Mind A143
——— To the Finland Station A6
WOODWARD C. VANN Reunion and Reaction A83
WRIGHT, G. ERNEST and FULLER, REGINALD H. The Book of the Acts of God A222
YEATS, WILLIAM BUTLER The Autobiography of William Butler Yeats A142
YARMOLINSKY, AVRAHM (Ed.) Soviet Short Stories A218
YOURCENAR, MARGUERITE Hadrian's Memoirs A108